Praise for *Parenting 4 S*

"*Parenting 4 Social Justice* is a great tool for paren___ about "isms" in our society, bringing together a ___ examples, and guided opportunities for reflection___ ___ social justice journey, there is something here for you to

—**Beverly Daniel Tatum, Ph.D.,** author,
Why Are All the Black Kids
Sitting Together in the Cafeteria? And
Other Conversations About Race

"*Parenting 4 Social Justice* is an excellent resource for preparing young people to survive, thrive, build community and work for justice. It gives adults the tools they need to combine their love for our children with their love for the world. The authors' stories are honest and insightful, the conversation examples are helpful and reassuring, the reading/listening/watching resources are invaluable, and the taking action suggestions are varied and doable. I'm excited to recommend this book to everyone who hangs out with young people and can't wait to give out copies to parents, teachers and youth workers I know."

—**Paul Kivel,** educator, activist, author of
Uprooting Racism and Boys Will Be Men:
Raising Our Sons for Courage, Caring and Community

"In this time of radical uncertainty and change, when nearly every day I ask myself 'yes, but what can I DO?' this book arrived at my door as a road map, a grounding rod and a much-needed guide for how to craft conversations and take action. I'm a better parent, caregiver and human because of this book, whose pages contain the seeds for an equitable, bright and beautiful future."

—**Robin MacArthur,** author of
Half Wild (Stories) and *Heart Spring Mountain*
parent of children ages 8 and 11

"At an historic moment when we are reckoning at a global scale with the rise of the right, the deep inequities of racialized patriarchal capitalism, white supremacy, anti-blackness and misogyny amidst a horrific global pandemic and inspiring widespread Black-led uprisings for justice, *Parenting 4 Social Justice* ' is a welcome resource for those of us who are striving to equip our children to understand and process the state of the world around them, to engage and take action as young people today, and to prepare them for the future that lays ahead of them."

—**Sha Grogan-Brown,** anti-racist, white,
queer, trans dad of a 5-year-old

"Young children begin to form their ideas about who they are and about diversity among people at an early age. This learning process is deeply influenced by the prejudices that circulate in our society. *Parenting 4 Social Justice* offers numerous ways for families to raise children who have empathy for people across our many kinds of diversity, and have tools for standing up for fairness and justice."

—**Louise Derman-Sparks,** author of *Anti-Bias Education for Young Children and Ourselves*

"*Parenting 4 Social Justice* offers parents a creative roadmap for raising socially-minded kids. Through the book's realistic prompts and examples of actual conversations, parents can learn to navigate and embrace talking (and taking action!) with their children on topics that may be uncomfortable but are timely and needed."

—**Shonda Smith,** Black woman (she/her/hers) raised in Brooklyn, now planted in NJ, parent of a 17-year-old daughter and 15-year-old son

"*Parenting 4 Social Justice* helped me tackle the difficult conversations I wanted to have with my children but didn't know how to get started. It made me think on a fundamental level about my own beliefs on race, class, gender, ability, capitalism and so much more (along with their interconnections). I got lost in the stories and perspectives and ended up realizing this is much more than tips to help kids, it is just as much a guidebook for adults to reflect on these issues as well. Highly recommended!"

—**Stevie,** heterosexual, middle-class- raised parent to kids age 11 and 7

"As a mother and social justice advocate, I'm often asked the 'hows' of raising socially conscious children by parents. *Parenting 4 Social Justice* is an incredible and heartfelt guide to intentional parenting, that teaches individuals how to raise a new generation of young activists."

—**Iliah Grant Altoro,** writer, activist, traveler, and mother to three badass critical thinkers. She is the founder of Negra Bohemian, a community dedicated to revolutionary mothering, intentional travel, raising global learners, and decolonized faith. www.negrabohemian.com

PARENTING 4 SOCIAL JUSTICE

Tips, Tools and Inspiration for Conversations & Action with Kids

After a Washington, DC Pride Parade, 2017.
PHOTO CREDIT: HUGH CLARKE.

PARENTING 4 SOCIAL JUSTICE

Tips, Tools and Inspiration for Conversations & Action with Kids

by Angela Berkfield
with co-authors Chrissy Colón Bradt, Leila Raven,
Jaimie Lynn Kessell, Rowan Parker, and Abigail Healey

Illustrations by Brittney Washington

GREEN WRITERS PRESS } *Brattleboro, Vermont*

Green Writers Press is a Vermont-based publisher whose mission is to spread a message of hope and renewal through the words and images we publish. Throughout we will adhere to our commitment to preserving and protecting the natural resources of the earth. To that end, a percentage of our proceeds will be donated to environmental activist groups and the author's organization: 10% of proceeds will go to The Root Social Justice Center, a grassroots organization that is growing the movement for racial justice. Located in Brattleboro, Vermont, The Root has a statewide and regional impact. The Root prioritizes POC leadership and is shifting resources to POC. Green Writers Press gratefully acknowledges support from individual donors, friends, and readers to help support the environment and our publishing initiative.

Giving Voice to Writers & Artists Who Will Make the World a Better Place
Green Writers Press | Brattleboro, Vermont
www.greenwriterspress.com

ISBN: 978-1-950584-10-9

COVER PHOTO: SYD SENNETT, S.SENNETT16@GMAIL.COM — RACIAL JUSTICE
RALLY IN BRATTLEBORO, VERMONT, ORGANIZED BY THE ROOT SOCIAL JUSTICE CENTER.

INTERIOR ILLUSTRATIONS BY BRITTNEY WASHINGTON.

ALL INTERIOR PHOTOS COURTESY OF
PARENTING 4 SOCIAL JUSTICE, BRATTLEBORO, VERMONT.

PRINTED ON PAPER WITH PULP THAT COMES FROM FSC®CERTIFIED FORESTS, MANAGED FORESTS THAT GUARANTEE RESPONSIBLE ENVIRONMENTAL, SOCIAL, AND ECONOMIC PRACTICES BY MCNAUGHTON & GUNN, A WOMAN-OWNED BUSINESS CERTIFIED BY THE WOMEN'S BUSINESS ENTERPRISE NATIONAL COUNCIL.

Dedications

Angela ~ For Birch and River, for my great-great-great-great grandchildren, and for all my teachers, mentors, and guides, including my parents, who made this book possible.

Brittney ~ For children like MJ who are closest to the joy and resistance that will transform the world; for our inner children still there, quiet and listening; for my own mothers, and to revolutionary mothering of and by us all.

Chrissy ~ For my mom, who always modeled engagement. For my ancestors, who made it possible for me, and for my children, who remind me that another world is possible.

Rowan ~ For Dane, who pushes me in all the right ways, even when it's hard.

Leila ~ For all those who mothered me, and for the wonderful child in my life who consistently teaches me to see the world through the lens of possibility.

Jaimie ~ For my children, who give me hope that the systems that have oppressed so many for so long really can be dismantled and society really can be remade in the image of equity and justice—legitimately—for all.

Abigail ~ For all the people who challenged my thinking along the way, and especially my son, who challenged what I thought it meant to be a parent from day one.

CONTENTS

Foreword by Autumn Brown ix
Foreword by Chris Crass xii
A Note about Language and Content xv

INTRODUCTION

BY ANGELA BERKFIELD

How I came to write this book *3* / What this book is about *6*
Who this book is for *12* / About the co-authors *12*
How this book is structured *14* / How you can use this book *16*
Take care of your heart and body *17* / Healing justice practice *19*

CHAPTER 1: SOCIAL JUSTICE (IN BRIEF)

BY ANGELA BERKFIELD

Quotes *21* / What is Social Justice? *22*
Privilege and oppression *33*
Distinction between diversity and social justice *40*
A note on culture *41* / What can I do? *44* / Healing justice practice *47*
Community of practice questions *47*

CHAPTER 2: PARENTING FOR SOCIAL JUSTICE

BY ANGELA BERKFIELD

Quotes *49* / What is Parenting for Social Justice? *50*
How do we parent for social justice? *58* / Healing justice practice *70*
Community of practice discussion questions *70*

CHAPTER 3: PARENTING FOR RACIAL JUSTICE

BY CHRISSY COLÓN BRADT AND ANGELA BERKFIELD

Poem and Quotes 73 / Our stories 76
The stories we are told are the stories we tell 81
Talking with kids 96 / Reading/listening/watching together 114
Taking action 116 / Healing justice practice 120
Community of practice discussion questions 123

CHAPTER 4: PARENTING FOR ECONOMIC JUSTICE

BY JAIMIE LYNN KESSELL AND ANGELA BERKFIELD

Quotes 125 / Our stories 126
The stories we are told are the stories we tell 136
Talking with kids 157 / Reading/listening/watching together 167
Taking action 171 / Healing justice practice 174
Community of practice discussion questions 175

CHAPTER 5: PARENTING FOR DISABILITY JUSTICE

BY ROWAN PARKER AND ABIGAIL HEALEY

Quotes 177 / Our stories 179 What is disability justice? 187
The stories we are told are the stories we tell 188
Talking with kids 194 / Reading/listening/watching together 206
Taking action 208 / Healing justice practice 211
Community of practice discussion questions 212

CHAPTER 6: PARENTING FOR GENDER JUSTICE

BY LEILA RAVEN

Quotes 213 / Story 215
The stories we are told are the stories we tell 222
Talking with kids 235 / Reading/listening/watching together 250
Taking action 253 / Healing justice practice 256
Community of practice discussion questions 256

CHAPTER 7: PARENTING FOR COLLECTIVE LIBERATION

BY ANGELA BERKFIELD

Quotes *257* / Story *259*
Collective liberation, intersectionality, and emergent strategy *263*
Talking with kids *277* / Reading/listening/watching together *286*
Taking action *287* / Healing justice practice *290*
Community of practice discussion questions *290*

CHAPTER 8: LOOKING BACK AND LOOKING FORWARD

BY ANGELA BERKFIELD

Quotes *291* / Taking time to reflect *292*
You've got this, and we've got each other *295*
Community of practice discussion questions *295*
Healing justice practice *296*

Appendix A: Social Justice Frameworks *297*

Appendix B: Definitions *304*

Resources *318*

Additional Resources *335*

(See supplemental material and Appendices C–J on our website.)

Social Justice Book for Kids *336*

Acknowledgements *354*

Author Bios and Family Photos *356*

FOREWORDS

BY AUTUMN BROWN

"Are you going to raise your child genderqueer?"

She was a young woman of color, younger than me I think, an anarchist organizer who had the lackadaisical air of a stoner. She asked me with such sweetness and innocence that the strength and belligerence of my response surprised even me. Defensively, reflexively, I clutched my infant as I exclaimed, "No! Given that this child was born male and will be white passing, my responsibility is to raise him to know what it means to move through a world that will perceive him as a white man!" Or something like that.

I look back on this moment with no small amount of chagrin, and a lot of self-compassion. I was only in the beginning stages of parenting, and therefore I knew nothing but believed otherwise. As the only person among my peers who was choosing to begin a family, and through incurring the bizarre judgments of many who were not, I was learning who my community was and was not. I was only just waking up to the harsh reality of the enormous distance between a proclaimed feminism, and a deeply practiced feminist, in my most intimate relationships. My political ideas, even, and perhaps especially the ones that were relatively binary, I clung to like a ship's mast in the storm that is becoming a mother.

I wish I could remember this young woman's name, so that I could apologize to her for having such a ridiculous response to what was, in actuality, a completely fair question. Years later, I can see so clearly how my response belied an area of true ignorance. My child, who was assigned male at birth, would quickly teach me how wrong I was. Indeed, not one but two of my children eventually came out as non-binary, both at so young an age that their self-knowledge on this front could hardly be questioned. If a three-year-old can tell you that they are neither a boy or a girl, who are you to argue?

Children are born knowing freedom. They will teach us that freedom if we are willing to slow down and listen, if we are willing to hold them close to us and learn alongside them, rather than exert control over their bodies, behaviors, thoughts, choices, and verbalizations at every possible moment. My eldest was my first teacher, but each of my children have taught me freedom.

The book you are about to read presupposes that parents have a role in shaping change in the world through the work we do in raising our children. But the stories and lessons contained here also posit the deeper truth that every parent knows: "Your children are not your children" (Kahlil Gibran). Our children are our teachers, often our unwilling teachers—because they resist the subtleties and confusion and lies of adults. They are always moving towards liberation, and in every breath seeking a future they access much more readily than they can access the past. Parenting for social justice is essentially about parenting for this kind of freedom.

Children are born caring about other people. Unlike sharks, and other ectothermic vertebrate species that produce self-sufficient offspring, humans have a biological requirement for care and nurturing. This does not end in infancy. Children exhibit a constant interest in care, nurturance, cooperation, empathy, and conflict resolution. It is only through deep social training—deep as in cellular, deep as in somatic, deep as in embodied—that children learn to be desensitized to the suffering of others, and to their own suffering. Parenting for social justice means opening the door on that trauma within ourselves and letting a different practice—a practice of reparenting ourselves, and of parenting our own children differently—heal the wounds of subjugation and violence that sit at the beating heart of that suffering.

We live in a world that is fundamentally shaped by subjugation and violence. One of the most insidious aspects of living under racial capitalism is the reproduction of subjugation within childrearing, and the way that raising children can be a site of reproduction of this same system. This system shapes us. It shapes every aspect of our lives. It shapes how we understand expressions of right and wrong, of discipline and punishment, of morality and justice.

Grace Lee Boggs famously asked that we consider what time it is on the clock of the world. It is an urgent time. If we are not actively reshaping conditions now, reimagining conditions now, there will be little left to fight for. We must ask ourselves, what kind of world are we shaping in our parenting? What kind of world are we reproducing? And what behaviors and beliefs are we reproducing within our children? Do we wish to reproduce acquiescence to this system of subjugation and violence? And if not, if we are to now create something different, then how free must our children be supported to be?

Whatever we have to share with our children, to help them on their freedom journey, we must also humble ourselves in the knowledge that our children will always take our freedom teachings to the next level. One of my children has had a years-long tendency to regress into a "baby voice," and it has always, always, driven me up the wall. One day, barely disguising my exasperation, I told her to use her nine-year-old voice. She said to me, "My voice is my voice, and I can use it how I want." And then she looked me square in the eye and said, "And you can't say anything to that."

Check and mate, young Padawan. In the final iteration of the Star Wars saga, Yoda tells Luke, "We are what they grow beyond. That is the true burden of all masters." I have gone rounds with this ancient truth, and I likely always will. Some lessons we must learn over and over again. Perspective gives us grounds for regret, but it also gives us grounds for change through small adjustments, and for acknowledging we are wrong. If we can do this then we, in turn, can teach our children that not only is it good and right to acknowledge mistakes, but indeed, the best we can hope for in life is room to continue growing. We have to be humble.

If we have any hope of changing the world, and earning our right to remain here, we are required to change our parenting. Instead of parenting towards a "norm" that keeps our children functional inside of supremacy, our call, our covenant with the earth, must be to prepare our children to shape change. I encourage you to read this important and timely book with an orientation of humility in the journey.

—AUTUMN BROWN, MARCH 2021

Autumn Brown is the proud and grateful mother of three living children, and one beloved child who transitioned. She is an artist, a writer, and a healing justice facilitator for social movements. Autumn is co-host of the podcast *How to Survive the End of the World*, and a worker-owner with the Anti-Oppression Resource and Training Alliance. www.iambrown.org.

BY CHRIS CRASS

"No, that's not right, that's racist."

As a young white boy, I grew up in a family that talked about racism and politics regularly. My far-right, racist grandfather would launch into his analysis of the country with Black and Brown people and Democrats at fault for every problem. As a three-year-old, seven-year-old, twelve-year-old, I would hear this worldview expressed in detail, as would my younger brother and my white cousins. But my Mom would argue back, "No, that's not right, that's racist." She would get cut off with misogynistic comments about "what would you know, you're a woman," from my Grandfather and Uncles, but she would continue to argue nonetheless.

My parents read books to me about Rosa Parks, Martin Luther King Jr., and Jackie Robinson. They told me about Cesar Chavez and the United Farm Workers. Much to my parents frustration, there was a time when I parroted my grandfather's rightwing views, just because I knew it would push their buttons. But when I was fifteen, and met another high school student who was a social justice activist—and soon thereafter the Rodney King verdict and uprising took place in Los Angeles—my mom's courageous "No" against my grandfather's racism, and the seeds my parents planted led to me to saying "Yes." *Yes* to social, racial, gender, and economic justice. *Yes* to joining justice organizations. And *Yes* to working specifically in white communities against racism and for racial justice.

As a parent now of two young white boys, I'm so grateful for this incredible book. *Parenting 4 Social Justice* is dynamite, a sacred offering, a manual, and a blessing.

Dynamite to explode the nightmare logic of systemic oppression that rationalizes and normalizes brutal injustice. A sacred offering that brings together vast knowledge and wisdom from liberation movements, ancestors, contemporary thinkers, and the hearts of parents—just like you—who love their kids and want to end the nightmare and build the dream of beloved community. It is a manual full of helpful insights, stories, recommendations, reflection questions, and guided practices to ground us and sustain us.

And it is a blessing, as the authors invite us to be with them on this journey, in this work, equipping us and encouraging us to be parents, joining together, for social justice, for a world where all our kids can get free in a society that loves, cherishes, resources, and cares for all of us.

Parenting provides so many opportunities to make mistakes, get it wrong, feel overwhelmed, and feel like failures. And while we know it's part of being a parent, it still sucks. For me, an important part of parenting for social justice is about being kind, generous, and compassionate with myself, loving and learning from my kids, and doing my best to practice my values in the culture of my family and with the relationships of my community and justice movements. For every five mediocre or failed attempts at meaningful justice conversations, there's one that went fairly OK, and then after some more, sometimes awkward efforts, there are really meaningful and engaged moments. But all the attempts, and moments, and what we learn and share in these experiences, helps build up family culture rooted in social justice values, and that's exactly what this book helps us all do, better.

"This is who we are, these are our people," I said to my three-year-old and seven-year-old boys as we stood on a hill looking out at the gathering of several hundred activists from around the South, at the historic Highlander Center in the mountains of East Tennessee. The gathering is intergenerational, multiracial, multigender, and rooted in anti-racism, feminism, and socialism. We've been here many times. "Highlander is where Rosa Parks, Martin Luther King Jr., Ella Baker, Anne Braden, Myles Horton, and John Lewis came together to build the Civil Rights movement," I share. "This is where Mom worked with auntie Tufara, where you were both at as babies, and now your aunties Ash-Lee and Allyn are the co-directors. And now we're here with family and friends, and with kids and adults who we get to meet for the first time, and we're all part of the movement for peace and justice, they all want to end racism and inequality, too."

"OK, OK, Dad . . . can we go find other kids to play with now."

"Yes, let's go play, and when we see people you know, or who know you, we'll stop and say hi."

Over the next few days, my kids will hear snippets of incredible talks by movement veterans and leaders, as well as ridiculous jokes from high school and college students. They'll run around and play and dance and be around people singing old and new movement songs. My primary goal isn't just what they'll learn in these experiences of social justice gatherings and protests, but also what they feel.

Supremacy systems are deeply committed to malnourishing us of justice wisdom, movement history, disconnecting us from movement leaders and the power of justice work making positive changes in the here and now. I want my kids to be nourished and connected—in their hearts, minds, bodies, and soul—with justice values, leadership, culture, history, and movements of today. I want them to learn about the history of systemic oppression and crucially, I want them to know about and experience movements for collective liberation and feel the way historic movements are legacies that present movements are building from.

In the months before the mass uprisings following the murder of George Floyd, the kids and I and their auntie Z! were going to weekly car caravan protests to get people out of jails, prisons, and immigrant detention centers in Kentucky as the COVID-19 pandemic intensified. The kids never wanted to go, but I would say that this was important, it was part of the school at home, and that they could watch a cartoon in the car. I'd tell them what the protests were about and point out people we knew who were leading the protests, and of course relate the protests to what Jedi do to fight the empire and what witches and wizards do to defeat Voldemort. They would usually respond, "Yeah, yeah, we know" and show little interest. Then the mass uprising began, and in Louisville, where we live, the movement for Justice for Breonna Taylor grew rapidly.

We went to marches and protests for Black Lives Matter, and on one of them, we took our white neighbors, who had never been to a protest before. With their bestie, a nine year old, in the back seat with them, the kids started talking about Black Lives Matter, Breonna Taylor, and being part of protests. I just listened in the front seat, as my kids talked—hearing past conversations they seemed only partially engaged in and hearing them express their own insights from past protests they had been to, as they oriented their friend on her first protest. Soon they were going to protests regularly and at one, a children's march, a Black woman elementary school teacher had all the kids take a knee while occupying an intersection. She said to the kids, mostly elementary school aged, mostly Black, that "as students, you are often learning about history, but today, you are making history."

As I march with my kids, I think of my Mom arguing with my Grandfather. She never changed his mind, but she knew I and the other white kids in our family were listening. I think of my Dad telling me about Cesar Chavez, even when I seemed uninterested, and what a difference it made.

As a parent, doing my best to bring social justice values into the heart of my family culture and kids' lives, reading and applying the wisdom of this book is vital. Both for what I bring to my relationship with my boys, but also for helping me and my kids join with our communities to take action for, fight for, and win social justice campaigns and collective liberation values in society.

—CHRIS CRASS, MARCH 2021

Chris Crass is the dad of River and August. He is a longtime social justice organizer, author, and educator with a focus on organizing in white communities for racial justice. He is the author of *Towards Collective Liberation* and *Towards the "Other America."* www.chriscrass.org

A NOTE ABOUT LANGUAGE AND CONTENT

Throughout this book, when we say parent we mean anyone who is caring directly for children, regardless of their specific relationship, including grandparents, aunts and uncles, and foster parents.

When we are talking about Black people we always capitalize the word Black. This is because Black people in the United States have very intentionally developed a Black identity and culture that, while not monolithic, is unifying as a group identity. Lowercase black refers to a color.

For similar reasons we capitalize Indigenous, which you might see used interchangeably with Native American, American Indian, or First Nations, also capitalized.

We capitalize Asian and Latinx for similar reasons.

We do not capitalize white, because there is no positive social identity developed around this term; in fact, not being aware of whiteness is one of the privileges and powers of whiteness. However, we recognize there are different views here and that language is shifting all the time. Capitalizing white can be seen as a step in an anti-racist direction because it names White as a racial identity, even though it is still not widely claimed as such. We are paying attention to all of the commentary on this issue and realize that a different language choice might make more sense a year from now.

Throughout the book we use POC, which stands for people of color, to refer collectively to the racial groups that are currently targeted by racism in the United States. These groups include African Americans and other people of the African diaspora, Asian/Pacific Islanders, Latinos, Native Americans, and people of Arab descent. Use of the inclusive term people of color is not intended to deny the significant differences within this grouping; it is used to challenge white supremacy and advocate for racial justice for all people who have been oppressed because of false categorizations of race.

We also use BIPOC, which stands for Black, Indigenous, people of color. The acronym is used for all people of color but specifically highlights Black and Indigenous because of "the unique relationship to whiteness that Indigenous and Black (African American) people have, which shapes the experiences of and relationship to white supremacy for all people of color within a U.S. context . . . It is used to intentionally undo Native invisibility and anti-Blackness, dismantle white supremacy and advance racial justice."[1]

This book was written over a four-year time span, with the bulk of the book being written in 2018. So you will notice there are some sources that are older, and some that are quite new, with the bulk of sources and references pertaining to events of 2018. Many things have changed since then, both on the micro and macro levels. On the micro level: the authors' kids are all older; and, we each have new circumstances in our personal lives (i.e., I was diagnosed with stage 4 breast cancer in 2020). And on the macro level: Joe Biden and Kamala Harris were elected to the U.S. Presidency and Vice-presidency in November 2020; the coronavirus pandemic has drastically changed our world; and, the racial justice uprisings of 2020-2021 have increased people's understanding of systemic racism and white supremacy. Still, so much of what is written in this book holds true and can be applied to the ever changing world we live in. Change is constant, and the need for social justice thinking and action remains relevant.

We hope that as you read this book, you are able to use the truths that can be applied to most any situation. Do share with us any ideas or ways you see our content can be improved and updated. We welcome your feedback.

1 The BIPOC Project, retrieved 2020. https://www.thebipocproject.org.

PARENTING 4 SOCIAL JUSTICE

Tips, Tools and Inspiration
for Conversations & Action with Kids

Two kids making Black Lives Matter signs together.

INTRODUCTION

BY ANGELA BERKFIELD

Tell the children the truth.
"Babylon System," BOB MARLEY AND THE WAILERS

My feet are on stolen land. I am descended from settler-colonizers. All the clothes on my body and the computer in my hands are somehow connected to the extraction of resources from Mother Earth and the exploitation of the labor of people in the U.S., and all over the world. I recognize that reality. I acknowledge the suffering I am connected to. And yet, I have the deepest belief that another world is possible. This book is dedicated to that world, a world we are co-creating right now through the way we interact with each other and with all living beings around us: connected, loving, transforming, healing, regenerating, equitable, peaceful, just.

How I came to write this book

Several years ago I was driving my friend Annique home from a party. We had known each other for year—she had taught my pre-birth class before my first son was born, and she was a midwife at my second son's birth. During the car ride she asked about my work, which at the time was facilitating social justice trainings with ACT for Social Justice. I had also co-founded The Root Social Justice Center in rural Brattleboro, Vermont, a few years prior. Because of what she knew about my work, Annique was asking me questions about racial microaggressions, about using gender-neutral pronouns, and about Black Lives Matter activism.

Then she knocked my socks off with a question: "Would you consider doing trainings for parents about how to talk about these things with our kids?" I stuttered, "Uhuhuhuh, I have no idea how to talk with my kids about this stuff, how could I teach others?" My kids were three and six at the time, and most days it was all I could do to keep them fed and bathed and get them to school and keep my temper under control, never mind translating social justice concepts into preschool language for them.

Annique thought I had more wisdom and skills about this than I realized. She followed up with questions that drew out my thinking about how I apply social justice concepts to my parenting. Through our conversation it became clear that while I don't have a magic wand, I have ideas influenced by my community work, and that bringing parents together to talk about our ideas could be helpful for all of us. By the time I dropped Annique off at her house I was already planning to bring the conversation we had begun to a broader group of parents and caregivers.

That started a journey of becoming more intentional about bringing social justice into my parenting. I checked out some social justice-related books from the library and asked for some others as Christmas presents (for me!). My instant favorite author was Jacqueline Woodson, who wrote *Brown Girl Dreaming*[1] and *The Show Way*,[2] whose books gave me a way to talk with my kids about the history of slavery while also recognizing the strength and resilience that are passed down through connections with ancestors. I found that *Rad American Women A to Z*[3] by Kate Schatz engaged my older son in talking about gender and also race in U.S. history. He ate that book right up when he was seven years old. And *Those Shoes*[4] by Maribeth Boelts nudged my kids to talk about class, race, friendship, and sharing. Those books opened up so many great conversations with my kids, even though they are usually more doers than talkers.

I began to notice opportunities to talk about social justice many times throughout each day. When my kids would ask me to buy them Nikes, I would talk about the harms of consumption and how our consumption is connected to unfair labor practices and the capitalist economy. When my kids would give their toys genders, saying stuff like "this dinosaur is a girl and this one is a boy," I would add "and this dinosaur is genderqueer." When we attended rallies for Black Lives Matter, instead of just bringing the kids with me I would prepare with them by talking about how all people deserve to be treated fairly, in terms that a three-year-old could understand. While buying food to donate to the local food drive, I would talk about how the minimum wage isn't enough for people to buy food, and that hunger is connected to the reality that there are people with way too much money. My heightened intentionality about talking about social justice with my kids opened up doors to chat with other parents about conversations they were having with their kids.

---

1 Jacqueline Woodson, *Brown Girl Dreaming,* (Waterville, ME: Thorndike Press, 2018). Written in prose, this is Jacqueline's personal story, appropriate for ages 9+.
2 Jacqueline Woodson,*The Show Way*, illus. Hudson Talbot, (New York, New York: G.P. Putnam's Sons, 2005). A powerful picture book for ages 4+ that tells Jacqueline's ancestral story from slavery until now.
3 Kate Schatz, illus. Miriam Klein Stahl, *Rad American Women A to Z: Rebels, Visionaries, and Trailblazers Who Shaped Our History . . . And Our Future!*, (City Lights, 2015). Using colorful artwork, each woman gets a page dedicated to a brief highlight of her life. From activists to artists to political leaders, this book has something for everyone.
4 Maribeth Boelts, illus. Noah Z. Jones, *Those Shoes*, (Candlewick Press, 2007). Jeremy wants a pair of shoes that many kids have, but his grandma doesn't have enough money. My kids pick this one up over and over.

My friend Abi Healey, co-author of Chapter 5, has been a key collaborator who has helped me stay true to my goals for parenting for social justice. Before she became a parent she was a part of the movement to close the School of the Americas[5] in Georgia. She now has two sons, nine and five, and she is a preschool teacher. In 2015 Abi and I began to write a blog about how we are incorporating social justice into our parenting, with the goal of inspiring and sharing resources with other parents. That same year, my local library agreed to host "Parenting 4 Social Justice Chats" (P4SJ) for parents to come together to talk about social justice issues.

Since then I have facilitated and co-facilitated[6] many P4SJ sessions and I hope to facilitate many more. Just as parents benefit from sharing support and tips about how to feed our kids, take care of our kids' physical health, and handle discipline and boundaries, we also benefit from supporting each other in talking about social justice issues with our children. I learn a lot from other parents and get ideas I wouldn't have thought of. My work on P4SJ has always been a project of mutual teaching, learning, and collaboration.

The idea for this book arose out of the P4SJ workshops and from a pilot curriculum that I wrote in 2016 for Oak Meadow, an organization that supports homeschooling families. Through those projects I found that there was limited material to support parents in parenting for social justice, so I decided to expand what I was already doing into a book that could be a resource for parents everywhere. Although my preference would have been to start with a diverse team of writers and to co-develop a book, I had already developed the existing framework. So, instead of letting perfect be the enemy of the good, I invited colleagues and friends with diverse identities who are parenting for social justice to co-author some chapters of this book and contribute examples from their lives in the form of short vignettes. The chapters on race, class, gender, and ability are all co-written by folks who have different and less-privileged identities than I do. However, the book is still heavy with my voice, which is not ideal because I can't help but tell this story from my perspective as a person with a lot of privilege in the current context. All of us writing for this book have tried to be as explicit as possible about the personal context that we are writing from and how that might affect our perspectives and ideas. My colleagues' contributions to this book make sure that throughout the book the stories, perspectives, and voices of many diverse parents are heard. They keep us heading towards a radical vision of justice. I acknowledge this doesn't erase the unequal influence resulting from my having developed the initial framework.

---

5 The School of the Americas is a U.S. military school that has trained military personnel from all over the world and especially from Latin America who have been directly involved in genocide and torture. For this reason School of Americas Watch has led an annual protest since 1990, demanding that the school be shut down. For more information: http://www.soaw.org/home.

6 Although I started facilitating by myself I now mostly co-facilitate with people who identify as people of color. In that way the facilitation team can support and reflect the experiences of a multi-racial space. Shela Linton, Mikaela Simms, Amber Arnold, and Chrissy Colón Bradt are people I co-facilitate with.

What this book is about—laying the groundwork for P4SJ concepts

There are many ways of parenting, and many philosophies to support us as parents in everything from how we discipline our kids, to how we get them to sleep, to what kind of education is most supportive for their brains and bodies and hearts. The particular focus that this book adds is how to bring social justice principles, frameworks, and action into everyday parenting, so that we equip our kids with the tools to be whole human beings and a new generation of change-makers.

The complex issues we are facing as a society show up in our kids' play, friendships, and conversation—new technology, social media, bullying, gun violence, mass incarceration, controversy over abortion, border walls to stop immigration, climate change. This book offers a foundational understanding of social justice so that when we are trying to solve those issues, or when we are talking about them with our kids, we are approaching the issues from a social justice framework. To do this well—in fact, to do it at all!—I need practice, ideas, and accountability in the form of people who will keep me on track and provide community and support along the way. Accountability is a key concept in social justice work and you will see it show up throughout the book (see Appendix B for the full definition).

Talking openly with our kids feels more urgent than ever in the age of a fascist-leaning president who banned people from entering the U.S. based on their religion and race and who separated immigrant children from their parents at the U.S.-Mexico border. How do we communicate openly with our children about these troubling issues? I find that it is easier to have brave conversations when we are already talking about our commitment to living in love rather than fear, our recognition of our individual power to make change, and the value of coming together in collective power. I also find that it is easier to talk about the horrors of what is happening in current events when we connect it to history and systems rather than just individual bad behavior, and when we are visioning and strategizing with our kids about how to create a just and equitable world. That feels very different than narrowly focusing on the failings of a president or the hope of electing a better one next time.

A foundational part of having these conversations is knowing how our own social identities impact our experiences (see Chapter 1 for more on privilege and oppression). As a middle class, white, cisgender female,[7] heterosexual, born into a Protestant family, English-speaking, U.S. citizen I recognize that I have a lot of unearned privilege and power. I was born into a society that privileges almost all of my social identities, both through law and in informal practice. Growing up I knew I had a good life—a loving family, strong community, very little (or well-hidden) drugs or violence or police surveillance in my suburban community, educational opportunities, a single family home that we owned, with room for a nice garden in the backyard. What I didn't know is that my privilege was connected to oppression—land stolen from the Indigenous people of that place, enslaved African and indentured European labor, policies such as the GI bill that benefited my family and excluded others, and on and on.

---

7 Cisgender female: assigned female at birth and still identify as female. For more description see Chapter 7, "Parenting for Gender Justice."

While my parents taught me to be kind, to love others as I love myself, to listen to others, and to solve problems through communication rather than violence, there were some important things that they did not teach me. I was not taught to see how my life circumstance was connected to the lives of others, and especially not to the problems I was seeing around me. I don't fault my parents. These realities have been intentionally covered up by those who hold power and wealth, through controlling the dominant stories we hear about American society. And people don't tend to go digging for them because digging is uncomfortable and risks bringing about change that is not entirely predictable. Now that I am a parent I am striving to tell my children the truth about injustice and their connection to it so they are equipped to do something about it.

After doing a lot of work unpacking my privilege, I recognize how much I am harmed by a society that creates advantage for some people and disadvantages others, that has oppression written into its operating system. I am harmed by being separated physically, socially, and emotionally from others based on skin color and class status; by feeling better than others; by knowing hardly anything about my ancestors; by knowing very little about the natural world and all the steps that go into meeting my human needs through natural resources; and by focusing on my individual growth and fulfillment instead of on the collective. I am also harmed because of the drugs and violence and health crises that are endemic in a society that values individual and profit over community and well-being.

I had the opportunity to hear Sherri Mitchell, a member of the Penawahpskek Tribe of the Penobscot Nation in Maine, speak. She talked about how the belief in our separateness from each other and from the world is foundational to the violence and injustice that we are experiencing as a country and around the globe. This separation has been used as a tool to maintain systemic oppression. As Sherri Mitchell writes in *Sacred Instructions: Indigenous Wisdom for Living Spirit-Based Change*[8]:

> The myth of separation is at the heart of the lies that we've been fed, and it supports all of the power structures that we have created. This illusion causes us to forget that we are connected to one another and to a divine source, which is embodied through us and put into action in the world around us. When we forget this truth and embrace the lie, it becomes possible for us to be at war with one another, and to be at war within ourselves.

We are interconnected with each other, with the earth, with our ancestors going back to the beginning of time, and with all who come after us, whether related or not. Sherri's wisdom has supported me in recognizing where separation is showing up in my thinking, and to shift to connected thinking and visioning. I'll give some examples to better illustrate this idea.

The separation I experience along race lines is particularly notable. The first time I remember this feeling of separation was when I was six years old in Des Moines, Iowa. My family lived in a neighborhood of single family homes of predominantly white families. A white neighbor of ours had a Black grandson who would come to visit on

---

8 Sherri Mitchell, *Sacred Instructions: Indigenous Wisdom for Living Spirit Based Change* (Berkeley, North Atlantic Books, 2018). I also participated in a workshop on trauma that Sherri led. She talks about how healing ourselves is a revolutionary act because we have also been separated from ourselves.

weekends. He and I were friends and played together a lot. He gave me a purple unicorn purse for my birthday. I loved that purse and I loved my friend. Yet I remember sensing a very strange energy from adults about our friendship. I was never told I couldn't play with him, but my memory is that I always somehow knew that adults frowned upon our friendship. And then I remember that he didn't come visit anymore, but I don't know why. When I think about this memory I feel an overwhelming sense of sadness and loss, my chest feels tight and my head starts to ache.

Can you recall the first time you noticed or felt separation based on race? What emotions and body sensations do you notice as you recall your earliest memory?

One of my more recent memories of separation based on race is at a conference I attended in St. Louis in 2018. This conference brings together people who are working towards a just economy—one that puts people and planet over profit. There are many people working in all kinds of ways on creating a cooperative and regenerative economy. They have made a big effort to center racial justice and the voices of people most impacted by injustice in leadership and decision-making positions. Having people of color (POC) in leadership also means that it draws many participants who are POC, yet white conference attendees are still the majority. While there are definitely strong relationships among white folks and POCs, there is still noticeable separation in how people tend to engage in the space. White folks, including me, were grappling with our privilege and trying to communicate more honestly about it. People of color were trying to explain the reality of how racism is showing up in their workplace, without being fully understood. Some of the workshops and panels co-facilitated by white folks and folks of color had a power imbalance, with white folks taking up much more space. At the same time, it was clear that people at the conference were aware of these patterns and working on addressing the many ways that racism shows up even in well-intentioned spaces. When I bring this experience to mind, I feel embarrassed and stuck, my body is tense and my heart has a physical ache.

What's your most recent memory of separation because of race? What emotions and body sensations do you notice as you recall that recent memory?

In between the first time I felt a sense of separation, and the most recent time, there have been countless times throughout my life that I have felt separated. The ripple effect of systemic oppression includes all of these moments of separation. When I let myself really and truly feel the impact of that, it opens up a wave of grief. How do I heal from this separation, how do I support my kids in healing, and how do we participate in collective healing? One of the first things we can do is notice and interrupt separation and the oppression it might cause.

I'm working on supporting my children to recognize how and when separation happens, so they can contribute to the collective work of repairing it in themselves, in relationships, in communities, and ultimately in systems. For example, I notice separation happening in the intense competition between my two sons. Instead of sharing and enjoying each other and coming up with new and better ways to play, much of their energy goes into competing with each other and being the "best." Until fairly recently, I thought this was an entirely natural part of sibling rivalry. After all, there are whole books written on competition among siblings! Through talking to folks from poor backgrounds, Indigenous folks, and people who have worked to unlearn the assumptions of the capitalist system, I have come to see that this dynamic is much more connected to winning the game of capitalism than to an inherent nature of sibling relationships.

So to interrupt this dynamic I name it when I see it: "I notice you are each trying to be the best." I ask consciousness-raising questions: "Is being the best important?" Then I suggest ways of cooperating: "Your brother is learning how to do this, could you show him what you know?" Or I provide a project they can do together: "Could you work together to make a card for your grandma?"

Another way that separation shows up is that my youngest son is already starting to separate from himself by engaging in self-hate. He says he wants to be his older brother. I interrupt this form of separation by holding his hands, looking him right in the eye and saying, "I want you to be you, I love you just the way you are. You are creative, you know how to make me laugh, you notice what all your friends like, you are good at connecting with animals, you are good at planting peas, you have a warrior spirit, and you give good kisses." He grins and starts bouncing off the walls again, as only he can.

I already know my kids are feeling separate from others based on race, class, disability, and gender. I can also see where they are able to repair that separation. One day my then six-year-old son came home from school and said, "Jude wants to be a girl." My nine-year-old son said, "So what. Anyone can be anything they want." In my head I thought, "YES! This parenting for social justice thing is working." Aloud I said, "Yeah, that's true. Jude can wear a dress to school today and be a girl. And he might wear a Spiderman suit tomorrow and be a boy again. Or he might not. We all have infinite possibilities of being. You be you. Jude will be Jude."

This isn't just about us as parents, because we don't parent in a vacuum. Friends, relatives, teachers, coaches, mentors, and others in the community play a really important role in our kids' lives and we can communicate with them about these issues too. A friend recently told me how her five-year-old, who is white, came home from school talking about the new girl in class being "mean and messy." The child didn't say anything about race, but the mom knew the new girl was Black, and the only Black student in the class. She asked her child to explain what she meant by "mean and messy." After getting some further description, the mom talked about how it is hard to be new and how the new girl might be trying to make friends. She then emailed the teacher to find out what was happening in the class, and asked the teacher to support the two kids in being kind to each other. The teacher emailed back right away to say that the new girl was adjusting quite well and that there seemed to be a particular spark between these two kids. She promised to keep an eye on their developing relationship. Sure enough, within a couple of weeks my friend's daughter was already thinking of the new girl as her friend. Was race a factor here? Probably, and even though the five-year-old wasn't talking about it, supportive adults were able to notice the separation that was happening and help the kids find connection.

Social justice is about power, whether or not we each have the ability to make decisions that affect our lives. In a parent-child relationship, parents have the most power. This power differential can create a separation between parents and kids. As a parent, I make important decisions that impact my kids' lives. In many situations, what I say goes. This power can be important for keeping our kids safe, but can also be misused to control or dominate them. When we don't name and address the power dynamics in our home, it is disingenuous to challenge the unequal and unjust power dynamics in society. Kids will see right through that!

In her book *Parenting for Social Change*,[9] Teresa Graham Brett talks about building relationships with kids based on respect rather than control. She writes, "We can choose to use our power to support, facilitate, and assist the growth of children in ways that affirm their personal power, dignity, and humanity." Her work has helped me gain clarity on how I want to parent. While it is important to me to set healthy boundaries in the home, it is also important that those boundaries are in many cases developed in collaboration with my kids, so they have a say in what happens in their life and so they feel affirmed in their humanity and decision-making power.

For example, last summer we took a media break as a family. We already have an hour-a-day limit, but the kids think about and plan for that hour all day long. I was exasperated by their focus on media. So we sat down and talked for about five minutes about how they were losing out on important time with friends and time outdoors because they were too focused on watching TV and playing electronic games. In our conversation we decided to take a media break for the summer, with a few exceptions. This was a respectful and mutual decision and affirmed all of our humanity and needs.

There are many ways that a parent can affirm children's decision-making power. *Can you think of an example of where you are able to affirm your child's decision-making power?*

It is important to note here that all kinds of circumstances, many of them related to class, race, ability, and family makeup, affect what makes most sense for each family. For example, maybe you can't let your kids decide what they want for breakfast when you're budgeting your food really tightly. It is particularly hard to affirm kids' decision-making power when you as a parent don't have much power yourself. Sometimes when we are in disadvantaged positions we have to teach kids to be okay with not having a choice. It can be important to name that reality, so that we and our kids don't internalize it as a problem with us personally, but that we understand the lack of choice as connected to unjust systems.

What we do at home matters. Conversations over breakfast, apologizing when we make mistakes, and making friends outside of our "neighborhood" all contribute to social justice. As adrienne maree brown writes in *Emergent Strategy*,[10] "What we practice at the small scale sets the patterns for the whole system." She continues, "I have to use my life to leverage a shift in the system by *how* I am, as much as with the things I do." My parenting for social justice practice is based on this principle. If I'm so busy attending activist meetings and protests that I'm not able to give my kids the love and attention they need, which creates connection instead of separation, then I am not creating a strong fabric for their future. There are times to contribute to the larger

---

9 Teresa Graham Brett, *Parenting for Social Change* (Tucson, Social Change Press, 2011).
10 adrienne maree brown, *Emergent Strategy: Shaping Change, Changing Worlds* (CA, AK Press, 2017).

community and societal change and there are times to be at home with my kids. I need to make room for both instead of putting one over the other.

In the past couple of years I've re-examined how I live my life. I had been running around stressed out and unable to recognize my own needs because I was so busy responding to the needs of others. I wasn't operating from a place of power—the ability to take action—but from a place of guilt and sometimes the inability to say no. I was depleted and was responding to my kids, my husband, and my co-workers from that depleted place. Once I recognized the need to take care of myself and actually began to do it, I began to show up for my family and my community with more patience, humor, and creativity. Addressing injustice and working for social justice is not always easy, and sometimes it is not rewarding in the short term. This is a long game. The issues we are trying to address have been around for many many generations. We may see some small successes in our lifetime, and we are also going to see many defeats. We need to take time for healing, singing, enjoying each other, dancing, being quiet, and envisioning the world we are striving for. Without time to take care of ourselves, it is hard to cultivate that vision for change.

A few years ago I heard Ash-lee Woodard Henderson, the co-director of the Highlander Center in Tennessee, speak on envisioning the world we are striving for. She said, "We move towards whatever our vision is, so it is crucial to have a radical vision for social justice."[11] She told a story about asking a group of high school kids what their vision was for change. They answered that they wanted to hold the police accountable for the way they were policing their neighborhood. She said, "That's great! Is that your highest vision? Are there police in your vision?" They went back into a huddle and when they came back they said, "There are no police, there's no need for police. Everyone will have the housing, food, meaningful work, and community that they need for a dignified life." Now that's a vision! By articulating that more radical vision, those youth can work on creating that world.

Sherri Mitchell talks about the importance of envisioning the world we want to create. She lives by what she calls the the 10-10-80 rule[12]: investing 10% of our energy in looking at and understanding what needs to be changed, 10% of our energy in holding back the tide of harm that is coming at us, and 80% of our energy envisioning and creating the world we want to live in. This rule keeps me on track, focused on envisioning the world I want to live in instead of continually getting pulled into a downward spiral of everything that is wrong. When I am able to live into that vision, I can bring that visionary energy and creative thinking into my parenting.

As I've been more intentional about making sure I have the right combination of quiet time (through hiking, meditation, yoga, and personal retreats) and people time (through inspiring conferences, organizing meetings, and talking with mentors), I've been increasingly able to cultivate a radical vision of justice, equity, and peace. Visioning is healing and it gives me the strength to show up for parenting and for the racial justice organizing work that I do.

---

11 Ash-Lee Henderson, co-director of Highlander Center, speech at CommonBound, July 2018.
12 Sherri Mitchell, public talk at the Brooks Memorial Library, Brattleboro, VT, May 2018.

Parenting for social justice is a journey. It is not about perfection or about being the "most woke" or the "best social justice activist." (Notice the separation present in those phrases?) It is about telling our children the truth, supporting connection instead of separation, and encouraging their radical visions for a just world. It includes having conversations about hard topics, noticing power dynamics, and paying attention to the small things. I'm glad you are joining me for this length of my journey and that I can join you for this part of yours.

Who this book is for

While there is much that anyone can learn from this book, it is intended for parents and other caregivers of children from birth to ten years of age. It is written for parents who would like to learn more about how oppression and privilege/advantage operate and impact all of us. This book will be helpful for anyone who wants tips, tools, and inspiration for bringing social justice into their conversations and actions with kids.

Depending on your context—urban, rural, surrounded by people who look like you or with people who look different from you, in the presence of socially liberal laws or socially conservative laws, living in the U.S. or somewhere else[13]—some stories in this book will resonate with you, and other stories you'll find are very different from yours.

Your identities will also impact which parts of this book are useful for you. All of us have things to learn about how oppression works and how it impacts us personally. This is a process of unlearning harmful messages that permeate our society and sometimes our own thinking. There will be parts of this book where you will learn something, and other parts where you could teach us.

As you read this book, I expect that you won't agree with me and the other authors on everything. There are many different "right" ways to do parenting for social justice. However, please hold me accountable if you see that my privilege is getting in the way of truth and justice. Your feedback will help further shape the vision of a world that is free from the chains of oppression and separation. Let's support each other, learn from each other, and be vulnerable. I'm committed to looking at myself honestly and with deep love. And I'm committed to doing the same for you. Thanks for being in this community of practice with me and with each other.

About the co-authors

This book has six co-authors and an illustrator as well as vignettes by 24 parents and caregivers around the U.S. As I mentioned earlier, I started writing the book and then I brought more people on board to contribute to the project. I reached out to people who I knew, either personally or through workshops I had led. I tried to think of people who represented diversity of races and nationalities, genders, abilities, and class

---

13 If you are not living in the U.S., this book may or may not be useful to you. It might be helpful for you in understanding a little bit more about the U.S. context since it has such a wide-reaching impact on the world. Some of what is in this book might apply to where you live; white supremacy, capitalism, and discrimination because of gender and disability are real in so many places around the world.

experiences. Many people I reached out to were not able to contribute because of timing or other priorities, and the book got stalled a few times until I could find the right person to work on a given chapter. The folks who said yes have been absolutely amazing to work with, and their analysis and vulnerability have pushed me to consider new ways of thinking and being. Here's a little background about us and how we each got connected to this book. You will learn more from each authors' writing in their chapters and also in the brief bios in the back of the book.

Abigail Healey (Chapter 5) lives nearby me in the Brattleboro, Vermont area and we are good friends. In fact, when our children were babies we lived in the same house for over two years! We bring similar perspectives in many ways, and yet we have very different parenting experiences. Jaimie Lynn Kessel (Chapter 4) lives a couple hours' drive from us in Waterbury, Vermont, although she is originally from West Virginia (in the Appalachian Mountain range). Back in 2018, she applied to be an intern for ACT for Social Justice, the training and consulting group I started. As an intern, Jaimie assisted with the transition of a Cross Class Dialogue Circle that I co-facilitated with Kendra Colburn, from an in-person only class into a virtual one. Jaimie and I became friends and when I asked her if she would co-write the economic justice chapter, it didn't take long for her to give an enthusiastic response. Chrissy Colón Bradt (Chapter 3) used to live in Brattleboro, Vermont and has been on the Board of Directors of The Root Social Justice Center for five years, even though she moved to Connecticut a couple years ago to take the position of Director of Diversity & Equity for a private pre-school-12 school. Chrissy and I have co-facilitated several workshops for parents and she was an obvious choice to coauthor a chapter on racial justice. Rowan Parker (Chapter 5) also participated in a Cross Class Dialogue Circle and lives in Northampton, Massachusetts. His contribution to this project has been invaluable because of the way he engaged critically and thoughtfully with the material and was able to address neurodivergence in the Disability Justice chapter. The gender chapter proved to be the hardest to find authors for, so we ended up with just one author rather than a team of two. This means the chapter doesn't provide two diverse perspectives on parenting for gender justice. However, Leila Raven (Chapter 6) has proved to be capable of rising to the challenge of penning a chapter on her own. Her writing is astonishingly full of powerful teachings on how gender oppression operates and tangible ways to practice gender justice with our families, informed by her grassroots organizing work in Washington, D.C., and New York. She was introduced to me by a colleague and friend of mine in southern VT, Sonia Silbert, who used to organize in Washington D.C.. Brittney Washington, Leila's friend and co-conspirator in Washington D.C., agreed to illustrate the parent and child conversations in the book. Her artwork is a beautiful and inspiring contribution to this book. The parents who wrote vignettes for the book are all people I know quite well and I'm honored and overjoyed that they agreed to share their experiences.

We live, work, play and parent in different communities with different sets of strengths and challenges. In this book we share our own stories so that you can be inspired to identify parallels and differences in your own communities. We know that each of us writing and reading this book parent and caregive in different contexts: from within different bodies, spirits, family systems, and communities, in cities or rural areas in different states, and regions. Please take what works for you, be curious about what is different from your experience, and leave behind whatever won't serve you. None of us are experts. We are adding our experiences and voices to a body of truth telling that we hope will contribute to this time of great transformation, of turning toward justice, of reaching out to connect with others to make all our lives more full, beautiful, and just.

How this book is structured

We have four overarching goals for this book. We believe that all of these goals will keep us on the path to collective liberation—so we can all be free!

Our first goal is to offer tools and direction in this next step in your social justice learning process. The second is to provide tips and support for asking big questions and having hard conversations about social justice issues with the children in your lives. Building on those conversations, the third goal is to inspire you to take bold action for social justice with your families. And finally, our fourth goal is to engage with challenging material and with each other (as co-authors, readers, and people reading this book together) in the spirit of love and possibility.

As authors, we will accomplish those goals by teaching about seven social justice principles (Chapter 1) and ways to build them into conversation and action in your family (Chapter 2). We will then apply those principles in four areas—racial justice (Chapter 3), economic justice (Chapter 4), gender justice (Chapter 5), and disability justice (Chapter 6). We'll tie it all together by connecting the key social justice concepts of collective liberation, intersectionality, and emergent strategy (Chapter 7). We'll close by reviewing what we learned together throughout the book (Chapter 8).

Each section in the book includes an experiential learning section: read/watch/listen, then reflect and generalize. When we take time to reflect on our own thinking and experience, it deepens our personal understanding of social justice, and strengthens our commitment to integrating social justice into our parenting.

Throughout the book, explanations from us, the authors, are illustrated with short stories of parents and caregivers from around the U.S. (although you will notice that many people are in Vermont because that's where I live, play, and organize) who are having social justice conversations with their kids. These conversations showcase parents' courage, creativity, and willingness to push through mistakes and to try again.

Let's start off with a story from Laura.

> **Laura Goldblatt lives in small-town Vermont with her two kids (ages three and a half and six and a half), husband, fluffy cat, and some friendly chickens. Some of the things she enjoys are biking with her family, reading novels, and getting to know people.**
>
> *Scene: My six-year-old child and I are in bed reading* Police Cars and Other Rescue Vehicles, *one of my child's favorites. We turn to a page that shows a person in handcuffs,*

with only their hands, arms, and torso visible. It's obvious that the person is of color and likely that they're male. It's the only picture in the book depicting someone of color, besides the one showing that "police officers can be anyone."

Me: Hmm, this picture really bothers me.

Child: [Stares at picture]

Me: I noticed that this person has darker skin than us, and almost all the rest of the people in the book have light skin, the kind that's called "white."

Child: Yeah, that one and that one and that one have skin like us. That one [pointing to handcuffed person] looks like the color of our friend.

Me: By having only one picture of a person with darker skin and having that person be in trouble, the book makes it seem like those are the only people who get in trouble, and like white men do all the good jobs. But that's totally not true, is it?

Child: No.

Mother: I wish there were more pictures in this book of people with all different skin colors doing the jobs.

Child: I think they should take out the picture of the person in handcuffs and just show some handcuffs. I don't like that picture.

Me: Is it scary to see a person in handcuffs?

Child: Yeah.

Me: I like a lot of the information in this book, but I want the library to try to find one with pictures of more people of different colors. When we bring this back to the library, would you help me talk to the librarian about that?

Child: OK.

Reflections: I wish I asked more questions when trying to talk with my child about important things, rather than lecture him, but it's a start! Also, I ended up returning the book by myself and would do that differently next time. I asked the children's librarian about it and other books like it. She said that the children's room has been intentionally working on its nonfiction collection with the purpose of having it fully reflect the humanity of all people. She said the "community helpers" section (police, rescue, firefighters, health care, etc) was under particular scrutiny for reasons just like what I brought up. She thanked me for bringing the issue to her attention and said it was really helpful when people speak up because the library understands better how its collection is seen by the community. She took this title off the shelf and after checking confirmed that all other books showing anyone getting arrested had been removed.

Laura's conversation with her son is a great example of how to respond to cringe-worthy books in the moment, and how to plan for braver actions in the future. Have you ever cringed when reading a book with a child? Maybe when reading some of your old favorites like Richard Scarry's *Busytown* books, or *Babar,* or *Curious George*? What did you do after the cringe? What would you do differently next time? Throughout the book after the parents share their stories you'll have an opportunity for that type of reflection.

There might be words or concepts in this book that you are unfamiliar with, or that you think about differently than how we are using the word. In some cases, the explanation or definitions will be included in the passage. When you see a term you're unfamiliar with that doesn't have an explanation, please refer to our description of our frameworks in Appendix A or our definitions in Appendix B for more information.

We refer to many resources throughout the book, and the resource section in the back of the book compiles them all in one place for easy reference. The resource section also includes a list of recommended children's books. One of the best ways to access those books is to ask your local library to purchase the books, so they will be available to many people in your community. Or if you have the means, you can purchase books and donate them to your local library.

How you can use this book

You can expect to spend upwards of three hours on each chapter. It may be helpful for your learning to set a schedule for when you will use the book, or to set a goal for how often you will finish a chapter so that it doesn't gather dust on your bedside table. For example, you could decide to spend lunchtime every Friday with the book and move through the chapters however quickly or slowly that takes you. Or you could decide you will complete one chapter every two weeks and finish the book in three months. Choose whatever will help you prioritize it in a way that works for you.

There are two main options for how to use this book. You can go through it at your own pace, either on your own or with a partner, relative, or friend. Or you can use the book with a "community of practice." If you will be reading this book within your family, here are some questions to consider before you start:

1. What is our timeline for completing the book?

2. Will we set a regular time for this learning or do it whenever it works into our schedule?

3. If we have kids over ten, will we ask them to discuss parts of the book with us?

When you engage with this book as a group, whether with one other family or ten other families, it will enhance your learning. First off, the book is less likely to simply sit on a shelf when you engage with a group. Second, you'll gain tips, tools, and inspiration from the others in the group. And third, you'll have others to hold you accountable for putting your goals into action.

There's a group in Marlboro, Vermont, that used this book as part of their community of practice. In the words of Robin, a mother who participated in the group, "This book was so powerful. About ten parents and teachers from my children's public school community studied it over the course of six months and met monthly to discuss what we had watched and read. The readings prompted deep, meaningful, and enlightening conversations about privilege, the very real economic disparity within our communities, empathy, and how to raise our children (and ourselves) to be self-aware, generous, and compassionate citizens of the world."

At the end of each chapter, there are questions you can use as a community of practice to reflect on what you learned. Whatever your community of practice looks like, here are some questions to answer before you start:

1. How often will we meet?

2. What will we do before we meet?

3. What will we do when we meet? (For example: watch film clips together, answer reflection questions together, or answer the more general discussion questions provided throughout the book at the end of each chapter.

4. Who will facilitate the meetings? Will there be one facilitator, rotating facilitators, or no facilitator?

5. What will our kids do while we meet? Will older kids join the conversation? Will we rotate childcare? Ask older kids to provide it? Pay for childcare?

6. Will there be food? How will that be organized?

7. Are there any accessibility needs we should be aware of (fragrance-free environment, language interpretation, ramp access, etc.[1])?

---

1 Suggestions for accessible events: https://www.sinsinvalid.org/news-1/2020/6/8/access-suggestions-for-public-events.

Another way to connect to a community of practice is through the closed group Parenting 4 Social Justice on Facebook: https://www.facebook.com/groups/2124078564584646. Join if you would like to engage with other parents around the world who are practicing parenting for social justice.

Take care of your heart and body

There are many benefits of bringing social justice conversation and action into your family, and there are also challenges. You will gain a more complex understanding of how your actions impact others, which improves your ability to find equitable and just ways of interacting. You will better understand yourself and your own experience, which will make you better equipped to support your kids in understanding who they are and what they are experiencing. Bringing social justice into your family will transform the way you understand and relate to those who have different life experiences from yours, which together with improved self-awareness, will make it possible for your family to connect with many different people. It will also increase your capacity to address injustice as it impacts your family, community, and world, which will create a safer, healthier, more equitable family, community, and world.

At the same time, social justice conversations can be uncomfortable and emotional, and can bring up past trauma for many of us. As you go through this book please do what you need to take care of yourself. Choose a pace that works for you. Find a good friend or even a therapist with whom you can talk about the painful and perhaps traumatic feelings that arise for you while doing this work. And if a spiritual practice is part of your life, it can be very supportive in moving through the emotions and trauma in a way that is healing. Prayer, meditation, singing, walking, sound healing, going to religious services, or reading holy texts or inspirational poems are all ways to gain perspective and grounding. Throughout this book we will share healing practices that are helpful for us.

Pretending that social justice issues aren't real and present is hurting us in ways that we aren't even aware of. Bringing them up can feel painful in the moment, yet it allows us to move through the feelings and find healing and freedom. You don't have to do this alone. Let's turn away from whatever is distracting us and turn towards what gets us connected to each other and to positive change. Let's roll up our sleeves and get our hands messy and mix in a few tears, rageful yells, belly laughs, and dance parties along the way.

A parent workshop facilitated by a parenting 4 social justice group.

Healing justice practice

Throughout the book you will find simple practices for noticing and moving through feelings and body sensations that come up. These practices will also support you in bringing your mind and heart and body back into the present moment. Many of these practices draw on work that is being done in the healing justice movement.

Leah Lakshmi Piepzna-Samarasinha, a well-known and respected disability justice activist, writes:

> Healing Justice as a movement and a term was created by queer and trans people of colour and in particular Black and brown femmes, centering working-class, poor, disabled and Southern/rural healers. Before "healing justice" was a phrase, healers have been healing folks at kitchen tables and community clinics for a long time— from the acupuncture clinics run by Black Panthers like Mutulu Shakur in North America in the 1960s and 1970s, to our bone-deep Black, Indigenous, people of colour and pre-Christian European traditions of healing with herbs, acupuncture, touch, prayer, and surgery.[14]

In this book we offer healing practices with the recognition that healing is a cultural practice connected to ancient ways of knowing. The healing justice movement comes out of oppressed communities and it is of utmost importance when using a healing practice to acknowledge where it comes from, and to ensure that using a certain healing practice is not cultural appropriation.[15]

In the social justice communities of practice that I am a part of, healing is foundational to the justice work we are doing. Healing from the traumas of being oppressed or oppressor allows us to be fully human, to recognize where the patterns of oppression still exist in us, and to move through the feelings and pain towards wholeness. This awareness allows us to be in relationship with others who are also doing this work. Because of how important healing is for justice we have woven healing practices throughout the book. There are so many wonderful and nourishing healing practices. We encourage you to find the practices that will best support you and your family in healing.

Let's start with this ***present-moment practice*** adapted from the beloved Buddhist monk, teacher, writer, and leader Thich Nhat Hanh:

---

14 Leah Lakshmi Piepzna-Samarasinha, "A Not-So-Brief Personal History of the Healing Justice Movement, 2010-2016," *Mice Magazine*, accessed April 9, 2019, http://micemagazine.ca/issue-two/not-so-brief-personal-history-healing-justice-movement-2010%E2%80%932016.

15 Cultural appropriation is when members from a dominant culture use cultural elements from a group that has been systematically oppressed. For an in-depth definition see Appendix B.

Get comfortable. Relax your body, roll your shoulders back, put your feet flat on the ground.

Feel the earth beneath your feet. Feel the earth holding you.

Take a deep breath in. Let it out.

Breathe in goodness and joy. Breathe out all of the thoughts and feelings that do not serve you.

Listen to the sounds around you.

Take a deep breath in. Let it out.

Notice the feelings that are present in you right now. Don't try to change them, just be with them. Let them know you see them.

Take a deep breath in. Let it out.

Be right here in this present moment. Be right here with who you are in this present moment.

Offer yourself a smile.

Take a deep breath in. Let it out.

Be still and quiet.

Continue breathing and noticing your feelings until you feel ready to move on.

Child making a sign at a protest.

Chapter 1

SOCIAL JUSTICE (IN BRIEF)

BY ANGELA BERKFIELD

*True compassion is more than flinging a coin to a beggar; it is not haphazard
and superficial. It comes to see that an edifice which produces beggars
needs restructuring. A true revolution of values will soon look uneasily
on the glaring contrast of poverty and wealth.*
—MARTIN LUTHER KING JR., "Beyond Vietnam" speech, April 4, 1967

*As long as poverty, injustice and gross inequality
persist in our world, none of us can truly rest.*
—NELSON MANDELA, "Make Poverty History" rally, 2005

*Another world is not only possible, she is on her way.
On a quiet day I can hear her breathing.*
—ARUNDHATI ROY, *War Talk*, 2003

Reflect
*Use the following questions as a guide to reflect on the quotes above. You can
write or paint and share your responses with someone, or just think quietly, whatever
works best for your learning style.*

1. When you think about social justice do you think more about individual-level
   solutions like providing for people who are hungry, or about systemic solutions
   like a restructuring of society, or both? What has shaped your thinking?

2. Can you feel the gravity of what Nelson Mandela is saying? What does this mean
   in your life?

3. Do you believe in the possibility of something different?

Person with a mask holding a handmade sign that says, "Injustice anywhere is a threat to justice everywhere!!" Credit: Shutterstock

What is social justice?

There are many ways to think about social justice. This is the definition I use because while it names what we need to stand against, it also presents a positive vision to strive for. As Ash-Lee Henderson said, "If you can't envision it, you're never going to get there."[1]

> A socially just world meets everyone's basic needs (food, housing, transportation, healthcare, education, job, etc.) in a dignified way; guarantees equitable distribution of resources; ensures everyone has a voice in the decisions that affect them; makes sure all people are physically and psychologically safe and secure; treats people from every background with dignity and respect; and supports the development of all people to their full potential. To achieve social justice we must stand in opposition to capitalism, exploitation, racism, and oppression in its many forms. We must engage in a constant practice of creating and recreating our actions so they are aligned with social justice principles.[2]

This definition lays out seven social justice principles and their opposites—the patterns we must work against in order to realize those principles. Let's look more closely at each principle.

---

1 Ash-Lee Henderson, co-director of Highlander Center, speech at CommonBound, July 2018.
2 ACT for Social Justice, 2013. Adapted from a classism definition by Class Action, August 2018, www.classism.org, and from social justice definition from "Social Justice in Intercultural Relations" course syllabus at SIT, taught by Janaki Natarajan, September 2007.

Everyone's basic needs (food, housing, transportation, healthcare, education, job) are met in a dignified way—as opposed to a society in which poverty, deprivation, and shame are accepted as normal.

The current reality falls far short of meeting everyone's basic needs in a dignified way. Poverty in the U.S. is increasing. There are currently 48 million people living with incomes below the federal poverty level (FPL) of $24,000/year for a family of four. The FPL is not an accurate measure for many reasons, not the least of which is that political opposition has prevented any updates that would keep the FPL up to date with inflation and changes to the cost of living.[3] If we were to use a more realistic number for the poverty level, the number of people living in poverty would double or even triple. Globally, poverty is even more extreme. Almost half the world's population—over three billion people—live on less than $2.50 a day. At least 80% of people live on less than $10 a day. More than 80% of the world's population lives in countries where the gap in income between rich and poor is growing rather than shrinking (including the U.S.).[4]

This principle is not simply about meeting people's needs, which can be done in a variety of ways. Social justice requires meeting needs *in a dignified way*. To do that we need to shift our collective beliefs about direct aid (such as that provided by government assistance programs and charity organizations), to reframe support for people's basic needs as an important part of an equitable society, instead of as something shameful that marks someone as not contributing "enough" to capitalist production. We need to end the massive handouts to the owning class, which take the form of tax breaks and loopholes. The wealthy need to contribute equitably through taxes to pay their share of all that is needed for a society to thrive. People need to be compensated fairly for their labor, and have access to the healthcare and childcare that they need not only to survive, but to thrive. We need to put the collective before the individual, so that it wouldn't be possible for some people to have mansions while others are homeless, for example.

Example of change: One suggestion for making this social justice principle a reality is the Universal Basic Income (UBI), a policy under which all citizens or residents of a country receive a regular sum of money from the government, with no stipulations. This differs from today's welfare system because society deems *all* people worthy of the same baseline income, and the quality of life it provides. Most people who receive UBI would still work at paid jobs, and whatever they earn would be "extra" beyond what's required to meet their basic needs. This gives people the freedom to not be in the paid labor force *all* of the time, and to spend time caring for kids and elders in their family, or pursuing artistic endeavors, etc., without fearing that they won't be able to eat.

---

3 Shawn Fremstad, "The Federal Poverty Level is Too Damn Low," *talk poverty,* September 13, 2016, https://talkpoverty.org/2016/09/13/poverty-rate-just-dropped-way-measure-poverty-wrong/
4 Anup Shah, "Causes of Poverty," *Global Issues,* September 28, 2014, http://www.globalissues.org/issue/2/causes-of-poverty.

There are also some very interesting and important critiques of the UBI,[5] one being that it does not alter the basic structures of capitalism that are wreaking havoc on people and planet. In other words, UBI alone does not solve the problem—but it can be one important piece of a solution.

Example of change: Cooperation Jackson, "an emerging vehicle for sustainable community development, economic democracy, and community ownership"[6] in Jackson, Mississippi. This network of cooperatives is very intentionally standing in opposition to oppression and exploitation, while creatively implementing the seven social justice principles. Cooperation Jackson creates affordable housing options like co-housing and paths to home ownership, launches worker coops and urban farms, facilitates ongoing study groups for community members to learn more about how to dismantle harmful systems, and so much more!

Principle #2

Everyone has a meaningful voice in the decisions that affect them—as opposed to disenfranchisement and power imbalances that give some people power over others

I was brought up to think that representative democracy gives people a meaningful voice, but the reality is different. The representative democracy in the U.S. is rigged in favor of those who have the most wealth. The interests of the wealthiest 0.1%—that's one in one thousand—control most decisions in the political arena. This is true on most local levels, as well as nationally. In 2015 the median net worth of U.S. Congress members was $1.2 million.[7] Dan Kopf, who writes about economics and statistics for *Quartz* (an online journal that calls itself a guide to the New Economy for people excited by change), says, "White individuals (81%) and men (80%) continue to dominate Congress, as they did back in 1972, but there is much more diversity today. At the same time, far more members enter Congress with personal wealth than was the case previously, and seven of the 43 who we have considered 'superrich' are women (16%) . . . Those in the other three groups we have looked at—African American, Latinx, and LGB—are far less likely to be wealthy than those in the other groups and in that respect are probably much more 'representative' of their constituents at the lower end of the income distribution."[8]

The people who make decisions about policies related to education, food, housing, welfare, social security, and prison and policing systems, do not have the same living conditions, nor similar interests, of the majority of people in the U.S. No wonder they vote for tax cuts to the rich. It is time to change who is making the decisions on a local,

---

5 Ellie Mae O'Hagan, "Love the idea of a universal basic income? Be careful what you wish for," *The Guardian*, July 23, 2017, https://www.theguardian.com/commentisfree/2017/jun/23/universal-basic-income-ubi-welfare-state.

6 cooperationjackson.org

7 Dan Kopf, "The Typical U.S. Congress Member is 12 Times Richer than the Typical American Household," Quartz, February 12, 2018, https://qz.com/1190595/the-typical-us-congress- member-is-12-times-richer-than-the-typical-american-household.

8 Richard Zweigenhaft, "Diversity and Wealth in Congress Today," *The Society Pages*, October 2, 2018, https://thesocietypages.org/specials/diversity-and-wealth-in-congress-today.

state, and national level. To do so will take a shift in values and a dedication of time and financial support to make it a reality. This brings to mind the movement cry "Nothing About Us, Without Us, Is For Us," which was coined by the disability rights movement in South Africa. It means that the people most impacted by oppression must be at the table participating in the decision-making process.

Example of change: What does this principle look like in practice? Since the 2016 presidential election there has been a big push by grassroots groups, such as People's Action, and Democratic groups, such as Emerge, for women, people of color, and LGBTQIA[9] folks to run for political positions. For these candidates to get into office and stay in office requires a lot of support and involvement from the communities they represent, to ensure they can compete with well-funded opponents and sustain their position in the face of threats and personal attacks. Without well-organized support, a newly elected representative from a marginalized community may not be able to be effective in the long term. For example, Representative Kiah Morris in Vermont was the only Black woman serving in the Vermont House of Representatives and a strong proponent of racial justice legislation. Although well-respected by many in the legislature and by constituents across the state, she resigned from the mid-term race in 2018 due to threats against her life by white-supremacists.[10] Legislators, local media outlets, and the non-profit sector in Vermont are now talking about how to ensure that legislators and all people of color in the state are safe and supported. Legislation to address the issue is currently being proposed.

Principle #3

All people are physically and psychologically safe and secure—as opposed to facing physical and emotional violence from individuals or systems.

If we put the first two principles into action it is more likely people will be safe. When people's basic needs are met and they have some power over what happens in their lives there is a reduction in violence, substance use, and isolation.

Equitable access to material resources is necessary for safety and security, but it is not all that's needed. We also need to shift the ideologies that permit and excuse violence. Because oppression is woven into the fabric of society, there is systemic violence against marginalized populations, with all kinds of justifications for the violence. Here are just a few well-documented examples:

- ❋ The National Council on Violence Against Women reports that one in four women and one in nine men experience severe intimate partner violence.[11] In a culture where sexual violence is the norm, people tend to blame the victim— her skirt was too short, she was asking for it, why didn't she say no?—instead of blaming the person who assaulted her. People in power, like judges and politicians, also indulge in this tendency, so it becomes embedded in law and policy, affecting everyone.

---

9 LGBTQIA: lesbian, gay, bisexual, transgender, queer, intersex, asexual.
10 Jim Therrien, "UPDATED: After threats, Kiah Morris withdraws from House race," *VT Digger,* August 24, 2018, https://vtdigger.org/2018/08/24/kiah-morris-withdraws-candidacy-bennington-house-race.
11 National Council on Domestic Violence, "Fact Sheet," October 14, 2018, https://ncadv.org/statistics.

❀ "Black girls face high and disproportionate suspension rates across the coun-try—and it's not because they are misbehaving more frequently than other girls," says Neena Chaudhry, director of education at the National Women's Law Center. "This uneven discipline is often the result of deeply ingrained racist and sexist stereotypes that push black girls out of school."[12] This trend is echoed in preschools as well.[13] Arguments used to justify this disproportionate punish-ment are that Black girls and women are angry, aggressive, or promiscuous, which, even if it were true, would not justify disproportionate punishment in a school-to-prison pipeline.

❀ Assaults in the U.S. (and other countries around the globe) against Muslims were up in 2016, according to a Pew Research Center Report.[14] Moral superior-ity arguments, such as "Muslims are terrorists," are used to defend these assaults. Regardless of morals, physically attacking people does nothing to solve the underlying issues, and it can be argued that it makes them worse.

Let's take the example of sexual assault. If we are to have physical and psychological safety we need to change both the physical reality, by following through on policies that protect women and everyone from abuse by holding abusers accountable (with an intersectional lens so that it doesn't turn into an excuse for disproportionate punish-ment of POC), and we need to change minds, through public awareness campaigns and by teaching consent in schools.

Example of change: The #MeToo movement has created a shift in consciousness in the U.S., with many survivors of rape and sexual violence coming forward to speak pub-licly about their stories and to demand accountability for the people who abused them. The movement has succeeded in winning some policy changes: more protections for low-wage workers, and in some state governments employees can now speak about sexual harassment in the workplace.[15] Of course it will take ongoing pressure for the policy changes to have the necessary teeth to actually reduce violence and harassment. #MeToo is an example of a social movement that changes hearts and minds, so that more people are advocating and voting for just and equitable policies and practices.

---

12 Lauren Camera, "Black Girls are Twice As Likely To Be Suspended in Every State," May 9, 2017, https://www.usnews.com/news/education-news/articles/2017-05-09/black-girls-are-twice-as-likely-to-be-suspended-in-every-state.
13 Rasheed Malik, "New Data Reveal 250 Preschoolers Are Suspended or Expelled Every Day," November 6, 2017, https://www.americanprogress.org/issues/early-childhood/news/2017/11/06/442280/new-data-reveal-250-preschoolers-suspended-expelled-every-day.
14 Katayoun Kishi, "Assaults against Muslims in U.S. surpass 2001 level," November 15, 2017, http://www.pewresearch.org/fact-tank/2017/11/15/assaults-against-muslims-in-u-s-surpass-2001-level.
15 Zoe Greenberg, "What Has Actually Changed in a Year," New York Times, October 6, 2018, https://www.nytimes.com/interactive/2018/10/06/opinion/sunday/What-Has-Actually-Changed-in-a-Year-me-too.html.

Resources are distributed equitably—as opposed to drastic inequality in income and wealth being the norm.

Right now the U.S. has a minimum wage, set by law at both federal and local levels, but we don't have a maximum wage. The U.S. government puts a lot of funding into policing the poor, while the rich get away with state-sanctioned robbery and murder. The wealthy have an increasing share of the economic pie, while more and more people fall below an already too low poverty line. This massive and grotesque unequal distribution of wealth harms all of us.

Richard Wilkinson and Kate Pickett have a whole body of research about how this wealth inequality is harming societies across the globe. Wilkinson says, "We showed that in more-unequal countries, with bigger income gaps between rich and poor, there is more of a whole range of health and social problems. Life expectancy tends to be lower, more obesity,[16] higher homicide rate, more people in prison, more drug problems, more mental illness. Basically what we showed was that all the problems that have what we call social gradients, problems that are more common down on the social ladder, get worse when you increase the status differences between us."[17] Wilkinson's research shows that this inequality in society affects everyone, regardless of income.

Guaranteeing equitable distribution of resources is possible, and has been within reach, but it requires political power. When Bernie Sanders ran for president he ran on the premise that economic equity is good for the U.S., and many Americans supported his platform. He is a proponent of progressive taxation,[18] in which the richest Americans and corporations would contribute equitably to the federal budget through tax policy. Progressive taxation would make it possible for all kids to have access to quality education, from preschool through college. It would also make basic health care coverage for all residents possible in the U.S. As it is now, one medical emergency or illness would put most people in the U.S. on a downward spiral into poverty.

Example of change: The campaign for universal health care has continued to grow over the past decade with many organizations involved in educating and organizing the public. All developed countries around the world, except for the U.S., already have a version of universal health care in place.[19] And according to a 2018 Reuters poll, 70% of Americans support the idea of universal basic health care.[20] In September 2017, Bernie

---

16 Obesity is a poor measure of health and has been used as an excuse to deny healthcare to fat people, who are disproportionately poor and/or POC. https://www.yesmagazine.org/peace-justice/fat-acceptance-movement-20190624.

17 Social Science Bites, "Richard Wilkinson on How Inequality is Bad," July 3, 2018, https://www.socialsciencespace.com/2018/07/richard-wilkinson-on-how-inequality-is-bad.

18 "Bernie Sanders on Tax Reform," On The Issues, August 16, 2018, http://www.ontheissues.org/2016/Bernie_Sanders_Tax_Reform.htm.

19 Thomas DeMichele, "The U.S. is the Only Very Highly Developed Country Without Universal HealthCare," Fact/Myth, updated January 31, 2019, http://factmyth.com/factoids/the-us-is-the-only-very-highly-developed-country-without-universal-healthcare.

20 Yoni Blumberg, "70% of Americans now support Medicare-for-all—here's how single-payer could affect you," CNBC, August 28, 2018, https://www.cnbc.com/2018/08/28/most-americans-now-support-medicare-for-all-and-free-college-tuition.html.

Sanders and fifteen other Democratic senators released a new bill to Congress for expanding Medicaid to cover all Americans.[21] Because of a Republican-controlled Congress, there is not currently enough political power to put these bills into law. But the popular support is there. Universal health care could happen if the U.S. Congress was more representative of the constituents or if the U.S. had a more direct democracy.

Example of change: Worker cooperatives are a very practical and possible way to ensure equitable distribution of resources within a business. There are many successful worker cooperatives and more are popping up all the time. One example is Cooperative Home Care Associates[22], which employs 2,300 home care workers in the Bronx. Over half of the workers co-own the cooperative business.

We have to be careful when creating new structures that the same injustices aren't just replicated in a new way. For example, a worker cooperative whose members are all white, able-bodied, cisgender men may represent a positive step for worker justice in a narrow sense, but in another sense it is not actually transferring wealth equitably since it is not creating justice for workers of many genders, races, and abilities. The cooperative must work to develop leadership for people who have been most impacted by oppression (Indigenous, Black, POC, poor, working class, queer, trans, youth, immigrants, formerly incarcerated or enslaved, etc.) so that wealth and power are shared more equitably throughout society.

Principle #5

People from every background are treated with dignity and respect, as opposed to stereotyping and assuming that some people are better than others.
Each person is valuable. Every single person.

Example of change: There are so many beautiful examples of humans treating fellow humans with respect and dignity. For the purposes of this section let's get honest with ourselves about a person who we need to treat with dignity and respect. *Bring to mind a person you have looked down on or judged. Then, think about how to transform that situation so that you are affirming the person's dignity and treating them with respect.*

I frequently drive by a man holding a sign, "Hungry, anything helps." It's an awkward place to stop and give money and so I don't. In my head I have thought, "Why is he at this intersection instead of a better one?" "I hope he doesn't walk by my house and rob me," "If he walks by my house I am going to have to talk to him, and I don't have time for that." Yep. I've thought all those things.

After a few weeks of driving by I finally stopped and talked with the man and let the cars drive around me. I learned that he sleeps in a tent throughout the winter and mostly enjoys it. He told me he'll stay in the area as long as he can make the money he needs to cover food and his other expenses, and he likes this area so he hopes to be able

21 David Weigel, "Sanders introduces universal health care, backed by 15 Democrats," Washington Post, September 13, 2017, https://www.washingtonpost.com/powerpost/sanders-will-introduce-universal-health-care-backed-by-15-democrats/2017/09/12/d590ef26-97b7-11e7-87fc-c3f7ee4035c9_story.html.
22 Policylink, "Modeling an Equitable Workforce with Cooperative Home Care Associates," Sept 2, 2019, https://equityis.exposure.co/modeling-an-equitable-workforce-with-cooperative-home-care-associates.

to stay. I didn't have any cash on me, but I promised to stop back when I did. I followed through on my promise. I hope I get to talk with him again sometime, to learn more of his story, and to share mine, too.

Engaging with him as a valuable human being felt so much better than the narrative that was going through my head. *How about you? How do you, or can you, transform your judgment into respect and dignity and shared humanity?*

Principle #6

All people are supported in reaching their full potential—as opposed to hoarding opportunities for some people over others.

The realities of an unequal society make it really hard for all people to reach their full potential, both because they lack the opportunities and the material resources necessary to do so, and also because of the emotional and health impact of being disrespected and devalued. Living with racism, poverty, sexism, homophobia, and ableism and oppression often causes trauma, which can be passed through our genes to the next generation.[23] Trauma has very real impacts on people, including ongoing negative impacts on physical and mental health.[24] We need to support individuals to heal from trauma. We also need to design systems to minimize trauma, and to repair the harm that is done. When we recognize that each person has value and potential, we design policies so that each person can thrive. What if instead of looking down on certain jobs or roles in society, we valued all the many ways in which people contribute their talents, skills, and care. What if all work was respected and compensated at a livable rate?

Example of change: The National Domestic Workers Alliance (NDWA) is advocating for this value shift and for policies to back it up, specifically with regard to the labor of people who work in other people's homes as housekeepers, nannies, in-home healthcare providers, and more. This is a powerful statement from the domestic workers: "We are the women who care for this country. We are black, we are women of color, we are immigrants. Behind closed doors we face harassment, abuse, and discrimination. We are uniting with women everywhere so that all workplaces are safe and dignified. We are unstoppable."[25]

Examples of change: Two policy changes would dramatically change the possibilities for millions of people. One policy is universal access to quality early childhood care. A Center for American Progress report provides information by state on current access to quality early education, and how improved access would benefit the state's

---

23 This is called epigenetics. To learn more, listen to Rachel Yehuda, one of the leaders in this body of research. Krista Tippett with Rachel Yehuda, "How Trauma and Resilience Cross Generations", On Being, July 30, 2015, https://onbeing.org/programs/rachel-yehuda-how-trauma-and-resilience-cross-generations-nov2017.

24 This diagram developed by the Ryse Youth Center in Richmond, CA, is helpful in understanding the impact of childhood and community trauma on a person's health outcomes. Ryse Youth Center, "Adding Layers to the ACES Pyramid, What do you think?" April 7, 2015, https://www.acesconnection.com/blog/adding-layers-to-the-aces-pyramid-what-do-you-think.

25 October 30, 2018, https://www.domesticworkers.org.

children and economy overall.[26] One example of a positive implementation of this policy is in New York City where Mayor Bill De Blasio started public pre-K for four-year-olds in 2014.

Another policy is universal access to college. College has increasingly become necessary to get a job that will pay the bills. And yet, the cost of college has increased dramatically and 70% of college students graduate with a significant amount of loans, with average student loans borrower $37,172 in debt when they graduate.[27] A June 2018 poll shows 78% of Americans support free public college for low and middle income students.[28] More and more states are providing tuition for some free college, whether it is two years at a community college or four years at a state college. The Campaign for Free College Tuition is just one of many organizations that are fighting for a shift in opportunity for college.

Principle #7

We respect our interconnectedness with the natural world, as opposed to presuming that the world is here for us to use without consequence.

One of my favorite writers and humans, Robin Wall Kimmerer, is a citizen of Potawatomi Nation and a botanist. She writes in *Braiding Sweetgrass*:

> I asked my 3rd year students in the Environmental Protection degree to rate human interaction with the natural world and they confidently said that humans and nature are a bad mix. Later in the survey they were asked to rate positive interactions between humans and the natural environment and the median response was none. I was stunned they couldn't think of any positive interactions between humans and the environment. As the land becomes impoverished, so too does their vision. How can we move towards ecological sustainability if we can't imagine what that path feels like? If we can't imagine the generosity of the earth?[29]

We need a deep cultural shift to turn us away from extraction and towards regeneration. Can you imagine the generosity of the earth? Do you think your children can? Mother Earth is a part of us and we are a part of her; our well-being depends on her well-being. Yet we pave over wetlands, slash and burn vast forests, dump trash everywhere, use toxic chemicals to grow food, and overfish the lakes and oceans. We continue to extract fossil fuels—oil, coal, natural gas—despite the overwhelming evidence

---

26 Simon Workman and Jessica Troe, "Early Learning in the United States: 2017," Center for American Progress, July 20, 2017, https://www.americanprogress.org/issues/early-childhood/reports /2017/07/20/436169/early-learning-united-states-2017.

27 Abigail Hess, "Here's how much the average student loan borrower owes when they graduate," CNBC, February 15, 2018, https://www.cnbc.com/2018/02/15/heres-how-much-the-average-student-loan-borrower-owes-when-they-graduate.html.

28 Morley Winograd, "Support for Free College is Remarkably Stable, Free College Now, July 9, 2018, https://www.freecollegenow.org/poll_stable_support_june2018.

29 Robin Wall Kimmerer, *Braiding Sweetgrass* (Milkweed Editions Canada, 2013).

of climate change caused by the emission of CO2 released into the earth's atmosphere when fossil fuels are burned. Even though many people around the globe now recognize the consequences of fossil fuel extraction and are calling for dramatic changes in our energy systems, the leaders of corporations and of the U.S., along with other countries that profit from selling fossil fuels, are not changing course. In fact they are ramping up extraction.[30]

Example of change: There are many ways that people are turning away from unsustainable actions and towards renewable and regenerative actions. On fractracker.org you can see a map of 350 communities worldwide that have set tangible goals to transition away from fossil fuels.[31] Another example is a repair cafe, where people come together to share their skills to repair items that would otherwise go to the landfill. Community members help each other to fix their cars, bikes, sweaters, tables, refrigerators, and even electronics. Repair cafés are a way to reduce consumption, shift our relationship to the extractive economy, and build community. There are 750 repair cafes all over the world.[32]

Example of change: Resistance to the fossil fuel industry is a key factor in moving toward a more positive relationship with the natural world. One well-known recent example is Standing Rock. From April 2016 to February 2017, Native American water protectors and their allies camped out at Standing Rock to challenge the Dakota Access Pipeline, which was slated to carry oil from North Dakota to Illinois.[33] [34] The pipeline was built within half a mile of the Standing Rock Reservation and under the Missouri River and Lake Oahe, the main water source for the reservation and millions of others downstream. Although the protest was broken up in February 2017, and the pipeline began piping oil in April 2017, Standing Rock was a key resistance moment. It was a time when many people were able to join together to say no to the extraction of resources and to educate the public about the way that the corporate fossil fuel industry works, and how the government so often supports corporate interests, by waiving permitting and Environmental Impact Studies. Although the pipeline was built, the protest built momentum that others are carrying forward.[35]

---

30 Emily Atkin, "Trump, Putin, and the Race for Artic Oil," *New Republic,* April 25, 2018, https://newrepublic.com/article/148095/trump-putin-race-arctic-oil.

31 https:// www.fractracker.org/2018/06/the-resistance-movement.

32 Sofie Backker, "Solution: Repair Cafe," This Changes Everything, accessed July 30, 2019, https:// solutions.thischangeseverything.org/module/repair-café.

33 "Dakota Access Pipeline Protests," Wikipedia, accessed July 30, 2019, https://en.wikipedia.org/wiki/ Dakota_Access_Pipeline_protests.

34 Sam Levin, "Dakota Access pipeline: the who, what and why of the Standing Rock protests," The Guardian, November 3, 2016, https://www.theguardian.com/us-news/2016/nov/03/north-dakota-access-oil-pipeline-protests-explainer.

35 See https://mn350.org/pipeline-resistance-team/ for an example in northern Minnesota where Native American activists, including Winona LaDuke, are resisting a pipeline being built through Ojibway land.

Reflect
Use the following questions as a guide to reflect on the seven principles above. You can write, paint, share your responses with someone, or just think quietly, whatever works best for your learning style.

❀ While reading this section what feelings or body sensations were you aware of?

❀ What questions do you have about the seven social justice principles and the changes needed for them to become a reality?

❀ Where could you find out the answers to those questions? If some of your questions don't necessarily have an answer, what might help you to continue processing the information you've gained?

Privilege and oppression

To better understand the need for social justice it is important to understand the concepts of privilege and oppression. A privilege and oppression framework recognizes that oppression harms everyone, both those who are oppressed and those who have benefitted from oppression. Oppression functions at the societal level, yet it shows up in our personal lives and results in negative feelings and in trauma. Guilt, shame, rage, internalized superiority, internalized inferiority, and hate are just some of the feelings that happen as a result of oppression. We often feel personally at fault for those feelings, but really the onus is on systemic oppression.

Have you ever experienced feeling "different"? Have you been discriminated against or treated unfairly because of that difference?

Have your children experienced feeling "different"? Have they been discriminated against because of that difference?

This feeling of difference is common. Many of us feel different at one time or another. Sometimes there is unfair treatment, or discrimination, because of that difference. Discrimination can happen at an individual level, like when one store owner decides not to hire people with a non-U.S. accent. Oppression is the broader system of institutions, laws, and cultural norms that enables widespread individual discrimination.

Oppression is when a whole group of people is systematically discriminated against because of a characteristic they share. Oppression is connected to historical and systematic benefit for one group of people at the expense of another. The current system of oppression we live in has been built on historical patterns of oppression that have made it possible for white, owning-class, Christian, abled, cisgender[36] men to amass and maintain wealth and power. Historical examples of this systemic oppression

---

36 Cisgender men: men assigned male at birth who still identify as men. See Chapter 7.

include enslavement of African Americans in the U.S. (and much of the Western hemisphere), the holocaust against the Jews and other marginalized groups in Germany, laws that prohibited women from voting in the U.S. until the 1920s, and cultural norms that have promoted unnecessarily institutionalizing people with mental and physical disabilities. Although many specific policies have changed for the better, oppressive patterns continue. Current examples include policies targeting immigrants who are Black and Latinx for deportation and in some cases separating parents from children in detention centers, a ban on immigrants from Muslim countries, a widespread "rape culture" that normalizes sexual violence, especially of men against women, and continuing to institutionalize people with mental illness.

Oppression operates on internalized, interpersonal, cultural, and institutional levels:[37]

Internalized: When individuals believe harmful messages about their role in a system of oppression, we refer to that as internalized oppression. For example, as a person with lighter skin you might believe, consciously or unconsciously, that you are better than your peers with darker skin—that's *internalized superiority*. As a person with darker skin you might believe that your peers with lighter skin are more beautiful, smarter, or capable than you—that's *internalized inferiority*. Both internalized inferiority and internalized superiority are part of internalized oppression.

Individual: Individual-level oppression shows up in acts of discrimination and harassment, including as microaggressions. Microaggressions such as name-calling and not using the gender pronoun people have requested are brief and commonplace interactions that intentionally or unintentionally communicate bias and reinforce a system of oppression (See Appendix E on our website).

Cultural: Cultural-level oppression shows up as taken-for-granted norms (such as, men can take up as much space as they want), assumptions (such as, if you are white you are American), stereotypes (such as, Black equals criminal), common knowledge (such as capitalism is the best way to organize an economy), media depictions that are harmful to some social groups while normalizing others (such as, the depiction of Muslims as terrorists and Christians as nonviolent).

Institutional: Laws, policies, and practices of institutions such as schools, hospitals, prisons, banks, nonprofits, and governments that have a differential impact on some social groups. Here are just a few examples of the many manifestations of institutional-level oppression: restrictions on who counts as "family" in hospital visitation, policies in human service organizations that prevent people being served from being in leadership, differential referral to special education, and redlining. Redlining is when banks and other institutions refuse to offer mortgages or offer worse rates to customers in certain neighborhoods based on their racial and ethnic makeup, literally drawing a red line around those neighborhoods.

---

37 Maurianne Adams and Lee Anne Bell, with Diane J. Goodman and Khyati Y. Joshi, Teaching for Diversity and Social Justice, 3rd ed., New York: Routledge, 2016. A go-to book for understanding social justice frameworks and concepts (even if you aren't going to teach about them!).

We can't describe a system of oppression without talking about the corresponding privilege or advantage, which is inherently linked to oppression for other people. The natural result of keeping some groups of people down is that people who do not have that characteristic are awarded unearned privilege, although to different degrees depending on their other identities. You might not be in the small group of people who have amassed great wealth (1% of U.S. Americans), or have legislative or even work-place decision-making power, but you likely still have other privileges. Often the people in the privileged group have no idea they have privilege. It is like the air they breathe, they don't even have to think about it.

This comic by Toby Morris (reprinted with permission) does an amazing job of laying out how privilege works. This is just one frame, but if you search "Toby Morris, privilege," you can find the whole comic strip.[38] In short, Richard and Paula are living parallel lives, with very different access to resources and very different life outcomes. Neither of them seems to understand how larger systems are impacting them. Richard has access to family support, quality education, financial resources, emotional encouragement, and connections. When he succeeds in life he thinks it is because he worked hard. Paula, on the other hand, has parents who are working hard to pay the bills, so she has to take care of herself and has to work at a young age instead of dedicating herself to her studies. She just can't seem to get a leg up in life, and sometimes she might even think it's because she's not trying hard enough. Can you relate to either of these examples?

Let's look at privilege using a couple of examples

In the U.S., Christianity was written into our official motto in 1956, "In God We Trust." Even though the separation of church and state is in the U.S. Constitution, "Congress shall make no law respecting an establishment of religion, or prohibiting the free exercise thereof . . . "[39] chances are that if you are not a Christian you do not have as much

38 Laura Willard, "A short comic gives the simplest, most perfect explanation of privilege I've ever seen," Upworthy, January 20, 2016, http://www.upworthy.com/a-short-comic-gives-the-simplest-most-perfect-explanation-of-privilege-ive-ever-seen. Comic reprinted with permission from the author.
39 U.S. Constitution, First Amendment, Establishment Clause.

power to affect the circumstances of your life as your Christian neighbor (unless you have significant wealth). Muslims have been especially demonized, targeted, and hated, often in government-sanctioned ways like the 2017 ban on immigrants from majority-Muslim countries. Muslims who run for government positions are targets of racial slurs and death threats. Jews are also targeted in the U.S., and sadly the Anti-Defamation League reported a 60% rise in hate crimes against Jews in 2017.[40]

Many Christians (including me, until I was in my 20s) have no idea that they have privileges because of their religious beliefs. Some of those privileges are being able to assume that everybody has heard of your religion's core beliefs and practices, being able to cross international borders with ease, being able to practice religious beliefs publicly, and not having to worry that someone might bomb their place of worship. The concept of intersectionality is important here; in the U.S. a white Christian has more privilege than a Black Christian. A very real example of this are the numerous, violent, and deadly attacks on Black churches.

For more on the power that the Christian church has around the globe you can read *Living in the Shadow of the Cross: Understanding and Resisting the Power and Privilege of Christian Hegemony,*[41] by Paul Kivel. This book reveals the ongoing, everyday impact of Christian power and privilege on our beliefs, behaviors, and public policy.

Here's another example of how privilege and oppression work in the U.S. context. Anyone who was not assigned male at birth, or who does not now identify as a man, is the target of oppression. Women/queer/trans folks get passed over for jobs, are not paid equally for equal work, are not promoted, are not supported to take maternity leave, and continue to suffer horrific sexual, physical, and emotional violence, which often goes unaddressed. Men hold the majority of decision-making positions in the U.S.—in national, state, and local politics, as well as in workplaces.

Many cisgender men have no idea that they have privileges like being hired over women applicants, being promoted on the job, being listened to when they say something, not having to watch their backs when they are alone out in public, not having to deal with sexual harassment in the workplace, and, being able to use violence to get what they want without suffering any consequences. Again, the concept of intersectionality is important here; the privilege a man has also depends on his race, ability, and class.

It is important to remember that patterns of privilege and oppression are not a natural way of organizing the world. It might seem natural because it's what we know, but this system of oppression was created, and we can create something different. In fact, we already are! There are many ways that people have joined together throughout the centuries to fight inequality and injustice and to make great gains for people of color, for women, for queer folks, for people with disabilities, for religious minorities, and for youth. Throughout this book you will learn more about the ways people are showing up for justice.

---

40 Anti-Defamation League, accessed November 6, 2019, https://www.adl.org/what-we-do/anti-semitism/anti-semitism-in-the-us.

41 Paul Kivel, *Living in the Shadow of the Cross: Understanding and Resisting the Power and Privilege of Christian Hegemony* (Gabriola Island, BC, Canada, 2013). Kivel also wrote *Uprooting Racism, Boys Will Be Men,* and *You Call This A Democracy?*—all important books for social justice learning.

Oppression has harmed, and continues to harm, all of us. As I shared in the introduction, some of the ways I personally am harmed include being separated from others based on race or class status, inaccurately feeling like I am better than others (subconsciously), knowing hardly anything about my ancestors, knowing hardly anything about the natural world, and a tendency to focus on my individual growth and fulfillment instead of on the collective. I also am harmed because of rape culture, because of a culture of fear, because of the drugs and violence and health crises that are endemic in a society that values individual and profit over community and well-being. As a result I often feel guilty, fearful, inadequate, small, and powerless.

What can we do with all the feelings that come up when talking about privilege and oppression? We can recognize the feelings, name where they come from, and then use them to motivate us to make change for ourselves, our families, and all humanity. Healing comes from recognizing that this is bigger than any of us individually. And it comes from being honest about the emotions we are feeling and looking for the root causes of those emotions. For many people healing comes from taking collective action to change a political and economic system that is oppressive, and from envisioning and creating a socially just system.

Although it is normal to have feelings in response to injustice, some of our feelings are much more intense and become embedded in our psyche so that they affect us long after the event that caused the feeling is over. This is called trauma (see page 90, and can be individual (like being in a car accident) and/or linked to systems of oppression (like the Holocaust and oppression of Jews for centuries). Trauma can happen as a result of one event, multiple events, or harms that a whole group of people have experienced that can be passed from generation to generation through epigenetics if unresolved. Trauma has adverse impacts on our health, mental, physical, emotional, or spiritual well-being. There is a huge body of work related to healing trauma. What feels important to say here is that because so much trauma is caused by the oppressive system we are living in, it is crucial to make that connection when we are working on healing individual trauma. It is also imperative that we begin to heal and repair the traumas caused by systemic oppression. We recommend reading *My Grandmother's Hands: Racialized Trauma and the Pathway to Mending Our Hearts and Bodies* by Resmaa Menakem[42] for both an understanding of racialized trauma and for healing practices.

Privilege and oppression: what is my experience?

The chart on the next page shows which social groups are privileged and which are oppressed in the U.S. context.[43] This is not a complete list; there are identity groups not indicated here. The list gives us a place to start, however, in building awareness and starting the conversation.

---

42 Resmaa Menakem, *My Grandmother's Hands: Racialized Trauma and the Pathway to Mending Our Hearts and Bodies* (Central Recovery Press, Las Vegas, NV, 2017). If you have a chance to go to hear Resmaa speak or attend a healing retreat, it will be well worth your time.

43 Adapted from the Think Again training "Teaching for Diversity, Inclusion & Justice," professional development training in Marshall, WI, 2019. Used with permission. Also adapted from "Quadrant-1-SJE-Core-Concepts-and-Terms-Slideshow," M. Adams & L.A. Bell with D.J. Goodman & K.Y. Joshi (2016). Teaching for Diversity and Social Justice. Web resources Ch. 4, Quadrant 1. New York, NY: Routledge.

Social Group Identity/ System of Oppression	Privileged Group	Conditionally Privileged	Oppressed or Targeted Group
race / racism	white people	some people of color who can pass as white	Asian, Black, Latinx, Native or Indigenous
socioeconomic class / classism	owning class, professional class	middle class	working class, poor, working poor
biological sex (assigned at birth) / sexism	men	some transgender people who pass as men	women, nonbinary transgender people
gender / trans oppression	cisgender men and women	transgender people who can pass as cis, cis-people who are gender nonconforming (butch women, femme men)	transgender, genderqueer, nonbinary
sexual orientation / heterosexism	heterosexual people	bisexual people who pass as heterosexual in current relationship	lesbian, gay, bisexual
ability / disability	temporarily able-bodied people	people with temporary disabilities	people with physical, psychological, and/or other disabilities, in-cluding chronic illness
religion / religious oppression	Protestants	Roman Catholics (historically)	Jews, Muslims, Hindus, Animists, Atheists, Buddhists
age / ageism	adults	young adults	elders, young people
language	English as a first language	English as a second language	all other languages

Your turn:

Step 1
Look at the above chart that outlines social identity groups (race, class, sex, gender, sexual orientation, ability/disability, religion, age, language) and the spectrum of priv-ilege or oppression within those groups. Circle the approximate place where you would be in each of those identity groups. Think about the current hierarchy of oppression in society and where you have privilege, and where you are oppressed. The intention of this activity is to open up a conversation about how privilege and oppression work in our society and in our personal lives. The lived reality is rarely so neatly in boxes. Nevertheless, this chart can help us to see where we might have privilege that we weren't aware of. This awareness is the beginning of positive change, both in interpersonal relationships and in making societal change. This chart is designed for the U.S. context. Depending on where you live around the world, this chart may or may not make sense

for you. In this chapter we've described the systems of oppression as they play out in the U.S., and in other parts of the world oppression operates similarly but with different groupings and details. The U.S. system also impacts the whole world because of U.S. imperialism.

Step 2

Once you recognize where you have privilege it can be helpful to learn more about how that privilege is at work in your everyday life, and also some ways you can interrupt it. The North American Students of Cooperation (NASCO) has developed an anti-oppression action guide[44] that is useful in looking at when and how you can be an ally, or be in solidarity with people who are oppressed. It includes privilege checklists,[45] as well as lists of ways you can be an ally.

1. Use the NASCO resource (or another similar resource),

2. Find the privilege lists that apply to you and circle the privileges you have. You may not have all of them because of your other identities. For example if you are middle class or upper class, find the *Class Privilege* list.

3. Find the ally lists and circle the things that you need to work on. For example if you are middle class or upper class find the *Being a Class Ally* list.

4. If none of these lists apply to you, think of an area where you have privilege, whether because of your age, religion, language, nationality, skin tone, ethnicity, or something else, and come up with a list of the privileges you have and how to be an ally in that area.

Reflect
Use the following questions as a guide to reflect on your own experience with privilege and oppression. You can write, paint, share your responses with someone, or just think quietly, whatever works best for your learning style.

1. Give examples of how you have experienced oppression because of your identities.
2. Give examples of how you have experienced privilege because of your identities.
3. What feelings and body sensations does this reflection bring up for you?
4. What will support you in working through those feelings? It could be taking a nap, going for a walk, talking with a friend, finding a therapist, joining a study group on privilege and oppression, etc.

---

44 North American Students of Cooperation, "Anti-oppression Action Guide", accessed July 2018, https://www.nasco.coop/sites/default/files/srl/Action%20Camp%20Packet_0.pdf. There are other such resources out there that get updated from time to time. Find a resource that works for you.

45 Checklists can be helpful, yet it is important to remember that this is lifelong learning. Just because you check off all the things on a list, doesn't mean you don't have more to learn!

5. How can this awareness help you to support your kids in the areas where they have privilege and in the areas where they might experience oppression?
6. How do you think this awareness of oppression and privilege can help you to show up for justice?
7. What are three things you will work on to show up in solidarity with or to be a better ally in the places you have privilege?

Distinction between diversity and social justice

You've probably heard the phrase "diversity and inclusion." **Diversity** practice is the process of understanding each other in all our complexity and moving beyond simple tolerance to embracing and celebrating the rich dimensions of identity contained within each individual. **Inclusion** work prioritizes involvement in and access to existing structures for all people, where the inherent worth and dignity of all people is recognized. An inclusive organization promotes and sustains a sense of belonging; it values and practices respect for the talents, beliefs, backgrounds, and ways of living of its members—but it's still the same organization as it was before the diversity and inclusion reforms. Diversity and inclusion can be important steps in working towards social justice, although without a social justice framework these efforts often fall far short of what is needed.

If we simply "include" people who we identify as "diverse" in our organizations, which have been structured by the existing systems of oppression, then we are not actually transforming those organizations or how oppression will manifest in them. For example, if a school board that has been all white since its inception "includes" a person of color on the board, but does not change its norms, power structures, and communication habits, then the other members are unlikely to truly understand or act on what the new board member has to contribute. And, as happens so often in "diversity" efforts, that board member is likely to quit because they don't feel heard, or worse.

While we definitely want to be recognizing and celebrating diversity and valuing the dignity of all people who are part of an organization, we must move beyond diversity and inclusion to working for social justice. To achieve social justice we need to dismantle the current heteronormative, capitalist, white supremacist, ableist, patriarchal system and to create a just and equitable system. Our goal is to transform these harmful systems, and the ways in which they show up in our workplaces and communities and families, so that people of all races, ethnicities, class, ability, gender, sexuality, political ideology, religion, language, and nationality have dignity and respect and human rights in a system that is built for them.

I use the concept of *re-centering* instead of *inclusion*. Instead of just widening our circles to fit more people inside, we must take the center off of the white, middle-class, cisgender male norm so that the people joining the circle aren't just being asked to fit into current norms. We are re-centering what is normal. Andrea Smith explains,

> As critical race theorist Kimberle Crenshaw has noted, it is not enough to be sensitive to difference; we must ask what difference the difference makes. Instead of saying, how can we include women of color, women with

disabilities, etc., we must ask what our analysis and organizing practice would look like if we centered them in it. By following a politics of re-centering rather than inclusion, we often find that we see the issue differently, not just for the group in question, but everyone.[46]

Expanding on the same example about the school board, if the community re-centers the people who are most marginalized in their school and community and prioritizes having many of those voices on their school board, it will change how the whole board thinks about meeting all students' needs. Recentering requires shifting norms and talking openly about how power works on the board. For example, if Robert's Rules of Order are used it likely means using a more horizontal and transparent (everyone knows how to participate) way of communication. Another example might be finding more open and transparent ways for the board to interact with parents, instead of requiring that people come to evening meetings without childcare if they want their voice to be heard. If people of color are recentered, instead of included, on the board, then it is likely to benefit not only how the board functions, but also what the school is able to accomplish in supporting students of color, which will benefit the learning environment for everyone.

Reflect
Keeping in mind the difference between inclusion and recentering described above . . .

1. Think of a specific time you felt excluded. What was that like? What would it have felt like to be included? How about centered? What would have needed to happen to be centered?
2. Think of a specific time you included someone. What was that like? What would have needed to happen to center that person?

A note on culture

This book does not focus on culture. However, culture will come up throughout the book, so I'm including a note here to clarify what I mean when I talk about culture. There is a large body of writing on this topic, much of which is problematic because it does not name how larger systems of oppression shape culture. So, if you want to better understand the concept of culture from a social justice lens I would recommend the following resources. In *Anti-bias Education for Young Children and Ourselves*[47] by Louise Derman-Sparks and Julie Olsen Edwards, there are concrete examples of how to engage with young children about culture and around cultural differences. In *My*

46 Andrea Smith, "Without Bureaucracy, Beyond Inclusion: Re-centering Feminism," LeftTurn, June 1, 2006, http://www.leftturn.org/without-bureaucracy-beyond-inclusion-re-centering-feminism.
47 Louise Derman-Sparks and Julie Olsen Edwards, *Anti-Bias Education for Young Children and Ourselves* (Washington DC: NAEYC, 2010).

Grandmother's Hands[48] Resmaa Menakem provides an understanding of the toxic culture that white supremacy has created and exercises for healing from it.

A culture is a shared set of norms, values, and ways of life that we've developed over centuries and millennia to help us make sense of the world around us and survive in it, and/or to take and maintain power. Culture includes language, food, religious beliefs, artistic expression, beliefs about what happens after death, assumptions about the economic system, relationships to nationhood and patriotism, norms about gender and family roles, relationships to work, child-raising practices and so much more. Some parts of a culture are very obvious, like what holidays we celebrate. Other parts are very deep and hard for us to even notice or articulate when asked, like our beliefs and assumptions about the economic system.

A culture is shared within a community, whether large (like an ethnic culture) or small (like a city's or even a neighborhood's unique local culture). Certain aspects of a culture may be very consistent within the community (like using silverware, hands, or chopsticks to eat food) and others can vary widely (like opinions about how to raise children). Culture is complex and we have to be careful not to make assumptions about someone's cultural beliefs or practices just because we know one thing about them, like where they live, or what language they speak.

In the U.S., one culture has more power than others, the culture of white, class-privileged, heteronormative, able-bodied Christians. This is the dominant culture. Those of us whose cultures line up with the dominant culture rarely notice that we even have a culture; our culture is what feels "normal" or natural to us. It is often when we are faced with cultural differences that we have the opportunity to notice our own cultural beliefs and practices. If we are open enough to recognize that our beliefs and practices aren't the only way of doing things, we have the opportunity to expand our worldview and learn from others. Expanding our awareness is not always easy, and it is an important part of living in a diverse world.

Cultures are shaped by the larger forces around us that impact what we need to survive and thrive. In the U.S., oppression based on class, race, gender, sexuality, and disability has been the norm since its inception. These patterns have shaped cultural beliefs and practices, both in the dominant culture and in the cultures of marginalized groups. Some cultural practices emerge from resistance to oppression, some cultural practices perpetuate oppression, and some do both at once. One example of a cultural practice that both aligns with and resists oppression is the singing of African American spirituals. Singing spirituals was a source of comfort and of passing messages during times of slavery, while at the same time aligning—unintentionally and probably inevitably—with the erasure of African religions among enslaved people. Another example of a cultural practice resulting from and perpetuating oppression is the U.S. holiday of Thanksgiving. The narrative of the invented holiday glosses over the atrocities of the genocide of the Indigenous people of this land, and turns it into a story of friendship and sharing. The story and rituals of the holiday rally people around the myth that the Native Americans welcomed the Pilgrims. This myth perpetuates the belief in manifest

---

48 Resmaa Menakem, *My Grandmother's Hands: Racialized Trauma and the Pathway to Mending Our Hearts and Bodies* (Central Recovery Press, Las Vegas, NV, 2017).

destiny, that white people from Europe were destined to own and dominate the Americas.

Here are a couple of personal examples: In my family, frugality is a cultural value which we can trace directly back to the great depression and my great-grandparents' experiences as farmers in the dust bowl area of Kansas. They did not lose their land and I'm not sure why—I'd better ask! What I do know is that to survive that time they developed extreme frugality that was passed to my grandparents, my mom, then to me and my brothers. An example of a cultural belief that arose out of oppression, and has ended up perpetuating oppression, is how my family gave up their Danish and Irish culture and traditions for American culture and traditions. Once they emigrated they became white. This assimilation into a culture of white supremacy was key to survival and to being awarded the privileges of being white Americans.

As parents we pass on our cultural beliefs to our children. We can do this in a way that implies our cultural beliefs are the only right ones, or the best ones, and that other cultures are inferior, or we can pass on our culture in a way that says, "This is how we make sense of the world. There are other ways of making sense of the world. It is good to keep learning from others! They have gems to share." And when our cultural practices harm others (like the Thanksgiving narrative), we can, and must, reject or transform those practices. We can look beneath the surface to ask why we believe what we believe and what histories and systems have shaped our cultural beliefs and practices in order to recognize where they might perpetuate injustice. We can ask these questions with our children. Developing this critical thinking is a central part of parenting for social justice.

 Reflect

- ❈ How is the explanation above similar to or different from the way you had previously thought about culture?
- ❈ Name some features of your own cultural beliefs and practices (language, food, religious beliefs, artistic expression, beliefs about what happens after death, beliefs about how the economic system works, your relationship to nationhood and patriotism, beliefs about gender, work, how you raise our children, what holidays you celebrate, etc.).
- ❈ Which aspects of your culture align with the dominant culture and which don't?
- ❈ Which aspects of your culture do you think about often? Which do you rarely think about?
- ❈ What are some ways your cultural beliefs and practices impact how you interact with people who have cultural beliefs and practices that are different from yours?
- ❈ Why do you believe what you believe? How might history and systems have shaped your cultural beliefs and practices?

What can I do?

As Nelson Mandela says, "As long as poverty, injustice, and gross inequality exist in our world, none of us can truly rest."[49] The injustices we experience today are connected to a political and economic system that concentrates wealth and power in the pockets of a few, while causing hunger, homelessness, and a mass extinction of species. These injustices are not new, but they also are not inevitable. They were created by humans and humans can create a world in which justice and equity are the priority. The path to social justice is not easy, because power does not give up without a fight, but it is a beautiful path when we are on it together.

The more organized we are as communities and movements—the more we come together with others to make change—the more likely we are to succeed. You've probably heard about, or even participated in, movements of people all over the world resisting injustices such as police brutality, corporate monopoly of seeds/media/surveillance, mass incarceration, climate injustice, and the abuse of immigrants. You might have participated through signing petitions, making donations, protesting, or spreading the word on social media or through conversations with your family. These are all ways that we resist what is harming people and the planet. When people come together to stand up against concentration of power and wealth, connected by the vision of social justice, they achieve big victories (think women's right to vote, requiring a minimum wage, and the end of Jim Crow laws).

Here's a historical example of people coming together to make change. Have you heard of the Freedom Rides? In the spring of 1961, Black and white protesters from around the U.S. came together to end the illegal practice of Black and white segregation on interstate buses in the south. In one action of the Freedom Rides, protestors got on a bus in Washington, DC, to ride to New Orleans and never made it. The protestors were beat up in South Carolina and their bus was set on fire in Alabama. This brought national and global attention to the civil rights struggle. The Freedom Rides motivated many people to join the struggle and contributed to ending segregation in the south.

Here's a present day example of people coming together to make change and my own personal connection to that change. Walmart is making huge profits while its compensation of employees is low even by retail standards. As of 2010 the Walton family had more wealth than the bottom 42% of American families combined.[50] Advocates for justice have called attention to Walmart's patterns of mistreating workers. So, I have made a decision to avoid shopping at Walmart. However, I know that if I don't connect my individual choice to larger change, it will have little to no impact. There are many people who must work at Walmart in order to pay their bills, and many others who see buying cheap goods at Walmart as their only option for having a good life. My individual choice gives me peace of mind, but if I want to have a bigger impact I can join with

---

49 Nelson Mandela, speech, February 3, 2005, http://www.mandela.gov.za/mandela_speeches/2005/050203_poverty.htm.

50 Josh Bivens, "Inequality, exhibit A: Walmart and the wealth of American families," Economic Policy Institute's Working Economics Blog, July 17, 2012, https://www.epi.org/blog/inequality-exhibit-walmart-wealth-american.

campaigns for holding Walmart accountable, such as the Fight for 15 campaign.[51] In this way the impact of me refusing to shop at Walmart is magnified and contributes to system change. People coming together is bringing about change. The Fight for 15 has already won raises for 22 million people.

While people are resisting they are also creating a just and equitable world through housing co-ops, food co-ops, community restorative justice practices, art for healing, green energy, community barter, and so much more.

I love getting *YES! Magazine*[52] because it highlights all of the beautiful solutions that people are creating right now. Editions of *YES!* have focused on creative housing solutions that people are developing or re-popularizing in response to the affordable housing shortage, ways that land is being reclaimed by Indigenous people, and how credit unions are putting resources into equitable community development.

To achieve social justice there are actions we can take at different levels. Personally, we can continue our learning. Interpersonally, we can share what we are learning with our friends and family. In our wider circles we can bring equity into our workplaces and community organizations or start new organizations based on a social justice framework. We can join local or larger movements for justice. Within each of those levels there are so many ways to be involved, from the small daily actions of learning more and having conversations with our kids, to larger-impact, non-violent direct actions such as sit-ins.

Here is a partial list of actions that we can take. Each of us will take different actions depending on who and where we are.

WHAT WE CAN DO!

Personal healing and growth:
- Continue studying and learning.
- Practice self-care and healing from oppression and trauma.
- Pray. Meditate. Be still.
- More . . .

Speak out against injustice in your family, school, workplace, or town.
- Talk with your kids.
- Name microaggressions when they happen.
- Write letters to the editor.
- More . . .

Advocate for just policies in your school, town, state, and/or nation.
- Start petitions, or sign petitions that others have started.
- Attend school board meetings.
- Join an equity, diversity, and inclusion committee.
- More . . .

---

51 Fight for 15, "About Us", retrieved April 2019, https://fightfor15.org/about-us.
52 *YES! Magazine*, https://www.yesmagazine.org

Support people who are surviving injustice.

- ❋ Share a meal with a friend in need.
- ❋ Share financial resources with friends and community members in need.
- ❋ Write a letter to a prisoner or to someone who has been a target of hate.
- ❋ More . . .

Join local organizations that are working to advocate for just and equitable policies.

- ❋ Get a new job!
- ❋ Serve on a board.
- ❋ Offer childcare, transportation, and food.
- ❋ Donate.
- ❋ More . . .

Join organized social justice campaigns. Participate by:

- ❋ Being on a planning committee.
- ❋ Going to a rally.
- ❋ Joining a non-violent direct action (such as a sit-in).
- ❋ Donating.
- ❋ More . . .

Participate in creating the world we want to live in.

- ❋ Get outside your neighborhood. Make friends with people who have very different experiences than you.
- ❋ Make art and music and share your creations with others.
- ❋ Plant community gardens.
- ❋ Put up solar panels.
- ❋ Organize community meals and host block parties.
- ❋ Engage in community dialogues about challenging issues.
- ❋ Practice restorative/transformative justice when you've harmed someone, or been harmed.
- ❋ Share resources generously.
- ❋ More . . .

 Reflect

Use the following questions as a guide to reflect on action for social justice. You can write, paint, share your responses with someone, or just think quietly, whatever works best for your learning style.

- ❋ What gets in your way of thinking about or taking action for social justice?

- ❋ How, if at all, do you think your actions are connected to the actions of others?

- ❋ In what ways are you envisioning and engaging in what is possible, even while you are resisting what is harmful?

Healing justice practice

Light a candle and breathe.

Thinking about social justice, privilege, and oppression can be overwhelming and bring up a lot of emotions—grief, sadness, trauma, guilt, shame. To process all those emotions I have a daily mindfulness and meditation practice of lighting a candle and breathing. It started as a ten-minute practice and now, on days when things feel especially hard, I might sit and breathe for up to an hour. This helps me to be connected to my body, to quiet my mind, and to be aware of other living beings and a larger truth of interconnection.

Gratitude jar:

This is a great practice to do with kids. Every day, write down something you are thankful for on a piece of paper and put in your gratitude jar. Whenever you have the feeling of scarcity (not having enough or being enough), or are overwhelmed by all that is harmful in the world, you can take a gratitude (or more than one!) out of the jar and read it to remind yourself that there is also good.

Community of practice questions

If you are reading this book with a group, here are questions to guide your reflection on the chapter. To learn more about communities of practice, you can refer to page 17.

1. What new information or ideas did you learn from this chapter?
2. What questions do you have about social justice?
3. Share what you learned about yourself from the privilege and oppression exercise.
4. What have been your somatic/body sensations and responses throughout this chapter?
5. What have you been doing for social justice lately?
6. What else would you like to do?

Illustrator Brittney and child MJ on the first day of sixth grade.

Chapter 2
PARENTING FOR SOCIAL JUSTICE

BY ANGELA BERKFIELD

Education either functions as an instrument which is used to facilitate the integration of the younger generation into the logic of the present system and bring about conformity, or it becomes the practice of freedom, the means by which men and women deal critically and creatively with reality and discover how to participate in the transformation of their world.
—PAULO FREIRE, *Pedagogy of the Oppressed*[53]

I was a wonderful parent before I had children. I was an expert on why everyone else was having problems with theirs. Then I had three of my own . . . They finally wore me down. And though it was the last thing I ever dreamed I'd be doing, I joined a parent group . . . I came home with a head spinning with new thoughts . . . Direct connection between how kids feel and how they behave. When kids feel right, they'll behave right. How do we help them to feel right? By accepting their feelings.
—ADELE FABER AND ELAINE MAZLISH, *How to Talk So Kids Will Listen, and Listen So They Will Talk*[54]

Our [kids] need us to be their allies every day, each step of the way, working these issues out together. Whether it is youth culture or family culture, toy guns or real guns, discipline or self-discipline, the challenge is still how to teach them to stand for compassion and justice and to stand with those who are organizing for change.
—PAUL KIVEL, *Boys Will Be Men: Raising Our Sons for Courage, Caring and Community*[55]

---

53 Paulo Freire, *Pedagogy of the Oppressed* (New York: Herder and Herder, 1972). This is a foundational book for collective liberation movements.

54 Adele Faber and Elaine Mazlish, *How to Talk So Kids Will Listen & Listen So Kids Will Talk* (Harper Collins: 1980). They now have this book for parenting kids 2–7. I have to pick this book up at least once a year for a refresher on how to talk with my kids so I can stop pulling my hair out!

55 Paul Kivel, *Boys Will Be Men: Raising Our Sons for Courage, Caring and Community* (Gabriola Island, B.C.: New Society Publishers, 1999). Although published in the early 90s, this book is still relevant in providing on-point questions and a solid framework for parenting boys.

 *Reflect*

1. How did the education you received as a child encourage you to respond critically and creatively to the world around you, or not? How do you encourage your children, and/or the children you care for, to respond critically and creatively to the world around them, or not?

2. Have your children asked questions about issues of inequality and justice? If so, what has been your response? If not, why might that be?

3. How have you received parenting support, whether from a group, hotline, therapist, or family member? How might parenting for social justice support be helpful for you?

4. Reflect on your ability to accept children's feelings. What makes it hard? What would make it easier to accept their feelings? Are any of their feelings connected to injustice?

5. What are some of the parenting for social justice issues that are coming up in your house? What has been your response?

Note: Throughout this chapter and book when we say "parent" we mean anyone who is caring directly for children, including grandparents, aunts and uncles, teachers, foster parents, and childcare providers.

What is parenting for social justice?

As a parent or caregiver who cares about people and the planet, how do I raise children who interact with the world in a way that is conscious, connected, and equipped to make change?

Author Chrissy and her son Maceo at the playground.

Days are filled with kisses and tears, whining about what's for dinner, scrambling to get on coats and boots so we aren't late to work and school, skirmishes over whose turn it is to pick a TV show for the day, pretend sword fights, and wiping noses for the monthly cold. Parenting presents so many daily challenges that it can feel overwhelming to also address social justice issues like the school-to-prison-pipeline and the separation of children from parents in immigration detention centers. Yet we are parents who have woken up to the reality of injustice in our world, our communities, and our homes, and we want to do something about it. We also want to raise kids who are able to show up for justice.

Parents have many roles. When we parent the whole child we consider physical, emotional, spiritual, and interpersonal needs. We pass on our beliefs about how to relate to the natural world. We teach tools and skills for making sense of the world and for surviving in it, such as how to stay safe, warm, dry, and how to read and count. How we parent our children is connected to our cultural values, which are connected to larger systems that impact us, including systems of privilege and oppression.

Often we are not aware of those larger cultural influences on our beliefs and values, and how those beliefs show up in our parenting. A first step in parenting for social justice can be becoming more aware of the ways we think and how that is impacting what we are teaching our kids. We can then check in to see how social justice, and the systems of privilege and oppression we were thinking about in Chapter 1, are impacting our family. Once this has entered our consciousness, it becomes clearer how to talk with our kids about social justice and how to support them to get through any challenges related to social justice.

I use a series of questions to bring this into my awareness. Following is a diagram of that process of questioning which helps me to examine how I am keeping social justice present as I am parenting the whole child. There are six main areas where I am passing on my beliefs: emotional, spiritual, interpersonal, physical, tools, and the natural world. I am careful not to compartmentalize, recognizing that my cultural values and beliefs infiltrate all areas of life. In each area it lists a general question, and then a question more specifically oriented to social justice values. Overall, the social justice questions follow this pattern: How is injustice impacting my child's ability to take care of their needs? How can they get over those barriers? How is injustice impacting the other people in their life? How can I support kids in being equipped to stand up for justice?

Emotional: What am I feeling? How do I take care of my emotional health? How has injustice impacted my emotional health and that of others? How can I take care of these emotions?

Spiritual: What do I believe about what I cannot see or prove? What do my spiritual beliefs say about injustice? How does understanding social justice strengthen my spiritual beliefs?

Relationships: How do I get along with and connect with the people in my life? How does injustice make it hard to connect with others? How can I connect across barriers?

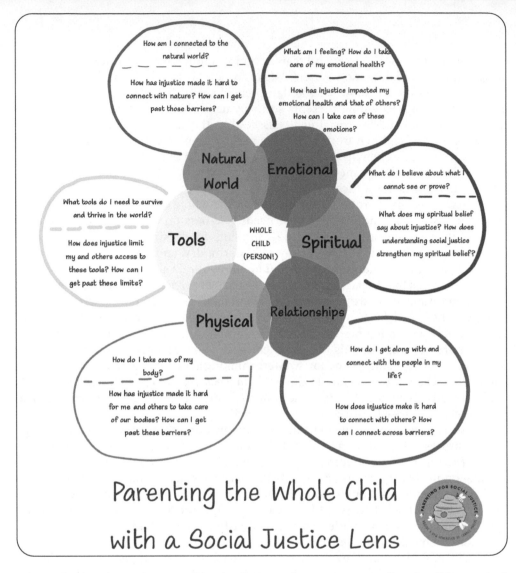

Parenting the Whole Child with a Social Justice Lens

Natural World: How am I connected to the natural world? How has injustice made it hard to connect with nature? How can I get past those barriers?

Emotional: What am I feeling? How do I take care of my emotional health? How has injustice impacted my emotional health and that of others? How can I take care of these emotions?

Spiritual: What do I believe about what I cannot see or prove? What does my spiritual belief say about injustice? How does understanding social justice strengthen my spiritual belief?

Tools: What tools do I need to survive and thrive in the world? How does injustice limit my and others access to these tools? How can I get past these limits?

WHOLE CHILD (PERSON!)

Physical: How do I take care of my body? How has injustice made it hard for me and others to take care of our bodies? How can I get past these barriers?

Relationships: How do I get along with and connect with the people in my life? How does injustice make it hard to connect with others? How can I connect across barriers?

Physical: How do I take care of my body? How has injustice made it hard for me and others to take care of our bodies? How can I get past these barriers?

Tools: What tools do I need to survive and thrive in the world? How does injustice limit my and others' access to these tools? How can I get past these limits?

Natural world: How am I connected to and impacting the natural world? How has injustice impacted my connection with nature? How can I get past any barriers?

zOpportunities for reflection from a social justice framework are always present, and these questions help to bring that to our attention. Chances are, in the places where our kids have less privilege we are already more aware of what is going on—where they are being picked on, when they need advocacy, or a shoulder to cry on. In the parts of life where we (or our kids) have privilege, we might be forgetting to ask these questions because privilege makes it harder to see how injustice is operational.

I'll give a personal example of how I apply these questions. My son is middle-class, able-bodied, and white. Although he is shy, he is a popular kid and has always had friends. I have never worried about his social life at school. However, the social justice framework encourages me to think more broadly about his experience, so that I can support him in forming relationships across difference, as well as recognize injustice and do something about it. If I ask the question about relationships: How does injustice make it hard for him to connect with people in his life? I start to notice how his friendships are with people who have similar class markers, similar racial identity, and the same gender identity. One of his best friends has a disability and I have noticed that as they have gotten older it has been harder for them to find things they both like to do, which is related to ability and also personality. This question helps me to see beyond what I had been noticing. It gives me an opportunity to think about how I can support my son in connecting with people across difference. And it has helped me to open up conversations with him about forming friendships with people who have a different experience than he does. When I am feeling brave I talk with him about how larger systems of injustice are making it hard to connect across difference (see sample conversations in upcoming chapters).

You might use these questions to better understand what is underneath the emotions your child is having. For example, your kid comes home from their friend's house feeling really frustrated, and you talk with them about their feelings. You might also ask (maybe to yourself, or maybe you can talk with them) how injustice has impacted their emotional health. Were there dynamics of privilege and oppression present that could be causing their frustration? These are things to notice, and hopefully at some point, when it makes sense, to talk about.

Parenting for social justice means talking with our kids about hard stuff. This prepares them for some hard realities. It also normalizes challenging conversations and gives them skills for making the conversations easier. Yet we often avoid difficult topics because we don't feel we have the right tools, because there aren't easy answers, or because we want to protect our kids for as long as we can from the hard realities of life. This book aims to support you with more tools to build your resilience for these conversations.

There is more and more support out there for talking openly with kids about topics like resolving conflict, consent, racism, gun violence, gender pronouns, and wealth inequality. The *Let's Talk*[56] guide by Teaching Tolerance supports high school students to talk about race, racism, and other difficult topics. While designed for the classroom, you can bring some of the ideas into your parenting conversations. Another resource is from Common Sense Media, *How to Talk To Kids About Difficult Subjects*,[57] which provides age-appropriate advice for kids 2–6, 7–12, and teens.

---

56 Teaching Tolerance, *Let's Talk*, accessed October 10, 2018
http://www.tolerance.org/sites/default/files/general/TT%20Difficult%20Conversations%20web.pdf.
57 Caroline Knorr, "How to Talk to Kids About Difficult Subjects," February 20, 2018 https://www.commonsensemedia.org/blog/how-to-talk-to-kids-about-difficult-subjects.

Once we recognize that something is an important issue to be talking about it can be easier to have brave, messy conversations. Here's an example of a time my son's teacher got brave in addressing gender stereotypes in the classroom. When I arrived to pick up my son from school she beckoned me over, "I have to tell you what happened today," she whispered. Uh-oh, I thought. "Some kids started making fun of your son for bringing a pink mermaid backpack to school. So I called everyone into the big circle and we talked about what it feels like to be made fun of. Lots of kids could relate, and they told stories of when they were made fun of. Then we talked about whether there is such a thing as girl and boy colors, and there was lots of debate and frustration at not being able to like all the colors. At the end I offered that any kids who had made fun of your son could apologize. They all did! It was the best. Thank you so much for giving our class this opportunity to have this conversation." My son continued to wear his mermaid backpack to school the rest of the week without any issue.

The teacher's response is such a great example of engaging in a hard conversation in a way that normalizes apologizing, asking questions, and makes the concept of gender norms easier and easier to talk about. If she had instead ignored what was happening or just said, "There are no boy and girl colors," it would have been harmful to my son and the other kids. Instead she addressed it as an opportunity to build skills and understanding. The way his teacher handled that situation could very well have altered the trajectory of my son's life.

This teacher was aware of the long-term impacts of bullying and discrimination because of gender and so it was worth it to her to address what was coming up in the moment. But often, when we are not as confident about the issue, it can be harder to address what is happening in the moment. There are topics we are more comfortable with and others where we need more information before we can have a conversation with kids.

Our kids' feelings are a good guide for where to start. Think back to the quotation from *How to Talk so Kids Will Listen and Listen So They Will Talk* at the beginning of this chapter: "When kids feel right, they'll behave right. How do we help them to feel right? By accepting their feelings."[58] Many of the emotions our kids experience are related to social injustices. Our kids are bullied (and/or are bullying others) for being "different" or for having disabilities; our boys are being made fun of (and/or are making fun of others) for wearing skirts to school or acting girly; in many subtle ways the culture influences kids to see white skin as better; and in most schools they aren't learning the skills to engage respectfully with difference or to stand up for justice. Society gives our kids strong messages about who belongs and who is an outsider, who is strong and who is weak, who is worthy and who is worthless. These messages impact our kids more than we might realize.

For instance, my son's friend had made her own costume for Halloween. She had worked hard on a pretty funky and powerful princess design. Right before going trick-or-treating she was hanging out with four boys who started making fun of her "girly" princess costume. She ended up not wearing it because she was embarrassed. Her mom recognized there was a gender power imbalance happening and encouraged her to

58 Adele Faber and Elaine Mazlish, *How to Talk So Kids Will Listen & Listen So Kids Will Talk* (Harper Collins: 1980).

take her power back by wearing her costume. She didn't put her costume back on that night, so the mom felt failure in the moment, but hopefully there was a more long-term lesson that came out of that night.

These moments might seem small, and inconsequential, and our kids might brush them off as no big deal. However, the cumulative effect has a life-long impact on our kids' self-confidence, their connection to people across difference, their ability to recognize patterns of injustice, and their ability to do something about it. Our response is really laying the foundation for them to be advocates for social justice in their own lives, and in the lives of people around them, in the communities they are living in, and for social justice on the larger systems level as well.

One of my favorite books for working with young children is *Anti-Bias Education for Young Children and Ourselves*.[59] It is very helpful because the concepts are age appropriate. However, it's important to pause here and make a distinction between anti-bias education and social justice education. A social justice framework recognizes injustices in the way society is organized, and works to change an unjust system. An anti-bias framework focuses on beliefs and judgements that individuals internalize and how they impact behavior at an interpersonal level. These biases and judgements are connected to the larger unjust systems, and if we change those biases at an individual level it will definitely have an impact. However, individual behavior should not be seen as the source of the problem. We need to be sure to always be connecting the problems that show up at an individual level to the larger systems of heteropatriarchy, ableism, capitalism, and white supremacy, which influence the biases that people hold.

Anti-bias education does provide a solid foundation for children to begin thinking about concepts that can contribute to creating a socially just world. Louise Derman-Sparks and Julie Olsen Edwards outline the four main goals of anti-bias education[60] as (each child will):

1. **Demonstrate self-awareness, confidence, family pride, and positive social identities.**

2. **Express comfort and joy with human diversity; accurate language for human differences; and deep, caring, human connections.**

3. **Notice unfairness, have language to describe unfairness, and understand that unfairness hurts.**

4. **Demonstrate empowerment and the skills to act, with others or alone, against prejudice and/or against discriminatory actions.**

We will be weaving those goals throughout the book: developing positive self-identity, connecting across differences, building skills for noticing and naming unfairness, and taking steps to act against discrimination. We will be connecting these four goals to the seven social justice principles outlined in Chapter 1.

Now that social justice is on your mind, you are likely to try conversations or actions that you might not have tried before. If you get stuck, that's okay. You can

---

59 Louise Derman-Sparks and Julie Olsen Edwards, *Anti-Bias Education for Young Children and Ourselves* (National Association for the Education of Young Children, 2010).
60 Derman-Sparks and Edwards, *Anti-Bias Education*, pg. xiv.

always say "I don't know" or "let's look that up" or "let's ask my friend." The nice thing is that you get to try again later today, and again tomorrow, and probably the next day. Kids' questions provide an opportunity for us to continue our own learning and bring that learning into our ongoing relationship with them.

Here are two examples of courageous and complex parenting-for-social-justice conversations:

Ariel Brooks is from Santa Fe, New Mexico, and now lives in Boston. After many years as an educator, she is now working to advance sharing economies and economic democracy. In her spare time, she does creative upcycled sewing, helps run a community gardening collective, and pets her affectionate cat.

Scene: I'm sitting with my daughter Anne, who's almost five, in the breakfast area at a hotel early in the morning. Fox News is on the TV, with coverage of a confrontation between police and a crowd of onlookers after a police officer killed a man in Chicago. Anne and I are both white.

Anne: What are they showing on TV, Mama?
Me: They're showing a lot of people who are angry because the police killed a man.
Anne: Why are they angry?
Me: Because in our country, the police kill a lot more people with brown skin than with white skin.
Anne: Why . . .
At this moment, Fox News shifts to a story about a seagull that stole a man's wallet and Anne is immediately distracted. I'm sleepy and in the kind of hotel where they show Fox News, so I do not continue the conversation.

Scene: Later the same day at a summer festival, Anne and I are waiting for a shuttle to the parking lot when we see two white police officers walk past.

Anne: Mama, why are the police killing more black people than white people?
Me: Well . . . racism. The police have ideas that people with brown skin are more dangerous.
Anne: Why, Mama?
Me: Maybe they grew up in a different time when their moms and dads didn't talk to them about how it's important to get to know people instead of deciding about them because of the color of their skin.
Anne: (Pointing to another police officer, with dark skin) So is that man in danger?
Me: Well, maybe not so much, because he has a uniform on, and sometimes people see a uniform as a clue that another person is "safe" or "good"—but yes, black people are in more danger from police than we as white people are, because of the color of their skin.
Anne: So, even Eliott [an African American boy from her school]?

Me: Mostly kids aren't seen as dangerous, but yes, when he becomes a grown up.

This exchange continues at length, with Anne wondering whether there's a difference in safety for black men versus black women and whether the issue is related to Donald Trump's belief that "white people are better than black people" as she's come to understand it.

Me: I'm really glad that we talk about important things like this, but it actually makes me sad to talk about these hard things for a long time. Can we talk about this some more later?

By this point we've reached the car, and Anne lets me know she's OK to return to the conversation later. Two weeks after the initial conversation, Anne brought it up again and I asked her how we'd gotten on the subject. She remembered right away, reminding me of the hotel and the TV. The way things stick in these kids' brains!

Kristen Elde is a 40-year-old cis white woman who lives in Northampton, Massachusetts, with her husband (36, white) and son (5, white). She loves poetry, running, and working for social change with her family.

Scene: I'm with my kid in his room, helping him get ready for bed.

Kid: I'm the boss of my own body, right?
Me: Absolutely, honey. We talk about that a lot, don't we?
Kid: Yeah.
Me: It's really important to your dad and me that you feel in control of your own body. So, your dad and I, and sometimes your grandparents, help you in the bathroom with things that involve your body, and we love giving you hugs and kisses and tickling you when you ask us to. But your body is yours and only yours, and you can always let people know if they're touching you in a way you don't want.
Kid: Yeah, like I can do a fist bump instead if I want.
Me: Yes, that's true. We talk about how even with family members who are loving and caring, if you're saying hello or goodbye to them, you don't have to give hugs or kisses if you don't feel like it. There are other ways you can show your love, like with a fist bump or a high-five or kind words. And just like you get to make those decisions about your body, other people also get to make decisions about theirs. So if you're playing around with another kid at daycare, maybe tickling or wrestling or something, and they decide they don't want to be touched anymore, it's important that you respect that. Do you know what I'm saying?
Kid: Yeah. Tracy's the boss of her body. Joe's the boss of his body. And also Logan's the boss of his body.
Me: Exactly.

Reflections: Following this conversation, I felt pretty good about it. As usual, I saw room for improvement in the form of using fewer words, but for the most part my kid had seemed interested in what I was saying. I admittedly worry about my kid going off on tangents and topics running away from us if I pause too long or ask him his thoughts, but I know it's important to try to involve him in a meaningful way if any of this stuff is going to speak to him. Also, as I remind myself, I'll be living with this person for at least another thirteen years so know I'll have plenty of opportunities to follow up.

Reflect

These are examples of how these conversations could have gone and are not meant to be examples of a perfect approach (no approach is perfect!).

1. How do these two conversations connect to the parenting for social justice questions? How do they address the anti-bias goals?
2. What else could these parents have said or done?
3. What would that conversation have looked like in your family?
4. What could you ask your child to better understand their experience and/or perspective?
5. What are some hard social justice conversations you have with your kids? What hard conversations have you avoided? What would help you to have those conversations?
6. How are you currently bringing social justice into your parenting? How about anti-bias goals? How else would you like to bring social justice and anti-bias goals into your parenting?

How do we parent for social justice?

Parenting for social justice is going to be different depending on who you are, where you live, what your family makeup is, what your relationship with your kids is like. Overall I say—just do it! Be creative and uniquely you! There's no right way to do this, and I don't want you to get tripped up on lists of what to do and what not to do. When you make mistakes, apologize and try again.

Also, I want to offer some of the tools I use in bringing social justice into my parenting, tools I work with parents on in the workshops I co-facilitate. I've organized the tools into these five areas:

1. Be kid appropriate.
2. Use experiential learning.
3. Find what works in your family.
4. Know where you have influence.
5. Set goals (and revisit them).

1. Be kid appropriate

People often ask, "How early can I talk with my kids about difference and injustice?"

My intuition says to start in utero, and research supports that. According to Erin Winkler,[9] Derman-Sparks and Edwards, and Beverly Daniel Tatum,[10] as well as many other leaders, it is important to start these conversations when your kids are very young, because they are already picking up on difference and how their caregivers respond to difference.

Winkler writes, "In a study that followed approximately 200 black and white children from the ages of six months to six years, Katz and Kofkin (1997) found that infants are able to nonverbally categorize people by race and gender at six months of age. The infants looked significantly longer at an unfamiliar face of a different race than they did at an unfamiliar face of their same race. The researchers argue that, because this finding is very consistent in six-month-olds, "initial awareness [of race] probably begins even earlier" (Katz & Kofkin, 1997, p. 55)."

Louise Derman-Sparks and Julie Olsen Edwards write about children's identity development based on a combination of research and the work of many experienced early childhood educators. I've paraphrased some key findings from their work[61]: Children pick up on differences in skin color as early as six months old. By two years, they are using gender labels and applying names of colors to skin. By three, they are asking questions about their own and other people's physical attributes. By four, they have internalized their own social identities—race, ethnicity, language, gender, class, and dis/ability.

Anti-bias teaching is important in providing children with positive and appropriate responses to difference, whereas "colorblind" approaches that encourage children to "not see race" are harmful, because they don't recognize children's lived experience. When you begin to use anti-bias teaching, there is an increase in talking about difference, because repetition is how kids learn. Integrating anti-bias thinking and language will take work at first. But after a year or so, you will find that it has become part of how you do things.

Continuing our own learning about race, class, gender, disability, and so on is key to being able to provide this learning for our kids.

As Beverly Daniel Tatum writes in *Why Are All the Black Kids Sitting Together in the Cafeteria?*,[62] young children are aware of differences based on race, gender, class, and ability as early as three years old. It is important that we are ready to have a conversation with them when they ask about those differences, and that we bring it up even when they aren't asking. So often we ignore or silence the conversation. Tatum's chapter on conversations about race with preschoolers has been helpful for me and for so many

---

61 Louise Derman-Sparks and Julie Olsen Edwards, *Anti-Bias Education for Young Children and Ourselves* (National Association for the Education of Young Children, 2010).
62 Beverly Daniel Tatum, *Why Are All the Black Kids Sitting Together in the Cafeteria? And Other Conversations About Race* (NY, Basic Books, 1997, 2017). Written over 20 years ago, this book is still highly relevant, informative, and inspiring.

other parents. We need to assume that our kids are noticing difference even if they aren't talking about it, and be proactive to make sure they are beginning to form critical consciousness around such differences. Critical consciousness is developed when we apply critical thinking skills to our current situations, which allows us to have a deeper understanding of our material and social reality. This understanding makes it possible to come up with and put into practice creative ways to solve our problems.[63]

As a parent with privilege, I find it especially important to remember that I need to be talking with my kids about social justice issues. I know that parents who are feeling the sting of oppression are talking with their kids about social justice issues out of necessity. Maybe it's because people are being killed on their block, or because they have to migrate to another country, or because they have to visit the food shelf weekly, or because they have to navigate daily stares or even insults. Even though those aren't daily realities for my family right now, our lives are connected to those realities so it is my responsibility to be talking about social justice with my kids. Having these conversations can be awkward, and it might feel like it is interrupting their peaceful childhood, but it is imperative if we are going to shift the current systems of oppression. I'm more worried about how I could mess up by avoiding these conversations with my kids than I am about messing up the conversations.

Following the lead of kids helps with knowing what is age appropriate for them. Often it is adults who are more uncomfortable with honest conversations than kids. The conversation that Ariel had with five-year-old Anne might seem advanced for her age, but Anne led the conversation and asked the questions, so it is absolutely appropriate for Anne. Beverly Daniel Tatum writes about a similar conversation she had with her preschooler.[64] It is not unusual for four- and five-year-olds to want honest and in-depth answers to their hard questions.

We recommend that you start conversations too, instead of just waiting for your kids to bring it up. In each of the following chapters we give examples of conversations about race, class, gender, disability, and collective liberation that parents are having with kids at various ages between 3 and 10. We also provide other resources from books, blogs, and organizations that can give you further ideas for starting and sustaining age-appropriate social justice conversations with your kids.

Another question related to age-appropriateness that people often ask is "at what point can we bring our young kids to social justice events and protests?"

Where I live there are lots of families who come to rallies and protests with kids, starting when they are babies. I think this depends on what protests and rallies are like where you live. Only you know what your kids and you are ready for. It can help to find out from the organizers of the rally if it is a family-friendly rally, if there is going to be nonviolent direct action, and if they are expecting any skirmishes from counter-protestors or police.[65]

As our children get older, the way we bring social justice into our parenting will change. Parents know their kids—how they communicate, how they learn best, and what their limits are. In thinking about how to bring social justice principles and

---

63 For more on critical consciousness see Appendix A, pp 298.
64 Daniel-Tatum, *Why Are All the Black Kids Sitting Together in the Cafeteria?*, pgs. 118–120.
65 For more on kids at rallies/protests, you can read a blog post I wrote in 2016 (*see Appendix C: https://www.parenting4socialjustice.com*).

teaching into your family, I recommend that you trust that intimate knowledge you have of your kids and the kids you are caring for. Kids will be in different places then their age peers, just like with math or reading or potty training. It's all okay.

Your turn:

Here are two helpful tools for kid-appropriate conversations and action based on four areas of anti-bias education: identity, diversity, justice, and action.

❋ Designed for preschoolers, *Starting Small*[66] by Teaching Tolerance, a project of the Southern Poverty Law Center, has many creative activities to try. Read Chapter 1 (*see Appendix D: https://www.parenting4socialjustice.com/*) and try one of the suggested activities.

❋ Teaching Tolerance also developed an *Anti-Bias Framework*[67] of what to talk with kids about for each grade level from kindergarten through high school. Read through the sections of the framework (*see Appendix D: https://www. parenting4socialjustice.com/*) and find the place your kids are in. It might be with the corresponding grade level, and it might not.

1. Which of these goals and outcomes have you been working on already?
2. Which of the goals and outcomes would you like to work on?
3. Based on your experience, write your own scenarios into the framework.
4. In your understanding, how does working on these anti-bias goals in your family contribute to creating socially just systems and structures?

2. Use experiential learning

We use the experiential learning cycle[68] throughout this book and suggest following the same cycle as you parent for social justice. Learning is connected to experience, and effective learning includes all four of these components (not necessarily in this order)—do something, reflect, generalize, plan the next do-ing. No one stage is effective on its own.

Do Something

experiential learning cycle

Plan

Reflect

Generalize

---

66 Teaching Tolerance, *Starting Small: Teaching Tolerance in Preschool and the Early Grades* (Southern Poverty Law Center, 1997). http://www.tolerance.org/sites/default/files/kits/Teachers_Study_Guide.pdf.
67 Teaching Tolerance, *Teaching Tolerance Anti-Bias Framework* (Southern Poverty Law Center, 2004), http://www.tolerance.org/sites/default/files/general/Anti%20bias%20framework%20pamphlet.pdf.
68 David A. Kolb, *Experiential learning: Experience as the source of learning and development* (Vol. 1) (Englewood Cliffs, NJ: Prentice-Hall, 1984).

1. **First, do something.** Read a book with social justice themes, have a hard conversation, serve food at a soup kitchen, write a letter to a prisoner, talk with a community member, watch your low-income neighbor's kids while the parents work, show up for a racial justice rally, or take any action toward social justice that feels within your reach right now.

   Example: My kids and I read *Fiona's Lace* by Patricia Polacco.[69]

2. **Then, reflect.** Reflect on what happened and what you learned. You might use journaling, art work, making a video, and/or music to process and reflect.

   Example continued: We talked about how our ancestors came from Ireland during the same time period in which the story takes place, and for a very similar reason as the characters'. We brought out our family tree and traced our ancestry back to Ireland.

3. **Next, generalize.** What does this learning mean in general? How does what I/ we saw or heard connect to other learning we've been doing? How does it connect to current events, or to history?

   Example continued: We talked about how Ireland was a colony of England and how the food that Irish workers produced was sold for the profit of the English government. While the people who were growing the food were poor and starving, and having to migrate to the U.S. to get jobs that paid enough to meet their basic needs, the English government was getting rich. We talked about current-day examples of the people who are migrating to the U.S. from Mexico and Central American countries because of trade policies that are making the U.S. corporations and government richer and Mexican farmers poorer.

4. **Finally, plan.** How will what you've learned influence further action? Make a plan for your next action that includes what you just learned.

   Example continued: We decided to learn more about our ancestors and why they came to the U.S.

5. **Take your next action!**

   Example continued: We had a conversation with the kids' grandparents to find out more about our family's story, and we began to fill in the family with more information.

---

69 Patricia Polacco, *Fiona's Lace* (Simon & Schuster Books for Young Readers, 2014).

Here's another example of the experiential learning cycle. The writer, Amber Paris, is a white, middle class, female living in rural Southern Vermont with her husband and her three homeschooling children (now 13, 10, 5). She loves learning alongside her children, painting, creating collaborative community art and spending time in nature.

1. *Do something.* Our white family (kids aged 10, 7, 2) went to a Black Lives Matter rally. Before we went, we talked about why the rally was important.

2. *Reflect.* After the rally, I asked the kids what they thought about it. My seven-year-old remembered some of the chants and songs and the call for justice. My ten-year-old was very quiet, working in her own way through issues of injustice.

3. *Generalize.* We talked about how rallies are happening all over the country asking that police be held accountable for killing people because of the color of their skin. Our action is connected with the actions of others. We talked about the history of racism in the U.S. and how it continues today.

4. *Plan.* We decided to show up for future rallies. And we decided to do some history lessons from the Zinn Education Project to further our learning about the history of racism and showing up for racial justice in the U.S.

5. *Next action!* We directly built social justice into our homeschool curriculum and opened that learning group up to other homeschoolers in the area in an effort to educate around these issues. We also, through rallies and direct action/service work, continued/continue to participate in the conversation and work around social justice in our area.

On a clean piece of paper, write an example of how you've used the cycle of experiential learning in your family, or how you could:

Do something.

Reflect.

Generalize.

Plan.

Next action.

3. Find what works in your family.

Different things will work for different families, depending on the ages of your kids, their temperaments, the other activities in your house, the perspectives and opinions that different household members hold about social justice, and your personal and family experiences with oppression. The following elements contribute to the success of family conversations and actions:

Timing: Find a time in the day when people are at their best, and keep your conversations and action within a time frame that works for the ages and temperaments of your kids. Plan for what your kids will need to be present and comfortable. For example, in my family when we go to a rally that is at dinner time, I make sure to bring food for my kids (and some food to share, too).

Consent: Don't force the conversation if the kids aren't interested or if they are resistant. Create an opening for conversation—for example, by asking a question or two before and after reading a social-justice-related book. If the kids don't take the opening, let it go and try again another time. Creating the opening is educational in itself, even if the conversation doesn't go very far at that time. It invites new kinds of thinking and sends the message that you are available for that kind of conversation. The same goes with taking action. Create opportunities to do social justice activities together, but don't force it. This way our kids won't resent social justice activities as competing with other interests. For example: I asked my kids to go to a rally in support of Palestine, and my son said it was at the same time as a ball game he wanted to go to. I suggested we go to the first part of the rally and the last part of the ball game, and he agreed. (If only it were always that smooth.)

Love: Parenting for social justice is based on love—love for our kids, love for others who are in harm's way, and even love for those who harm us. Some of the greatest advocates for social justice talk about love as central to their action, including Martin Luther King, Malcolm X, bell hooks, Valarie Kaur, and Van Jones. Dr. Martin Luther King Jr. said, "Power without love is reckless and abusive and love without power is sentimental and anemic. Power at its best is love implementing the demands of justice, and justice at its best is power correcting everything that stands against love."

Let's love our kids unconditionally, even if they say or do something that makes us feel disappointed. And let's talk with our kids about the people we love who are struggling for their rights. If you can't think of anyone you know who is impacted by social injustice, think of ways to get to know more people with different experiences than you. And then, let's take action inspired by love. One example is the local Love Brigade in my town, which has now spread across the U.S. The group organizes people to write postcards and sends them to people who have survived attacks and insults based on their race/ethnicity, immigration status, gender, or sexual orientation. This is a very practical and community-oriented way to get kids educated about the issues and show them how to take action through love. Start a Love Brigade where you live!

Belief in kids: Believe that it is possible for kids to know the truth and to create a better world. There are many kids who offer great examples of what is possible for kids to do. Two kid activists who inspire my family are Malala Yousafzai[70] from Pakistan, who is standing up for the rights of girls and women, and Xiuhtezcatl Martinez of Earth Guardians,[71] who is a climate activist and protector of the earth. Read books about kids fighting for social justice. Watch social justice videos made by kids. Go to events planned and run by kids.

Play: One of the best ways to communicate social justice concepts to kids is to play. This is a hard one for me; I much prefer to talk. However, I have a friend who spent many years as a preschool teacher and she has been coaching me on playing with my kids. When my youngest breaks out into pretend gunplay, I play too (sometimes). And then, I talk about how it feels to hold a pretend gun, and why many people wouldn't want to play guns, and why consent is important when engaging in gunplay. Or I play soccer with my oldest, and talk about playing as a team. Sometimes, we even pretend to solve the world's most pressing issues through a game of soccer. We are playing, having fun, and learning about social justice, all at the same time.

Working for social justice is not only hard, it is also beautiful and fun and creative and rejuvenating. So let's have fun! Break out into a spontaneous dance party. Take action with friends. Create stories, art, and music. When you go to social justice events, wear superhero costumes, bring a drum to play while you march, or make giant puppets to bring with you.

Community of practice: As you go through this process of bringing social justice into your parenting, find others who you can connect with to share what is working and what isn't, and together find the resources and support you need. For example, in my community, I facilitated a series of parenting for social justice chats over the course of a year. Out of those chats, a community of practice has formed, and families are continuing their learning together. They are able to respond quickly to support each other and our community. When one family was going to be evicted, the community fundraised to make it possible for the family to stay in their home. Another time, the school district was going to cut the funding for the position of Equity & Diversity Coordinator. With only 24 hours' notice, in a town of only 12,000 people, over 60 showed up to a school board meeting to share why they believed the position was crucial. Their action saved the position from being cut (this time)!

All of the above elements—timing, consent, love, belief in kids, play, and community of practice—contribute to the success and sustainability of bringing social justice into your parenting.

---

70 https://www.Malala.org.
71 https://www.Earthguardians.org.

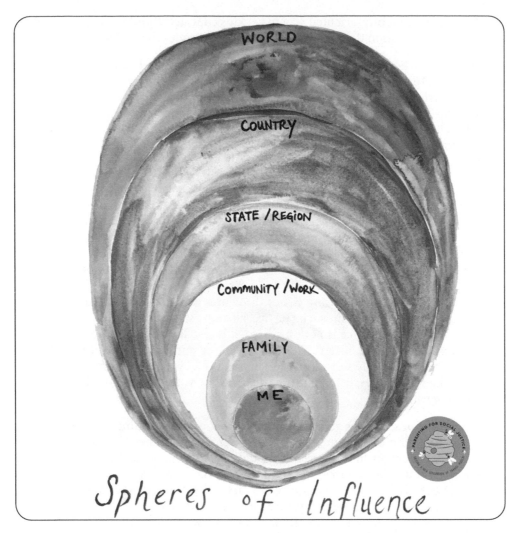

Spheres of Influence

Using this chart think about where you have influence.
(see Appendix E: https://www.parenting4socialjustice.com/)

4. Know where you have influence.

A lot has to change for the dream of a socially just home, community, country, and world to be realized. We each have the power to make change, even if we haven't learned to recognize or access it yet. Our kids have the power to make change, too. This spheres of influence diagram, used by many organizers and educators, helps us think about the places where we have influential power. There are six circles: the inner circle is me, the circle around it is family and friends, the circle around that is community/work, the circle around that is state/region, then country, and the biggest circle is world. Where are you already using your influential power? I like to start by looking at where we are already using our power, and then expand from there and set goals (next section) for where else we would like to use our influence to make change.

For example, here are ways that I use my influential power in each sphere:

1. *Myself:* Spend time researching social change theory and how change has happened throughout history. Turn off my phone for one hour a day to focus entirely on my children. Meditate/pray daily for peace and justice. Do practices to heal from the trauma of white supremacy culture.

2. *Family:* Read social justice books with my kids. Raise money for social justice work. Pick a social justice action and do it together, even when it's not easy. Join the local chapter of 350.org's MotherUp! program.

3. *Community/workplace:* Show up to five rallies a year. Support BIPOC[72] racial justice organizing. Donate to key local social justice organizations. Speak out truthfully about social justice issues. Join the diversity committee at my kids' school, or in my town.

4. *State/region:* Show up for two statewide events, like a lobby day for raising the minimum wage. Donate to key statewide social justice organizations. Sign petitions. Support state- and local-level politicians who are working for economic and racial justice issues.

5. *Country:* Donate to key social justice organizations. Show up to one national rally. Sign petitions. Listen to *Democracy Now!*[73] twice a week. Vote.

6. *World:* Donate to key social justice organizations. Sign petitions. Bring global information and connections into my conversations, teaching, and advocacy. Connect local social justice organizations with similar organizations/campaigns internationally.

This book focuses primarily on change in the personal and family spheres. What we do on a small level has a ripple effect on the community and world. We might spend five years of learning about our own privilege or about how we have internalized oppression based on gender/race/class/disability, before we are ready to show up as leaders for making change. Or it might be a matter of weeks. Each person is different. Educating ourselves is crucial, as long as we connect that education to continued action. It is important to use our influence to impact larger change, and throughout the book, we refer you to other relevant resources for organizing to change our communities and our world.

Finding our role in social justice movements can feel overwhelming. Here are some tools I've found useful to counteract overwhelm:

❀ Find small, doable steps to accomplish. (The next section of this chapter will support you in coming up with bite-sized goals.)

---

72 BIPOC: Black, Indigenous, people of color (see Appendix B for definition).
73 https://www.democracynow.org.

* Practice healing justice. (Each chapter concludes with a healing justice practice. I'm going to do the one at the end of this chapter as soon as I turn off my computer!)

* Connect with community for laughter and tears. (I love this one and practice it a lot.)

We might also have defensive thoughts that come up when we consider taking action for social justice, like "someone else is already doing it," "I don't know enough," "I'm not good enough," "I've already contributed enough," and so on. There are always plenty of reasons to do nothing *and* there are far more reasons to do something. To get through my defensive reactions I:

Remember that defensiveness is a normal reaction in a situation where I feel overwhelmed or afraid. It does not mean I'm a bad person.

* I have people who can let me know when they notice my defensiveness. We use code words, like "squirrel" and "bubblegum," so that it doesn't have to be a huge conversation in the heat of the moment.

* I have learned to apologize to people who might have been impacted negatively by my defensive reactions.

Let's push through the overwhelm and our defenses, and show up for change.

Not everyone will become a social justice activist, and that's okay. You know yourself and your family—find ways to contribute to change that work for you. There is room for *everyone* in the movement for social justice!

Parents Abby and Laura with their kids at a 350.org Mother Up rally.

5. Set goals (and revisit them)

In each chapter we'll ask you to set SMART goals for bringing social justice into your parenting. In Chapter 8, we will ask you to revisit the goals you set throughout the book, so record them somwhere you can find them later. SMART stands for specific, measurable, attainable, relevant, and time-bound. Here are a few hypothetical examples of SMART goals:

Example 1: My goal is to learn tools (specific) for having conversations about social justice issues (relevant) with my four-year-old and to have at least one (measureable) social justice conversation with her every week (time-bound). (This is attainable because we spend about a million hours together every week, and once a week gives me time to process and feel prepared for the conversation.)

Example 2: My goal is to make a plan (specific and meaureable) within the next month (time-bound) for supporting and advocating for my ten-year-old who is gender nonconforming (relevant). (This is attainable!)

Example 3: My goal is to show up to a racial justice rally (specific, measurable, and relevant) with my kids within the next two months (time-bound). (This is attainable!)

 Reflect

Use the following questions as a guide to reflect on the five sections above (Be Kid Appropriate, Use Experiential Learning, Find What Works in Your Family, Know Where You Have Influence, Set Goals). You can write, paint, share your responses with someone, or just think quietly—whatever works best for your learning style.

1. These sections contain a lot of suggestions. What do you want to keep in mind when bringing social justice into your family? Write a note and put it in a place that will remind you!

2. What are your learning goals for your work with this book? Make them SMART goals!

3. If you haven't already invited others to join you in reading this book, who could you invite?

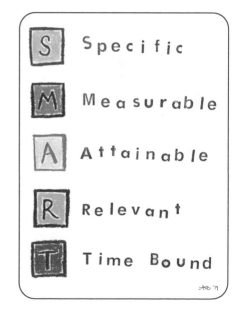

S Specific

M Measurable

A Attainable

R Relevant

T Time Bound

Healing justice practice

"I Am Enough," adapted from Kaiilama Morris's Breath of the Heart practice[1]

Sometimes, maybe all the time, life can feel overwhelming. We can so often feel down on ourselves, on our kids, and on the people around us. The truth is that we are each valuable, special, loved, and "enough."
This meditation is a chance for us to be in touch with that truth.

Get comfortable in your body, whether seated on a chair or on the floor or lying down. Breathe deeply in that position for at least five minutes. I suggest using a timer so that you don't get anxious about time, but of course you can continue longer than five minutes if you want to. While you are comfortable and breathing deeply, repeat in your mind or aloud "I am enough." When you are ready, come back into your body, aware of your surroundings.

You might want to take some time to journal or make art afterwards.

---

1 Breathoftheheart.com

Community of practice questions

If you are reading this book with a group, here are questions to guide your reflection on the chapter. To learn more about community of practice, refer page 17 in the Introduction.

1. What are some social justice conversations you've been having in your family lately?

2. What questions do you have about parenting for social justice?

3. What are you already doing to bring social justice into your parenting? What else would you like to do?

4. Share your learning goals for this book and how you came up with them.

5. What have been your somatic/body sensations and responses throughout this chapter?

Abby and Laura's daughter, Lucy, at The Climate March in Washington, DC.

"Trayvon could've been me." Illustrator Brittney's child, MJ, at a racial justice protest, Washington, DC.

Chapter 3
PARENTING FOR RACIAL JUSTICE

BY CHRISSY COLÓN BRADT AND ANGELA BERKFIELD

We march every day
BY ALYSSA BROWN[1]

Some of us march every day.
We've been marching for centuries.
Into rooms where all eyes are on us
But no one smiles
Into jobs where our qualifications are constantly in question
Into jobs where we are forced to choose between our dignity and our paycheck
Into schools where we are simultaneously invisible and under a microscope
We march through spaces we are told we don't belong
For some of us, that space is a high level executive position and
For some of us it is a bathroom
For some of us it is a sidewalk
In spite of our anger, and fear, and disappointment
We gather our splintered pride around us
Over and over again
We march even when it feels like crawling
With the strength and will of our ancestors
We march
Over obstacles
And through barriers
We don't have special chants
We don't hold signs
We don't wear pink hats or safety pins
We wear
Our black skins
Our brown skins
Our gender non-compliant bodies

---

1 Alyssa Brown, LCSW, Free To Be Therapeutic Services
"We march every day," unpublished (2019).

Our fat bodies
Our hijabs
Our wheelchairs
Our "disabilities" visible and invisible
Our ancestors' pain
Our love
Walking around in these othered bodies
Our resistance is individual and collective
Our resistance is every day
Our resistance is massive
Billions of us march
We march on every town
We march every day
We march because we have no choice
For us, it's march or die
More money would be nice
But we march in defiance
We claim the right to breathe
We claim the right to live
We claim the right to know joy
We claim the right to know peace
Right now
In these bodies
Every day we march
Our revolution is loving ourselves in the face of hate
Our revolution is loving each other in the face of hate
"Resistance is in our DNA"
We were born for this time
We are ready
Because
Every day we march

"I don't worry that [my son] will be killed by police while playing in a park.
In front of a store. While walking home with Skittles. While driving.
With his hands up. Because my son is white."
—ALYSSA HADLEY DUNN[2]

"It's funny (in a laugh-to-keep-from-crying way) because, while my husband
and I are both Latino, my skin is much darker than his. When Lucas was born,
I jokingly said that I wished he was darker so he would look more like me.
As he has gotten older, I have felt relief about his lighter complexion. Although

---

2 Alyssa Hadley Dunn, "On Mothering White Kids to Know #BlackLivesMatter: Our Silence Is
Continued Violence," (*Huffington Post*: July 7, 2016). https://www.huffpost.com/entry/on-mothering-
white-sons-to-know-blacklivesmatter_b_577e85bce4b03288ddc57d79?te=Atlantic.

he will never be perceived as white, I think that having lighter skin will benefit him in life. It will make him seem less 'aggressive' and 'threatening' to others."
—AILEN ARREAZA[3]

"Beloved community is formed not by the eradication of difference but by its affirmation, by each of us claiming the identities and cultural legacies that shape who we are and how we live in the world . . . We deepen those bondings by connecting them with an anti-racist struggle."
—BELL HOOKS[4]

Author Angela's son (at right near BLM sign) on his father's shoulders, Brattleboro, VT, 2015.

Reflect

Use the following questions as a guide to reflect on the quotes above. You can write or paint and share your responses with someone, or just think quietly, whatever works best for your learning style.

1. How does the race and skin tone of your kids impact how you parent them?

2. How does your race and skin tone impact how you parent your children?

3. What racial justice issues are on your mind?

4. What is your personal and ancestral experience with resistance to racism and white supremacy?

5. Are you part of an anti-racist community? How does that shape how you parent your kids?

---

3 Nani Arreaza, "Talking About Ferguson with Our Little Boys," (Parents Together: Aug. 28, 2014). https://parents-together.org/talking-about-ferguson-with-our-little-boys.
4 bell hooks, *killing rage: Ending Racism* (Holt Paperbacks, 1996, p. 265).

Our stories

There are infinite stories of how we experience race, yet there are common themes. The co-authors of this chapter will each tell a piece of our stories. These stories set the stage for learning about race and for our roles as parents in teaching our kids about race and racial justice. We each continue to peel back the many layers that make up our stories to better understand our thinking and our actions. We trust that in reading our stories you will think about pieces of your own story in a new way

Chrissy

I was born in Newark, New Jersey—"Brick City"—a city infamous for its racial riots, its failing schools, its murder and car theft rates. This is also a city that has served as a haven to generations of immigrants from Portugal, Spain, Italy, and South and Central America. This is a city that thrived during the Industrial Revolution but was quickly abandoned during times of suburbanization. This is the city I was born in, grew up in, learned to read in, built relationships in. It was here that I experienced and learned about racism.

The baby of five children, I grew up in a housing project in "down Neck Newark"— the Ironbound section. I was raised by a village in a single-parent home, to a fiercely Puerto Rican mother. I am 17 years younger than my oldest sibling and by the time I was of school age, my mother was well aware of the disparity between the schools available in our neighborhood and those in whiter districts. The search for an adequate education began. From the time I was very young, I can remember being coached to lie about our address. My mother would find a friend, a colleague, a confidant, use her address and promptly send me to schools with whiter classmates, better books and programs, and cleaner facilities. When the commute would get too difficult, or someone would start lurking around our fake address, she would begin the search for a new confidant and school again. Inevitably I was discovered to be out of district, and my mom would work two jobs or sacrifice minor luxuries in order to pay for a Catholic school tuition until she found another way to get me into a quality public school. At the entry interviews for the Catholic schools I heard things like "We don't want any trouble here. Our kids are good. We do our work here." These comments came with each move, despite the fact that I loved school and rose to the top of the class wherever I found myself. I worked hard, because my hard work was all I could use to prove I was worthy of the education we were stealing. When I ask my mom today why she chose that particular path to access education she says, "The school near us was bad. You were smart. You deserved better."

I grew up in a world where I learned to interpret *better* as white. No one ever explicitly said that better was white, but everywhere I looked this was the case. Every school out of district left me as the only or one of two children of color in the room. Every white friend I made lived in what I perceived as a nicer home, had nicer clothes, took vacations. These families owned small businesses, had access to these schools that I snuck into, and their families pitied me. That feeling was palpable and ever-present.

Growing up, when someone would say I was Black, my mom instructed me to respond, "No, I'm tan." Too young to understand what was being communicated in this statement, I proudly corrected peers, teachers, and even family members. A light-skinned Afro-Latina, my mom had herself learned the colorism that is prevalent in Latinx[5] communities. When extended family would meet me for the first time, they would always ask, "Is her father Black?"

"No," my mother would say. "He's West Indian. From Trinidad." This qualifier somehow making his Blackness acceptable.

In fifth grade, when I took my first standardized test, I found myself paralyzed. Staring at the first page that requested I fill in the box that corresponded with my race, I was stuck. Confused. It had been made clear to me that I was not Black. I knew from years of schooling that I was not white. I did not know what West Indian meant and there was no category that reflected what I understood myself to be. I went home that day and asked my mother. She said, "Check the white box. We're just as good."

White was better. Everything I had learned about my racial, ethnic, and class background told me, white was better.

Let's fast forward. My mother's pursuit of a better education leads us to an access program that eventually leads me to a small, independent boarding school in Newport, Rhode Island. The shock was massive. Now, it was clear. White *was* better. My peers lived lives I had never encountered, not even on TV. They had chauffeurs, they played sports I'd never seen, they traveled to worlds I only learned about and they seemed at ease in this foreign place. They moved through spaces with a kind of untouchability that I had never really experienced before. Even my peers of color seemed to come from families that owned homes, that took vacations. Although they were black and brown, their lives at least in class markers resembled the lives of the white kids I read about and saw on TV.

But it was here, in this tiny boarding school, miles away from anything or anyone familiar, that I learned how beautiful, how resilient, how Black, Latina, and worthy I was. During these four years I was confronted with constant microaggressions and assumptions. I was faced with some of the ugliness that lurks beneath the surface of seemingly progressive mindsets. But I had teachers, advisors, mentors who introduced me to W.E.B. Dubois, Langston Hughes, Beverly Daniel Tatum, and Richard Wright. It was here that I first read Zora Neale Hurston, Frederick Douglass, Malcolm X. It was here that I researched Operation Bootstrap[6] and made sense of a story I'd heard growing up about how our family came to the mainland. It was under the guidance of these mentors that I was able to make sense of the messages, misperceptions, and structures that had led me to think that white was better, and it was here that I began to unravel that insidious spider web of lies.

Today, I am a mom. My son is four. I am married to a white man. My son is biracial; he is white passing. I still remember the first time he mentioned our different skin

---

5 Latinx is a term used for a person of Latin American origin or descent (used as a gender-neutral or nonbinary alternative to Latino or Latina). This term has risen out of college campus organizing and first appeared online in 2004. (remezcla.com, 2018).

6 Operation Bootstrap was industrial planning in Puerto Rico starting in 1948 that was based on external capital and tax exemptions and prompted rapid industrialization. While there were immediate economic gains, it also resulted in a large wave of immigration to mainland U.S. by the 1970s.

shades. It was a Saturday morning. We were lying in bed. He touched my skin and then he touched his dad. "You're brown, and daddy is not."

I nodded. "Yes, we have different skin shades. Mommy is brown, sometimes called black. Daddy's skin is paler, more like peach, sometimes called white. What is your skin like?"

"Mine is like daddy's," he said. Then he said, "I like your skin, mommy."

"Thank you, bud. What else is the same and different?"

We began to play this game almost every day. In the mirror, after his bath. What is the same and what is different? He would notice we both had curly hair, but his was yellow. He would notice his eyes were like Daddy's, his nose like Mama's. He loved to play this game, and for me this was the beginning of our conversations about race. Those conversations have continued with books, and I am committed to continuing these conversations throughout his life.

In our home, we are deliberate about the books we read, the shows we watch, the media we consume. We are intentional about my son's playdates, his activities outside of school, and how we interact with the broader world. First and foremost, I want my son to know that he is beautiful, that he is multiracial, that his ancestors are Taino, Spanish, German, African. I want him to feel pride, but also recognize his privilege and the power he holds to work for racial justice. As a mother, this has felt complicated and nuanced. I've had to continually explore and pay attention to my biases, to my assumptions, to what I communicate. Where we live, the schools he attends, the media he consumes—all of these, for me, have the potential to send him messages, positive or negative, about who he is and where he's from, and I feel an obligation to think about that and to shape a more racially just world for him and for humanity.

Here are some of the lessons I teach my son:

❀ I am teaching my son the multiracial bill of rights.[7]

❀ I am teaching my son to live and operate in a racially unjust world: to recognize inequity, to understand how he may be perceived by others, and to stay safe, but also to be courageous in the name of justice.

❀ I am teaching my son what allyship looks like, and how to occupy that space.

❀ I am teaching my son to be open, to keep learning, to ask questions, and to be adaptive.

❀ I am teaching my son that his power is in community, and community is all living beings.

❀ I am teaching my son that when the community is harmed, we are harmed, and we have a responsibility to support the healing of ourselves and others.

❀ I am teaching my son to know his ancestry. As I learn more, I want to teach him more and teach him to commune with his ancestors.

---

7 Maria P. P. Root, ""Bill of Rights for Racially Mixed People," www.safehousealliance.org/wp-content/uploads/2012/10/A-Bill-of-Rights-for-Racially-Mixed-People.pdf.

Angela

I grew up in an all-white family with Danish, Irish, English, and German ancestry that I know hardly anything about. I still don't have anybody in my whole extended family who is a person of color. I married a white man who also grew up in a white family and doesn't have any people of color in his extended family. I grew up in a suburb of St. Paul, Minnesota. I went to a high school of about 2,000 students, which was over 95% white. Growing up, I only had a few friends of color. My access to learning about people from different racial and ethnic cultures was through hosting foreign exchange students from Japan when I was in elementary school, supporting an immigrant family from Russia when I was in high school, a two-month family trip to Israel in 9th grade, and a one-week church mission trip to Mexico in 11th grade.

This context shaped my understanding of racism. I thought (and was taught) that racism was a thing of the past. The Civil War ended slavery, the struggle for civil rights was won in the 1960s, and we are all one human race. I had no idea that a mere ten miles away were neighborhoods of Black, Native American, and Latinx folks who were having a completely different life experience than I was. In many cases they did not have access to the same opportunities, to "good" education, decent and affordable housing, safe neighborhoods, or health care. Their neighborhoods were heavily policed, and in the 1980s and 90s many men in that neighborhood were being imprisoned because of the "war on drugs." No one in my family or classrooms talked about that reality, nor our connection to it.

All that is to say, no one taught me to understand racism, notice racism, be aware of my own racial identity and privilege, or to be aware of how privilege and oppression are connected, much less to stand up for racial justice. I often wonder where I would be now if I had actually learned about injustice and the tools to show up for racial justice when I was growing up.

My parents encouraged me to have friends of many races and ethnicities, but they didn't talk about racism or whiteness. My parents *did* teach me important building blocks for being civically aware, engaged, and responsive. They taught me to be kind and non-violent, to share (including donating 10% of my income), say I'm sorry, listen to others, listen to myself, be confident, love everyone, and to love learning. I'm so thankful for all they taught me and for how it has formed a solid foundation for being able to hear about and respond to injustice.

I also learned about suffering and poverty and need. "Helping" is the tool I was offered to respond to that need. I served in soup kitchens, food shelves, homeless shelters, and on mission trips. Yet during all of that volunteering I was not taught to think critically about why there was so much need. No one helped me understand the connection between the imbalance of resources between the rich and poor. I was certainly not taught to connect the suffering I saw to racism, white supremacy, colonization, and capitalism. I was not taught that my privilege came at the expense of other people and the earth. I was not taught my own ancestral stories and teachings, and didn't even recognize that as a lack. In college I studied social work and Spanish, and in spite of the relevance of racism to those fields I was not taught about present-day racism and my connection to it.

It wasn't until many years later, in my graduate program, that I learned about racial identity and about how oppression functions to maintain white supremacy. I had been collecting puzzle pieces through years of cross-cultural interactions, working as a social worker, and backpacking throughout Southeast Asia and Central America. It only took three weeks of classes with Janaki Natarajan for me to put all the pieces together. I had worked in Minneapolis, with Latinx youth struggling to stay off drugs; in Puerto Rico, with women recovering from drug addiction; in Thailand, with refugees escaping from an oppressive government in Burma; and in Ecuador, with Indigenous tribes struggling to maintain their culture and language in the face of oil and mining companies. The experiences were all different, but white supremacy and capitalism were the connection. The manufacture of the belief that white people are supreme has justified and upheld the conquering of continents, stealing of lands, and genocide of peoples, which have made wealth accumulation possible for the elite.

So I promised myself that when I had kids, I would tell them the truth. And I did, when they were very young. I remember looking for good social justice books for my two year old and coming across *The Great Migration: An American Story*[8] by Jacob Lawrence. The book is about factory jobs opening up in northern states in the 1930s and 40s and Black families migrating north to escape continued persecution in the South. I read this book with my son when he was two, which in retrospect, I'm not so sure was age appropriate. (In fact, I waited until my second son was six years old before reading it with him.) We also read other books about race and participated in local rallies for racial justice. I didn't know what kind of impact these experiences were having on him. But then apparently out of the blue, when my first son was four, he asked, "Mom, why don't white people and Black people like each other?" We were at a city park in Burlington, Vermont, and he had been watching a group of Black youth playing ball. I'm not sure if he had picked up on dynamics in the park or if he was just thinking back to the books that we had read and putting those ideas together in his head in that moment.

I said something like, "It's complicated and it is because of a long long history since way before you or I were born. But you and I can change that. We have friends who are Black. And we go to the protests for Black Lives Matter in our town. We are part of long-term organizing for racial justice in our area. I am committed to change, and I hope you'll commit to making change too."

As he and my second son get older, they still haven't committed to making change, at least not visibly, and at least not in the way they are committed to soccer and hockey. And not in the way that I've seen other kids their ages commit to social justice. That's OK. I still teach them about history, about how our family has benefitted from historical realities, and how we have been harmed. I teach them to keep learning, how to heal, and how to take action.

Quite honestly, it would be easier not to be talking about racism. It isn't a noticeable issue or problem in my kids' daily lived reality. They think their experience in a

---

8 Jacob Lawrence, *The Great Migration: An American Story* (The Museum of Modern Art, New York, HarperCollins Publishers, 1993). Suggested for ages 8 and up. It is a simple and powerful book that can be helpful in illustrating connections between race and class and causes of migration.

95% white rural community is normal. They think they are normal. It is important to me to interrupt that thinking. They haven't had their hearts broken yet, and it's hard to think about being the one to break their hearts by telling them about racism. But I know that it is from that place of heartbreak that there will come the motivation for change. I also know that for many people heartbreak isn't a choice.

When my kids were nine and six, I started reading more in-depth books about history with them. We read a book about Sitting Bull and books about the transatlantic slave trade. They started to ask more questions. My youngest said, "We are white. We did that." My oldest added, "We are so messed up." I responded, "Yeah, well, it is complicated. There have been many white people who have fought against slavery and on behalf of the Native Americans. I'm not actually sure what our family's position was. Our family came to the U.S. after slavery had been officially ended and they lived in the North. They did benefit from the money this country made off of slavery. They definitely benefited from the forced treaties with the Native Americans. Your grandparents were farmers in Kansas and Iowa, where—" "Mom! Keep reading." And that's how it typically goes in my house. They only let me talk for about two minutes, and there isn't much conversation, but they certainly pay attention.

Talking with my kids is one thing, but I think they learn the most from my actions and from the things we do together. As a co-founder of the local racial justice organizing collective, I am often at meetings and events and protests and gatherings that are related to racial justice work. I have found a "beloved community," like bell hooks talks about in the quotation at the beginning of the chapter—a community engaged in anti-racist practice. I want for this community to be a beloved community for my family as well, but so far it isn't. They join me sometimes, but usually they don't want to. I'm not going to make them do something they don't want to do, because that is sure to leave a negative imprint on their minds. I do continue to invite them, though. I think my youngest is coming around! He sometimes even puts on his Root Social Justice Center T-shirt.

The stories we are told are the stories we tell

As parents it is important for us to understand race, racism, whiteness, and white supremacy because it is affecting our families right now, and it will continue to have a dramatic impact on our children's lives. For the purpose of this book we are summarizing what we see as the main points that can support us in having an understanding so we are prepared to talk with our kids. We highly recommend continuing your learning and maybe even researching with your kids. There are many resources at the end of the book to support that learning. (See page 318.)

System of White Supremacy

The idea of race was created centuries ago for the purpose of amassing and maintaining power and wealth, and it has infiltrated all of the institutions in the U.S. and even around the globe. Race was socially and politically constructed; it does not have a biological basis. "Modern consensus of evolutionary biologists is that our species does not have enough genetic variability among its populations to justify either the identification of geographically based races or of evolutionarily distinct lineages."[9] Yet here we are in the 21st century with this huge weight of the cumulative impact of the construction of race and resulting system of white supremacy. In the white supremacy system white people are continuously given advantages over non-white people (the definition of who is and isn't white has shifted over time) and white bodies are held up as the standard by which all other bodies are judged. This false measurement has been used to justify all kinds of exploitation, violence, and oppression.

When we better understand the history of why and how race was socially and politically constructed, who is benefitting, and who is being harmed, we are better equipped to show up for racial justice. It becomes easier to see racism, or systemic advantage because of race, showing up in many ways—racist jokes that family members make, hateful rhetoric about Muslims, the poisoning of water on Native American reservations and in Flint, Michigan, the practice of dehumanizing immigrants, the more subtle ways that white supremacy culture functions in everyday interactions, privileging the needs and voices of people with white skin, and on and on.

Let's use the following iceberg analogy (see image on the opposite page) to better understand how racism functions as a tool for white supremacy and what is required for racial justice. This analogy reminds us to look beyond the tip of the iceberg to see how the whole system functions. You will find this iceberg on our website in worksheet form. (*see Appendix G: https://www.parenting4socialjustice.com/*). It would be helpful to fill it out as you go through this section.

All people in the U.S. are on this boat, which has rammed into the iceberg created by a system of white supremacy. People of color, poor and working-class folks and recent immigrants are on the bottom levels of the boat where there has been a gaping hole for centuries with water pouring in. The most hideous impacts of white supremacy are visible here and those who have survived have developed a keen awareness of how white supremacy works, as well as survival tools. Owning-class folks, who are mostly white along with a few people of color, are on the top deck and are either unaware of the hole that white supremacy has caused, or like to pretend it isn't there. The rest of us are somewhere in the middle. The reality is that white supremacy is sinking the boat and the vast majority of us are going down with it, so we need to work together to patch the hole and to get to land.

Above the water is interpersonal racism—crossing the street out of fear when you see a Black man, racial slurs and jokes, and displaying racist symbols like swastikas or confederate flags. Also above the water are some less-obvious manifestations of racism, like children's books featuring mostly white characters. This is also where we see racial microaggressions: unintentional individual-level actions that are insulting, demeaning, or dismissive to people of color. Behaviors like asking a Latinx or Asian person, "Where are you from?" or touching Black people's hair and exclaiming, "You are a credit to your race," are all common microaggressions. Microaggressions might not

---

9 Joseph L. Graves, "Race Does Not Equal DNA," *Teaching Tolerance*, Summer 2015, https://www.tolerance.org/magazine/summer-2015/race-dna. This article puts the science of race as a social construct into layperson's terms.

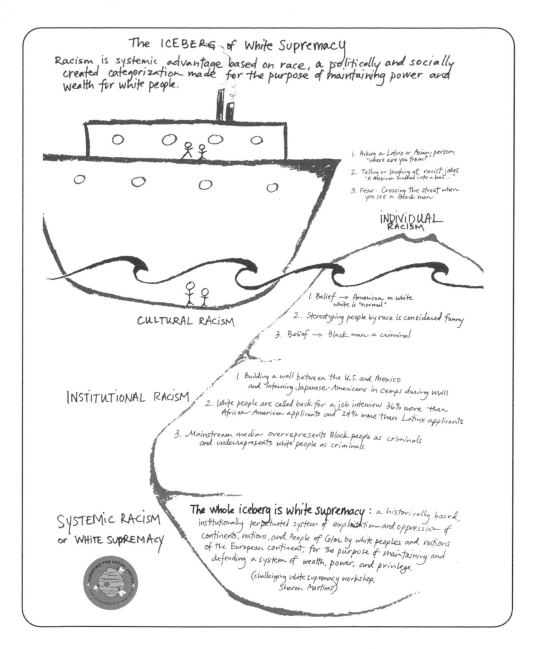

The ICEBERG of White Supremacy

Racism is systemic advantage based on race, a politically and socially created categorization made for the purpose of maintaining power and wealth for white people.

1. Asking a Latinx or Asian person: "where are you from?"
2. Telling or laughing at racist jokes "A Mexican walked into a bar..."
3. Fear: Crossing the street when you see a Black man

INDIVIDUAL RACISM

CULTURAL RACISM

1. Belief → American = white white is "normal"
2. Stereotyping people by race is considered funny
3. Belief → Black man = criminal

INSTITUTIONAL RACISM

1. Building a wall between the U.S. and Mexico and interning Japanese-Americans in camps during WWII
2. White people are called back for a job interview 36% more than African-American applicants and 24% more than Latinx applicants
3. Mainstream media overrepresents Black people as criminals and underrepresents white people as criminals

SYSTEMIC RACISM or WHITE SUPREMACY

The whole iceberg is white supremacy: a historically based, institutionally perpetuated system of exploitation and oppression of continents, nations, and People of Color by white peoples and nations of the European continent, for the purpose of maintaining and defending a system of wealth, power, and privilege.
(challenging white supremacy workshop, Sharon Martinas)

seem like a huge deal, but when a person experiences them every day, multiple times a day, for many years, it adds up and creates toxic overload. Experiencing daily micro-aggressions requires that a person repeatedly and constantly defend their worthiness, humanity, and right to occupy space. It is exhausting, maddening, and disheartening and has very tangible impacts on physical and mental health.

Can you think of more examples of interpersonal racism above the water? Write them on the iceberg worksheet.

Try this!
In Appendix E (*https://www.parenting4socialjustice.com/*), you'll find a list of common microaggressions based on race, gender, and class. Find the racial microaggressions on the list, and notice:

1. Which of these things have you said?
2. Which have you been on the receiving end of? How have you responded?
3. Which have you heard directed at others? How have you responded?

Let's continue . . . Right below the waves is cultural racism, the ways racism shows up in cultural beliefs and values. Developed over centuries and millennia, our cultural beliefs and values are how we make sense of the world around us and survive in it. White supremacy has had a profound impact on our beliefs and values, distorting them in ways that are so subtle that they look like innate cultural attributes. One such belief is that white is pure, clean, and beautiful. In our culture American equals white (thus asking people of color "where are you from?"). On the flip side, a cultural belief is that black is dark, dirty, and ugly. In our culture black equals criminal. You can hear this black and white pattern in the way that people use white and black to talk about inanimate objects and even animals. Angels (considered good and pure in U.S. American culture) wear white, while devils and witches (considered evil in U.S. American culture) wear black. Another cultural belief is that stereotyping people by race is funny. Many of the jokes that are told whether in public or private are related to race.

Despite our prevalent association of Blackness with negative, violent, and bad, there remains a widely held belief that we live in a post-racial society. Some white people believe it is racist to talk about skin color so they say, "I don't see race," or they point to policies and practices that do not mention race as evidence of our post-racial society. This is called racial color-blindness, and is another example of cultural racism.

Can you think of more examples of cultural racism? Write them on the iceberg worksheet.

Let's continue . . . As we drop down even further into the sea, the iceberg widens considerably to encompass all of the institutions in the U.S., symbolizing that institutional racism holds more power than interpersonal racism because it is built into every institution, every aspect of life. This has an immense power in shaping how people of color experience life. The examples used on the iceberg image are:

1. **National security:** Building a wall between the U.S. and Mexico. Japanese Americans interned in camps during WWII.
2. **Human resources and hiring practices:** White people are called back for a job interview 36% more than African Americans and 24% more than Latinx applicants.[10]

---

10 German Lopez, "Study: Anti-black Hiring Discrimination so Prevalent Today as it was in 1989", Vox. September 18, 2017, https://www.vox.com/identities/2017/9/18/16307782/study-racism-jobs.

3. **Media:** Mainstream media overrepresents Black people as criminals and underrepresents white people as criminals.[11]

Here are a few more examples: the U.S. constitution did not give Black men the right to vote until 1870, nearly one hundred years after the constitution was ratified. Black folks have been blocked in many ways from voting, even after the civil rights movement in the 1960s won major voting rights victories, and this continues today in the form of restrictive voting requirements that disproportionately affect Black voters. Another key way that Black, Indigenous, and people of color (BIPOC[12]) have been systematically discriminated against is through the home buying process. Banks have used redlining practices to deny loans to BIPOC. In fact, they are still doing that today.[13]

Can you think of more examples of institutional racism? Write them on the iceberg worksheet.

We just said that racism is built into the institutions in the U.S.. In another sense, it's also the case that institutions in the U.S. created race and racism. That's what we mean when we say that race is socially and politically constructed. We'll use two examples to illustrate that. The first example is Bacon's Rebellion in 1676, which is often pointed to as a turning point in America's racial history. Nathaniel Bacon was a white wealthy landowner in Virginia who was in disagreement with the Governor over how to respond to Native American raids on plantations. He wanted to counterattack the Native Americans for their raids on the colonies so that he and others could expand their land ownership. We could spend time on that, but we won't for now. The point here is that Bacon put together a militia made up of indentured Europeans and Africans as well as enslaved Africans to raid nearby Native American villages. Months of conflict ensued and Bacon's militia eventually burned Jamestown to the ground. The fact that a multiracial militia had this much power when they joined together, and was influencing other uprisings throughout the colonies, caused the establishment and the governing decisionmakers at the time to panic. So they changed the policy on the importation of enslaved people. A priority was given to bringing more Black African slaves, and fewer white European indentured servants. More laws were written to favor European indentured servants and give some freedoms, while making slavery of Black Africans more permanent. The colony's goal was to reduce the power that a multiracial alliance had in challenging those in power.

Governments still create policies that intentionally divide people who rise up against injustices (or who are just trying to help out other human beings). The second example we'll give is in the current-day U.S. When Trump was president, he instituted draconian immigration laws and practices, such as separating asylum-seeking parents from their children at the U.S./Mexico border. Trump dramatically increased deportation of people

---

11 Dr. Travis L. Dixon, "A Dangerous Distortion of Our Families: Representation of Families by Race in News and Opinion Media", Color of Change. January 2017, https://colorofchange.org/dangerousdistortion.
12 See Appendix B for BIPOC definition.
13 Aaron Glantz, "We Exposed Modern Day Redlining in 61 Cities. Find Out What's Happened Since." Reveal Center for Investigative Reporting, October 25, 2018, https://www.revealnews.org/blog/we-exposed-modern-day-redlining-in-61-cities-find-out-whats-happened-since.

who do not have citizenship. Many people who support fair and just immigration policy change responded to these policies and practices through protests and lawsuits. An example of a policy that divides people is a federal law that makes it illegal to "harbor" people who are not in the U.S. legally.[14] This law applies to anyone who houses, employs, or transports someone who they know is in the U.S. illegally. A current use of this law is against a 36-year-old teacher, Scott Warren, in Tucson, Arizona, who had three felony charges brought against him for helping migrants.[15]

For a better understanding of institutionalized racism we recommend watching *Race: The Power of An Illusion*, a California Newsreel documentary that provides a solid framework for understanding the construction of race.[16]

Let's continue . . . Returning to the iceberg, a combination of factors has combined to create this deadly iceberg of interpersonal, culture, and institutional racism. That combination of factors is the ideology of white supremacy, which is pervasive and upholds the continuation of racism in all its forms. White supremacy is not just the KKK or militant white nationalist hate groups, although white supremacy definitely rears its head in hateful individuals and groups. It is primarily a thought system in which being white is valued above any other ethnic or cultural heritage. On the extreme end this ideology is used by those in power (sometimes explicitly and often implicitly) to justify exploitation and even genocide of people based on their race. But no one in the U.S. is immune to the culture of white supremacy because it gets reproduced in subtle ways and is very pervasive. Many people who would not consider themselves white supremacist and would speak vehemenently against genocide, including some people of color, have bought into this system in one way or another and have no idea that it even exists. It is like the air we breathe. Tema Okun has developed a list of characteristics of how white supremacy shows up in our culture: perfectionism, fear of open conflict, either/or thinking, individualism, power hoarding, and more. (*see Appendix H: https://www.parenting4socialjustice.com/*).[17] This list is important for us to begin to understand more deeply how "whiteness" works and how it is perpetuated, even in those of us that are working for racial justice.

So how does whiteness work? We'll illustrate with stories from our families. When my (AB) ancestors came to the U.S. four generations ago, they had to relinquish their Irish and Danish heritage to become "American" and reap the full benefits of being seen as white instead of ethnic. Some folks with lighter skin—the Irish, Greeks, Polish—did not become "white" until relatively recently. This is in contrast to my (CCB) ancestors who are Indigenous to the island of Puerto Rico (Taino), of

---

14 Catholic Legal Immigration Network, "Harboring: Overview of the Law", accessed 9/21/19, https://www.disciplesimmigration.org/wp-content/uploads/2017/02/Harboring-Memo.pdf.
15 Miriam Jordan, "An Arizona Teacher Helped Migrants: Jurors Couldn't Decide If It Was A Crime", New York Times. June 11, 2019. https://www.nytimes.com/2019/06/11/us/scott-warren-arizona-deaths.html.
16 *RACE—The Power of an Illusion.* Produced by California Newsreel in association with Independent Television Service; written, produced and directed by Tracy Heather Strain; edited by Randall MacLowry, Cob Carlson. (2003/2012, San Francisco: California Newsreel), documentary film.
17 Tema Okun, "Characteristics of White Supremacy Culture", dRworks, retrieved October 18, 2019, http://www.dismantlingracism.org/uploads/4/3/5/7/43579015/whitesupcul13.pdf. You can find more on white supremacy culture at http://www.dismantlingracism.org/white-supremacy-culture.html.

African descent and of Spanish heritage. They were subjugate and oppressed and not perceived as belonging. Recent generations of Puerto Ricans moving to mainland U.S., were mostly Black folk who were fooled off their land and given one way tickets to New York City, and who were and continue to be perceived by people with white privilege as "other," as not belonging. Some of my relatives (CCB) with lighter skin, who could pass as white, were able to assimilate into American culture, but like Angela's ancestors, had to give up obvious signs of their ethnicity, such as their language, in order to do so. Even at great personal cost, there is pressure to enter whiteness whenever possible. People with darker skin and with Indigenous features do not have the option of assimilating. Whether from the African continent, or the Asian continent, or from Central and South America and Mexico, people with black and brown skin are still seen as "other" in the U.S. Many folks whose ancestors came to this country long before mine (AB) did are still asked on a daily basis, "Where are you from?"

Inherent in this iceberg is the system of privilege for white folks that results from oppression of people of color. People who identify as white, or can pass as white, benefit from a system that is organized around the belief that white people are better than people of color. Some white people benefit more than others from this system, depending on their other identities, such as class position, gender, ability, nationality, and so on. For example: A person who is white, and who receives government benefits like food stamps and subsidized housing, has privileges because of race (like not being followed around in a store or racially profiled by police), but is also experiencing oppression because of class (not having enough resources to meet basic needs in a dignified way and the stigma and criminalization that often goes along with that). We all live our identities intersectionally; one identity does not define our whole experience as a person. (For more on this, see p 261)

Here's another example of how identities intersect: a woman of color who is Christian and uses a wheelchair experiences oppression based on gender, race, and disability, but also has religious privilege in this country. Intersectionality is not additive. You don't just weigh the number of marginalized identities against the number of privileged identities. They interact in complex ways, so that being Christian doesn't exactly "lessen" the impact of ableism, for example, but it makes it play out differently and grants some unrelated benefits besides.

For racial justice to be possible it's important to notice where we have bought into white supremacy and how it is keeping us from being willing to show up for racial justice. We need to shift our thinking and actions, and here are two activities to help us do that.

Try this!

1. On a piece of paper, write how you identify for each of these eight social identities: age, ethnicity, gender, race, religion, sexual orientation, ability, and socioeconomic class.
2. Next to each identifier, note whether your identity is preferred and granted more privilege in America (refer to chart on page 38).

3. How do each of those identities intersect with race? Give examples.
4. Can you think of specific times when you had privilege because of this identity? Times you were denied privilege because of this identity?
5. What if anything surprised you about this activity?

Now try this . . .
1. Read through the characteristics of white supremacy culture. *(see Appendix C: https://www.parenting4socialjustice.com/)*
2. Star the characteristics that you notice in yourself.
3. Write down an example of when you notice that characteristic showing up in you.
4. Circle the antidotes you think will work for you to counter that characteristic.

Race and ethnicity—who gets to be white?

The political construction of race is complex, and racial categories, based primarily on outward physical characteristics, have changed over time depending on how those in power use the concepts. Ethnicity is also socially and politically constructed and refers to a person's identity linked to cultural practices, language, ancestry, and the region or nation a person's ancestors come from. Ethnicity refers to the identification of group members based on such shared heritage and distinctiveness that make the group into a "people."[18] Race and ethnicity function distinctly in the U.S., although they are related.[19]

For example, when the Irish first immigrated to the U.S. they were looked down on and considered second class citizens and even subhuman.[20] As recent immigrants they did not have all the benefits of white privilege. In fact, some people pushed for halting the immigration of the Irish and rescinding their right to vote. The Irish did, however, have the benefit of not being a permanently enslaved class. Over a period of decades they were able to assimilate into "whiteness"—a racial category—even though some people with Irish heritage still identify *ethnically* as Irish.

People of Jewish heritage who are white passing and of European heritage (not Spanish and not Jews from any other continent) have similarly been seen at times as "less white" and targeted as ethnic minorities in the U.S. At other times they have been able to assimilate into whiteness and receive the benefits of white privilege. Other groups of immigrants to the U.S. have been considered white at first, and then that classification changes. For example, when people of Arab descent and identity fill out the U.S. Census they either have to check the box for white, Black, or "other," essentially erasing their ethnic heritage.[21] Yet they still don't have the same white privilege as peo-

---

18 Louise Derman-Sparks and Julie Olsen Edwards, *Anti-Bias Education for Young Children and Ourselves* (Washington DC: NAEYC, 2010).

19 For a simple and visual explanation of the difference between race, ethnicity, and nationality watch this video "Race, Ethnicity, Nationality and Jellybeans" by Eliana Pipes: https://www.youtube.com/watch?time_continue=146&v=CqV3CK6QfcU&feature=emb_logo.

20 Brando Simeo Starkey, "White Immigrants Weren't Always Considered White—and Acceptable," *The Undefeated*, February 10, 2017, https://theundefeated.com/features/white-immigrants-werent-always-considered-white-and-acceptable.

21 Sarah Parvini, Ellis Simani, "Are Arabs and Iranians White? Census Says Yes, But Many Disagree," *LA Times*, March 28, 2019, https://www.latimes.com/projects/la-me-census-middle-east-north-africa-race.

ple of Hungarian, Spanish, and Greek descent. In a white supremacist culture their (on average) darker complexion and hair and eye color make them a target of racism, on both interpersonal and institutional levels. Especially after the 9/11 attacks at the World Trade Center in NYC, people with darker complexions who "look like" they are from the Middle East have been the target of racial discrimination and violence.

The ability to assimilate into whiteness can diminish the importance of the role that one's ethnic heritage plays in one's life. For recent immigrants to the U.S., ethnic identity is very present. For some groups this changes over the generations as they assimilate into identifying as African American, Asian American, Latinx, or White. For other groups, maintaining their identity as Mayan, Hmong, or Kurdish is of utmost importance. For more on race and ethnicity and the complicated history of who gets to be white in the U.S. we recommend reading *A Different Mirror*[22] by Ronald Takaki.

Try this!

To think more about the biases you might have about different racial and ethnic groups we encourage you to try the following exercise.[23]

1. On a sheet of paper, create a list of five to eight racial and ethnic groups. For example, you might write white, Black, Asian, Jewish, Latinx, Middle Eastern, Vietnamese, Native American, and so on. You can choose whichever racial and ethnic identifiers you would like. In fact, we suggest you repeat this exercise multiple times, perhaps changing some of the identifiers each time.

2. For each identifier, set a timer for five minutes. Write down every stereotype, joke, or assumption you've heard about this group of people. Keep going until the timer goes off.

3. Next to each stereotype/joke/assumption, write down where and when you think you first heard or learned it.

4. Now, reflect:
   a. How did it feel to complete this exercise?
   b. What surprised you about where and how you learned stereotypes and assumptions about racial/ethnic groups?
   c. What does this exercise make you think about the way that your children are experiencing the world? What do you want to talk with them about or teach them?

This exercise makes us aware of the implicit and explicit biases we've learned throughout our lives. We understand this exercise can be uncomfortable, and we believe that discomfort is a sign that we are learning something, that our brains are being stretched. We recommend you repeat this exercise at a later date to see if you gain any new awareness. You might add other kinds of group identifiers, such as religion, gender, and class.

22 Ronald Takaki, *A Different Mirror: A History of Multicultural America* (Back Bay Books, New York, 1993).
23 Adapted from Eddie Moore, Ali Michael, and Marguerite W. Penick-Parks, *The Guide for White Women Who Teach Black Boys*, (Corwin, 2018).

Racism is trauma

Many of us, across all races, have been separated from our ancestry and from the wisdom passed down from the beginning of time. For Indigenous peoples who have never been colonized, the stories are shared from one generation to the next, linking each generation going all the way back to the beginning. But genocide, displacement, forced migration, and assimilation into whiteness have interrupted that ancestral linkage for many people. We each carry trauma from our separation from our ancestors. And our traumas are all connected to those of each other.

I (AB) have the stories of my parents and to some extent my grandparents, because my grandpa (a farmer who went to college to become a preacher) wrote a "self memoir" before he died. But I have no knowledge, no memory, no stories of my ancestors before that. I can feel that trauma deep inside me. I have been working on healing this ancestral trauma and I am overjoyed to be reweaving a spiritual connection with the seven generations before me. This connection with my ancestral heritage is an important part of my process of disinvesting in whiteness and white supremacy.

As a child, I (CCB) loved to listen to the stories of elders in my community. As soon as I was able to write, I began interviewing those elders. While I learned about their lives as children, I felt a sense of sadness that so much was lost in our migration and assimilation. I do not have concrete information about my great grandmother—a woman my aunt describes as living in a small dirt hut, as a healer of her community, as a dark-skinned woman with long, jet-black hair. I am saddened that I do not know how my blond and green-eyed grandmother's ancestors arrived in Puerto Rico or the lineage that results in my father's flame-red hair and freckles. I am aware of the historical trauma that lives in my veins and of the ways in which a desire to access the privileges of white supremacy convinced my mom not to speak Spanish to me and led my grandmother to stop planting the healing herbs of her childhood. I see the vestiges of that ancestral knowledge in my aunt's home altar, but mostly that knowledge and connection feel absent. I too have recently been working on communing with my ancestors, on uncovering our stories, on learning our rituals, and on celebrating this lineage and the strength, resilience, and healing power in it. I want this for my son and I believe that our collective ability to connect to our ancestors and to heal this trauma is critical for racial justice.

We have both been separated from our ancestral heritage because of colonization, the process by which nations and people in power exert their dominance over a group of people and their land. Think of the colonizers of America who took this land from Indigenous people, massacred those people, and forced assimilation on those who remained, forcefully removing their young to boarding schools where they were taught how to be "civilized." Throughout history we can see the ways in which colonizers take over land and resources and wreak trauma and havoc on the people who were already inhabiting that land. This continues to happen today through gentrification of cities and neighborhoods, and putting oil and natural gas pipelines through reservations and rural towns.

This has happened over and over again throughout history. For the last 600 years the colonization project has been most intensely led by countries and people of the

European continent, and then by the U.S. The United States was formed through the occupation of what is now the East Coast by the British, and then the resistance of the colonies to the crown. Later, the U.S. took over (and in some ways re-colonized) lands that had been colonized by the Spanish and French. The colonizers exercise their power by subjugating the people, pillaging communities, and effectively erasing people's way of life through forced conversion to the religion of the colonizer, through an erasure of their native tongues and by inflicting pain and trauma on those people. Colonization affects not only our material reality but also cultures, languages, beliefs, religious practices, food, and medicine—everything. This causes trauma. We know that this trauma does not end with the generation that is initially colonized, but is passed down through the generations and serves to reinforce white supremacy. The trauma remains lodged in us, unless we actively work against colonized beliefs and actions.

Uncovering how our minds and bodies have been colonized supports us in recognizing where that thinking is seeping into lessons we teach our children. Some values of colonization that come out in what we teach our children include:

- *It is admirable to suffer.* Even if you believe it is admirable to suffer in a spiritual sense, the way in which this value has been disseminated through colonizer culture does not serve the individual or community, but instead has been used to serve those in power.

- *Hard work is important.* While effort can be a virtue in itself, again, this virtue has been taken advantage of in ways that serve those who are in power through exploiting labor.

- *The individual is more important than the collective.* When people are divided and looking out for themselves above the collective, it is much easier to divide (and conquer).

- The language, foods, and beliefs of the colonizers are normal and best. And the colonizers' home country is the best. Recently a relative asked my son which country was the best. He shrugged his shoulders. The question asker said, "The U.S. is the best." Of course, it's not always taught that explicitly. (AB)

And then we need to be teaching our children how to create something new, just, decolonized. Lessons for a decolonized world:

- *Critical thinking.* We ask critical questions to develop a consciousness about the world.

- *Interconnection.* We are interconnected and part of a whole. When anyone is harmed, we are all harmed.
    - *Ancestry.* Being in touch with our ancestors, including knowing how they benefitted from or were harmed by oppression, helps us to better understand how we are interconnected.
    - *Nature.* Respecting the cycle of life through growing a garden and composting also teaches interconnected thinking.

↬ *Alternatives to capitalist consumption.* Being conscious of how and what we consume is important because what we do impacts the earth and other human beings. Utilizing alternative economies such as the gift economy,[24] bartering, and DIY (do it yourself) teaches us there are other ways of consuming that are less harmful to others.

❀ *Honoring difference.* There are many ways of being in the world—language, foods, beliefs, nationality—and all are valuable.

 Reflect

1. How have you experienced trauma because of white supremacy and racism?
2. When you think about trauma because of white supremacy and racism what feelings and body sensations do you notice?
3. What are you currently doing to heal that trauma? What else would be helpful for your healing?

Complexities

Colorism

"You almost pass the brown paper bag test," a boyfriend joked (CCB), evoking the colorism so present in communities of color. The brown paper bag test has a long history in the Black community. It is said that this test of skin color was used as a requirement of admission into exclusive clubs and organizations within Black communities. This preference for lighter skin and more European features is called colorism.

Colorism is defined by Alice Walker as "prejudicial or preferential treatment of same raced people based solely on their skin color."[25] We can trace the origins of colorism to slavery, where lighter-skinned people with straighter hair and more European features were sold for more money and coveted as indoor workers in the owners' home. They were no less enslaved, but were usually treated better and did not suffer the same kinds of brutal outdoor labor as their darker-skinned cousins. This preference for lighter skin and European features, imposed at first by white masters, became internalized and expressed within the Black community itself, first in slavery and still today. We can see colorism playing out in Hollywood casting, in beauty pageants, and even in the criminal justice system. Lighter-skinned people of color are more likely to be cast as leads in films, are often cited as more beautiful, and receive less restrictive criminal justice sentences on average.

Colorism rears its head within and across communities of color. It was colorism that led my (CCB) mother to instruct me to call myself tan and not Black. It is colorism that privileges people of color with more European features and lighter skin over darker-skinned people of color (but not over white folks). Take a moment to consider the famous Black actresses you can name. How many of them would pass the heinous brown paper bag test?

---

24 Goods and services are gifted, instead of bought or exchanged. To learn more: https://www.gifteconomy.com.

25 Alice Walker, *In Search of Our Mothers' Gardens* (Mariner Books, 1983).

Of course, at the root of colorism is white supremacy. Colorism is another symptom of this same system of oppression—a way in which lightness and whiteness get preferential treatment and are read as more favorable, more worthy, and better than darker skin. Colorism shows up in our media, in our families, and in our schools. As an educator (CCB) I see this all the time in our schools' casting of students of color in theater productions. It is often our lighter-skinned students who are given lead roles in plays and musicals or solos in choir performances. I am keenly aware of the way colorism affects my son in particular. I am often disrupting comments from family members about how "good hair" and "light eyes" make him handsome.

As parents, we need to be just as aware of this phenomenon as we are of racism more generally, and actively work against it. Be conscious of the ways in which you too might be showing preferences for lighter-skinned people of color.

Do the books you read and the media you watch with your child feature a range of skin shades? Are you more likely to comment on someone's attractiveness if they are a light-skinned person of color than if they're darker? How are darker-skinned people portrayed and depicted in the media you consume? How are you lifting up the stories and images of dark-skinned folks of color?

Opportunity Hoarding

Opportunity hoarding is when people with race and class privilege provide the best for their children even when it means that children who do not have race and class privilege will be even further disadvantaged. It is one way that well-intentioned white people participate in the continuation of racism.

Margaret Hagerman, the author of *White Kids: Growing Up with Privilege in a Racially Divided World,*[26] researches progressive white parents. Her research shows that those parents teach their kids about race when it's convenient, but pull them out of uncomfortable situations such as racial tensions in a neighborhood or school, sometimes even changing schools or houses to avoid racial confrontation. This is problematic in that the white child learns that they are able to avoid that kind of problem whether by changing schools or by moving, when the majority of their classmates of color don't have that option. When asked in an interview how she thought that could change, Hagerman said,

> I really think—and this might sound kind of crazy—that white parents, and parents in general, need to understand that all children are worthy of their consideration. This idea that your own child is the most important thing—that's something we could try to rethink. When affluent white parents are making these decisions about parenting, they could consider in some way at least how their decisions will affect not only their kid, but other kids. This might mean a parent votes for policies that would lead to the best possible outcome for as many kids as possible but might be less advantageous for their own child.[27]

---

26 Margaret A. Hagerman, *White Kids Growing Up with Privilege in a Racially Divided World* (NYU Press: 2018).
27 Joe Pinsker, "How Well-Intentioned White Families Can Perpetuate Racism," Atlantic, Sept. 4, 2018, https://www.theatlantic.com/family/archive/2018/09/white-kids-race/569185.

This is related to the concept of separation we've been talking about throughout the book. We are connected to each other, and if we can begin to notice that connection we will make different choices, ones that are better for all of us.

In learning about opportunity hoarding, I (AB) have begun to notice where I am complicit, even though it has not been intentional. For instance, I moved to a town that is considered upper class and white. I moved here because of the better than average public school, which included free preschool. I could have lived in a nearby town and contributed to improving the public school there, which has a much higher percentage of students of color and free and reduced lunch students. But I didn't make that choice. I am continuing to wake up to the way that my race and class privilege greatly influences not just how the world treats me and my kids, but the choices that I make.

Racial justice

Racial justice is when the iceberg melts all the way, eliminating white supremacy and all its manifestations. Or maybe we just get that boat going in a different direction. Then we sail the liberated seas! Although, we still gotta rearrange who is on the bottom of the boat and who is on the top (see Chapter 4).

Racial equity is when race doesn't determine whether or not you get hired, whether or not you get arrested, whether or not you receive quality health care, whether or not you get a loan to buy a house, whether or not you are elected for office, whether or not you can vote, or whether or not you are regarded as a human being. Racial equity is when we acknowledge that race is a window into the experience of your ancestors, but that it does not determine your value as a human being or your ability to access what you need.

Racial equity is part of racial justice. Racial justice requires addressing the root causes of inequities, not just their manifestation. It is the proactive reinforcement of policies, practices, attitudes, and actions that produce equitable power, access, opportunities, treatment, impacts, and outcomes for all.

Remember how we talked about the 10-10-80[28] rule in the introduction? When we are following this rule 80% of our energy goes towards living into our vision for justice. It can be hard to actually envision racial justice, when we've been living in an unjust and oppressive society for so many hundreds of years. Thankfully there are many groups who are working on that vision for a racially just world. Many different groups that are part of the Black Lives Matter movement came together to put together a policy platform for racial justice. They put a lot of time into visioning and putting that vision into words. The Movement for Black Lives policy platform[29] is a visionary and specific road map for all of us, no matter what social justice issues we are working on. Let's tune in to that vision . . .

---

28 The 10-10-80 rule is used by Sherri Mitchell, author of *Sacred Instructions*, in prioritizing where we put our energy: 10% on understanding the problem, 10% on resisting the problem, and 80% on visioning and creating what we want instead.

29 Movement for Black Lives Policy Platform, accessed July 12, 2018. https://m4bl.org/policy-platforms/.

Your turn:

- ❋ Read: The Movement for Black Lives Policy Platform[30]
- ❋ Watch: "Understanding Race in the 21st Century"[31] (nine-minute video)
- ❋ "The Myth of Race, Debunked[32]" (three-minute video) with Jenee Desmond Harris
- ❋ Head to your local library and check out one or more of these books or ask them to get a copy if they don't already have one:
    - ↪ *Why Are All the Black Kids Sitting Together in the Cafeteria?* by Beverly Daniel Tatum (1997 or 2017 edition)[33]
    - ↪ *Parenting for Liberation: A Guide for Raising Black Children* by Trina Greene Brown[34]
    - ↪ *Raising White Kids: Bringing Up Children in A Racially Unjust America* by Jennifer Harvey[35]
- ❋ Read: Dismantling Racism: 2016 Workbook.[36] In particular, pages 9–14 provide a brief timeline of the history of the construct of race and racism.

Reflect

1. Consider your own racial identity. When were you first aware of race? What was that experience like? How did you feel?
2. How does the way that Beverly Daniel Tatum thinks about race differ from how you think about race? What, if anything, surprises you about her thinking?
3. Reverend David Billings talks about preaching to the choir, a familiar analogy for only talking to people who already agree with you and who consistently show up for practice every week. He says that the choir is important, and that the choir needs pep talks! What gets in your way of joining the choir, or of showing up for practice every week? What inspires you to show up?
4. Both Beverly Daniel Tatum and Reverend Billings say that one of the solutions is for white parents to talk with their kids about race very early, instead of protecting them. They suggest that kids have the ability to understand and

30 Movement for Black Lives, https://m4bl.org/policy-platforms/.

31 "Understanding Race in the 21st Century," PBS News Hour, May 10, 2016. https://www.pbs.org/video/understanding-racism-in-the-21st-century-1470184215. This clip spotlights Reverend David Billings of the People's Institute for Survival and Beyond.

32 Jenee Desmond Harris, "The myth of race, debunked" (video), Vox, Jan. 13, 2015. https://www.youtube.com/watch?v=VnfKgffCZ7U&feature=youtu.be&ab_channel=Vox

33 Beverly Daniel Tatum, *Why Are All the Black Kids Sitting Together in the Cafeteria?* (New York: Basic Books, 1997, 2017).

34 Trina Green Brown, *Parenting for Liberation: A Guide for Raising Black Children* (Cuny, NY: The Feminist Press, 2020).

35 Jennifer Harvey, *Raising White Kids: Bringing Up Children in a Racially Unjust America* (Nashville: Abingdon Press, 2017).

36 dRworks, Dismantling Racism, 2016 Workbook, accessed October 15, 2019, https://resourcegeneration.org/wp-content/uploads/2018/01/2016-dRworks-workbook.pdf.

integrate the concepts of fairness and justice. Are you able to talk with your kids about race and racism? If not, what is holding you back? If so, are there topics that you avoid?

5. How can you use/apply the Movement for Black Lives policy platform in your life and work?

6. After learning more, now what questions do you have about race and racism in America?

This is such a huge topic and continuing our learning is crucial. Check out the resources page for more films, articles, books, and websites.

Talking with our kids about race and racism

We don't have to have this all figured out before we talk with our kids. We don't have to have answers. Courage, sincerity, and the willingness to learn with our kids is enough.

Most of us, and white folks in particular, have not been taught how to talk honestly and constructively about race, so we just avoid it. But we know that kids pick up on the racist messages all around them, both subtle and overt, whether or not we talk about it. Kids have an innate sense of fairness and justice, and the unequal valuing of people in our society doesn't make sense to them. Giving kids a historical and present-day context both of the problem and of the vision for justice is important for their under-standing so they can have a strong sense of self and their place in the world, and so that they can start to learn the tools they need to show up for racial justice.

No matter what race or ethnicity you are, it is really heartbreaking to talk about the violence carried out to ensure the continuation of white supremacy—people who bomb Black churches and Jewish synagogues, police officers who kill Black men with their hands up in surrender and are then acquitted, a political system that intentionally cages millions of people in for-profit prisons and detention centers, including separat-ing detained parents from their children. We want to protect our kids from this violent reality. However, our avoidance has serious ramifications. We cannot solve a problem if we keep avoiding it, and we cannot prepare our children to face and change the realities of the world if we hide difficult truths. Violence is a daily reality for many people in the U.S. and around the world. So let's start seeing it and talking about it. Our kids are part of the present and future world, so let's get them in on this discussion and action as early as possible.

As parents of kids of color, we have to talk to our kids about race and what it means to grow up in a racialized society. We might already be talking about race with people in our racial group, but we will also still need to examine our learned biases and internalized racial inferiority so that we can communicate across races from a place of awareness and reflection. We have a choice in what we teach kids about race. Do we only teach them how to survive in a racist society (which is already a lot)? Or do we also teach them where racism comes from and how to fight for racial justice?

As a mother, if I (CCB) ignore this work, I leave my son vulnerable and risk his sense of self.

I want my son to develop a strong sense of self worth, to honor and celebrate his identity so that he can cope with the racialized messages he will encounter throughout his life. At the same time, I want him to recognize his resilience and power in confronting racism and in being an advocate for change. I find that being in community with other parents of color who are actively thinking about what this looks like provides me with perspective, language, and approaches to try at home. In addition, intentionally doing my own work—reflecting on my identity and my position in the world—helps me develop the language, stances, and skills I want to transfer to my son.

As white folks, we have to be really intentional in talking with our kids about race and what it means to grow up in a racialized society. The privilege of whiteness in a racist society has blinded us to the ways we benefit from racism. To continue to recognize how whiteness works it is really helpful to meet with other parents or white peers, especially groups that have accountability to POC-led anti-racist groups. We too have a choice in what we teach kids about race. Do we only teach them to be kind to people of all races? Or do we also teach them where racism comes from and how to fight for racial justice?

As a white person raising white kids, I (AB) recognize how easy it is to avoid talking about race. I notice many white people around me talking about kindness and compassion and civic engagement as a stand-in for talking about issues of racial injustice. These three qualities are good, but they do not go far enough. They do not ensure that the root causes of injustice are named and addressed.

It is much easier and often more politically correct to say "We are all the same!" than "In our society it is harder for Black and Latinx folks to get good housing, good food, well-paying jobs, educational opportunities, and to find justice in a court of law. All humans are valuable, race has nothing to do with value. Our family is showing up with lots of other people so that every person will be treated fairly and justly and have the food, housing, jobs, and education they need. And we advocate for reparations for past harm that has been done." I realized early on in my parenting that I would have to be very intentional about keeping the conversation about race and racism open and relevant in my children's lives. I can now see the fruit of those early conversations. They are noticing and naming racism when they see it, and they are also naming where they see the need for justice.

Learning about racial identity development provides context for us to better understand where we and our kids are at in our own racial identity development so that we can continue the growth process.

Racial Identity Development
We all have to negotiate our identity over time. Throughout our lives, each of us will repeatedly explore the question, "Who am I?" Our identity formation is a result of our interactions among ourselves, others, and our social environment. Understanding the basics of racial identity development can help you get a sense of how your child is experiencing their racial identity now. Considering where you and they are in your racial identity development can help you choose how to approach conversations about race.

Scholars and activists have developed various identity development models to help us understand how different parts of our identity evolve over time. You can find a helpful summary of racial identity models at the Racial Equity Tools website.[37]

Here are a few things to keep in mind about racial identity models:

❀ Some of the early racial identity development models were created based on the experiences of Black college students in the 1970s. Subsequent models have been adapted from this original model, sometimes based on a presumed similarity of Black experience to other racial identity development experiences that may not always hold true.

❀ These models can be a tool for making meaning of one's experience; they are not diagnostic measurements. They may not hold true for every individual's experience.

❀ Although the models overlap, there are differences in the stages for white folks, for people of color, for specific groups of people of color, for biracial children and so on.

❀ Although the stages of each model appear as linear, in reality we can move back and forth or even cycle through them throughout our lives.

❀ Instead of trying to diagnose a stage or move faster through the stages, we recommend using this as a tool to help make meaning of your experiences and those of your child.

Racial Identity Development for People of Color

For people of color the stages of racial identity development begin at pre-encounter, where a person has internalized the dominant narratives about the value of whiteness and has not yet become fully aware of race and racism. This stage is generally disrupted when the person begins to encounter racism and can see the effect of racism on their lives. It is in this encounter stage that a person realizes that they cannot be white, or rather that they cannot attain the privileges that come with whiteness. This realization may then lead to a desire to steep oneself in one's culture (racial and/or ethnic) and to actively push away the markers of whiteness. For some, this pushing away might be coupled with feelings of anger and animosity toward white people. As the person becomes more secure in their racial identity, their pride becomes less defensive and more open. The person can engage in meaningful and reflective dialogue with white folks, and can form close relationships with white people who understand the systemic nature of racism and who are empathetic and active allies. In the final stage, one can then begin to leverage one's racial or ethnic identity for social change. A strong and healthy sense of in-group belonging allows a person to connect with the struggles of people in general and to specifically feel driven to seek justice for their racial/ethnic group. In this stage, the individual is able to build cross racial relationships and work towards racial justice.

---

37 Racial Equity Tools, Racial Identity Development Theory, accessed October 2019, https://www. racialequitytools.org/fundamentals/core-concepts/theory. There are tools for white, Black, Asian, Latinx, Indigenous, biracial, and multiracial identity development. Find the tools that support your learning.

Racial Identity Development for White Folks

The stages for white folks are similar to that of people of color. White folks begin at a stage of "colorblindness"—the sense that racial identity holds no bearing on one's life. In this stage, called contact, there is not conscious racism. This initial stage (contact) mirrors the pre-encounter stage described for people of color. In the second stage of disintegration, the person is then confronted with evidence of racism that challenges their preconceived notions of the world. When this happens, guilt and shame often appear. If one does not attend to these feelings of guilt and shame, there's a risk of moving into the reintegration stage. The reintegration stage is characterized by a blame the victim mentality. People may express sentiments like "if people of color are arrested more, it's just because they are more likely to commit crimes." With active work, this person may move into the stage of pseudo-independence. It is in this stage that the individual recognizes racism and its impacts and attempts to be a "good" white person. In this stage, people have a tendency to rely on people of color to confront racism and stand by to validate and encourage people of color. This individual has not yet figured out how to be anti-racist and white. As this person is held accountable to their role, they enter a state of immersion. It is here that the individual becomes focused on being a good anti-racist and begins to reject white folk who are not as aware or anti-racist as they are. The final stage, known as autonomy, mirrors the final stage for people of color. In this final stage an individual is able to be both white and an anti-racist, recognizing that it is possible to develop both a positive white racial identity and work toward racial justice with white folk and with people of color.

When we talk about race with our children and with other adults, it can be helpful to hold these stages in mind as we think about what kinds of conversations, movies, and books might help people move through feelings of anger, shame, and sadness to feelings of pride and agency.

For example, for children of color in the pre-encounter and encounter stages, sharing stories about the accomplishments of individuals of color can help them develop a sense of pride and gain language for describing and honoring their racial identity. As children grow more aware of racism, it is helpful to share stories of resistance and resilience of people of color, to teach them ways to push back against racism in their world, and to also share stories of white anti-racists and allies who have worked for racial justice. Supporting our kids of color in understanding that there are white folk who actively work towards racial justice will help them see the potential and promise in cross-racial friendships.

Recently (CCB), a friend recounted the story of how his third-grade child of color wrote a thoughtful essay about the racism inherent in many Disney movies. Her white teacher responded with positive affirmation and reminded her that she had left out Dumbo. This child is well past the early stage pre-encounter. She's aware racism exists and she can see it, but she's also a third grader and will undoubtedly cycle through the stages as she grows and develops. Moments such as the one with this teacher are empowering and affirming for her racial identity development. Supporting our kids of color in using their voice to speak out against injustice and then affirming them when they do will help them develop a positive sense of self and a commitment to racial justice.

White kids need support too. I (CCB) had an interesting conversation with a high school freshman where I work. He had sent a text to a friend, letting her know that while he liked her, he could not date her because she was Black. When prodded, he admitted his parents would not be pleased and that he did not want to subject his friend to their racism. At the same time, he struggled to understand why his text had upset his friend so much. In his mind, she must know he did not hold the same views. We had a very interesting and thoughtful conversation about race, intent, impact, and internalization. I was glad we had an opportunity to unpack this moment and help him create a more nuanced understanding of the situation.

Talk to your kids early and often about race. Read stories that feature racially diverse characters. Give your kids the tools to see racial inequity and the skills to speak out against it at age-appropriate levels. Reading and sharing stories of white anti-racists and activists help white kids move through stages of guilt and shame and feel a sense of empowerment and interdependence.

Age-appropriateness

Kids pick up on the concept of race much earlier than they are able to verbalize it. Erin Winkler is a sociologist and professor at the University of Wisconsin–Madison, and her research consistently shows that kids as young as three have already started to learn and express racial biases. There are age-appropriate ways to talk about racial inequality and to give children of all races and ethnicities the tools they need to show up for justice.

Winkler gives these tips for age-appropriate conversations about racism:[38]

❋ Get comfortable talking about race and racism with other adults, so you can talk with kids about it too. If we are going to interrupt biases it is essential to be talking with our kids about race from the time they are born.

❋ Ask questions to better understand where children's statements are coming from. For example: "tell me more about that," "what do you mean when you say that?", and "can you show me?"

❋ Use the concept of fairness, which is clear and powerful to young children and empowers them to respond to unfairness.

❋ Empower kids by pointing out people in the community who are addressing inequality, and have them participate with you in efforts to address inequality. For example, work with the school library to ensure adequate representation of characters of color in their children's book collection.

❋ Connect the past with the present and the future. For example, when you go to a protest for immigrant rights, talk about past immigration laws and patterns. Learn what people are doing to work for just immigration laws. If you aren't sure, do some research with your kids.

❋ Model anti-racist behaviors. Children watch and learn from everything we do. For example, when your uncle makes a racist joke at a holiday dinner, let him

---

38 Erin Winkler, "Tips for talking to children about race and racism," *Buzzfeed*, June 11, 2017, https://www.buzzfeed.com/erinwinkler/tips-for-talking-to-children-about-race-and-racism.

know (in front of the kids) that that is hurtful to you and to many people you know and care about.

❀ Encourage complex and critical thinking. When children are taught to pay attention to multiple attributes of a person at once, research shows that their levels of bias are reduced. Encourage kids to recognize that each person is multidimensional. For example, say your child comes home saying LaShawn is good at basketball because he's Black. You could respond, "Well, LaShawn is also tall for his age, went to basketball camp, and has a big sister who plays basketball, so it seems like there are several reasons why he's so good at it."

Conversations will look differently depending on all the complexities of your and your kids' identities and experiences. As you become more comfortable and knowledgeable, your social justice conversations will change. It's like riding a bike—some people need to practice a lot before they can ride comfortably, while for others it seems to come naturally, and still others need to modify their bikes to work with their bodies. If it feels uncomfortable at first, don't worry, it's all part of the process of learning anything new. Louise Derman-Sparks, in *Anti-bias Education for Young Children and Ourselves*, writes about how when you begin to use anti-bias teaching, there will be an increase in talking about difference—this is how kids learn rules/limits about behavior. Integrating anti-bias thinking and language into parenting will take work at first. But after a year (more or less) you will find that it has become part of how you do things.[39]

Conversations about race and racism are challenging because they bring up our own traumas and experiences. When we put into words the inequity and injustice we experience, see, and even participate in, we can feel a lot of emotions. In these conversations we also need to support our kids in navigating any emotions these conversations bring up for them. It helps to be honest with your children about what you know and how much more you have to learn. It also helps to be honest about your feelings and help them identify their feelings. Acknowledging and tending to the very powerful feelings that come up when engaging in racial justice work is important to sustaining engagement.

Here are a few sample conversations of age-appropriate conversations you might have with preschoolers and elementary-age kids, whether white or of color, to get you started thinking about how conversations with kids might go. These examples include lots of things that you can say, but in a real conversation you might not say them all at once.

If your child has black or brown skin . . .
With your preschooler:

> **Child:** My skin is brown. Perry's is white.
>
> **Parent:** Yes, people have different skin shades. There is something special in skin that can make it darker. It's called melanin. Can you say that word? It's a

---

39 Louise Derman-Sparks and Julie Olsen Edwards, *Anti-Bias Education for Young Children and Ourselves* (Washington DC: NAEYC, 2010).

big science word! Your skin is brown because you have more melanin than Perry does. Let's read *I'm Your Peanut Butter Brother.* Do you remember in that book the boy talks about many different skin shades? Let's read it and find our skin shades in it!

With your elementary-age child:

Child: Perry called me burnt popcorn.

Parent: How did that make you feel?

Child: Mad. I think he was talking about my skin.

Parent: I'm sorry that happened to you today. That would make me mad too. It sounds like Perry hurt your feelings. Perry said something mean and he said it about your skin shade—something you were born with and will always be part of you. That can really hurt feelings.

Child: Uh huh.

Parent: You have brown skin. People sometimes call folks with brown skin Black. Your skin is beautiful and special. It has lots of melanin in it. Melanin is a pigment that makes skin darker.

Child: Do you have it?

Parent: Melanin? Yes I do! What do you think we should do to let Perry know that he hurt your feelings and to teach him about melanin? I could speak to your teacher and we can come in and use paint to talk about melanin and make our signature skin shades. What do you think? I also know a fun book we could read about different skin shades.

With your elementary-age child:

Parent: How was your day?

Child: Ok. We talked about slavery today.

Parent: Oh? Want to tell me more?

Child: We talked about how white people brought Black people from Africa to America as slaves. They treated Black people badly and put them in chains.

Parent: Yes. We've talked a little bit about this before. How are you feeling?

Child: After, on the playground Morgan and some other kids were coming to me and saying "I'm so sorry. I'm so sorry."

Parent: Oh. What did you say? How did that feel?

Child: It felt weird! I'm not a slave and they didn't do anything. It made me feel kinda bad. I told them to stop.

Parent: Yes, I can understand how having your friends say they are sorry to you about slavery can make you feel bad and weird. You're right. You are not a slave and they don't have to apologize to you about slavery. Why do you think they said they were sorry? They know this happened a long time ago.

Child: I dunno. Maybe they feel bad because it was white people who did it.

Parent: Maybe. When we talk about racism and slavery there are a lot of feelings that can happen. Sometimes people feel guilty or ashamed and sometimes they feel angry or sad. It sounds like your friends were feeling guilty.

Child: But they didn't do anything. And I'm free.

Parent: Yes! You're right. You are not enslaved. We know because we've been talking about it, that even though there is no longer slavery in this country, that there is still inequity. Do you remember what that means? And there is still racism. I wonder if your friends can see the ways the world is still unfair for Black and brown folk, and they might not yet know how to talk about that or how to feel about it or what to do about it.

Child: I don't want to talk about it with them.

Parent: I can understand that. These are things even adults have a tough time talking about. I have an idea. What if, when you feel ready, we invite your friends to our next Black Lives Matter chapter meeting or to the next march? I am happy to talk to their parents about this. I think, if it's okay with you, I'll also give your teacher a call and see if I can offer some suggestions about activities or books to read or conversations to have. Would you feel okay if I came in and did an activity with your class?

Child: I want to think about that.

Parent: Okay. Listen, you are a brave, smart, strong young woman. I'm impressed that you can name these complicated feelings. Let's practice some things you can say to your friends if this happens again.

Child: Okay. Can we do that later?

Parent: Yes. You do not have to feel bad about slavery. You come from a people who are strong, resilient, and who fought back and continue to fight against oppression. Your ancestors and your grandmother have done so much to fight against oppression. You want to hear one of my favorite stories about your grandmother? . . .

If your child is white . . .

With your preschooler:

Child: His skin is dark.

Parent: You are very observant—good at noticing things. That man has brown skin that people in our country call Black. People have many different colors of skin. All skin is beautiful. You have peachy skin that people in our

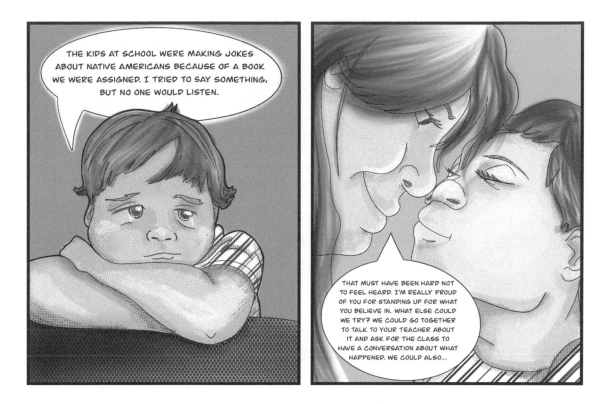

country call white. Let's draw a picture of our skin. Here are lots of art supplies. Let's find the color that most closely matches our own skin. We might have different colors of skin, but did you know that our blood is the same color? What else is the same and different about us as humans?

With your elementary-age child:

Child: The kids at school were making jokes about Native Americans because of a book we were assigned. I tried to say something, but no one would listen to me.

Parent: That must have been hard to not feel heard. I'm really proud of you for standing up for what you believe in. What else could we try? We could go together to talk to your teacher about it and ask for the class to have a conversation about what happened. We could also bring in a few books about Native Americans that do a better job of telling the truth about the past. What do you think?

With your elementary-age child:

Child: Enzo is mean. He should go back to where he came from.

Parent: What do you mean, he should go back where he came from?

Child: I don't know, Rex was saying that about Enzo.

Parent: Sometimes when people say that they are making an assumption that the person is a recent immigrant from another country. This is a very mean thing to say to a person. In fact, we call that a racist comment, meaning that it contributes to a society where white people are considered good and people who are not white, or who are Black, Latinx, Indigenous, or Asian, are considered bad. We want to end racism because it hurts all of us. I hope the next time you hear someone say that you are able to let them know they should stop talking that way.

Child: Well Enzo was being mean.

Parent: So you should be mean back to him?

Child: Well, no.

Parent: What else could you do next time Enzo is being mean?

With your elementary-age child:

Child: Did white people really do all those things—killing Native Americans, hanging Black people?

Parent: Yes, they really did.

Child: Did our family do that?

Parent: Well, our family hadn't immigrated to the U.S. until the time of the Civil War, sometime in the 1860s. And while we don't have reason to believe they participated in the direct killing of people, it is clear that they bought land that was stolen from Native Americans.

Child: White people are stupid and bad.

Parent: It sounds like you might be feeling guilty. Guilt is an icky feeling we get when we recognize we have hurt someone, whether directly or indirectly, and it's going to be really hard to change what happened.

Child: Yeah, I feel really bad.

Parent: Humans do some pretty awful things to each other. It is really hard to think about and understand. And it is important to learn about so that we can stop it from happening in the future. Throughout human history, people of all races have hurt each other when they have the power to do that. When we understand history better we can see when injustice is happening now and we can stand up for justice. People are doing that right now, like Alicia Garza, one of the co-founders of Black Lives Matter, and all of the white folks who are part of Showing Up for Racial Justice, which is supporting the work of Black Lives Matter.

In the previous section, we talked about the Black Lives Matter (BLM) policy platform. It can be empowering to talk with our young kids about the BLM movement and the platform. Laleña Garcia,[40] a preschool teacher in Brooklyn, New York, gives an example of how to introduce BLM. Here is an excerpt:

> While adults can obviously talk about any of the principles (and many of us already do) without mentioning the Black Lives Matter movement, we can also mention the movement as a group of people who want to make sure that everyone is treated fairly, regardless of the color of their skin. We can say something along the lines of, "The Civil Rights Movement, with people we know about, like Martin Luther King, Jr. and Rosa Parks, worked to change laws that were unfair. The Black Lives Matter movement is made up of people who want to make sure that everyone is treated fairly, because even though many of those laws were changed many years ago, some people are still not being treated fairly." The idea of police violence is frightening to young children, and the same way we don't discuss the violence which met Civil Rights activists, I would not discuss this kind of violence with our youngest children.

Here are some real-life conversations related to race that parents/grandparents are having with the kids in their lives.

The writer, a white, working-class, queer, cis gender woman, lives in smalltown Vermont with her wife and two kids (ages five and one). She likes dancing, hiking, biking with her family, and working for racial and social justice at the state and national level.

Scene: We are sitting in a café eating pie, where we had stopped to ask for directions to a hike. The following conversation started totally out of the blue after we'd spent a couple of months talking about racial and gender equality.

Sam: White boys and Black girls aren't equal.
Mom: Do you really think that? And why did you say that?
Sam, *mumbling*: I don't know, sometimes I just forget.
Mom: Well you know the truth, that boys and girls are equal and Black people and white people are equal, right?
Sam: Yes.
[Sam runs off to the next thing.]

Later we revisit the conversation with him about how what we say matters. He is testing us constantly right now on many topics.

---

40 Laleña Garcia, "How to Talk with kids about the Black Lives Matter Movement," accessed August 13, 2019, https://eeuschool.org/wp-content/uploads/2020/06/How-to-talk-to-young-children-about-the-Black-Lives-Matter-Guiding-Principles.pdf.

Nelis: I have been in the U.S. for 22 years. I came from Tabasco, Mexico, with my twin daughters and their father when they were just a year old. We decided to come to the U.S. because of my daughters' medical condition and twice were lied to by lawyers that we would get visas. I now live here undocumented. I gave birth to my youngest daughter twenty years ago. I have two grand-daughters, seven and one year old—my greatest joy. I am just another human being with the willingness to work, study, and live without being labeled a criminal.

In this scene I am driving my granddaughter, age six, home from school and we are listening to songs.

Esme: Do you have a mom?
Me: Yes, I do have a mom.
Esme: Is she my grandma too?
Me: Yes baby, she is more like your great grandma.
Esme: Mama, can we go see her? Can she come live with us?
Me: No mami, she doesn't have a paper to get on a plane and come visit us.
Esme: Why mama?
Me: Our country is a little bit harder to get papers for, so maybe when you grow up you can visit her.

One day I talked to a lawyer about my possibilities to move to Canada. Esme overheard me talking to him. I found her crying behind the couch because she didn't want me to go away. Esme said if I left she would never see me again because I was going to leave to another world. It broke my heart. She said the president was mean, and she decided to write my mom a letter. I showed my mom the letter over a WhatsApp video call. Esme talked to my mom on the call and after that she was talking to me about bringing her home to us and hiding her so I didn't have to go away. I had to promise her that I would never go. Once in a while, she still talks about going to visit my mom, she just doesn't know my mom passed away.

Hun Taing is a Cambodian genocide survivor and refugee to the U.S. She has biracial Black and Asian twin girls who are three and a son who is six. She has spent the last twenty years fighting for social, economic and racial justice as an organizing director for SEIU, field director for ACLU, and now as the equity & inclusion manager for Multnomah County Health Department. She's a Buddhist mindfulness practitioner in the Thich Nhat Hanh tradition, integrating principles of interbeing, non-discrimination, and equanimity into her social justice work. She is a conflict transformation and trauma healing specialist whose life purpose is to transform her own intergenerational violence and trauma and support others to do the same.
H = six-and-a-half years old

M = Mama
D = Dad

On July 4th, H came into the house with a U.S. flag from my neighbor and was chanting USA! USA! USA! I freaked out, and that evening D and I talked with H about what USA meant to us.

M: We do not chant USA in this house.
H: Why?
M: The U.S. has done many hurtful things to people. Remember when we talked about colonizers?
H: If the U.S. is the bad guy and the colonizer then why do we live here?
D: We didn't choose to come to the U.S. People from Europe came to Africa and forced us to come to the U.S. . . . .
M: Mommy's family came because there was a war in our country . . .

We then shared a brief history of slavery and the U.S. bombing of Cambodia.

Phoebe Gooding is a biracial Black woman raising her two multiracial boys in Vermont. She is an environmental and racial justice advocate, climate activist, educator, lifelong learner, organizer, and visionary.

Scene: I'm at a Black Lives Matter rally with my two boys, ages nine and eleven. Earlier, while heading to the rally in our small New England town, my older child told me he didn't want to go, that he was scared, and that he didn't want to get killed. I told him that's how many young Black boys and men feel every day just going to school or the store or even church. I was nervous as we piled into the car with our Black Lives Matter signs at the ready. We walked through the downtown area chanting "hands up, don't shoot."

Older child: [Walking past the local movie theatre] Mom, they're playing *The Secret Life of Pets*. I really want to see that movie.

[I continue to chant, thinking about how it is that my son can be talking about going to the movies at a serious time like this. I'm ready to shush him when a woman, another mother, starts talking to him.]

Woman: You know, I saw that movie recently with my son and it was really funny.

[My son smiles, letting go of my hand, and proceeds to chat it up with this lovely stranger. I feel myself loosen up as I watch my son start marching with his sign held high, chanting loudly and still smiling. Later, as we're leaving the rally, my children both tell me they had fun.]

Reflections: What an amazing experience this was, and such a good lesson for me that living in the moment need not diminish the seriousness of the matter; in fact, on that day, it solidified even more why we were there. And it helped me remember that my kids are just that—kids. It was a beautiful thing for my son to connect with a community member and be silly, be happy.

Ray Sylvester is a cisgender white man who lives in Northampton, MA, with his wife and five-year-old, both of whom are white. He's a writer, editor, and movement educator.

Scene: It's my son's bedtime and we're reading Malala's Magic Pencil *by Malala Yousafzai, the young Pakistani woman who has spoken out about the treatment of girls and women under Taliban rule in Pakistan. After the Taliban unsuccessfully attempted to assassinate her for standing up against them, she made it her life's mission to, as the website of the Malala Fund, the foundation set up in her name, says, "[work] for a world where every girl can learn and lead." We get to a page that describes how the Taliban banned Pakistani girls from going to school. The illustration depicts a woman and a girl walking down an unpaved road while two Taliban soldiers with guns stand watch.*

Me: These two women are wearing a headscarf. Many Muslim women wear a headscarf, and sometimes a scarf that covers their whole face. Some choose to wear it, while in other places they have to.

Kid: Why do they have to?

Me: Well, because in those countries, that's the law. But the Muslim women you see in our country are most likely wearing it because they choose to.

Reflections: So many questions went through my head during this short exchange. Do I understand enough about the use of the headscarf in varying political contexts by Muslim women around the world to explain it to my kid in a way that will make sense to him? How much can he understand about the idea that some women may choose to do something that is forced on other women elsewhere? Does he see the paradox . . . or am I just overthinking things? Is it possible to do this topic justice given my uncertainty about my own knowledge and his ability to understand the complexities of it? In the end, I realized that not being faced with these kinds of self-reflective questions when trying to explain a complex topic involving power, gender, religion, politics, and freedom of choice to your child would have been much more unfortunate.

Reflect

After reading through these conversations, we invite you to spend some time reflecting. These examples are not meant to demonstrate perfect responses, but rather to encourage us to think about the ways that we are talking with the kids in our care.

1. What felt familiar to you?
2. What surprised you?
3. How might you have responded in similar circumstances?
4. What could you ask your child to better understand their experience and/or perspective?
5. What are you wondering now?

Your turn:

Check out these resources, which include tips on talking with kids about race.

❋ "100 Race Conscious Things to Say to Your Child to Advance Racial Justice"[41] (*see Appendix I: https://www.parenting4socialjustice.com/*). This is a go-to list for when we're looking to talk with our kids about race-related topics.

❋ "Teaching Young Children About Race,"[42] a resource from Teaching for Change

❋ EmbraceRace.org is an excellent resource for book suggestions and hosts monthly webinars geared to parents and teachers. They are committed to helping caregivers develop children who are "brave, informed and thoughtful" about race.

Reflect

Think of a time your child asked a question or made a comment about race. What was your response? How would you like to respond if you had that opportunity again?

1. How do you talk with your kids about a current event that is connected to racism?

2. Think about a book, project, or lesson your child has been a part of at school that might have contained implicit messages about race. What were those messages? From whose perspective was the project created? If your child were to do this assignment again, how could you help expand their understanding to include more perspectives?

3. What questions do you have about talking with your kids about race and racism?

---

41 Raising Race-Conscious Children, "100 Race Conscious Things to Say to Your Child to Advance Racial Justice," June 2, 2016, http://www.raceconscious.org/2016/06/100-race-conscious-things-to-say-to-your-child-to-advance-racial-justice.

42 Teaching for Change, "Teaching Young Children About Race," July 8, 2015, https://www.teachingforchange.org/teaching-about-race.

Reading/listening/watching together

Reading, listening to, and watching content with kids is an excellent way to get the conversation about race started and keep it going. It is important to choose many different kinds of materials for our kids to learn about racial justice. Choose resources that are **mirrors** of a child's personal experience, **windows** into the experiences of others, and **doors** into whole new worlds of what could be possible.[43] Use the concept of mirrors, windows, and doors to talk about the stories with your children. Help them see how their lives are both the same and different from the characters they encounter. Help them feel and see their connection to a broad spectrum of identities. This concept of mirrors, windows, and doors is important no matter what age we are!

As you are looking for resources, make sure to include:

- ❋ material about and written by Latinx people, Native Americans, African Americans, and Asian Americans; about people of all races showing up for justice; and about people who live all over the world
- ❋ material about hard historical truths, books about the challenges people of color face today, and books about social change that adults and kids are making
- ❋ material that illustrates people of color experiencing ordinary facets of life like family, gardening, sports, music, and work
- ❋ material about your ancestors (or people like your ancestors) before and after they immigrated to the U.S.

Be mindful of accidently curating books and media experiences that only depict a single story of what it means to hold any particular identity. The reality is that there is much diversity of experience within each racial identity group.

There are big lessons to be learned from books, and asking the right questions can help you and your kids go deeper in your conversation about important social justice issues. This can be applied to listening to music and watching movies too. Here are some ideas for open-ended questions to ask your kids, adapted in part from the Lexile Framework for Reading.[44]

Before you read:

- ❋ What makes you think this book is going to be interesting?
- ❋ What do you think the book is going to be about?
- ❋ Does this book remind you of anything you've already read or seen?

After you read:

- ❋ What is similar to your life or experience? What is different?
- ❋ Do you know anyone who might have experienced this?
- ❋ If you were [a specific character], what would you do? What would you feel?
- ❋ How do you think [a character] felt when [an event] happened?
- ❋ What do you wish was different in this book?

---

43 Adapted from Maria José Botelho and Masha Kabakow Rudman, *Critical Multicultural Analysis of Children's Literature: Mirrors, Windows and Doors* (NY: Taylor & Francis, 2009).
44 "21 Questions to Ask Your Child About a Book," Lexile Reading Framework, accessed August 13, 2019, https://lexile.com/parents-students/tools-to-support-reading-at-home/21-questions-ask-child-book.

❀ What is one big lesson you've learned from this book?
❀ How would the world be different if all people acted like [a character]?
❀ What questions do you have?

Your turn:
Choose three books from the book list below (or other similar books) to read with your kids, and practice asking questions like those above.

Read

Ages 0–3
> *Feast for 10*, by Cathryn Falwell
> *I'm Your Peanut Butter Brother,* by Serena Alko
> *My People*, by Charles R. Smith, Jr.
> *We March*, by Shane W. Evans

Ages 3–6
> *All the Colors We Are: The Story of How We Got Our Skin Color*, by Katie Kissinger
> *Bein with You This Way,* by W. Nikola-Lisa
> *Chocolate Me!* by Taye Diggs
> *Last Stop on Market Street*, Matt de la Pena
> *Love,* by Matt de la Pena

Ages 6–10
> *Crown: An Ode to the Freshcut*, by Derrick Barnes
> *La Frontera: El Viaje con Papa / My Journey with Papa*, by Deborah Mills, Alfredo Alva, and Claudia Navarro
> *Let's Talk About Race*, by Julius Lester
> *Not My Idea: A Book About Whiteness,* by Anastasia Higginbotham
> *Rad American Women A to Z*, by Kate Shatz
> *Rosa*, by Nikki Giovanni
> *Sitting Bull: Lakota Warrior and Defender of His People,* by S. D. Nelson
> *The Show Way*, by Jacqueline Woodson

Listen *(see P4SJ playlist on Spotify)*

> "Latinoamérica," by Calle 13 and Toto La Momposina
> "Liberated," by DeJ Loaf and Leon Bridges
> "Nina Cried Power," by Hozier, featuring Mavis Staples
> "Somos Sur," by Ana Tijoux and Shadia Mansour
> "What's Going On," by Marvin Gaye
> "We Rising Up," by Climbing PoeTree
> "Occupy," by Rising Appalachia
> "We Shall Overcome," by Mahalia Jackson

Watch *(third grade and up)*

> "The Children's March"[45] (41 minutes; you can get this on YouTube in its entirety)

---

45 The Children's March, accessed November 5, 2019, https://www.youtube.com/watch?v=5enZRwbnISQ&ab_channel=ExtinctionRebellion.

"Because I'm Latino I Can't Have Money? Kids on Race"[46] (4 minutes)
Ruby Bridges, a 1998 Disney film about the true story of the six-year-old who
    was the first Black child to integrate the all-white schools in New Orleans

The following DVD titles are not readily accessible. Ask your local library to purchase
to make them available to more people:
    Unlearning "Indian" Stereotypes, a Rethinking Schools and Council on Inter-
        racial Books for Children, DVD, Native American history through the eyes
        of Native American children: https://www.zinnedproject.org/materials/
        unlearning-indian-sterotypes
    I'm Not Racist, Am I? http://www.notracistmovie.com

 Reflect

1. What feelings and body sensations came up for you while reading/watching/
   listening?
2. What did you learn about yourself and/or your kids from reading/listening/
   watching together?
3. What else do you need to know to have further conversations about race and
   racial justice with your kids?
4. What are you wondering about?

Taking action
How can you turn all this learning into action?

- ❀ Keep learning.
- ❀ Heal from trauma.
- ❀ Read/listen/watch and have conversations with your kids.
- ❀ Talk with people who have a similar racial identity to you—share your story of
  awakening, what you're working on, and why you care about racial justice.
- ❀ Be intentional about spending time with and forming strong relationships with
  people in your community who are working for racial justice.
- ❀ Hold your child's school accountable for what they're teaching.
- ❀ Get involved in local work for racial justice.
- ❀ Support national and global campaigns for racial justice.

Keep learning. Learning IS action. There is power in reading and talking with your kids
about race. There is power in saying, "I don't know. Let's find out!" We can learn with
our kids. What we think impacts what we do, so we need to commit to continually
unlearning the harmful biases that are in our minds, and learning the truth about race,
racism, and racial justice that will contribute to freedom.

---

46 Kids on Race, WNYC, July 2015, https://www.youtube.com/watch?v=C6xSyRJqIe8&feature=youtu.
be&ab_channel=WNYC.

Heal from trauma. Sherri Mitchell has said that healing ourselves is a revolutionary act.[47] The trauma we have all experienced because of racism and white supremacy is real. How can we practice healing for ourselves and encourage healing practices for our children? We must first recognize the trauma we carry and then, depending on who we are and what our needs are, begin taking steps toward healing.

> For me (AB), healing racial trauma means putting together the puzzle pieces to learn how my family has benefitted from racial oppression, and grieving that injustice through tears, meditation, and journaling. It also means going to somatic breath therapy for the past four years to unlearn the "white savior" response to guilt, and to energetically reconnect with my ancestors.

> For me (CCB), healing racial trauma is a continued process of learning. It means always asking questions of my elders. It means uncovering the stories of my family history, honoring my ancestors with an altar of their photos, and journaling and reflecting on the gifts my ancestors have given me. It means honoring my heritage by intentionally building deeper, more honest relationships with extended family. It also means noticing and working against internalized racial inferiority. It means recognizing when those patterns are at play, naming them, and making conscious choices. Each day I remind myself that the work I do is done in honor of those who came before me.

Read/listen/watch and have conversations with your kids. This is action! And you've already started doing this in the previous section.

Talk with people who have a similar racial identity as you—share your story of awakening, what you are working on, and why you care about racial justice. It is really important to make sense of our stories and life experiences. Taking the time to journal about your racial and ethnic identity and to share stories with peers will help you build connections, grow your comfort with talking about race, and place your life story in context. Form a group of peers who are interested in growing together. Read, watch, and listen together, and then talk. Depending on the racial identities in the group, you might talk about colorism, opportunity hoarding, or any other related issues.

Be intentional about spending time with and forming strong relationships with people in your community who are working for racial justice. Seek out groups and organizations that are working toward racial justice and diversity. Good relationships take time, so don't get discouraged if you feel like you aren't making strong connections right away. The goal is for our families to be better equipped to be in solidarity with each other and to challenge injustice in our communities—it's hard to do this when we don't even know each other.

---

47 Sherri Mitchell, *Sacred Instructions: Indigenous Wisdom for Living Spirit Based Change* (Berkeley, North Atlantic Books, 2018).

Something we often hear from white folks in the workshops we facilitate is "But we don't have any friends who are people of color. How do we make friends with people who are different from us?" Our response to this is that while it is a good thing to have friends with a different racial identity from you, to achieve racial justice it is actually more crucial that you are involved in action for racial justice. In fact, there is a growing body of research that shows that merely exposing young children to people of different races and ethnicities does not guarantee that the children will internalize messages about racial justice or that they will maintain cross-racial friendships as they reach the upper elementary years.[48] A study out of New York University found that teachers and schools played a critical role in preventing this pattern. Teachers with strong racial literacy skills and who actively examined their own biases created classrooms that fostered cross-racial friendships.[49] And if you are involved in racial justice action and are continuing to work on your privilege as it shows up, then it is likely that friends of color will come naturally into your life.

Hold your child's school accountable for what it is teaching. In many of our schools the curriculum, particularly our history curriculum, has not changed in decades. As you read more books with your children and learn more about the histories of peoples of color, advocate for a more racially just curriculum. Connect with your kids' schools about the books they are reading. What's in their library? What do they read in the classroom? If these books maintain the dominant white narrative, this would be a good time to talk to the school and other parents about replacing these with socially just books. Ask questions about the perspectives and voices in the curriculum. Whose history are they telling? Advocate for more books that center the experiences of people of color. Ask about how the voices and perspectives of folks of color are being honored and highlighted. Push for the curriculum to move beyond tokenizing theme months (e.g., Black History Month) and instead to integrate discussions of race and racism into students' daily lives. At home, when your child is working on a school project, support them in researching the contributions and perspectives of people of color.

Get involved in local work for racial justice. Wherever you live, there are bound to be social justice groups. If not, get something started! Here are a few examples of organizations we (CCB and AB) are involved in. There are many ways to be involved in each—providing childcare, donating generously, joining committees, showing up for rallies and lobby days, providing mutual aid when requested . . .

The Gathering for Justice (gatheringforjustice.org) is building a movement to eliminate the racial inequities in the criminal justice system.

---

48 James Moody, "Race, School Integration and Friendship Segregation in America," *American Journal of Sociology*, vol. 107, no. 3 (November 2001): 679–716.
49 Rachel Harrison, "Interracial Friendships Decrease over Time in Elementary and Middle School, with Teachers Playing a Hidden Role," NYU, June 6, 2016, https://www.nyu.edu/about/news-publications/news/2016/june/interracial-friendships-decrease-over-time-in-elementary-and-middle-school.html.

The SHIFT and SHARE are student groups I'm involved in (CCB), and **Youth 4 Change** and **AWARE** are student groups I'm connected to (AB). These groups don't have websites to share but are examples of student groups that exist in many schools around the country that are supporting students of color and raising awareness about racial justice issues. Look for a student group in your area to either connect your kids with or support in other ways.

The Root Social Justice Center (therootsjc.org) is building a movement for racial justice by building power for people of color and shifting resources to POC-led organizing. It has a youth group, a media project, a monthly social gathering for people of color, a monthly BIPOC caucus in tandem with a white caucus of racial justice allies, and educational forums for the community. It is based in southern Vermont and works with folks all over the state and region.

Migrant Justice (migrantjustice.net) organizes very successfully with undocumented migrant farmworkers in Vermont for basic human rights and dignity. It has received national attention for some of its work.

Support national and global campaigns for racial justice. National and global issues can feel distant, yet from a social justice perspective we know that we are all interconnected. For this reason it is important to learn about ways that national and global groups are working for racial justice and to support their work. You can get started by signing petitions, showing up for national actions, organizing a local chapter of a national organization, sending donations, and hosting teach-ins, and in all kinds of other ways. Most national organizing groups have designed ways for people to plug in from wherever they are.

Black Lives Matter (blacklivesmatter.com/getinvolved) has an official website that outlines the principles of the movement and ways to support. There are chapters all over the U.S.

Showing Up for Racial Justice (showingupforracialjustice.org), through community organizing, mobilizing, and education, moves white people to act as part of a multiracial majority for justice with passion and accountability. There are chapters all over the U.S.

#Not1More (notonemoredeportation.com) builds collaboration between individuals, organizations, artists, and allies to expose, confront, and overcome unjust immigration laws.

Idle No More (idlenomore.ca) calls on all people to join in a peaceful revolution, to honour Indigenous sovereignty, and to protect the land and water. Based in Canada.

Reflect

1. How are you working for racial justice in your community? How do you involve your kids?
2. What else would you like to be doing? Make a SMART goal—one that is specific, measurable, attainable, relevant, and with a time limit (see page 69).

Examples:

"My SMART goal is to take an action to support Indigenous sovereignty in the next two weeks. First, I will learn more about the Idle No More Campaign for Indigenous Sovereignty with my kids. We will look at the website together. We will read the articles and resources from their website. And if there is action that the campaign is asking us to take, like signing a petition, donating, or showing up for a march, we will decide as a family how to respond to those asks."

"My SMART goal is to invite the migrant family at our local farm over for dinner next week. We met because our kids are on the softball team together."

"My SMART goal is to talk with my brother about the Black Lives Matter movement, because he keeps talking smack about it in front of my kids."

 Healing justice practice

Ancestral Healing (Angela)

This healing practice shifted my relationship to my ancestors, and to my anti-racist practice, in a very powerful and long-lasting way. The practice comes from the Healing Justice Podcast, hosted by Kate Werning.[50] First, listen to the hour-long conversation #14, "Ancestral Healing for Anti-Racist White Folks," with Jardana Peacock and Kelly Germaine-Strickland. Then, do the Practice #14, "Ancestral Connection for White Folks with Jardana Peacock and Kelly Germaine-Strickland."[51] It will take about a half hour. Links for both of those are at www.healingjustice.org.

---

50 Jardana Peacock and Kelly Germaine-Strickland, "Ancestral Healing for Anti-Racist White Folks," interview by Kate Werning, *Healing Justice*, January 30, 2018, podcast, 1:08:24, accessed through https://irresistible.org.
51 Jardana Peacock and Kelly Germaine-Strickland, "Ancestral Connection for White Folks" hosted by Kate Werning, *Healing Justice*, February 1, 2018, podcast, 30:09, accessed through https://irresistible.org.

Touching the Earth, adapted from a Plum Village Practice[52] (Chrissy)

In gratitude I bow to this land and to all the ancestors who made it available. *(Bell, all touch the earth.)*

I see that I am whole, protected, and nourished by this land and all of the living beings that have been here and made life easy and possible for me through all their efforts. I see all those known and unknown who have made this country a refuge for people of so many origins and colors, by their talent, perseverance, and love, those who have worked hard to build schools, hospitals, bridges, and roads; to protect human rights; to develop science and technology; and to fight for freedom and social justice. *(Bell, all stand up. Take three breaths.)*

I touch my African American ancestors, you who were enslaved and brought to this land, who poured your blood, sweat, and tears on this land, whose unrewarded labor helped make this country an economic world power. *(Bell, all touch the earth.)*

I am in touch with the crippling violence and inhumanity that my African American ancestors faced every day, the loss of your land, language, culture, family, and freedom, and how you always found ways to resist, to subvert oppression, to maintain your humanity, through soulful singing, prayer, humor, slave revolts, communities of escaped slaves, as well as through political struggle, a strong commitment to education, and economic empowerment. I aspire to preserve, nourish, and pass on your strength, patience, perseverance, love, forgiveness, humility, your creativity and innovation in agriculture, inventions, history, music, dance, art, the sciences, sports, oratory, literature, religion, civil and human rights activism, and community spirit. I see Sojourner Truth, Harriet Tubman, Frederick Douglass, George Washington Carver, Garrett A. Morgan, W. E. B. DuBois, Langston Hughes, Ernest Just, Roger Arliner, Rosa Parks, Dr. Martin Luther King Jr., Malcolm X, Audre Lorde, Ella Baker, Fannie Lou Hamer, John Henrik Clarke, Ivan Van Sertima, and all others known and unknown inside of me, and in gratitude I honor you all. *(Bell, all stand up. Take three breaths.)*

I touch my European American ancestors, you who came to this land to find freedom from political and religious oppression and poverty, who came seeking a new vision of society. *(Bell, all touch the earth).*

I touch the deep insight and compassion of these ancestors: the Quakers, Abolitionists, peace activists, and the great conservationists. I am aware that many of you European American ancestors lost your fortunes and even your lives to resist the oppression of people of color. At the same time, I touch the great suffering experienced by some of you in my ancestry who were misguided in their views, whose

---

52 Kenley Neufeld, "Racial Divide and a Buddhist Response", Dec. 14, 2014, https://medium.com/mindfulness-and-meditation/racial-divide-and-a-buddhist-response-b28e5f804cdf.

belief in your superiority led to the decimation of Native peoples, the horrors of slavery, and the exclusion of people of color. I pour all this suffering on the earth and ask the earth to help me transform it into wisdom and compassion. I aspire to preserve, nourish, and pass on your courage in coming to an unfamiliar land, your strong faith and commitment to democracy, your perseverance, respect for the arts and ingenuity. I see Abigail Adams, Abraham Lincoln, Jane Addams, Benjamin Franklin, William Lloyd Garrison,

Susan B. Anthony, John Dewey, Amelia Earhart, Dorothy Day, Albert Einstein, Helen Keller, Woody Guthrie, Ralph Carr, Isadora Duncan, Myles Horton, Andrew Goodman, Michael Schwerner, Howard Zinn, Jane Goodall, Paul Farmer, and all others known and unknown, inside of me, and in gratitude, I honor you all.

(Bell, all stand up. Take three breaths.)

I touch my Latino/a ancestors of this land, you who are the children of the indigenous peoples of the Americas and the Spanish colonizers, some who for centuries lived on and built up roughly half of the present-day U.S., and some who immigrated from Central and South America more recently.

(Bell, all touch the earth.)

I touch the blood, sweat, and tears you have poured on to this land as farm laborers, skilled artisans, teachers, politicians, architects, and activists. I am in touch with the suffering of my Latino/a ancestors due to war and racist policies, like the deportation of two million Mexican American U.S. citizens during the Depression, as well as loss of land and culture. I am in touch with the United Farm Workers movement to end dehumanizing conditions for migrant workers, and I feel this collective energy, courage, intelligence, and dedication nourishing and supporting me to also do my part. I aspire to preserve, nourish, and pass on your strength, patience, perseverance, love, forgiveness, humility, humor, your creativity and innovation in the arts, your tradition of nourishing food and taking care of family. I see Cesar Chavez, Dolores Huerta, Emiliano Zapata, Pablo Neruda, Simon Bolivar, Rigoberta Menchu, Sandra Cisneros, Emma Tenayuca, Gloria Anzaldua, Rodolfo (Corky) Gonzalez, Sonia Maria Sotomayor, and all others known and unknown, inside of me and in gratitude, I honor you all.

(Bell, all stand up. Take three breaths.)

I feel the energy of this land penetrating my body, mind, and soul, supporting and accepting me. I vow to cultivate and maintain this energy and to transmit it to future generations. I vow to contribute my part in transforming the violence, hatred, and delusion that still lie deep in the collective consciousness of this society, in all ethnic groups, so that future generations will have more safety, joy, and peace. I ask this land for its protection and support.

(End with three sounds of the bell.)

Community of practice questions

1. What have been your *aha!* moments in this chapter?

2. What have been your successes in talking/reading/taking action for racial justice with your kids?

3. What have been your struggles?

4. What have been your somatic/body sensations and responses throughout this chapter?

5. Share your SMART goals. How can the group support you in achieving your goal?

6. What else do you want to learn?

Solidarity with Standing Rock rally, Brattleboro, VT, 2016.

SUSU commUNITY Farm, in Brattleboro, VT, is dedicated to offering a life affirming space that nourishes and centers the liberation of Black, Indigenous, People of color, and that builds a sustainable and thriving culture in Southern Vermont. Learn more and support this visionary project at https://www.facebook.com/susucommunityfarm

Chapter 4

PARENTING FOR CLASS & ECONOMIC JUSTICE

BY JAIMIE LYNN KESSELL AND ANGELA BERKFIELD

One day we must ask the question, "Why are there forty million poor people in America?" And when you begin to ask that question, you begin to question the capitalistic economy. And I'm simply saying that more and more, we've got to begin to ask questions about the whole society. We are called upon to help the discouraged beggars in life's marketplace. But one day we must come to see that an edifice which produces beggars needs restructuring. It means that questions must be raised. You see, my friends, when you deal with this, you begin to ask the question, "Who owns the oil? Who owns the iron ore? Why is it that people have to pay water bills in a world that is two thirds water?" These are questions that must be asked.
—DR. MARTIN LUTHER KING JR., 1967,
Southern Christian Leadership Conference

When I give food to the poor, they call me a saint. When I ask why the poor have no food, they call me a communist.
—DOM HÉLDER CÂMARA

I'm not preparing our kids for a gentle world, full of interesting and stimulating experiences. I'm getting them ready to keep their damn mouths shut while some idiot tells them what to do. I'm preparing them to keep a sense of self when they can't define themselves by their work because the likeliest scenario is that (unlike doctors and lawyers and bankers) they will not want to. I'm getting them ready to scrap and hustle and pursue happiness despite the struggle.
—LINDA TIRADO, *Hand to Mouth: Living In Bootstrap America*[1]

---

1 Linda Tirado, *Hand to Mouth: Living in Bootstrap America*, (Berkley: Putnam, 2014).

Reflect

Use the following questions as a guide to reflect on the quotes above. You can write or paint and share your responses with someone or just think quietly, whatever works best for your learning style.

1. What issues related to poverty are on your mind? What are some ways that the economic structure causes or contributes to those issues? Do you talk with your kids about the issues?

2. What are you currently doing for economic justice in your own life and in your community?

3. What are some ways you talk with people in your life about your own class experience? How about with your kids?

4. How does your class experience impact how you parent?

Our stories

These stories set the stage for learning about class and the economy and for our roles as parents in it. We each bring a unique perspective because of our own class locations and how those locations have shaped our experiences. We each continue to peel back the many layers that make up our stories to better understand our thinking and our actions. We trust that in reading our stories you will think about pieces of your own story in a new way.

Jaimie

As has been the case for my mother and her mother before her, I have spent my life in generational poverty. Although there are many "official" definitions of poverty, I would define poverty as a state of being that is caused by a lack of usual or socially acceptable amounts of money (or access to the material possessions that money can buy) and/or an inability to access an appropriate level of resources to sustain one's participation in society, and in which the individual or group experiences feelings of guilt, shame, anger, sadness, and inadequacy that affect their quality of life. To me, generational poverty is simply the continued state of such poverty across the lifespans of multiple generations within a family system.

I am from West Virginia. There are many things that I could say about my upbringing in WV regarding my family's lack of access to resources and my personal experiences of poverty. Suffice to say that we had access to food most of the time (but it was always of low quality), access to housing the majority of my life (but it changed frequently, such that I attended four elementary schools, four middle/junior high schools, and two high schools by tenth grade), and the stress that each member of my family felt due to our poverty was apparent to me even as a child. We were all drowning in a river of stress, trying to swim through it and mostly failing. I know that it certainly *felt* like I was failing.

By the time my 18th birthday arrived, I was many walking statistics of poverty all wrapped into one: I had been a high school dropout (without it being my choice in any way), had been homeless, had a teenage pregnancy, became a teen mother, and was living in a HUD housing complex in Charleston, WV, called Washington Manor. The level of shame and guilt that I carried with me over how society viewed me simply because of my circumstances, rather than the content of my character, was extremely heavy.

After the birth of my son, I attempted to return to high school to earn my high school diploma. At first I attempted to attend an alternative school program that was designed for teen mothers. I went to the location listed only to discover that the program had been shut down due to lack of funding. Disappointed, I attempted to enroll in a traditional high school but was informed by the board of education in Kanawha County, WV, that I would not be allowed to do so, because I had been out of school for more than one calendar year and therefore was no longer eligible for earning a high school diploma in West Virginia, only a GED. I felt angry that I was being denied access to education for such an arbitrary reason.

My first saving grace came in the form of my son's paternal grandfather. He and his wife hailed from a higher economic class and social status than I did and this made it possible for them to "rescue" both me and my son when I was the ripe old age of 18. I moved with my then-six-month-old son to Vermont to live at a residential facility called the Lund Family Center, where I utilized an educational program to earn my high school diploma.

Moving across the country with my baby, when I was still a child myself in many ways, was scary. Upon arriving in Vermont, I moved into the Lund Family Center's residential program. My son and I lived there with about 20 other pregnant and/or parenting young mothers. The living situation at Lund was not exactly positive. This was prior to Lund's renovations to their property and the building had asbestos and mold. Lund required all of the women in the residential program to apply for food stamps and cash assistance, and then every dollar was given to Lund to help pay for your stay in the program. The quality of food we were receiving was not very high and we were not allowed to have food in our bedrooms. Each young mother was given only $10 per week of "allowance" by Lund staff (despite the fact that each of us were receiving state grants via the Reach Up program that were going directly to Lund) and Lund required us to purchase not only our own toiletries, but also our own supplies of diapers and baby wipes for our children. Had it not been for my son's grandparent's continuous financial assistance, my son and I surely would have suffered even more than we did. We were not allowed to exit the building without permission from staff. After moving out, I realized how much of a resemblance my experiences at Lund bore to the experiences of someone who is incarcerated in prison.

The aspect of Lund's program that I did appreciate was the New Horizons educational program. Using that program, I completed my last two years worth of high school credits during the six months that I lived at Lund, so that my high school diploma would say that I finished "on time." The sense of pride I felt when I attained this goal was immense and has actually been one of the driving thoughts that has propelled me forward in life: if I could do *that*, I am certainly capable of surmounting this next challenge, whatever it might be.

I now have four children. My son, who identifies as gender-fluid and uses male pronouns, is now 16 years old and is on the autism spectrum. My second-born child, who identifies as nonbinary and uses they/them/their pronouns, is 14 years old and has ADD and possibly Borderline Personality Disorder (she is too young currently to be diagnosed). My third-born child is 6 and is the only one of my children I do not have sole custody of (her father and I divide time with her equally). My fourth child is 6 months old and her father and I are married and co-parent all of the children together.

The financial challenges of having children are huge for all parents. It is even harder when you are the only parent, especially if you are poor and rely on welfare to attempt to make ends meet. Trying to keep up with all of the bills every month is difficult. There have been many times when it was impossible, which is bound to happen when providing even the most basic of needs for your family requires living "outside of your means." I can't count the number of times that my electricity, gas, phone, and/or cable has either been shut off or was soon to be shut off. I am no stranger to a disconnect notice and the accompanying panic that follows receiving such a notice.

Parenting amid these financial difficulties is like riding an emotional rollercoaster. I have felt angry and sad that my children have had to deal with the consequences of poverty, despite my best efforts so far to shelter them from those consequences. I have been filled with dread and apprehension when dealing with landlords or case managers or anyone that was in a real or presumed position of authority over me and who held my life and the lives of my children in their hands. The lack of control over my own life and the lives of my children has been a major source of stress in my life. The level of distress, anxiety, unease, and tension that I have felt as a result of living in poverty has been difficult to navigate, especially while simultaneously trying to raise three small humans. The countless hours spent lying awake in bed, worrying about how I was going to afford gas for my car to get to a doctor's appointment for one of my kids or having to decide which bill was more important to pay (gas or electric?!) has cost me so much in terms of time and energy.

When people are under chronic stress, like that which is caused by experiencing poverty, the neurons in their prefrontal cortex (the part of the brain which deals with decision-making that doesn't get fully formed until you are in your mid-20s to 30s) actually lose some of their synaptic connections. I can definitely attest to this phenomenon in my own life. When I have been completely stressed out, worrying about how I was going to provide for my children financially (food, clothing, education, etc.), it felt like my brain just couldn't work efficiently. My ability to plan and problem-solve was greatly diminished and it felt like it took so much energy just to exist; just to be present in the moment felt nearly impossible at times. Experiencing major depression was also par the course, because it is extremely difficult to feel hopeful about the future when it feels like all of the odds are stacked against you (which they *are*).

Currently, I am on the verge of transitioning to a new level of poverty that feels affluent in comparison to the level of poverty that I have spent my entire life at. I am definitely still poor. I can't afford car repairs of any kind (even an oil change requires major financial planning) and without my Section 8 voucher, my family would be homeless; but I can buy toilet paper right now without worrying about it breaking the bank, which feels like I am winning at life.

The way that I run my household is distinctly different from the ways that my mother ran the households of my childhood. This manifests in many ways, including the messaging regarding class and socioeconomics that I convey to my children versus the messaging that my mom conveyed to me and my siblings growing up.

The messaging that I received about money as a child/adolescent was that money was simultaneously both the root of all evil and the gateway to happiness. I was woefully aware that we had no money growing up. I grew up angry that other people had things that we did not and was especially angry that the world was trying to tell us that it was *our fault*. The people I saw who had access to food, better housing, name-brand clothing, and new toys certainly did not deserve to have such things over me and my family based on some moral grounds. If anything, in my childhood experiences, those who had more than me were generally not good people; they were usually the ones bullying others.

I wanted to teach my children that the entire concept of money is bonkers to begin with. The fact that people have literally died over these small pieces of paper is lunacy. Unfortunately, short of owning property back in the woods somewhere that the government or corporations aren't interested in stealing and that also happens to have fertile land that can be worked for a small-scale farming operation, or joining a commune of some kind, if you live in America you don't have much of a chance of escaping capitalism or the worship of the "almighty dollar." And so I am stuck—as are many others—attempting to carve out a life for myself and my family that is socially just in an economy that is unjust.

Author Jaimie's son, Paul (12), at the March for Science in Montpelier, VT 2017. "Those who are unaware of the past are doomed to repeat it."

Coming from the background that I have, it is of vital importance to me that I pass on to my children the cultural knowledge I have gained while living in poverty. Having access to class privilege in the form of having a college degree (I am the first person in my entire family to graduate from college) and by way of former relationships (upper middle class family—think three-story house on a hill, two-car garage, and ALL OF THE TOYS), I also feel the importance of passing on the cultural knowledge I have gained as a result of having attained such privilege.

I am not wealthy today, and it is not because of any moral failing or lack of hard work ethic on my part. In fact, I have worked my ass off to even get this far. I am poor today because my white ancestors of Irish/Scottish/English/Dutch ancestry did not own enough land/slaves to gain prosperity and/or they didn't own any rights to oil fields or railway lines. And my Indigenous ancestors were forced off of their land by colonizers.

Although I now have access to class privilege through my education and relationships, I am still very much living in poverty at this time and the access to privilege that I have gained is by no means a reliable indicator that I will rise completely out of poverty. It isn't even a reliable indicator that my children will rise out of poverty, but it definitely gives them an advantage that I did not have access to in my childhood.

It is important to me that my children understand that poverty is not a choice—it is a LACK OF CHOICE—and that no amount of hard work is guaranteed to lift you out of poverty. "Lift yourself up by your bootstraps" is a myth; it is actually a lie told to poor people to turn what is really systemic inequality into a private moral failing. You are not inadequate because you are poor, any more than someone is automatically a good person because they happen to have money and resources.

I inform my children of the realities of living in poverty on a daily basis. Children are able to handle much more than we as parents typically think they can. Our children are growing up in a globally connected society with more access to information than any of us had access to at our children's ages. Unfortunately, not all of the information posted online is accurate or age-appropriate. This means that our work is cut out for us in completely different ways than it was for our parents or grandparents.

When I first started thinking about what examples I could use for this chapter to really showcase the ways in which I teach my kids about economic justice, I asked my 12-year-old daughter for examples they could think of, and they responded, "You talk about money and stuff ALL THE TIME, how am I supposed to come up with one example?!" I laughed because they are not wrong. Every chance I get, I am talking about equity and equality, whether it's about economic justice, ecological justice and sustainability, human rights, and/or a million things in between.

When my oldest two children come home from (public) school, having just been taught a civics unit where they are learning about how our government supposedly operates, I do the work to correct the inaccuracies they learned. As we sit around my dinner table every night, after sharing stories about how our days have gone, my family dismantles all kinds of complex concepts like white supremacy, the patriarchy, colonialism, slavery, racism, global warming, and economic inequality. I talk about what is happening in the world with the kids in the exact same ways that I talk to other adults about the same subjects: both factually and passionately. I express freely my fears and encourage the kids to do the same. I do vision work with them as well, by talking about what we think a just society would look like.

To parent your children regarding economic justice is to learn the truth about the economic systems at play in our society and how systemic oppression operates to keep certain people down while allowing others to rise, and then teach your children those truths in ways that make sense to them.

Even though I work really hard with my kids to teach them about economic equity and social justice issues, I am hardly perfect at any of this. My children are still inevitably taught things regarding economic status that I might not want them to actually learn, simply because they are going to pick up on my biases. We are all works in progress.

I will leave you with one last slice of wisdom that I have gained from a lifetime of poverty that is applicable to all, regardless of your economic status: as long as you are trying your very best with what you have at your disposal, you're good. Work with what you've got. Work within your means, whether your means are sleeping on friends' or family's couches or vacationing in the Hamptons; it doesn't matter. Be a good human and teach your children to be good humans too.

Angela

My class story is quite different from Jaimie's story. I grew up in the Midwest, in a suburb of a metropolitan area. My parents both had college degrees and throughout my childhood my dad was working on his doctorate. We didn't have much money growing up because my dad was a pastor of a small church and my mom chose to stay home while we were young and homeschool my brothers and I until we were in third grade. Yet we were never hungry and owned a modest three-bedroom home. Both of my parents helped us with our homework throughout our schooling. We had a garden, learned how to sew and use a hammer, took camping trips in the summer, and went to visit our extended family on the farm for holidays. Life was pretty good and I never thought about or questioned whether or not the economic system was working, because it was working just fine for me (although I did wish I could have the Guess jeans my friends had and go on trips to the "cabin" up north).

It is important to connect my class privilege to the experiences of my ancestors. On both sides of my family, my ancestors emigrated from Western Europe (Denmark, Ireland, England) in the mid-19th century for economic reasons. They were able to access rich farmland in the Midwest at very cheap rates because of the Homestead Act of 1860. The land had recently been stolen from the Sac and Fox Native Americans. This access to land, which was passed down through generations, along with the houses, tractors, and barns needed for continuing to earn more capital, allowed my family to accumulate more property and a modest amount of wealth that was passed on to my parents and to me.

Many experiences I had throughout high school and college—volunteering at soup kitchens and homeless shelters, a trip to Mexico to build a church, a trip to Guatemala to build an orphanage, a Habitat for Humanity trip to Kentucky, volunteering for a summer in inner city Chicago—taught me that not everyone had such benefits. Through those trips outside of my bubble of security I learned that poverty was real and needed to be addressed.

"Helping" was the tool that I was taught for addressing poverty. It was taught with the best of intentions, which was to make sure that people who were suffering had food and a place to stay. However, there was no teaching about poverty as connected to systemic oppression, nor was I given the tools for challenging and changing systemic oppression. I was taught how to feed hungry people, but not to ask why people were hungry, nor to feel confident in challenging the source of the problem or envisioning an economic system where people weren't hungry.

As someone who desperately wanted to help others, I went to college for a social work degree. In my decade of being a social worker I had the honor of working alongside people who were survivors of domestic abuse, in recovery from heroin addiction, and taking refuge from oppressive dictators. The people I worked alongside were supporting each other in meeting basic needs, in healing from trauma, and in advocating for human rights and system change. This solidarity work changed me and primed me for a graduate education that put all of the puzzle pieces together. I quickly recognized how the capitalist economy concentrates wealth at the expense of the poor, people of color, and the earth without a care for what it is destroying. That education instilled in me a responsibility to join with others who are working to change that system, to work for justice and equity.

Since that time I've been involved in many actions for justice, from co-founding The Root Social Justice Center for local racial justice organizing, to facilitating trainings on racism and class, to joining in actions for the rights of migrant workers and climate justice. It is all good work, yet I recognize that my class upbringing can get in the way of joining with people from oppressed class backgrounds to make change. I must continue to learn how class shows up in my thinking and actions. I've built in accountability from others in my community to support me in this lifelong learning.

I'm now a mom. I'm raising two white, cisgender boys (at this point) who are middle class and who have owning-class privilege. They have relatives who are in the 1%, which means they have privileges I could never have even imagined existed when I was a kid, like five-star beach vacations and all the Lego kits they could want. I'm raising my kids to be change-makers. I want them to be compelled to change a system that on face value is working very well for them. This feels like a tall task, and I'm doing my best to rise to the challenge.

I'll give an example. When my oldest was eight he watched lots of soccer on YouTube during his daily hour of screen time. It was a good way for him to spend his time. He paid close attention and tried out the mind-blowing moves on the soccer field, which is his favorite place to be. At one point he had a friend over, and after playing soccer for an hour they went into the den for screen time. After a while I went to check in. I was shocked to find they were watching a video about famous soccer players' houses. The video was comparing the house the player grew up in to the house they live in now. Many players, most of whom were people of color, grew up in poverty and are now among the wealthiest people in the world, and they had houses to match that shift in class status. It was a classic celebration of rags-to-riches stories. The video was unashamedly glorifying wealth.

Awe and adoration were all over the boys' faces. These young kids are already buying into the myth that wealth is the goal of life. And they were planning their futures accordingly. It made me sick to my stomach. I couldn't stop myself from commenting. "What if instead of building mansions, those players redistributed the money they were making so that their family members and friends could live in safe neighborhoods and have running water?" They gave me a funny look, which was hard to read. It probably meant "bug off, mom."

I want my son to dream. Yet it is important for all of humanity and for the planet that his dreams are based in reality and are about collective good, instead of just about good for himself. Then, if he ever does become a famous soccer player, he can use his wealth to contribute to a more just and equitable society, instead of on his own aggrandizement. Or better yet, advocate for a change in the way that the sports-industrial complex[2] is structured, using the bodies of incredible athletes (many of whom are POC) to make millions and billions for the already wealthy (majority white), not to mention corporate control of athletes and fields.

I have a responsibility to teach my sons about the reality of inequality. They are unlikely to learn about it in public school. And they certainly aren't going to learn it from watching mainstream media. So after I saw them watching the YouTube video on mansions, I decided to show them (eight and five years old at the time) a video about wealth inequality in America.[3] The video explains graphs that show how unequal the distribution of wealth is in the U.S. After watching, we talked about where our family falls on those graphs and where other people we know fall on those graphs, including the famous soccer players. I asked what they thought about the wealth inequality. My youngest had lots to say: "the rich people should spend all their money and then we'd all have all that money" and "we should take it away from everyone except for Neymar."[4] My oldest son simply took the computer cursor and took the film back to the part where all the money was distributed equally—this video's version of "socialism." I'm not sure what was going on in his head, but it felt promising that he was thinking about equal distribution of wealth.

We talked about where different houses fall on that economic wealth continuum: the Brazilian favelas on the far left, our trailer right around the 40% mark (based on what we can afford with our income), the house where we vacationed in the top 10% area, and Neymar's mansion on the 1%. My kids immediately placed Trump in the wealthiest 0.1% of people.

---

2 For more on this, listen to the Freakonomics podcast (http://freakonomics.com/podcast/sports-5) or read an article in Salon, https://www.salon.com/2013/02/08/the_sports_industrial_complex_is_bleeding_america_dry.

3 Politizane, *Wealth Inequality in America*, November 2012. https://www.youtube.com/watch?v=QPKKQnijnsM&ab_channel=politizane. As of 3/12/19 (has been viewed 22 million times).

4 Neymar da Silva Santos Júnior, a Brazilian soccer player who in 2018 was the third-highest paid, taking home $90 million.

For all of you out there with big houses or more than one house, this is not intended to be a personal critique. It is, rather, a critique of how our economic system and the value system that goes along with it has robbed us of our humanity. We are all hurting from this system, whether we know it or not. This critique is an attempt to move us towards sharing our resources more equitably and work towards equitable governance of our homes, our towns, our states, and our country. It is a challenge to all of us to look critically at how the societal messages about wealth have seeped into our homes and hearts without us even knowing it. It's time to return to community, to connection, to collaboration, to sharing. It is time for us to ask important questions about how much is enough.

When I was talking with my kids about different houses, I was not talking about how Neymar or Trump are bad people, but about how they are playing into an economic system that values bigger and more. I explained that we need to be careful to not fall into that value system so that we don't hurt others and ourselves. I encouraged them to ask critical questions (like the ones Martin Luther King Jr. asked in the quote at the beginning of the chapter) of an economic system that allows for such extreme wealth and extreme poverty.

This is not necessarily easy to do. There are three things I have found to be crucial in bringing this kind of conversation into my parenting. First is being honest about my class story with whomever I am talking with. Second is being intentional about forming friendships with people in different classes from me and supporting my kids to do the same. Third is volunteering with campaigns for economic justice, and finding ways for my kids to be involved in that work too.

I have worked to better understand my own class story—where I've had privilege/advantage in my lifetime, both in terms of resources and social capital and access to opportunities, as well as historical advantage because my ancestors came from Europe. I work on getting as honest as possible with myself about how I am consciously and unconsciously contributing to the system staying the way it is because it works for me. And then I share this story transparently, whenever it makes sense to. It is a story I'm telling my kids too, so that they have the real information they need to learn their own class story.

We are also intentional in forming friendships across class differences. Where we live, class is a stronger predictor than race for friendships (the town we live in is 95% white). In my kids' kindergarten classes, the class divide among peers was already noticeable. Kids from poor and working-class families played together, kids from middle- and upper-class families played together, and kids from private schools played together. How did I know? In our town you can tell by who is wearing Carhartts (for their working-class job) and who is wearing Patagonia (from an upper-middle-class income). That's a joke, but it's kind of true too. Dress is a strong class indicator.

Our kids watch us and they mimic us. If we spend time only with people in a similar class to ours, then our kids learn from that. And I mean this more in terms of the outward, observable attributes related to class cultures, not so much how much money people have. And when we prioritize forming friendships across ingrained class boundaries, they learn from that too.

Despite my attempts to encourage cross-class friendships, my kids mostly have close friendships with kids with middle-class markers. But I continue to support them in widening their circle of friends. I often have friends over who are poor and working class. We go to lots of parties and events with those friends and all the kids play together and have a great time. This feels weird to write about—and Jaimie let me know there is a "white, middle-class, savior" tone to it. In other words, Jaimie is detecting a hint of an attitude from me that I can help/save people from poverty by being friends with them. I didn't even notice that attitude in myself in this instance. I appreciate her holding a mirror up so I can see it there, a couple layers beneath the surface. Forming friendships across difference needs to be mutual in a genuine way.

Her feedback has me thinking. Forming cross-class friendships is in some ways similar to being intentional about making friendships with people who have a different racial identity. Being brought up with strong cultural memes about a "classless society" and colorblind racism ("I don't see race, we are all the same"), it is hard to break that silence and to talk about race divisions and class divisions in relationships. Yet we have got to build the skills for forming friendships across social barriers, which means messing up and learning from our mistakes. It is hard when we are busy. It is easier to call the parents whose numbers I already have, where I know my kids will have a good time, who I know will feed my kids the food I want them to have. Yet my effort to support my kids in building cross-class friendships now will be well worth it in the future. If my kids are going to be change-makers, this is a crucial piece of that puzzle.

Angela's kids at an annual worker's rights rally at the Vermont Statehouse, 2013.

We show up as a family for economic justice work. Since the kids were very little we have participated in an annual rally for workers' rights at our statehouse and in many rallies for immigrant rights in our state. The whole family participates in events at The Root Social Justice Center where many of the programs are directly connecting racial and economic justice. We participate in an annual campout to raise support for dignified housing for everyone in our community. The kids fundraise for that effort. The kids have also chosen for their volunteer focus to be with a local hub of 350.org. We will be doing exchanges with families in other parts of the country/region who are resisting pipelines. And we will also be talking about how economic justice and climate justice are intricately connected and supporting initiatives like the Green New Deal.[5]

I'm committed to interrupting the glorification of wealth for myself and my family, through continual learning, through intenti0onal transparency about my class story, through forming strong cross-class friendships, and through working with others for justice.

The story we are told is the story we tell

As parents it is important for us to understand class in the capitalist economy because it is affecting our families right now, and it will continue to have a dramatic impact on our children's lives. For the purpose of this book, we are summarizing what we see as the main points that can support us in understanding how unequal the economy is and in what ways this inequality functions, so that we are prepared to talk with our kids. We highly recommend continuing your learning and maybe even researching with your kids. There are many resources from pages 318–334 to support this learning.

What is class?

In the United States of America we hold up egalitarian values of justice, fairness, and freedom. We reject the idea of a rigid class society because that would be unjust, unfair, and definitely not free. Class tyranny is what immigrants from Ireland and Denmark, from Poland and Germany, were escaping when they came to this new land, right? The meme of a classless society has been pushed hard into our brains, similar to how the concept of a "post-racial" society has been pushed by the media, school curriculum, and messages we receive from all around us. Because of our collective belief in a classless society many people are surprised to find out how real class barriers are, and how racialized our society still is—and how inextricably interconnected the two are. At the same time, many people have been aware of class all along and have been doing their best to survive the horrible impacts of it, and fighting for justice in many different ways.

---

5 Check out this short video envisioning a world after the Green New Deal, a bold plan for creating jobs and revamping the U.S. for responding to climate change: Naomi Klein, "A Message from the Future with Alexandria Ocasio Cortez." *The Intercept*, April 17, 2019. Retrieved from https://theintercept.com/2019/04/17/green-new-deal-short-film-alexandria-ocasio-cortez.

Class is defined in various ways. We use this definition of class, adapted from a definition developed by Davey Shlasko of Think Again Training and Consulting.[6] This definition works for us because it includes both the structures that create class groups and how those class structures impact people, which is sometimes referred to as socio-economic class.

Class is . . .

⚜ relative social hierarchical ranking in terms of income, wealth, status, and power

⚜ a group of people who share similar roles in the economic system as particular kinds of workers, owners, and/or buyers/sellers/traders/consumers *(Think about the hierarchy of power in those roles: Who labors? Who owns and benefits from the labor of others?)*

⚜ the culture, knowledge, skills, and networks that come along with being part of a particular class group *(Think about the hierarchical ranking of culture, knowledge, skills, and networks: What kinds of culture, knowledge, skills, and networks are privileged and have advantage? Which kinds are oppressed?)*

⚜ inextricably connected with race, gender, and disability

In other words, class is complicated. Describing class categories can be helpful to better understand this definition. However, we want to avoid contributing to the idea that class categories are neat and tidy or that these are static categories. But it can be helpful to have a starting place from which to move into deeper conversation about how class works. We start with class categories adapted by Think Again Training from those that Betsy Leondar-Wright outlines in her book *Class Matters: Cross-class Alliance Building for Middle-class Activists.*[7]

Persistent poverty: people and families who chronically don't have enough income to meet their basic needs. This group includes people who are disabled, elders, currently or formerly incarcerated, homeless or living in substandard housing, single parents, and people who have been on public benefits for a long time.

Working class: people and families who earn hourly wages for their labor or the non-managerial work they do, and who have very little decision-making power in those roles. This work sometimes requires a two-year degree or vocational training, and might even require a college education.

---

6 Davey Shlasko & Toby Kramer. 2011. "Class Culture and Classism in Campus and Community Organizing." Paper presented at Presentation at Pedagogies of Privilege Conference, University of Denver. Think Again Training and Consulting: www.thinkagaintraining.com. Davey and I (AB) co-founded Cross Class Dialogue Circles in 2015, which are still going now! Check out the upcoming circles at www.equitysolutionsvt.com.

7 Betsy Leondar-Wright, *Class Matters: Cross-class Alliance Building for Middle-class Activists* (Gabriola Island, BC, Canada: New Society Publishers, 2005).

Upper-working class or lower-middle class, which we also refer to as buffer class: people and families with higher and more stable incomes compared to working class people, who have jobs that require skills gained through a college education or whose "low-skilled" employment is very stable. If they own a business it survives because of the owner's labor. They most likely have higher education in the form of a two-year degree or a BA. The people in this class serve as a buffer between poverty-class working-class people and the people in the wealthier classes, so that those classes rarely interact. This group includes professionals such as teachers, police officers, social workers, and correctional officers.

Professional middle class: people and families with higher incomes because of professional jobs and often because of investment income. A family in this class has at least one breadwinner with a four-year academic degree, a master's degree, and/or specialized skills that bring more income and more security than working-class families have. People in this class category typically have more autonomy and decision-making power, and might be in a management position within an organization or business. They still depend on their salaries to pay their bills to some extent, but might be able to afford more travel or luxury items. This group includes some doctors, many lawyers, and some CEOs.

Owning class: people and families who earn enough income from their investments, assets, and/or inheritances so that they don't have to work full-time to pay basic bills, although they still might. People who live modestly on investment income also belong to this class. A subset have positions of power that put them in the ruling class, the people who have major influence over national and global policy decisions.

Straddler: people and families from working-class or poor childhoods who now have more resources. Includes people who are the first generation in their family with a college degree. Those people who are upwardly mobile with a professional career are *assimilated straddlers*; others are *unassimilated straddlers*.

Involuntarily downwardly mobile: people and families with a professional-middle-class or upper-middle-class background, impacted by health crises, disabilities, addictions, crashed economy, war or other traumas, so that they live in poverty or working class as an adult.

Voluntarily downwardly mobile: People and families from professional-middle-class or upper-middle-class background with a college degree who choose not to pursue a professional career for political, artistic, environmental or other values.

A mix of the above: many people have complicated experiences that don't fit into these categories, such as being raised by parents with different class categories from each other, or experiencing changes in class during childhood.

WEALTH INEQUALITY IN AMERICA

OWNING CLASS
1% of US population (~3 million people)
$35-39% of US wealth
Annual household income ~at least $300k
Wealth = over $3,000,000
May work...but don't need to (living off dividends/financial instruments)

"THE WEALTHY"

PROFESSIONAL/MANAGERIAL CLASS
19% of the US population (most of the wealthiest 1/5)
55% of US wealth
Annual household income ~$100k-$300k
Wealth = over $344k
High-paid professionals ie CEOs, corporate managers, lawyers, doctors, financiers

POOR
40% of the US population
Annual household income under $40k
Zero or negative net wealth
Low status workers, people on public assistance, retirees, people who are unemployed, homeless, incarcerated...

BUFFER CLASS
40% of US population (lower middle class, upper working class)
5-8% of US wealth
Annual household income ~$40k-$100k
Wealth = over $56k
Teachers, social workers, police, nurses, skilled tradespeople

6. Chapter 4 - Parenting for Ecor
Google Docs

"THE RICH"

ACTUAL Distribution of Wealth in the U.S.

"THE POOR"

"THE 1%"

0%   10%   20%   30%   40%   50%   60%   70%   80%   90%   100%

This graph, taken from the "Wealth Inequality in America" YouTube video by Politizane in 2012[8] and with text by the training group Equity Solutions,[9] gives us an idea of how many people in the U.S. are in four class categories and what the wealth distribution looks like by class category.

These class categories can help us make sense of our own experience, as well as patterns we notice around us.

Let's go back to the definition of class, starting with "groups of people and their roles in the economic system." We can divide these groups into two main categories: owning class and working class. The owning class are those who own large corporations or real estate, or who directly benefit from the labor of the other main group, the working class. The working class must sell their labor to make ends meet. This setup has created immense inequality in wealth distribution. When we understand class in this way it is easier to see that the main problem lies with an economic system that allows the owning class to exploit the labor of the working class for immense financial gain.

However, this is not the way that people typically think about or talk about class, partly because the people who own the land, resources, and labor have used many tactics to keep us from thinking this way. One major tactic is "divide and conquer"— pitting different segments of the working class against each other. Division by race is the key method for fomenting class division, which allows the owning class to maintain power. In Chapter 3 we wrote about Bacon's Rebellion, just one example of poor and working class people coming together across racial division lines to challenge the

---

8 Politizane, *Wealth Inequality in America*, November 2012. https://www.youtube.com/watch?v=QPKKQnijnsM&ab_channel=politizane. As of 3/12/19, it has been viewed 22 million times.
9 Equity Solutions, www.equitysolutionsvt.com.

owning class. This kind of coming together in class solidarity has happened again and again throughout history, and the owning class finds ways to interrupt and prevent it.

Another way the powerholders have taken action to divide working class people is by creating a buffer class, or people who have just enough resources that they are not suffering in this economic system and are willing to play the role of serving the upper classes or keeping the lower classes in line. The buffer class still needs to work and so are still in the working class (within this definition of two main classes); however, they see themselves as separate and better than the lower classes. They typically identify as middle class and work as skilled tradespeople, teachers, police officers, social workers, and middle management.

This division of labor has resulted in strong class cultural markers (e.g., language, dress, education), which can look and feel a lot more complicated than the relatively simple inequality that class really is (a conflict between the owning class and everyone else). This makes it really hard to challenge the power structures that create inequality.

This brings us to the next part of how we define class: "the culture, knowledge, and networks that go along with a class identity." Socioeconomic class is not just about how much money one has, it's also about the class markers that go along with it: what level of education you have, what restaurants you go to, whether or not you can afford dental care, what clothes you wear, what jobs that will hire you, what kind of car you drive. Class is a combination of your access to resources, whether through income or assets, your relationship to work, whether you are respected and belong, and whether you have decision-making power in any given situation. Our class-stratified society privileges those with middle-class dress, education, and language, and oppresses those with poor and working-class markers. The way we look, talk, and act has an impact on how people and institutions treat us.

Because of how complicated class is, it is important not to make assumptions about people. People in any given class don't look a certain way. For example, if you grew up middle class but are currently unable to get a job, you might be temporarily poor and on public assistance. However, you still hold onto your "middle class" status because of your college education and your social capital, which may still make it possible for you to get called back for a job interview or get a car loan. Another example: you might be working class and have a relatively high wage because of being in a historically unionized industry, but you still get disrespected by those with higher status and the owning class is still fighting back against that and trying to lessen your voice and what you have access to.

When we talk about class, we must talk about race. The connection of capitalism and white supremacy is inextricable. Racism has made it possible for a small number of people (previously all white, now also some people of color) to maintain wealth and power (see Chapter 3). One statistic that clearly illustrates an outcome of centuries of economic oppression is the racial wealth divide. It is increasing as we write, with the median wealth of African American families at only $11,000, compared to the median wealth of white families which was $141,900 in 2013 (according to Census data).[10] This

10 United for a Fair Economy, *Closing the Racial Wealth Divide Charts*, accessed March 13, 2015 http://www.faireconomy.org/racial_wealth_divide.

racialized wealth disparity is directly linked to race-based labor policy and practices, such as chattel slavery of Black peoplefrom the mid-1600s through 1865, Jim Crow laws in the south from after the Civil War until 1965, fair wage policies that continue to exclude domestic workers and agricultural workers who are disporportionately Black and Latinx, and mass incarceration from 1970 through today and laws that make it nearly impossible for people with criminal records to get jobs.

There are so many more policies and practices that have contributed to this disparity. Racism is baked into every institution in the U.S. When we look at racism as part of the system of white supremacy, we see how all of these institutions reinforce each other, contribute to continued wealth for some white people, and strip wealth away from people of color, particularly Black, Latinx, and Native Americans. Yes, there are some people of color with wealth, but they are the exception to the rule and that is not going to change anytime soon, unless the U.S. takes serious action for reparations,[11] which is making monetary amends for the harm done through centuries of systemic racism.

It is important to point out that race is still a stronger predictor than class of the way someone will be treated by institutions in the U.S. One key example has to do with discipline in school. Studies show that students of color are expelled more often than white students, across socioeconomic classes.[12]

We also must talk about gender. There are many examples, but the gender wage gap is a simple way to understand the disparity in class by gender. The Institute for Women's Policy Research reports that in 2017, white women made $.80 to the dollar of white men doing the same jobs. At this rate, it will take 37 years for white women to gain pay parity with white men, and 102 years for Black women and 207 years for Hispanic women.[13] Another telling statistic is that single mothers are five times more likely to be in poverty than married mothers.[14] Policies and practices in the U.S. make it very difficult for single mothers: there is little if any maternal leave or paid sick leave, job schedules can be unpredictable, quality childcare is expensive and hard to find, and affordable housing is scarce. All of these policies and more impact whether or not a single mother is going to be able to thrive, or if she is going to be hanging on by a thread.

What is capitalism?

To start off, we want to acknowledge that this is a huge topic. We highly recommend that you continue to learn about the capitalist economy beyond our brief summary. We

---

11 For more on reparations we recommend you read Ta-Nehisi Coates' article, "The Case for Reparations," https://www.theatlantic.com/magazine/archive/2014/06/the-case-for-reparations/361631, and look at the Movement for Black Lives toolkit for reparations.

12 Nora Gordon, "Disproportionality in Student discipline: Connecting Policy to Research." A Brookings Institution report. January 18, 2018, https://www.brookings.edu/research/disproportionality-in-student-discipline-connecting-policy-to-research.

13 "Pay Equity & Discrimination." Institute for Women's Policy Research website, accessed March, 2021, https://iwpr.org/iwpr-publications/quick-figure/pay-equity-projection-race-ethnicity-2020/

14 "Half in 10 Report 2014—Poverty and Opportunity Profile." National Women's Law Center website, accessed June 30, 2019, https://www.nwlc.org/sites/default/files/pdfs/mothers-poverty-opportunity-profile.pdf.

recommend these accessible curriculums: Teaching Economics As If People Mattered,[15] Economics for the 99%,[16] Economics in Wonderland,[17] and Just Transition Zine.[18]

Class is directly connected to how the capitalist economy functions. What is an economy? Gopal Dayaneni from Movement Generation describes economy as "the management of home." *Eco* comes from the Greek word for home, and *nomy* from the word for management. This is helpful in shifting our thinking about economy from a big "out there" concept to something far more intimate and relatable. We each have practice at managing our own homes, although it is not always easy.

Now, let's expand our awareness to how our national home is being managed. For the last 500 years, the way we in the U.S. have managed our "home" (including all of the places the U.S. has controlled and influenced due to U.S. imperialism, definition on page 316) has been through the extraction of natural resources, the exploitation of labor (through slavery, cheap migrant labor, and mass incarceration[19]), and the belief in infinite growth (of GDP) as opposed to sustainable growth, all while denying the ecological and social consequences. This management system we currently live in is called capitalism, and more particularly, corporate capitalism, dominated by bureaucratic and hierarchical corporations. Robert Reich, a former secretary of labor and a prominent critic of capitalism, calls it supercapitalism.[20] He is referring to the dramatic shift beginning in the 1970s of corporate involvement in politics with the goal of shaping government regulations to benefit their shareholder interests. The interests of citizens have been lost in the shuffle at best, and have been willfully destroyed at worst.

The capitalist economy prioritizes profit, privately held wealth, growth, extraction, competition, and monopoly *over* well-being, the commons, sustainability, regeneration, cooperation, and diversity. Let's unpack each of these terms.

> *Profit vs. well-being:* Privately traded companies must make a profit for their shareholders in order to continue existing in a competitive marketplace. Business models in a capitalist system are designed to make a profit, not to ensure the well-being of humans or the planet. Making a profit is the bottom line. Some businesses are trying to shift this by using a "quadruple bottom line"—people, planet, profit, and purpose—however this is not the norm nor is it required in capitalism.

---

15 Tamara Sober Giecek with United for a Fair Economy, *Teaching Economics As If People Mattered: A High School Curriculum Guide to the New Economy.* (Boston, United for a Fair Economy, 2007).

16 Center for Popular Economics, "Economics for the 99%," 2014, https://www.populareconomics.org/wp-content/uploads/2012/06/EconomicsForThe99pct2014.pdf.

17 Robert B. Reich, *Economics in Wonderland: A Cartoon Guide to a Political World Gone Mad and Mean.* (Seattle, Fantagraphics Books, 2017). In an easy to digest fashion, Reich addresses complexities of how capitalism currently functions.

18 Movement Generation Justice and Ecology Project. *From Banks and Tanks to Cooperation and Caring: A Strategic Framework for a Just Transition.* Accessed September 30, 2019, https://movementgeneration.org/wp-content/uploads/2016/11/JT_booklet_English_SPREADs_web.pdf.

19 Able-bodied prisoners in the U.S. are required to work and are paid anywhere from $0–4.73/day. https://www.prisonpolicy.org/prisonindex/prisonlabor.html.

20 Robert Reich, *Supercapitalism: The Battle for Democracy in an Age of Big Business.* (Icon Books, 2008).

Privately held wealth vs. the commons: With private ownership of the means of production (agriculture, mining, industry, technology, entertainment, etc), any profits go to the owners and investors, instead of to the people who worked to create that profit. When wealth is commonly held, the profit goes to the people, either to the workers or to the residents of the state or country. One example of commonly held wealth is North Dakota's state bank: the annual profit goes back to the people of North Dakota.[21]

Growth vs. sustainability: In the capitalist economy, constant growth (of sales) is necessary to keep a profit margin. Corporations have done whatever they can to increase consumer spending. In 2018, corporations spent $223 billion on marketing in the U.S.[22] As a result of this intense push for profit we have become a consumer society. The U.S. has 5% of the world population and consumes around 25% of the fossil fuel resources.[23] Growth is prioritized, even when it means that we are degrading people's health and the sustainability of the planet. One example is that the ExxonMobil corporation knew about human-induced climate change as early as 1977, and they spent millions to cover up that research.[24] They have continued to extract fossil fuels, the primary source of climate change, because it has given them enormous profits, even though their own research confirmed it was threatening the safety of future generations.

Extraction vs. regeneration: Because profit and growth are required in this economy, corporations continue to extract resources instead of engaging in regenerative actions, which takes more time, care, and is not as profitable. Corporations extract coal, oil, uranium, diamonds, water, nutrients from the soil, wisdom from Indigenous communities, creativity from artists, and so much more. Corporations exploit people's labor even if it will make them unhealthy, and people are not justly compensated for their labor. Any excess resources are burned and dumped without care for how they impact the environment and people. Regeneration would prioritize using resources in a way that continues to be productive over time and does not cause damage to the environment or people.

Competition vs. cooperation: The capitalist economic model uses competition to motivate growth. Competition, rather than cooperation, is baked into what we value as a society. We teach kids about competition very early: most games, and

21 Stacey Mitchell. "Public Banks: Bank of North Dakota," *Institute for Local Self Reliance* website, July 2, 2015, https://ilsr.org/rule/bank-of-north-dakota-2. In the last 21 years, $400 billion in profit has been transferred to the state's general fund to subsidize education and reduce the tax burden on individuals and businesses.
22 "Media Advertising Spending in the U.S. from 2015 to 2022," retrieved June 30, 2019, https://www.statista.com/statistics/272314/advertising-spending-in-the-us.
23 "The State of Consumption Today," Worldwatch Institute. The Institute was wound up in 2017, after publication of its last *State of the World* report. https://securesustain.org/job/worldwatch-institute/.
24 Shannon Hall, "Exxon Knew about Climate Change almost 40 years ago," *Scientific American,* Oct. 26, 2015, https://www.scientificamerican.com/article/exxon-knew-about-climate-change-almost-40-years-ago.

many common conversation starters (e.g., "Who is the best player on your team?") and stories (e.g., Cinderella) are about competition.

Monopoly vs. diversity: This focus on competition in an economy that prioritizes profit creates an economy of monopolies instead of a diversity of companies. We have one or two companies that control all of our communications, a few companies that control our medicines, huge factory farms, and a few giant banks. This puts us all at great risk. Does "the banks are too big to fail" sound familiar?

You can see capitalism's priorities in the main way we measure whether or not our economy is healthy—the GDP, or gross domestic product. The sale of weapons, the number of people in hospital beds, the sale of fossil fuels, and the number of people in prison cells all reflect *positively* in the GDP. By this measure, the more people are hospitalized and incarcerated the *better* our economy is said to be doing. On the other hand, diplomacy, the number of people who are taking care of each other instead of being hospitalized, drug use prevention, education, and crime reduction have no reflection in the GDP.

The priorities of capitalism create dramatic wealth and income inequality. In 2014, 46.7 million people in the U.S., or 14.8%, lived below the federal poverty line of $23,492/year for a family of four and had a net worth of zero or less (that is, their debt exceeded their assets). At the same time, the net worth of the richest member of the *Forbes* 400 has soared from $2 billion in 1982 to $76 billion in 2015.

This is not the first time we've experienced such drastic inequality and it is not even unique to a capitalist organization of the economy. Throughout recorded history, when there has been concentrated wealth there has been rampant poverty, from the Roman Empire in the last two centuries BC, to Europe in the Middle Ages, to the U.S. in the 1930s. In capitalism, whether or not the inequality is extreme, inequality always exists. The way it is organized requires cheap labor and as such there has always been a wealthy class and an impoverished class. However, over the past five decades, from 1970 through today, economic inequality has become more extreme. A few reasons for this include deregulation in the corporate sector (e.g., removing regulations that protect citizens and environment so that corporations can increase their profit margin), tax policies that have greater benefit for the wealthiest Americans than for anyone else, and austerity policies, such as cutting food stamps, that continually cut public funds to people who need them most.

The wealth inequality in the U.S. today is echoed in many places around the globe, which is connected to the globalization of capitalism. This funneling of wealth to those who already have the most wealth has had global consequences because we have a global economy. The majority of us in the U.S. are already in tough times, or we are one paycheck away from tough times. Yet it is really important to be clear that the majority of people in the U.S. are wealthy when compared to the rest of the 7.7 billion people around the world, half of whom live on less than $2/day. Check out *Global Issues*[25] for statistics on global poverty and wealth.

---

25 Anup Shah, "Poverty Facts and Stats," accessed January 1, 2013, http://www.globalissues.org/article/26/poverty-facts-and-stats.

In short, making ends meet is getting harder and harder for the bottom 99%, even while the wealth of the 1% increases like never before. The ladder many of us have been taught to climb, for the purpose of gaining more money, status, or power, is not actually climbable; it is missing most of its rungs.

Of course, many people disagree with our analysis, for all kinds of reasons. For some it might be too radical, and for others not radical enough. We don't expect that every reader will agree with every point here, but we do ask that we all think critically about the current capitalist economy. We have not been taught how capitalism actually works, and those who benefit from it are deliberately keeping its functioning from the masses of people. They do this through tactics such as blaming individual bad actors and gaslighting those who put the blame on institutions. I (AB) talked with students who recently graduated from college with a degree in business, and they said that they never talked about capitalism during their four years. Their schooling taught them to succeed according to capitalist definitions, but not to understand capitalism.

The way we understand the problem impacts how we design solutions. Some of our favorite organizations to get information from about the economy, because they prioritize a critical lens and look at how race, class, disability, and gender are all connected, are United for a Fair Economy, the Economic Policy Institute, Movement Generation, Race Forward, and Policy Link.[26]

Class division

Capitalism creates class divisions. The basic premise of capitalism is extraction of "excess" value from labor. This means that some people gain from the exploitation of others. This kind of exploitation requires justification, such as believing that some people are less worthy than others, to excuse the unfairness and ensure that those who make up the buffer class, who are in managerial or middle-man positions, keep the system going through whatever means necessary. It also requires divide-and-conquer strategies, such as giving some groups of people benefits and leaving other groups behind, so that the majority doesn't rise up to overthrow this system that benefits a minority.

Different tactics have been used to foment class division. Divisions by race have been the most notably used tactics for the past 500 or so years. In the present moment we can see how the emigration of people from Mexico and Central America is being used to stir up anger among the white working class and direct it towards immigrants, rather than towards wealthy white elites who are benefitting from the exploitation of both immigrants and white working-class people. When we don't see other people as fully human, it is easier to feel like we deserve more than they do and in some cases to enact violence. Another tactic is subtle messaging in the media that instills a belief in the myth of a classless society where it is possible for anyone to be independently wealthy. This causes many people to be unwilling to challenge power structures because they believe they have a chance at a bigger piece of the pie. These and other tactics make it possible for this unequal economy to continue, even while the masses are being harmed.

---

26 http://www.faireconomy.org, https://www.epi.org, https://movementgeneration.org, https://www.raceforward.org, https://www.policylink.org.

We have all been receiving subtle and not-so-subtle messages about people who are different from us. These show up as biases that we hold against people because of their class. And if we aren't consciously working to interrupt those biases, we can discriminate against people based on their class. Discrimination based on class, or classism, is happening all the time. The Catalyst Project defines classism as "the policies, attitudes, behaviors, and beliefs that discriminate against and are used to disempower working-class and poor people. Classism is one way within a capitalist system that the concentration of power and wealth is maintained. It perpetuates the belief that people are poor because they are lazy and stupid, rather than exposing the nature of the capitalist system that relies upon exploitable classes to thrive."[27]

Class stereotypes are often talked about as an inherent feature of a group. For example you might have heard, "the poor are lazy," "the working class have a strong work ethic," "the middle class are focused on their own families," and "wealthy folks are business savvy." We might not even realize that something is a stereotype because it is such a commonly held belief. Like we wrote about on page 42, culture develops out of a need to survive and thrive within a larger context. The larger context in this case is the capitalist economic system, where class mobility is unlikely. Many commonly held stereotypes related to class are not based on inherent features of a group of people, but rather on tactics and skills that a group of people have developed to be able to survive and even thrive in the midst of an oppressive economic system.

If we are going to interrupt a harmful class system, we need to notice where and how we participate in thinking that blames people, even ourselves, for inequalities rather than blaming a larger system that is exploiting people's labor and disempowering people.

Massive economic inequality impacts peoples' lives in very real ways. Let's look at two potential lives you could have lived.

Your grandmother worked hard, day and night, in a factory. Her supervisor told her she was worthless and chastised her for taking breaks. The factory didn't pay her enough to cover basic necessities, and as soon as production dropped she was fired and had to stand in the breadline. Your mom was born into that situation, and had to drop out of high school early to contribute to the family finances. The restaurant where she worked paid too little to get by on and she supplemented that income with food stamps and welfare, where the social workers treated her like a leech, telling her she was trying to suck the system dry. You were born into that same life of working without being valued and never having enough. The company where you work pays you minimum wage and does not give you enough time off to take care of your mom, who now has cancer (probably related to chemicals she was exposed to from living in public housing next to a brownsite). There is almost no way out of this situation because the entire system is stacked against you. You are so busy trying to survive that there is little money, time, or energy left to change

---

27 Catalyst Project, Anti-Racism for Collective Liberation, from handout at workshop, Oct. 2008.

your life. There are even times when you feel so down that you believe what the system consistently tells you—that you don't deserve more.

Or (it's much less likely that this is your story):

Your grandmother inherited land from her grandfather and spent her youth learning how to play the piano, paint portraits, and put on parties. Your mother was born and was cultivated to have upper-class manners and had tutors to help with homework. Her parents encouraged her to go to one of the most prestigious universities and paid for the entire bill. You were born into wealth that had accumulated for at least three generations. You grew up going on annual vacations to the Caribbean, learning to play the violin with first-class teachers, and receiving your parents' credit card to go on shopping sprees. Although the whole world was handed to you on a platter, you feel frustrated and that "life is so unfair" when anything goes wrong in your life. After all, you worked hard to do well in school and you know the right people, so why didn't you get the job?

If you are that second person, it might be hard to want to look at reality more closely and to recognize that your wealth was somehow connected to the poverty of your peers. In the capitalist economy, where many people labor for the benefit of a few, it is very hard to change the unjust economic system because the people with the most wealth hold a lot of power and are invested in keeping things the way they are. They aren't inherently bad or greedy people, it's just that the way the system is set up is working for them and they're afraid of what would happen if someone else were making decisions, so it feels safer to keep things the way they are.

The people with little or no wealth may want to change things, but they have very little power individually and are so busy trying to survive that they don't have the time and energy necessary to take on the systems in place. Yet as we've seen, the poor far outnumber the rich. If all of the people in that position (the majority of people!) would come together and organize, they would have a whole lot of power to make change.

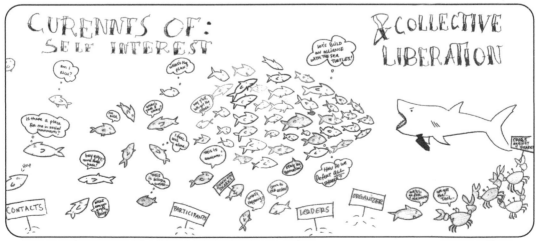

Drawing by Sarah Abbott of Resource Generation (https://resourcegeneration.org): a riff on a classic organizing meme.

When we come together we have power. But what does it take for us to come together? There are many great books out there about organizing. Check out the list that Social Justice Books has compiled.[28] This book you are reading now is not focused on organizing, but instead is about the personal changes we can make to be able to show up for community efforts, including through organizing. Larger societal change starts with how we as individuals think and act every day, which then inspires us to join movements. How we think and act has a profound influence on how our kids think and act, and it has a ripple effect on all those around us.

Economic justice: what is possible?

Economic justice is when the economy is organized in such a way that all people and the earth are treated fairly and with dignity and respect, they are not exploited or oppressed, and they have what they need to survive and thrive. Many definitions also include reparations (see page 315) for past harms of slavery and land theft. This is certainly not possible under the current version of capitalism and arguably not possible under any version of capitalism.

Visions of economic justice are motivating people to rise up to resist injustice and create new and just possibilities. Around the world, there are massive grassroots campaigns succeeding in bringing about changes in their local contexts. One example of this is the Fight for $15 campaign. Another is the campaign to resist oil pipelines being built through communities.

What solutions are people proposing? Within a capitalist structure there are many policies that people are advocating and fighting for that would make the current economic system work better for more people. As outlined in "Economics for the 99%,"[29] some examples of what people are demanding that would meet the needs of the 99% include full employment for all; health care for all; first-class K–12 education, preschool, and college for all; and eliminating discrimination that makes it hard for some groups of people to access employment. People are also demanding that the wealthy pay their fair share of taxes, get big money out of politics, support unions organizing, stop shipping jobs outside the U.S., and ensure everyone's right to vote.

In an economy that has continually stolen from Black people, Black people must be named in all economic justice efforts. The Movement for Black Lives has a well-laid-out economic justice policy platform[30] that speaks specifically to what is needed to ensure justice for Black people. The platform includes job programs, the right for workers to organize, renegotiating trade agreements, and on-the-job protections. Each of these reforms *could* be completed without changing the basic premises of capitalism. However, reforms that maintain private ownership, the profit motive, and the market economy can only be a temporary fix at best.

The capitalist economy was created by people. People can create a new economy: an economy that is just and equitable and where all people have their needs met and

28 https://socialjusticebooks.org/booklists/organizing.
29 Center for Popular Economics, "Economics for the 99%", 2014, https://www.populareconomics.org/wp-content/uploads/2012/06/EconomicsForThe99pct2014.pdf.
30 Movement for Black Lives, Economic Justice Platform, accessed October 15, 2019, https://m4bl.org/policy-platforms/economic-justice/.

can live dignified lives. There are alternatives to capitalism, where inequality is not a byproduct of how we manage our homes. Two of the alternatives to capitalism that people are working on are the solidarity economy and socialism.

Solidarity economy: The solidarity economy is grounded in the principles of solidarity and cooperation, equity in all dimensions (race, ethnicity, gender, class, sexual orientation, etc.), social and economic democracy, sustainability, pluralism (not a one-size-fits-all approach), and people and planet first. This alternative builds on existing and emergent practices, and makes room for many different ideas. Some solidarity economy advocates are market socialists (public or cooperative ownership in a market economy); some favor a democratic, participatory form of socialism; and some do not have an ideological position but are motivated by ethical principles or the simple need to make a living. "While some elements of the solidarity economy have existed for hundreds of years, the theoretical framework is very young and is still in the process of evolving and being defined. There's a growing global movement to advance it as an alternative to capitalism and its current form, the failed model of neoliberal corporate-dominated globalization" (adapted from Economics for the 99% zine and the U.S. Solidarity Economy Network website).[31]

This framework is exciting because of the multiplicity of solutions it allows for and because of the connections to international movements. The people and groups involved in this work are both visionary and connected to real on-the-ground change. I (AB) had a chance to see this firsthand at the Solidarity Economy Conference and through contributing to a book on the solidarity economy.[32]

The New Economy Coalition[33] is "a membership-based network representing the solidarity economy movement in the United States. We exist to organize our members into a more powerful and united force, in order to accelerate the transition of our economic system from capitalism to a solidarity economy." The multiple groups in this coalition are actively working on a just economy based on the seven social justice principles (described in Chapter 1): people are compensated fairly for the work they do, are able to meet their needs, have decision-making power, have physical and psychological safety, are treated with dignity and respect, are able to develop to their full potential, and prioritize an economy that takes into account humans' interconnectedness with the environment. This movement is being driven by an incredibly diverse coalition with a powerful vision for the future. They are weaving together theory and building diverse coalitions. The website of the New Economy Coalition is compiling many of those proposals and visions. Their biennial conference, Common Bound, is an opportunity to learn from people and groups that are putting these principles into practice, like Ujima.[34]

---

31 "Solidarity Economy," U.S. Solidarity Economy Network website, retrieved July 4, 2019, https://ussen.org/solidarity-economy.
32 Ed. Emily Kawano, Thomas Neal Masterson, and Jonathan Teller-Elsberg, *Solidarity Economy I: Building Alternatives for People and Planet* (Amherst, MA, Center for Popular Economics, 2009).
33 New Economy Coalition website, retrieved Feb. 5, 2019, https://neweconomy.net.
34 Ujima is an innovative Cooperative Economic Project in Boston. https://www.ujimaboston.com.

Socialism: Socialism aims to get rid of the problems of capitalism completely, rather than just make them less harmful. It does this by striking at their root causes: private ownership of capital and productive resources, the profit motive, and the impersonal marketplace. As described in *Economics for the 99%*:

> "In socialism, productive resources are owned by the community rather than by the top 1%, economic activity is oriented towards human needs and wants rather than profit, and people democratically plan what they are going to produce instead of letting the marketplace control their lives. By replacing private ownership of companies with social ownership, socialism puts the 99% in charge of the economy and ensures that production is guided by people's needs. Capitalism produces whatever increases the profits of the wealthy. Socialism produces whatever the citizen-owners of the economy want it to produce. And each person has an equal say."[35]

Socialism is continually vilified by the mass media and those who sit in seats of power in the U.S. Yet it has gained increased visibility and momentum recently with two young women. Kshama Sawant serves on the Seattle City Council, and is part of the Socialist Alternative Party. Alexandria Ocasio-Cortez, the U.S. House Representative for NYC 14th Congressional District, and a self-described Democratic Socialist. These two young women ran on socialist platforms and are pushing forward policies like raising the minimum wage and the Green New Deal.

At many times in history poor and working-class people have come together to make change in spite of the odds—to challenge the injustice of slavery, to form unions to end unjust working conditions, to challenge the privatization of the commons, to buy out their trailer parks from absentee landlords,[36] and more. Those in power have consistently used violence and repressive tactics to break up groups that have come together in the struggle for economic justice. Racial division is a core tactic used in U.S. capitalism to maintain economic power. One example of a repressive tactic that is about race and also about economic power is voter disenfranchisement of African Americans that happened from post-Civil War through the 1960s through the Jim Crow era. It continues today through gerrymandering or redrawing of political boundaries, erasing people from voter lists, and intimidation at the polls. The Civil Rights struggle brought people together in the 1950s and 60s across race and class divides to fight for justice. People have persisted in the struggle for voter rights through protests, through political advocacy and legal means, and even through non-violent direct action. The American Civil Liberties Union (ACLU) has been at the forefront of that struggle on the litigation side and there are many grassroots organizing groups that are mobilizing people.[37]

---

35 Center for Popular Economics, "Economics for the 99%", 2014, https://www.populareconomics.org/wp-content/uploads/2012/06/EconomicsForThe99pct2014.pdf (pg. 33).

36 Simon Montlake, "Trailer Parks Face Rising Rents," Oct. 26, 2018, https://www.csmonitor.com/Business/2018/1026/Trailer-parks-face-rising-rents.-This-one-s-residents-found-a-way-out. This is just one example: residents of a trailer park who formed a housing cooperative instead of accepting rising rents or being forced out of their housing.

37 You can learn more about some of those organizations here: https://www.bustle.com/p/8-voting-rights-organizations-to-know-before-the-2020-elections-roll-around-13156367.

Charity vs. solidarity

When we talk about economic justice it is important to clarify the role of charity compared to solidarity. **Charity** is when people who have more than enough choose to give away some of their extra to people who have less than enough. But it's not enough that the givers now don't have extra, and the recipients aren't still struggling. Charity often reinforces existing power dynamics, giving a sense of pride and empowerment to the givers and a sense of shame, forced gratitude, and disempowerment to the recipients. People who are able to give sizable donations to causes get to choose what their money gets used for while recipients of charity have little choice what kind of "help" they get, from whom, or with what strings attached.

Example: When I (AB) work at a food shelf or pantry, I donate a couple of my hours of time to hand out food to folks who need it. In exchange I get all kinds of benefits: I get props from people I know for being "a good person," I feel good about having spent my time helping people who are struggling, I might even get to put the volunteer work on my resume. Although the work of the food pantry fills a very real need, it does nothing to change the economic system that allows and requires some people to be so poor they can't afford food. Nor does it change the social judgement and stereotypes that lead many people to feel shame about needing to get food from food pantries. It lets me off the hook from asking the questions that Dr. King asked in the quotation at the very beginning of the chapter.

In contrast to the charity model, which is premised on separation, **solidarity** means walking *with* a person because our struggles are connected. From a solidarity perspective, when a person with plenty of resources shares those resources, it is with deep respect and connection, instead of pity or scorn. This sharing also happens on the terms of the person whose basic needs have not been met, not the person who has plenty. There is reciprocity—an exchange of skills and resources. There is also accountability for having more resources than is necessary and for shifting those resources towards mutual aid and collective benefit instead of personal benefit. Solidarity shifts the unequal power dynamics. It is a commitment to addressing the questions of Dr. King—to looking at the root causes of injustice and working together for justice, to effectively and resourcefully addressing the systemic issues that are impacting both people negatively.

Example: What solidarity looks like for me (AB) is when I know folks who are struggling with hunger, we talk openly about how the economic system is messed up, how so many of us are getting pinched, and how we share an investment in making sure they have enough food for their kids. We brainstorm creative solutions. I might go with them to the food pantry or to the soup kitchen, resisting separation, stigma, and shame. All food drives and food shelves should prioritize honest discussion about how the system sets some people up to be in need. I have to show up for systems change in ways such as signing petitions for universal school meals (so that all kids can eat daily without stigma), supporting low-wage workers who are on strike, and writing letters of support to the local paper. As a person with class privilege who is in solidarity it is important to be open to being held accountable for my actions. People need to be able to give me feedback about how my privilege is getting in the way of authentic relationship and real change. And if I'm not feeling uncomfortable because of how much I'm sharing (both in terms of time and financial resources), then it probably isn't enough!

Cross-class relationships

If we are going to have successful movements for economic justice, then cross-class relationships are especially important, because movements are made up of relationships. Forming relationships across class is physically harder and harder to do these days because of segregation by class, which has only increased in recent decades. Research shows that we live increasingly separate lives along class lines. In *Our Kids: The American Dream in Crisis,*[38] Robert Putnam illustrates this separation through people's stories and through data about how city demographics have shifted dramatically in the last 30 years to be more segregated along class lines. For many of us, we need to be very intentional about getting outside of our neighborhood if we are going to have cross-class friendships. This is hard to do if you lack resources, so the responsibility of developing most cross-class friendships must fall on those with resources to do so.

It can be emotionally challenging to have cross-class friendships. In these relationships we are constantly confronted with the reality that we have more than or less than our friend. We bump up against our rough edges, our rigidity, our entitlement, our intense emotions, and our cultural differences.

Yet in many ways, cross-class friendships that are built on solidarity improve our lives. They prompt us to share and be generous. They teach us about reciprocity and mutuality. Cross-class friendships are a constant reminder that people are having different experiences in the world, keeping us humble and flexible. They caution us that capitalism is not working for the majority of people. They can remind us that we are more than our circumstances.

Sometimes, in the case of someone with upward mobility, cross-class friendships with people who are lower on the economic spectrum can serve as a reminder of how far we have come socially. Some questions we can ask ourselves are: Is that a good thing? Does it help us feel more grounded in our history? Does it keep us connected and accountable? Does the relationship evoke some sort of feeling in us? We may be able to support a friend who currently has less class privilege by serving as a resource for social connections or more access to financial resources, and can sometimes serve as a bridge to a job or a relationship they are seeking.

In our P4SJ groups and cross-class dialogue circles, here are some tips that come up repeatedly for forming cross-class relationships.

What *not* to do:
When you have class privilege and are forming relationships with people who do not, be sure to avoid these mentalities:

☘ savior (I can save you from poverty),

_____

38 Robert D. Putnam, *Our Kids: The American Dream in Crisis,* (NY, Simon & Schuster, 2015). While he doesn't critique the economic system that is creating this divide, he does provide an important look at the symptoms and suggests solutions that can alleviate the immediacy of the suffering.

❀ pity (I feel sorry for you so I'm gonna be nice), and

❀ tokenizing (I need to have poor friends in my life so I don't look classist).

When you have less class privilege and are forming relationships with people who have more, some things to avoid are:

❀ expecting your more privileged friend to pay for everything because they can afford to, without ever having direct communication about it. and,

❀ expecting your more privileged friend to understand reality from your without having to explain very clearly to them how life actually works for you. One idea here is to point them to resources that will explain where you are coming from without you having to do all of the educating within the relationship—although realistically doing it within the relationship tends to be more effective.

What to do:

Be authentic. Authenticity means genuinely connecting with a person. One way to connect authentically is to find the things we have in common. Maybe we both like to cook or learn about new music or crack jokes. And then we build on our commonalities, finding ways to continue getting to know each other. In an authentic relationship we can be ourselves, even when it means having uncomfortable conversations. This is a commitment to working through any conflict that may arise because of that.

Try this:

❀ Think of a person who you connect with authentically. What are the qualities of that relationship? How does it feel? What are some things that you do automatically? Take a moment to jot down your thoughts.

❀ If you have a relationship in mind, then you already have some skills in connecting authentically with people. If you can't think of an example of a person you connect with authentically, there are great TEDx talks to check out on how to connect with others—the power of vulnerability, 10 ways to have a better conversation, the power of introverts, and more.[39]

❀ How do you use those same skills in connecting across difference? What else might you need to connect authentically (maybe a friend you share in common, maybe more time)? Again, take a moment to jot down your thoughts.

Take time to cultivate. There are many barriers to cross-class friendships, so we have to build these relationships over time. We both (JLK & AB) think of it as a social investment. Maybe it is intentionally sitting next to someone with different class markers than our own at the kids' baseball games over a couple of years instead of always sitting with people we're more similar to. And then after we've built trust and genuine liking of one another, maybe we invite the person to an event or over for dinner, or we do things together as families. There may be many uncomfortable moments—it's okay, that's where change happens. There are also lots of fun times to be had!

---

39 TEDx playlists—How to Connect with Others, retrieved August 2019, https://www.ted.com/playlists/367/when_you_re_having_a_hard_time.

Reciprocate. In cross-class relationships, we are always aware there is reciprocity—we give and we receive. As a person with class privilege, I (AB) am aware of the financial resources I have to offer, as well as the social capital (connection with people who have power and resources) and maybe other skills I can offer (like technology troubleshooting or grant writing). I am ready and willing to share these resources. Here are some of the amazing gifts I receive from my poor and working-class friends:

- ❀ Flexibility. I want things to start on time, and often there are reasons things don't start on time. I have received the gift of being okay with that. This has benefited me in cross-class relationships, and also in so many other ways in my life. I'm more flexible with my kids, my family, my workplace, you name it
- ❀ Resourcefulness. I learn so much from friends who have lived with less than me. Recently some friends taught me how to fill up my oil tank when I was going to run out of oil to heat the house. They knew who to call and what to do in the meantime. This benefitted me personally in that moment, increased my respect for my friends' deep well of practical and creative problem solving skills, and has encouraged me to think outside the box whenever problems arise.
- ❀ Delicious food. My most fun and delicious cooking experiences have been in cross-class and multi-racial groups. I have found that more time is spent preparing food and that meals are made in bigger quantities so that all people are taken care of (although definitely not always). And although it may not be local/organic/whatever, it is certainly tasty. Folks with less access to financial resources often seem to have a keen knack for making a tasty dish. Plus, food is such an amazing connector!
- ❀ Humor. I never laugh harder than when I'm hanging out with my poor and working-class friends, because they tend to have well-developed senses of humor and are less inhibited about sharing it. I think this is because of a direct daily experience of oppression and the need to survive it and thrive in spite of it. Humor is a coping strategy in times of hardship, but even when times aren't hard, humor brings joy and connection. It also makes me notice how some people in middle-class culture are taught to suppress humor or laughter in order to come across as dignified, but at such cost! The humor in cross-class relationships has helped me remember ways of connecting that I was trained out of.

I could go on and on. My life is so much more fun and beautiful and real and happy because of my friends who have less class privilege.

Be generous. Generosity is essentially the practice of giving freely, and there are many things people can be generous with. People with class privilege have been generous in sharing with me (JLK) by introducing me to new social contacts that I otherwise would have most likely never met given my economic status and social class. People have also covered expenses that provide some sense of respite or fun for my family that I did not have the ability to divert funds to, such as paying for my kids and I to take a ride on the Polar Express Train or for tickets to the Champlain Valley Fair. My (AB) friends who are poor and working class are extremely generous with gifts. I have so many examples. Yesterday a friend who comes from generational poverty gave me some social justice kid's books for my Parenting 4 Social Justice project. And I'm generous right back at her. I know she is struggling with making rent this month and so I offered to spot her until her paycheck comes through (she thought about it for a few days and then agreed to receive the loan).

Participate in mutual aid. Mutual aid is basically generosity, on a larger scale. Just like animals in the wild who form symbiotic relationships in order to not only survive but thrive, humans who form community support outside of government authority also survive and thrive. You help me out, I help you out, without the feeling that one offering is better than the other. Mutual aid is a missing piece of the puzzle in working for justice. So often we aren't in close enough relationship to each other to share directly with each other. People with resources can give money to organizations without ever having to talk directly with someone who would be receiving support. And people without resources have to go through a mid-level organization to get the resources they need. This arrangement does nothing to interrupt the unjust economy. Mutual aid requires relationship, and thus is necessary for both redistribution of resources in an unequal economy and for interrupting our current erroneous beliefs (e.g., poor people are lazy, rich people are stingy, there isn't enough).

These relationships across difference make our lives better in material and emotional ways, they make our communities stronger, they motivate us to participate in movements for justice, and they create the fabric for the just and equitable world we envision.

In summary

Class is a feature of the capitalist economy. This economic structure is inherently unequal and harmful. We each have a class story and position, and it is important to learn and be able to talk about our class identity. Capitalism is not the only possibility—a just and equitable economy is possible. People are (and have always been) resisting current harmful policies and organizing for just alternatives and a just economy. In working for a just economy is it crucial to shift from a charity mindset to a solidarity model. Investing in cross-class relationships is important for the foundation of economic justice movements. Let's do this! Get involved! Power to the people!

Your Turn:

  ❀ "Wealth Inequality in America"[40]
  ❀ "The new gilded age: Income inequality in the U.S. by state, metropolitan area, county," a report on inequality from the *Economic Policy Institute*.[41] This report

---

40 Politizane, *Wealth Inequality in America,* November 2012. https://www.youtube.com/watch?v=QPKKQnijnsM&ab_channel=politizane. As of 3/12/19, it has been viewed 22 million times.
41 Estelle Sommeiller and Mark Price, "The new gilded age: Income inequality in the U.S. by state, metropolitan area, and county", Economic Policy Institute, July 19, 2018, https://www.epi.org/publication/the-new-gilded-age-income-inequality-in-the-u-s-by-state-metropolitan-area-and-county.

includes a chart where you can see by state what the difference is between the income of the wealthiest 1% and the income of the bottom 99%.

❋ The Next System Project has a four-minute video about the need for a new economic system,[42] or if you prefer, read a few articles from their website.[43]

❋ Interactive website from Class Action on seeing class cultures. Take the quiz on class culture traits![44]

Then pick a few of these projects to learn about:

❋ **Poor People's Campaign:** A National Call for a Moral Revival is continuing Dr. Martin Luther King Jr.'s work—uniting people across the country against systemic racism, poverty, the war economy, and ecological devastation. https://www.poorpeoplescampaign.org

❋ **Fight for 15** is organizing food-service workers to advocate for increasing the minimum wage to $15/hour in the U.S. They have win after win. https://fightfor15.org

❋ Read about the power of worker owned co-ops as described by the **Democracy Collaborative**. https://community-wealth.org/content/worker-cooperatives

❋ **The Boston Ujima Project** is putting the solidarity economy into practice. https://www.ujimaboston.com

❋ **Honor the Earth** is protecting Native American lands with a vision of a sustainable future for Native communities. http://www.honorearth.org

❋ **Cooperation Jackson** is building a solidarity economy in Jackson, Mississippi, anchored by a network of cooperatives and worker-owned and democratically self-managed enterprises. https://cooperationjackson.org

Reflect

1. What is your class experience? What factors have impacted your class experience?
2. How is inequality showing up in your house? Is it making it nearly impossible to pay the bills? Is it making you say things like "we don't have the money for that" more often than you'd like? Or have you not even had to think about it?
3. What emotions and body sensations come up for you as you read and think about extreme wealth and poverty?
4. Which key values of the capitalist economy (profit, extraction, growth, individualism, competition, and monopoly) have you internalized, and where do they show up in your thinking and actions?
5. What are some things you are doing to shift your thinking and actions towards well-being, regeneration, sustainability, relationship, cooperation, and collective ownership?

---

42 "The Next System Project," March 30, 2015, https://www.youtube.com/watch?v=d6z4yDu3gc0&ab_channel=TheNextSystemProject.
43 The Next System Project website, retrieved Sept. 13, 2019, https://thenextsystem.org.
44 "Working for Social Justice Goes Better When You Understand Class Cultures," retrieved Sept. 13, 2019, http://www.activistclasscultures.org/#about-marquee.

6. What is your vision for economic justice? How would economic justice impact your family?

Talking with kids about class and economic justice

After reading all about class and the economy, you might be pondering how your class experience growing up and your class location today is impacting your parenting. Parenting for economic justice is important regardless of how much money we have, but just like with racial justice, it will look different depending on the amount of class privilege we have. We give our kids powerful messages every day in the ways that we talk about money, how we spend money, what we encourage them to do with money, how we respond to the very real basic needs of members in our community, how we show up for economic justice (or not!), and how we interact with people who have a different class background than we do. And those messages have been formed by the larger economic system we are all living in and our class location in it.

Having a better understanding of how class shows up in your own thinking and action is important for shifting the conversations in your house.

Your turn:

Here are some key questions to ask ourselves about the kinds of messages we are giving our kids. Take some time to reflect on these questions and jot down your answers.

- Do we teach our kids to put their own well-being above others (think of the game Monopoly)? Or to take action with the collective well-being in mind? (Try Co-opoly!)[45]
- Do we teach our kids to respect and value work done by janitors, laborers, childcare providers, and food service workers as much as the work done by doctors, lawyers, financiers, and managers? Do we believe in and talk about equitable compensation for the work that people do?
- Do we teach our kids to share what they have, not in an "I feel sorry for you" kind of way (charity), but in a "we are all in this together" kind of way (solidarity)?
- Do we teach our kids that there is not enough to go around (scarcity)? Or that there is enough for us all (abundance)?
- Do we teach our kids that the way things are today is the only way, no matter how awful it may be? Or to stand up for economic justice no matter how out of reach it may seem?

Sample conversations

Here are a few sample conversations to get you started in thinking about how conversations with your kids might go. These examples include lots of things that you can say, but in a real conversation you might not say them all at once.

---

45 On Toolbox for Education's website, retrieved Sept 13, 2019, http://store.toolboxfored.org/co-opoly-the-game-of-co-operatives.

If your family is poor or working class . . .

Here are messages you can pass on to your children from the time they are born:

"You are beautiful, smart, and courageous. Each human is beautiful, smart, and courageous. Do your best. We are all doing our best. We are connected to each person in our community; we take care of each other and we share. If another person is hurting, we are also hurting."

With your preschooler:

Child: "Momma, why can't I have my own room?"
Caregiver: "I hear that you wish you could have your own room. Right now, this is the amount of space that we have to work with and that means that you have to share a bedroom in the same way that we all share the kitchen."

Another preschool example:

Child: "Daddy, can you buy me a Barbie Dream House?"
Caregiver: "Honey, a Barbie Dream House is very expensive to buy from a store brand new. For the same price of one Dream House, Daddy could pay for a weekend getaway at a hotel with a pool for the whole family! And as much as Daddy wishes he could afford to do something really fun like that, right now, we have to focus on paying for all of the stuff we need as a family. Maybe we can start to save up a little bit here and there and try to find you a doll-house at the thrift store or at a garage sale in the summer."

With your elementary-age child:

Child: "Why can't I have Nike shoes?"
Caregiver: "I know that other kids at school have Nikes and that you not having them makes you feel really left out. However: #1. There are far more important things for us to spend our money on than name-brand shoes. #2. You have decent shoes on your feet right now and do not need new shoes. #3. Like we've talked about when we read that book about factories, the conditions in the factories where those shoes are made are awful, and the people who own Nike are making millions of dollars. Nike doesn't deserve our money. We will not support corporations that do not take proper care of their workers."

Another elementary-age example:

Child: "Mom, why are you out of work again?"
Mom: "Honey, it's gonna be okay, I'll make sure we don't have to go without heat again, I heard there is fuel assistance support from the state."
Child: "Okay, can I help? Maybe I could sell my bike."
Mom: "You can help by doing the dishes tonight so I can make some calls. Keep your bike, you need that. I want you to know that it really isn't fair that our family has to go through hard times like this. My boss doesn't want to give up his $300,000 salary so he lays off people like us when the company hits hard times. We gotta fight for better for us and for people like us—all people deserve to not have to worry about feeding their family.

If your family has class privilege (middle class, professional class, owning class) . . .

Here are some messages you can pass on to your children from the time they are born:

"You are beautiful, smart, and courageous. Each human is beautiful, smart, and courageous. Do your best. We are all doing our best. We are connected to each person in our community—we take care of each other and share. If another person is hurting, we are also hurting."

With your preschooler:

Child: "Why do we have to take this food to the food shelf?"

Caregiver: "We want to make sure everyone in our community has full bellies. We are sharing what we have with our neighbors."

Another preschool example:

Child: "I don't like him, he smells."

Caregiver: "Sometimes you smell, too! And how you smell doesn't have anything to do with how wonderful you are. That's true for your friend too. What do you like about him?"

With your elementary-age child:

Child: "Is _____ really hungry? There really is no food at their house?"

Caregiver: "Yeah."

Child: "Why?"

Caregiver: "It's complicated and there could be lots of reasons. But one thing we know is that what people are paid for the work they do right now is not actually enough to pay for rent, electricity, and all the other bills. Sometimes food is the one thing that people can cut back on. Often people will go hungry so they can pay rent and keep the house warm enough. It doesn't have to be this way. We could make sure that people are paid enough for their work to cover basic expenses. There are many ideas and one idea is the Universal Basic Income. Do you want to research more about it with me?"

Another elementary-age example:

Child: "Why can't I buy Nike shoes?"

Caregiver: "You have plenty of shoes. The conditions in the factories where those shoes are made is awful, and the people who own Nike are making millions of dollars. We want to do our best to avoid supporting that industry. I know you want the cool shoes, but it's not very cool to support corporate control. Change what is cool!"

Following are real-life conversations that parents are having with their kids. Here is a relatively simple and straightforward conversation:

> **Ei Ei Samai is a mixed identity mama, whose personal politics are shaped by a childhood in post-colonial Burma, adolescent years in Silicon Valley, and adulthood in the six continents in which she has lived, studied, and traveled. She has two boys, three-and-a-half years apart. Her primary professional mission is to make the world a safer, kinder, fairer place for children all over the planet through her contributions.**
>
> O = Four and a half year old, the asker of the whys
> M = me, mama, master answerer of the mentioned whys
>
> **O:** Mama, why is that guy sleeping there?
> **M:** He doesn't have a house to sleep in, honey.
> **O:** Why not? Why doesn't he get cold?
> **M:** I'll bet he does get cold. I think everyone should have a warm and safe place to sleep. What do you think?
> **O:** Yeah! Then they can have a place to keep their toys and they won't have to wake up when it's cold. And they can cook a little something and get up in the middle of the night and go pee-pee. And have a little snack if they want to.
> **M:** Hahaha. Yes, exactly! Wouldn't that be nice?

Below is a more complex conversation that partly has to do with class, but also with other identities and beliefs that are related to class identity. Issue-based politics, like whether or not you support abortion, is often related to one's class position. There are also class dynamics present in this disagreement even though it's not directly about class.

> **Written by SJ Muratori, a 43-year-old white, working-class, cisgender, queer woman.**
>
> *Scene: My almost-seven-year-old daughter, Vera, and I are walking our dog in our working-class neighborhood. We stop to chat with a neighbor who is setting up for a tag sale. Standing too close to me and my daughter, a sixty-something white man declares that the tag sale will benefit the local crisis pregnancy center and that we must support it.*
>
> **Man:** You know the center, right?!
> **Me:** Yes, I believe it's a place that tricks pregnant women who are seeking abortions into keeping their pregnancies.
> **Man:** Well we don't want abortions; abortions are murder!
> **Me:** Yes, abortions are sad, but not everyone can keep their pregnancy.

Man: [Continues with his "murder" refrain]

Me: [Holding my daughter's hand, walking away] Well I disagree.

Vera: [Out of earshot of the man] Mama, you and that man don't like each other?!

Me: No, sweetie, it's not that we dislike each other; we just disagree about women's bodies. I believe a woman should have full control of what she does with her body, including ending a pregnancy if she is not ready or able to have a baby.

Vera: What does that mean? And why was that man saying abortions are murder?

Me: Well, some people get really upset because they think an abortion is killing a baby, which is understandable, but often people's objection to abortion is more about controlling women than protecting a baby. [The blastocyst and then the fetus] can't live without the pregnant body, and often the body naturally aborts a fetus if it's not healthy enough, and that's not murder; that's best for everyone.

Vera: How does an abortion happen?

Me: Often through a procedure called a D&C, which is sort of like a little vacuum.

Vera: Does it hurt?

Me: Only a teensy weensy bit for some people.

Reflections: I did not tell my daughter that I had an abortion when I was 19. I did not tell her that she would not exist and that I would be an unimaginably different person today if I hadn't had one. I just breathed in thanks and a bit of sadness, thinking of all the young people/students I love and care for in my profession who are around the same age of the child I would've had and feel so grateful that I can be here for them and my daughter because I had access to a safe and legal abortion.

Claire Halverson is Grandma to six-year-old Annika and two-year-old Gavin, and she loves spending time with them. She is a professor emeritus from the School for International Training where she taught in the Social Justice in Intercultural Relations Master's program. She is currently a social activist engaged in issues of racial justice and aging.

My daughter Renya and her husband Aaron were talking with their five-year-old daughter Annika about how President Trump was separating parents from children who were coming into the U.S. at the Mexican border. They also told Annika that there were organizations close to the border who were working to change that and to help the families coming across.

Annika wanted to help out by having a lemonade stand, but since there weren't enough people coming by to buy lemonade, she and her parents came up with another idea. The parents would reach out to their contacts to see if they would send money to Annika so she could send it to RAICES (https://www.raicestexas.org). In exchange, Annika would send the people who donated a drawing of their family (see above). She raised $128 for RAICES and they sent an email thanking her and said they would post the story on their website.

Renya and Aaron realized this project was too abstract for Annika, because she didn't know the people who were donating or the people who would be the recipients. They wanted to do something more concrete and experiential, which is more age appropriate for a five-year-old (and for all of us). A church where they lived was delivering meals to people who needed food for Thanksgiving. They were cooking food for hundreds and hundreds of people. I went with Annika and we got to help out by cutting pies, loading up plates, etc. She didn't get to see where the food was going, but she got to participate with other people who were doing something to help out.

These kinds of experiences were also important to me when I was raising Renya a generation ago. When she was five, I took her to play basketball a few times at an inner-city YMCA in Milwaukee, where she was the only white girl among a group of black boys. She attended a desegregated school in Milwaukee. I also took her on a trip to Mexico where she had an experience that changed her perspective about poverty: when she spent her days in a childcare situation with a poor family. I believe it is important to support kids who are of a privileged status to have experiences that get them out of being in the dominant position.

By Annika, age 5

María Antonieta Jandres is a Latina lawyer and immigrant from Nicaragua who moved to the United States 12 years ago to continue her education. After being homeless, Maria graduated from San Francisco City College with the goal of giving her family a better future. She advocates passionately for childcare, housing rights, and campaigns to end poverty. María Antonieta wants to leave a legacy for young children and youth by helping the Latinos who come to her business looking for help with their legal or real estate needs, or just a friendly hand that can uplift their strengths.

María Antonieta and her three-year-old son got up early for a two-hour bus ride with other families to Sacramento for an annual convening of 600 families for Parent Voices, a childcare advocacy group. At the gathering they met with legislators and assembly persons to advocate for a Universal Childcare bill that would provide free childcare to families in San Francisco.

María brought her son with her for the advocacy day because quality and accessible childcare is really important to her. And her son knew they were there at City Hall to stand up for their rights. María knows that in leading by example, she can guide him and help him find his own voice. She also does this for many other people in her life.

She always tells her son, "Work hard to achieve your dreams. No matter what situation you are facing, you can overcome any obstacles."

Reflect

After reading through these conversations, we invite you to spend some time reflecting. These examples encourage us to think about the ways that we are talking with the kids in our care, and are not meant to be perfect responses.

1. Where did you notice class in the examples?
2. What could you ask your child to better understand their experience and/or perspective?
3. What felt familiar to you?
4. What surprised you?
5. How might you have responded in similar circumstances?
6. What are you wondering now?

Over a period of one week, notice the conversations about money, class, and other related issues that happen in your home and in your daily life. Journal or make art or music if it helps you to remember and process what you are hearing. After a week or so, think on the questions below.

1. What are some conversations you've had about money in your house recently? What did you do well? What would you change next time?

2. What are some conversations you think are important to have with your kids? What else do you need to know in order to have that conversation? Where will you find that information?
3. Think of a person in your life who you can talk with about money and class, someone who can hold you accountable and challenge you to think about economic justice. Make a plan for talking with that person about what you are learning.
4. If you are part of a practice group, share the different conversations you are having.

Reading/listening/watching together

To shift the messages that our kids are receiving we can read books, listen to music, and watch videos/films that illustrate cooperation, collective ownership, valuing all kinds of work, sharing, and a world in which everyone can meet their needs.

Remember to pick resources that are **mirrors** of a child's personal experience, books that are **windows** into the experiences of others, and books that are **doors** into whole new worlds of what could be possible.

Your turn:
Here are some of our favorite books/songs/shows for starting conversations with our kids about class and economic justice. Choose three to read/listen/watch with your kids. Use these questions as a guide for conversations before and after.

Authors Angela and Abigail read Those Shoes *by Maribeth Boelts to their kids, 2015.*

Before:
❋ What makes you think this book is going to be interesting?
❋ What do you think the book is going to be about?
❋ Does this book remind you of anything you've already read or seen?

After:
❋ What is similar to your life or experience? What is different?
❋ Do you know anyone who might have experienced this?
❋ If you were [a specific character], what would you do? What would you feel?
❋ How do you think [a character] felt when [an event] happened?
❋ What do you wish was different in this book?
❋ What is one big lesson learned from this book?

Read

Ages 0–3

> *Counting on Community*, by Innosanto Nagara
> *Feast for 10*, by Cathryn Falwell
> *Giving Thanks: A Native American Good Morning Message*, by Chief Jake Swamp
> *The Teddy Bear*, by David McPhail

Ages 3–6

> *Night Job*, by Karen Hesse
> *The Streets Are Free*, by Kurusa
> *Those Shoes*, by Maribeth Boelts
> *Town by the Sea*, by Joanne Schwartz and Sydney Smith
> *Two White Rabbits*, by Jairo Buitrago

Ages 6–10

> *Brave Girl: Clara and the Shirtwaist Makers Strike of 1909*, by Michelle Markel
> *Brick by Brick*, by Charles R. Smith Jr.
> *Crenshaw*, by Katherine Applegate (fourth grade and older)
> *Harvesting Hope: The Story of Cesar Chavez*, by Kathleen Krull
> *I Can Hear the Sun*, by Patricia Polacco
> *Just Juice*, by Karen Hesse
> *La Frontera: El Viaje Con Papa / My Journey with Papa,* by Deborah Mills, Alfredo Alva, and Claudia Navarro
> *Muskrat Will Be Swimming*, by Cheryl Savageau
> *¡Sí, Se Puede! Yes, We Can!: Janitor Strike in L.A.*, by Diana Cohn
> *The Benefits of Being an Octopus*, by Ann Braden (fourth grade and older)
> *The Hundred Dresses*, by Eleanor Estes

Listen (see P4SJ playlist on Spotify)

> "Come All You Coal Miners," by Bela Fleck and Abigail Washburn
> "Daughter's Lament," by Carolina Chocolate Drops
> "Hammer and a Nail," by the Indigo Girls
> "Solidarity Forever," written by Ralph Chaplin, popularized by many artists including Pete Seeger
> "The Revolution Will Not Be Televised" by Gil Scott Heron
> "This Land Is Your Land," by Woody Guthrie

Watch

We tried to find shows to recommend on class. We really did! The reality is that there are very few shows that we feel represent poor and working class people in an accurate, respectful, non-stereotypical way, or that don't glorify wealth and "climbing the ladder." We couldn't find shows/movies that name the systems that cause poverty. In most shows people are stuck trying to pull themselves up by their bootstraps or hustle their way out of poverty or make it in a dog-eat-dog world, and when they can't it is depicted as a character flaw or bad luck. Other shows might subtly critique power dynamics, but the messages are too indirect or sarcastic for kids to pick up on and they just perceive it as bad luck.

What we (JLK/AB) do with our kids, and what we encourage you to do with yours, is to ask questions about whatever you are watching with your family that helps them learn lessons about class that the show's creators didn't necessarily intend them to learn. For example, we ask questions like:

1. How does this show relate to your life? What's similar and what's different?
2. What's missing from this show? For example: "I see that it does a good job of having women in lead roles, but I don't see anyone in a lead role who is surviving poverty."
3. Does this portrayal seem accurate? For example: "We see a lot more big houses than homeless people in the shows we watch. Why is that? Why do you think some people live in mansions? Why are some people homeless? Would it really be possible to live in a big, new suburban house on a grocery manager's salary?

In addition to these general critical thinking questions, you can learn to recognize and point out to your kids some common class-related tropes. We want to highlight a few types of shows or movies that have particular flavors of hidden classist messages.

Rags-to-riches or riches-to-rags stories like *Annie, Cinderella, Blank Check*, and *The Little Princess* depict people in poverty who through luck and hard work end up wealthy, or at least further up on the class ladder by the end of the show. Or sometimes the opposite: they start off wealthy and then through bad luck or bad choices end up in poverty. This theme is harmful because it keeps people hoping for that lucky break, blaming themselves for not having been able to change their current circumstances, or afraid to lose what they have. When watching these shows with your kids, you can ask: What do you notice about how kids are treated differently depending on how they dress and where they live? Do you see that in real life? Do you think kids really live like that? What would it feel like to go from having nothing to having anything you could want? What about the friends and family who were left behind? Is it okay for people to have that much? Could it be different?

Shows that highlight working-class people often gloss over the real-life challenges or further ingrain harmful stereotypes. There are a couple shows that do a better job.

❋ *Everybody Hates Chris,* a parody on Chris Rock's life, won critical acclaim for addressing important race and class issues with humor (for kids nine and older).

❋ And Rosanne Barr aside,[46] old episodes of the show *Rosanne* do a good job of showing the life of a white working-class family. The show doesn't gloss over the challenges or stereotype working class folks in a harmful way, particularly the early seasons. The show is definitely still relevant today and worth watching with kids over seven years old.

---

46 Rosanne as a person has said many controversial things in recent years about the Trump presidency and her own transphobia. Her show on ABC was cancelled because of a racist comment she made. Instead of writing her off completely, this is a chance to talk about intersectionality with your kids and the complexity of people's experience and what they believe.

Popular cartoons are also full of messages about class, because the people who created the shows live in a society where everything is related to class! Let's look at two shows to think about how class shows up and how we can support our kids in noticing those messages.

⁂ *SpongeBob SquarePants* (age 5+): SpongeBob is always so happy working as a cook at the Krusty Krab. But in real life people who hold those jobs don't make enough to live comfortably at all, so how believable is SpongeBob's happiness? What would it be like if all people made enough money at their jobs to live comfortably? Plankton craves all the power, he wants to control everyone around him. Does this remind you of anyone you know or know about in real life? What do you think are some ways we can spread a very different message, one of teamwork and compassion, in our own lives?

⁂ *The Simpsons* (age 8+) portrays the "American Dream" of a white suburban family with a father working outside the home, stay-at-home mom, three kids, and a dog and a cat in a three-bedroom home. The father, Homer, contributes very little to housework or raising the kids, while the mother, Marge, finds much of her work unappreciated.

How is our family similar? How are we different? What are some ways that other families live? The grandfather lives in a nursing home, where he and the other elderly residents often are neglected by the outside world because they're seen as no longer having important things to contribute. The phenomenon of nursing homes is linked to class—the more money you have, the better care you get. You might even be able to stay at home and have in-home care. It is also linked to culture. For some families, many of whom are recent immigrants, elders are taken care of in the family home, which then makes it hard for adults in the family to earn income. How is putting our elders in nursing homes connected to capitalism? What do you think we lose out on by not acknowledging what people who have been alive for many years have to offer? What would have to change for older people to be more respected and even honored, as they are in Indigenous cultures and in other parts of the world?

And two more shows/movies that do a better job than most of presenting poor and working-class characters and families in a respectful and non-stereotypical manner:

⁂ *Coco* (all ages): The movie *Coco* is about a boy in Mexico whose working-class family makes shoes. While the family doesn't have middle-class resources like in the U.S., they do own their own small business and it appears that they have enough to get by. The boy Coco is searching for his father, who he thinks might be a famous musician, but then he finds out that his father is someone entirely different: a poor, forgotten musician. It is a story about the importance of family over wealth or fame, connecting with ancestors, and unconditional love.

⁂ *Charlie Chaplin* (all ages): Charlie Chaplin shows are from the first half of the 20th century and illustrate the connection of money and power and the relationship between workers and owners. Kids really love and relate to his shows because of his slapstick humor.

Reflect

1. What did you learn about yourself and/or your kids from reading/listening/ watching together?
2. What else do you need to know in order to have further conversations with your kids about economic justice?
3. How can you turn this learning into action for economic justice?

Taking action

How can you turn all this learning into action?

❁ Keep learning.
❁ Heal from trauma.
❁ Read/listen/watch with your kids and have conversations about what you are learning.
❁ Talk with people from a similar socioeconomic class—share your story, what you are working on, and why you care about economic justice.
❁ Be intentional about spending time with and forming strong relationships with people in your community who are working for economic justice.
❁ Get involved in local work for economic justice.
❁ Support national and global campaigns for economic justice.

Keep learning. Learning is action. Learn your own class story; keep peeling back the layers of the onion to get to the truth and complexity. Notice how bias gets in the way of forming authentic relationships with people of different class backgrounds. Notice how your own perception about the economy and your place in it impacts your ability to have open conversations with your kids.

Heal from trauma. The traumas we have all experienced because of racialized capitalism are real. Practicing healing for ourselves and encouraging healing practices for our children is important.

Read/listen/watch with your kids and have conversations about what you are learning. You've already started doing this! Believe in the power of reading and talking with your kids about class and the economy.

Talk with people from a similar socioeconomic class—share your story, what you are working on, and why you care about economic justice. Affinity groups (meeting with people who share our social identity) can be helpful in broadening our understanding of our experience and in holding us accountable to shifting our perspective. In affinity groups we can often be more honest about our internal dialogue without the danger of re-traumatizing people who have been oppressed or of inviting criticism/pity/tokenization of people who have more privilege than us.

Be intentional about building relationships with people working for economic justice. Whether it is resisting foreclosures or advocating for universal health care, or creating alternatives like time banks and community land trusts, when we put in the time to support efforts for economic justice in our communities, strong relationships across class can follow. These efforts are often coalitions of people of all classes. So this is a place where you can get to know people with a different class experience than you.

Get involved in local work for economic justice. Wherever you live there are bound to be groups working for economic justice. If not, get something started! Here are a few of the groups and efforts we are involved in:

> **Equity Solutions**, which hosts Cross-Class Dialogue Circles for people of all class backgrounds and experiences to come together to better understand their class stories, to build skills for cross-class communication, and to gain skills for showing up for economic justice. There are virtual circles, so you can participate from anywhere. (Internet search: Cross Class Dialogue Circles Davey Shlasko.)

> **The Vermont Workers' Center** is a democratic, member-run organization dedicated to organizing for the human rights of the people in Vermont, currently focusing on universal health care. (https://www.workerscenter.org)

> **Time-banking** is a kind of money. Give one hour of service to another person and receive one time credit. For one person to earn a time credit, however, someone else has to agree to give it. Timebanking happens when a network or circle of members have agreed that they will give and receive credits for services that other members provide. (http://timebanks.org/what-is-timebanking)

> **Community land trusts** provide lasting community assets and permanently affordable housing opportunities for families and communities. (http://cltnetwork.org/faq)

Support national and global campaigns for economic justice. National and global issues can feel distant, yet from a social justice perspective we know we are all interconnected. Here are a few good places to start:

> **The Coalition of Immokalee Workers** organizes for economic justice for migrant farmworkers across the U.S. (http://ciw-online.org)

> **The National Domestic Workers Alliance** organizes for economic justice for domestic workers. (https://www.www.domesticworkers.org)

Resource Generation organizes young people with wealth and class privilege in the U.S. to become transformative leaders working towards the equitable distribution of land, wealth, and power. (https://resourcegeneration.org)

Grassroots Global Justice Alliance is organizing to build power for poor and working communities and communities of color in the U.S. and globally. (http://ggjalliance.org)

Grassroots International advances human rights to land, water, and food around the world. (http://www.grassrootsinternational.org)

Spend at least 30 minutes exploring three of the above organizations or resources or finding organizations that arc local to you.

 *Reflect*

1. What are ways that you are working for economic justice? How do you involve your kids?
2. What else would you like to be doing? Make a SMART goal—specific, measurable, attainable, relevant, and with a time limit. (See page 69 for explanation.)

Examples:

"Our family goal is within the next week to ask our local library to order five to ten books on the book list that they don't already have. We will read the books as a family."

"My goal is to recognize when I have negative thoughts about people who are poor and to interrupt the assumptions I am making. I will remind myself that poverty is directly connected to the accumulation of wealth. Within the next two weeks I will find an accountability buddy to check in with about the assumptions I am making."

"My goal is to heal from the pain of generational poverty and to support my kids in loving themselves despite the messages they are getting from others. I will do this through a daily gratitude practice as a family starting today and by attending the monthly meetings of a local campaign for affordable housing starting next month."

"Our family goal is to set up a meeting with other families next month to talk about the food drives we have been organizing. We want to suggest that we do our food drives while providing education about the economy and how we are all in this together."

Healing justice practice

Jaimie: **Recognition of Truth**

This practice aided me in my journey through Goddard College. I partially attribute my graduation to it! It is also what I have utilized in my equally challenging journey of going from surviving to thriving.

In both my bedroom and the small section of my living room that I have dedicated as my "office" (both locations that I find myself in frequently), I have dry-erase boards filled with quotations. I never actually write down who made the statement, because it isn't about who said the words, it's about how I *felt* when I either heard the words or read them somewhere.

When I hear or read something that I instinctively recognize as *truth*, I write it down. Whenever I feel that moment of truth, when it feels like I have been hit in the gut with a ball of energy, I add it to one of the boards.

Currently, my boards say things like:

- You *always* have time to breathe.
- You are further ahead than you think.
- Nothing in nature blooms all year; be patient with yourself.
- Behind every failure is an opportunity that someone wishes they had missed.
- There's no better way to make something unspeakable than not to name it.
- They wanted me to feed the poor people, but I wanted to ask why are there poor people to feed.
- I have no problem remembering where I came from. The thing I'm trying not to forget is where I'm going.
- I know what my breath is for.
- It would be a shame to give up now.
- Find yourself, lose yourself, and then find others—how to be a human.
- You deserve success.
- Check In: Am I operating out of scarcity (or fear) or am I operating out of giving (or love)?
- Money can't buy you happiness, but it pays for the pursuit.
- Understanding is not approval.
- You gotta nourish to flourish.
- The more vulnerable you can be, the more human you are *being*.

Write down any truth that you recognize on a daily basis, and have your children do the same. Maybe at dinner you can each share the truths you have discovered on your own, then combine them on your own whiteboard or poster to reflect back on whenever you need to hear a little truth, or to share with others when they might need a little truth.

Angela: **Loving Kindness Practice**

This loving kindness practice is adapted from *metta*, an ancient and widely-practiced Buddhist compassion meditation. You can practice it by yourself, and it is also an excellent practice to do with your kids. I do this with my kids at least a couple times a week before bed.

Sit comfortably, with your eyes closed, and calm your breathing.
Say or think these phrases during the practice:
May I/you/they be safe and free from injury.
May I/you/they be free from anger, anxiety, and fear.
May I/you/they be peaceful, happy, and light in body and spirit.

You repeat these wishes, directing them first to yourself and then towards different people in your life.

1. Start by directing the phrases to yourself.

2. Next, direct the metta/loving kindness towards someone you feel thankful for or who has helped you.

3. Now direct the metta/loving kindness towards someone you feel neutral about—people you neither like nor dislike.

4. Next, direct the metta/loving kindness to someone you don't like or who you are having a difficult time dealing with.

5. Finally, direct the metta/loving kindness towards everyone universally: may all beings everywhere be safe and free from injury.

Community of practice questions

1. What have been your *aha!* moments in this chapter?

2. What have been your successes in talking/reading/taking action for economic justice with your kids?

3. What have been your struggles?

4. What have been your somatic/body sensations and responses throughout this chapter?

5. Share your SMART goals. How can the group support you in achieving your goals?

6. What else do you want to learn?

Chapter 5

PARENTING FOR DISABILITY JUSTICE

BY ROWAN PARKER AND ABIGAIL HEALEY

*All bodies are unique and essential. All bodies are whole. All bodies have
strengths and needs that must be met. We are powerful not despite the
complexities of our bodies, but because of them. We move together,
with no body left behind. This is disability justice.*
—PATTY BERNE, disability activist and co-founder of Sins Invalid

*Instead of telling disabled kids 'you can do anything you want if you put your
mind to it,' I think we should tell them 'the things you are capable of doing matter.'
A person can't live on increasingly strained hope that someday
they'll be good enough, especially if all you ever do is tell them who
they are and what they do now is worthless.*
—ANNIE SEGARRA, disability activist

*Students with disability desperately need this type of authentic social interaction
with a wide variety of peers in order to develop self-esteem and a sense of
belonging to a larger community beyond the world of disability.
We can't expect students, or teachers for that matter, to suddenly
overcome their discomfort just because they have a student with disability
sitting in their classroom. We need a "next step" solution toward the
eventual goal of a truly inclusive school system and society.*
—LORIE LEVINSON, disability activist and educator

 Reflect

*Use the following questions as a guide to reflect on the quotations above. You can write or
paint, and share your responses with someone or just think quietly, whatever works best
for your learning style.*

1. What are your experiences with the disability community? Are you or your
   children living with disability? Do you or your children have friends who are
   living with disability? Do your kids attend integrated classrooms?

*Families come in all different forms, some kids have disabilities,
some parents have disabilities. There are many ways of loving
and being together. Credit: Shutterstock.*

2. How does your background with regard to disability affect how you view people with physical or developmental disabilities?

3. How do you approach accessibility in activities you organize?

Sierra signing her speech at a Climate Strike Rally at Santa Fe Capitol—the Roundhouse. (Photo by Global WE; see story on page 203)

A note on terminology

This chapter is written primarily for parents who are nondisabled. We hope that others will be able to take away from it useful perspectives and ideas, but nondisabled parents of children who are nondisabled are the primary target audience. Abigail writes as an able-bodied parent of a child born with a physical difference, and Rowan writes as a neuroatypical person with chronic pain who works with children with developmental concerns. In this module, we talk about physical differences, developmental delays, and mental illness primarily as "disability," even though it is not the preferred terminology for all people living with these experiences. We use "disability" broadly with the understanding that some might prefer not to be labeled that way, because it helps us talk about the commonalities across a wide range of experiences. We recognize the limitations of language in our expression of complex issues, and we trust your capability in managing this challenge to fit your community's needs. This module is limited in scope. Disability justice is diverse and includes a range of viewpoints that would be impossible to fit within a single chapter. We include many resources in this chapter and in the resource list on page 335, so you can expand your learning about disability justice.

When referring to people with disabilities, except for autistic people and Deaf people, we will use person-first terminology, as in "people with disabilities," or describe the specific disability if it is relevant. For autistic people, we will use identity-first terminology as is generally preferred within the autistic community (i.e., "autistic people" rather than "people with autism"). Within Deaf communities and the field of Deaf studies, Deaf with a capital D describes the identity of a person who is part of Deaf culture, while small-d deaf refers to the inability to hear; therefore we will use "Deaf" when referring to culture and identity, and "deaf" when describing the hearing impairment. We recognize that not all people who share these traits prefer this terminology; for this chapter we are using the terms most commonly requested by the respective communities they refer to. When applying the concepts from this chapter, we recommend that readers have conversations with people in their own communities about the terminology they prefer for themselves.

Our stories

Rowan

I grew up in a family where being "smart" (intellectual, clever, knowledgeable) was prized above almost everything else. My twin brother and I were both early talkers, early readers, and more comfortable speaking with adults than with other children. My parents encouraged our curiosities and intellectual pursuits. While these are all positive values on the surface, the heavy emphasis on intellectualism came with some downsides.

One negative aspect of this focus on intellect was the way my parents talked about others. Often, their go-to insults were related to judgements about people's intellect, which implicitly positions people with intellectual disabilities as less-than and unworthy of respect. They also highly prized self-reliance and independence, and those values leave out people who need support in their daily activities.

The way we talked about "intelligence" gave me a warped idea of the worth of people with intellectual disabilities that I am still working to unlearn, and that negatively shaped my behavior towards them. One incident stands out and still causes shame when I think back on it. I was at my weekly church youth group meeting and we were assigned partners to discuss a topic. There was a girl with Down syndrome in the class and when my youth group leader told me I would be paired with her, I made a face. I remember feeling that it was unfair for me to have to work with someone like that. I remember my youth group leader admonishing me, but I don't remember what she said, and my attitude did not change at that point.

The idea that we should always be paired with people similar to us in ability is a dangerous one. It creates divisions between people who have shared goals and should be working together. Social justice movements are often split by these tiny, invisible cracks that make it that much harder to create a better world.

These subtle lessons about intellect and worth have affected my ability to parent appropriately with disability justice in mind. As a foster parent, I care for children from varied backgrounds. We have many interactions that I feel go well, in which I am able to impart my values—respect, compassion, empathy, honesty—in appropriate ways. Other times, I've found myself stuck, or miss an opportunity to address an issue. One example happened when a child who was living with us needed transportation to school, and the only space available was in a VanPool (usually used to transport students with mobility-related disabilities). He was very resistant to this, and when pressed he said, "Kids will make fun of me. They always make fun of the VanPool kids and say they're 'SPED,'" a derogatory abbreviation of special education. It was clear that he didn't want to be associated with special education students, specifically kids with disabilities.

I wish I had taken this opportunity to talk to him about his views of people with intellectual disabilities. I could have asked him, "What exactly do they say about special education kids?" That might have made him uncomfortable, but he might also have told me about some of the ableist things his peers were saying so that we could think through them together. We could have talked about people he knows who are non-neurotypical and explored his attitudes towards them, as well as towards people who might say things about those friends and family members. To address his concerns about being made fun of for taking the VanPool, we could have talked about a script to use with peers who said negative things to him.

That is what I wish I had done. Why didn't I do it? I was concerned about allaying my child's concerns and convincing him to take the bus, because I would not be able to drive him to school due to my work schedule. He had only lived with us for a few weeks, and I didn't feel comfortable having a potentially emotionally charged conversation with him. I was not taught to have those kinds of conversations and didn't have a model for it in mind before that moment. As social justice-minded parents, we need to support each other in getting over these barriers and making these conversations smoother and easier through practice. If we don't create a culture in which these conversations happen regularly, we do all of our children and our community a disservice.

My mental health began to deteriorate in middle school, with symptoms beginning when I was in middle school. Sometimes I was productive and gregarious, and other times I was isolated and irritable. My grades went down, and I spent a lot of time in the school nurse's office managing headaches and anxiety attacks. In high school, I also developed a chronic pain condition in my hip, which made it even harder to focus. Add to this the fact that I had just come out as queer in a relatively conservative school, and I found myself almost unable to function academically. Things began to make more sense once I received a biopolar diagnosis in college, but I was struggling for years without any sense of what was wrong with me; no one seemed to think I had any "real problems," so I assumed I was just inncompetent or lazy.

As a child who had always identified as smart and as good in school, my academic emotional struggles were devastating. My parents didn't understand, either. They knew I was smart, a voractious reader, and a deep thinker; they didn't understand why that wasn't translating to good grades. I hear this sentiment a lot from friends who also have mental health issues. People tend to see us as lazy or willful. If you can do something well some of the time, why can't you do it well all of the time? Today, the people in my community talk about things like mental illness and executive dysfunction on social media all the time. When I was in middle and high school, however, authority figures and peers did not have language connecting mental illness to everyday struggles, and it was easy to view my behavior as laziness or a lack of effort or interest.

Once I started finding words for what was "wrong" with me—why I couldn't seem to be consistent, why my thought patterns weren't the same as other people's—once I found words like "neurodivergent,"[1] I was able to shift away from blaming myself. The vocabulary I have acquired while studying child development has been extremely helpful in undoing my internalized ableism. Categorizing my struggles with this new vocabulary is freeing. The judgemental label of "clumsiness" becomes a motor planning issue; difficulty making decisions is a break in executive processing; sensitivity to loud noises and bright lights isn't weakness, it's a sensory processing difference. Everyone experiences these struggles to some extent, and shifting from negative to neutral language when describing them normalizes my experience. It allows me to move forward when I come to an obstacle. Instead of blaming myself or deciding that a task is impossible, I reframe the issue and plan around it. I give myself extra time to plan physical activity; I ask for help with organizing and prioritizing tasks at work; and most importantly, I'm gentle with myself, allowing myself to take this time and not passing judgement on my abilities.

I discovered that I have a special talent of seeing the world from different perspectives. This has served me well in my work. I'm a developmental specialist in early intervention, meaning I work with infants and toddlers with developmental delays or disabilities. I also support parents in understanding and supporting their children's development. Often, that means helping them manage their reactions to their child's behaviors. We talk about how the world might feel different to their child based on their child's sensory processing. We look at things that might be too bright, too loud, or too uncomfortable for the child that the adult may not even notice. By taking the child's perspective and reframing their behavior as a way to communicate, caregivers find more empathy for the child and are better able to help them cope and thrive.

I spend a lot of time thinking about what disability really means, how people learn, and how to interact with people who experience the world differently than I do. Many of the children I work with receive an autism diagnosis. Parents usually bring them in for testing at my urging. I mentor these parents as their children are given these diagnoses that are upsetting to them, that disrupt their life narrative for their children. I emphasize that the important thing is looking at the world through the eyes of their child and empathizing with their child's struggles and strengths. I get to help parents and caregivers find their way through their ableist preconceptions to a place of empathy and appreciation of their child. It's offered me a roadmap for undoing my own ableisn, too. Sometimes, I get to imagine what I would've liked my own parents to hear as I was growing up—a powerful exercise in emotional repair.

One thing I do to help unravel my internalized ableism is to consume media created or presented by disabled people. In the Facebook group "Autistic Allies," autistic adults provide information and opinions to parents of autistic children. The

---

[1] Neurodivergent is a term meaning those with mental differences such as autism, depression, ADD, etc. In some contexts the term is used specifically to refer to autistic people, but other groups have adopted it as a catch-all term for having brain function that is different from the "norm."

web series *The Specials*[2] documents the lives of several young adults with Down syndrome as told in their own voices. Disabled people of all kinds have written books, made movies or videos, and written blogs about their experiences. From activist blogs to autobiographies, these own-voices materials help me see people as they wish to be seen, and to humanize people whom my cultural upbringing told me aren't fully people. I still have a long way to go in unlearning, but I have made a commitment to do everything I can reteach myself and to learn a new way to see the world and disability.

I still struggle with my mental health. I have difficulty following through on projects and being organized, and my energy levels fluctuate. I often irritate my partner with my circuitous thought processes or my tendency to get stuck on one difficult task, especially if that task would not be difficult for her. I have trouble making phone calls and communicating with people in a timely manner, which can make things hard for me at work. To deal with these challenges, I talk openly about what I am having difficulty with and create systems to help me get organized.

Beyond my daily challenges, I fear the stigma attached to my diagnosis. Although I'm out as transgender at work, I rarely talk about being bipolar. I hide my disability out of a fear that people will treat me differently—to not take me seriously, to assume that I am somehow inferior to them because I am bipolar. I internalized those fears as a child. I try to speak up to challenge these ideas when I can. For example, if a coworker refers to someone as bipolar or ADHD in a negative light, I challenge their use of the word. The same goes for other negative references to psychological conditions that do not affect me, such as schizophrenia. I hope that by pushing people to examine their assumptions about mental illness and disability, I can make a world that is safer for me and for others like me.

One thing my mental health issues have given me is a lot of patience for other people. I empathize with people who are not efficient at their jobs or who don't get back to me right away, and I understand that everyone is doing their best at any given moment, even if their best is not meeting my particular needs. I can be part of an anti-capitalist society where everyone contributes what they can without worrying about whether someone is contributing "enough." That is what unlearning ableism is all about—making the world easier, safer, and more connected for everyone.

Abigail

I grew up white, middle-class, able-bodied, and cisgender—in other words, fully a part of the dominant culture in the U.S. I also grew up in the 1980s and 1990s as part of the "colorblind culture," in which recognizing or naming differences among people was frowned upon. The dominant narrative among white people at the time was that if we see everyone as human, and do not notice racial differences (and, I believe, disabilities), then we all will be the same and the world will be a much better place. The message was reinforced through songs, books, posters, and the total absence of conversation around race or disability. I learned early on that I shouldn't voice questions or observations

---

2 *The Specials* is a TV show about five friends with intellectual disabilities in Brighton, UK, who share a house together: https://www.the-specials.com.

about people being different from me, simply from observing that the adults in my life didn't engage in these conversations.

The first time I remember an adult in my life explicitly talking about race was as a teenager, when a Black neighbor said in casual conversation that her best friend was white and that they didn't have any problems with each other. I remember feeling like this conversation was a bit illicit, and I didn't know how to respond or what to think. For me, this silencing of honest conversation around race influenced my thinking on disability as well. Special ed students in my schools were on a completely different program, and not part of the larger school culture. Children with disabilities who were mainstreamed into my classrooms seemed like trouble-makers, and there was no conversation around why unfamiliar or disruptive behaviors were happening. The lack of explanation led me to form my own opinions, without support from adults. Like most kids, I believed my experience to be the norm, and that everyone should be like me. Without guidance to teach me otherwise, at least with regard to disability, I developed an ableist perspective.

In my childhood, I had a few great opportunities to develop friendships with people with disabilities: notably, the brother of a good friend from elementary school who had cerebral palsy, and a middle-school classmate who was deaf (because I don't know the person now and don't know if she identifies as part of Deaf culture, here I will use the word "deaf" instead of "Deaf"). These relationships were hard because they came with unfamiliar challenges that I was unequipped to manage without support. Some relationships take extra work, and the pathways I might have used to get to know someone with a physical difference or a disability were unfamiliar to me.

As a child, my lived experience—that there are differences between people that are visible, such as race and ability—contrasted with the messages I received (that if I could ignore these differences, the world would be better). I saw that my friend's brother with cerebral palsy was different than mine, but because I'd been taught that everyone was the same or that I should treat everyone the same, the mismatch between what I'd been taught and what I was seeing felt confusing and frightening. As a child, I didn't have the internal resources to overcome this confusion, and so it was easier to just ignore the boy with cerebral palsy in favor of easier, less-confusing relationships. In middle school, my deaf classmate and I exchanged phone numbers and talked once through the help of an adaptive phone that she had. The logistics of the exchange felt awkward; I was not a socially confident child and gave up quickly. I wish somebody had said to me, "This friendship is going to require some extra steps. That's okay. It's worth it and it's right that you take those extra steps to meet this person halfway." I didn't get that guidance, and I backed away from the relationship.

Rather than teaching children that we're all the same and then shushing them when they ask in public why that person over there is fat, short, missing a leg, walking with a limp, in a wheelchair, screeching and flapping his arms, or whatever difference they notice, we can and should fill in the gaps in their knowledge. In these moments, children are genuinely asking us for information about the world, and there is nothing wrong with their curiosity. Children can be given information in a way that is respectful both to them and to the person about whom they are commenting. Rather than the false message that all people are the same, we can share with them and celebrate the ways that people are different, and what those differences might require of us. How can we approach, support, befriend, and learn from people who are different from us? How can we walk children through the extra work needed to create a relationship with a classmate who is different than they are, whether because of brain chemistry, an extra chromosome, race or class difference, hearing impairment, a developmental delay, or a physical difference?

I am the mother of two children, ages six and ten. My older son was born with physical anomalies that affect his arms and hands and his face and ear, as well as his hearing. When he was very young, some visiting family members proclaimed that they didn't even notice the difference, as if to assure me that I had nothing to worry about. I was not worried about his physical differences, nor was I apprehensively watching people's reactions and hoping they wouldn't notice him. I knew that people did notice his differences, and that was okay with me. Having two people who loved my child tell me that they didn't even notice a significant part of his body felt strange, disingenuous, and like a devaluation of who he is.

This is the disability version of colorblind racism—claiming we don't see differences rather than addressing how those differences impact our relationships with one another, as well as people's ability to access public spaces, education, and community events. My child's unique body is part of who he is and it affects the way he operates in the world and the way the world relates to him. There is no way to separate him from the physical anomalies that he was born with; we can't know who he would be without his unique experiences, but I assume that he would be a completely different person, as would I be a completely different parent without him and his experiences to guide me. I don't want people not to notice or to pretend not to notice his body. I want them to notice him, and to see the amazing ways that he has learned to function and thrive in a body that is different than a typical child's. I want them to expect him to excel, to push him toward greatness, and to understand when he does things differently than typical kids.

The first time I really understood that parenting a child with special needs[3] would require me to step up to the plate in a different way was when my child was very young. He wasn't nursing well, he cried constantly, and he was skinny. I knew in my bones that something wasn't right, but my midwife continually assured me that everything was fine. "You were made to do this, and he was made to do this," she said again and again. I figured out that my baby was starving at about six weeks of age. Unfortunately, what the midwife had meant was that typically developing babies were made to breastfeed effectively, and she wasn't able to see that there might be some different motor functioning at work that made it hard for my son to nurse. I realized then that I had to be an advocate for my child as a unique individual who may never follow the rules or developmental patterns that the typical child follows. This continues to be true.

---

3 While I use "disability" in most of this section, I don't use it in reference to my son, because it is not a description with which he identifies. I use "special needs" here because that is a more comfortable identity for him.

Parents and educators who work with children with disabilities can expect that these children will solve challenges differently than typical children do. Our responses to these children and our classroom strategies for them should be developed with an appreciation for each child's unique abilities. Our expectations of children with disabilities can be high, but they shouldn't be based on the expectations of a typically developing child.

Parenting my son, it has been very important to me to normalize his experience, for him and for those in his community. He has a rare combination of physical differences that could lead to him feeling isolated. Creating a community of support for him felt very important, so we wanted to make sure that we were spending time with other people with similar physical differences. For example, as a family we've attended the Helping Hands gathering outside of Boston for eight of his ten years. This gathering brings together families of children with upper limb differences for a weekend at a hotel. The hotel is full of children with some degree of limb difference, ranging from a few missing fingers to quadruple amputees, all of them confidently swimming, making art, and chasing each other around the halls of the hotel. Like with other marginalized groups, gatherings like this are incredibly important for kids with disabilities. Having a safe space where others can understand and support your experience is invaluable to creating a secure identity.

As a family, we have always talked openly and freely about his body. As a result, he was able to advocate for himself and answer people's questions confidently and securely from a very young age. He is empowered to answer differently depending on how he is feeling; sometimes he answers people's curious questions with a short one-word response, sometimes with a longer explanation, and sometimes with humor or sarcasm. When he was first starting school, he and I went into his classroom with X-ray pictures, an old cast, and some baby pictures and gave a presentation so that the children could ask questions and have their concerns alleviated. This helped to establish a base of support among his peers, whose new knowledge allowed them to become allies.

As my son gets older and more independent, my role in his life has shifted. Increasingly, he is responsible for his own story. Several years ago on the playground a group of older children surrounded him, commenting and asking him questions. They weren't unkind, just aggressively curious, and so I held back and waited for his response. I asked him later what he would have liked me to do in that situation and what he would want from me in the future. Would he like for me to step in? "It's okay, Mom," he said matter of factly. "I do this all the time."

The world is curious and nosy and bossy, and people are, in turn, callous, kind, and ignorant; as his parent, I cannot change this and it's not my job to protect him from everything. My job as his parent is to help him develop confidence and to feel empowered to own his story, and to tell it when he wishes to, in whatever way he chooses. As an ally, my job is to listen, to educate his teachers and community members, and to be in community with others with disability, even when it takes work. As parents of able children, our role is to help our children develop the strategies and tools they need to be in relationships with children who are different from them.

In addition to my older child, I also parent a child who at this point is typically developing. Like other children, he stares and wonders and is curious when confronted with people who are different from him. Like other parents, I often stumble and feel embarrassed and don't know what to say when he is vocal or obvious about this in public. However, with lots of practice and reflection, I can respond decently at least half the time in the moment and almost always later, after I've given myself time to think about it. I find that relationships and honest conversations are the most important tools that I have to counteract any negative reactions he might have. To encourage honest conversation, I might say something later like, "I saw that you noticed the person in the grocery store who was in the wheelchair. It's not okay to point and stare, because it could make the person feel uncomfortable, but it is okay to notice differences and to talk about them with me. Do you have any questions?" Alternately, I might respond positively in the moment by saying something like, "Oh, yeah, that kiddo uses braces. Isn't that cool? Maybe she wears them because she needs extra support to walk. We can say hi to her by waving and giving her a smile." Because of the relationships he has with his brother, with the children he meets each year at Helping Hands, and with his cousin who has Down syndrome, I think that it is easier for him to be empathetic towards people who experience unwanted negative attention in public.

We talk a lot as a family about how other people don't get to decide what people with disabilities are or are not able to do, that only the person can decide that. A common public response to my older son, especially when he was younger, was overprotection from strangers, especially other children. Older children used to regularly try to stop him from climbing a tree or hanging from the monkey bars, out of concern; witnessing such interactions has guided my younger son's understanding that he cannot place limitations on others. We also read books that feature complex characters with disabilities, and talk about their experiences. I talk regularly about the way that our community is set up, and try to notice when facilities are not accessible or could be challenging for people with disabilities, even if they don't affect the people in our family. If I keep this in mind and talk about it as much as I think of it, then (I hope) my children will have it as part of their regular internal dialogue as well.

My internalized ableism is definitely with me and I am always striving to unlearn old beliefs and form new ways of thinking. I try very hard not to feel any shame when I make a mistake, but instead learn from it and commit to new ways of thinking and behaving. Even as I work on this chapter, I am humbled again and again as I recognize ways that I have failed to be an ally for folks in my community who have disabilities, or remember conversations with my children that could have gone differently if I had been better educated or had committed myself to disability justice earlier. Each time this happens, I take a deep breath and try to imagine myself doing things differently next time. I find it very helpful to read essays and blog posts by people with disabilities; these have been crucial in challenging my assumptions and helping me to see the world in new ways. I can also participate in and help establish a community that is in contrast to the capitalist society at large; this disrupts the dominant culture that expects all people to be productive and instead values interdependency, relationships, and connected community.

Author Abigail's son, Emmett with her niece, Annabelle.

What is disability justice?

What is disability justice? It's not just about awareness, or even accessibility, though both of those are important. It's about creating a new world, one in which our liberation, happiness, and success are bound up with one another's.

We know we want our children to behave appropriately around people with disabilities and to include them in our community, but disability justice is so much more. At its heart, disability justice is about people with disabilities having agency, including the power to choose where they live, with whom they interact, how they exist within community. Much of the disability justice movement focuses on the social model of disability, which is the idea that disability is not a problem in itself, but rather that people face difficulty and discrimination within an inaccessible environment. Many people with disabilities are not looking for a cure or a way to become nondisabled, and feel that emphasis on cure is an erasure of their identities; this is especially prevalent in the Deaf and Autistic communities.

As with any social justice movement, the fight for disability justice is complex and varied; not all disability advocates agree on what is best or necessary for the disability community. Some people with disabilities, especially very painful ones or ones that limit participation in community, do want a cure or better treatment. Access needs do not always overlap and may even contradict each other at times, such as when one person needs low lighting due to sensory processing needs and another needs bright lighting in order to see. The disability justice community focuses on honoring and understanding those differences; the point is not to be completely uniform in our definition of a perfectly accessible space, but to be aware of differences in the community and to find ways to make space for all people with disabilities.

The most important piece of disability justice, as in all social justice movements, is the centering of disabled voices. The phrase "nothing about us without us" in its modern usage originated in the disability rights movement.[4] While it is important in all social justice movements, this concept is especially important to stress within the disability rights movement because so much of the time our stories are told by nondisabled people and disabled narratives are ignored. Many people with disabilities have their lives limited or controlled by nondisabled people. This is especially true for people with mental illness or intellectual disabilities, who may be forced to receive unwanted treatment or be seen as dangerous, or may have very little agency and be infantilized by nondisabled people. Even supposedly positive portrayals of people with disabilities often fall into what those in the movement call "inspiration porn," in which people with disabilities are held up as "inspiring" or "brave" simply for living with their disabilities, which removes agency and further dehumanizes people with disabilities. The disability justice movement seeks to give everyone agency, to give everyone a voice, no matter how marginalized.

The story we are told is the story we tell

Why do we have such a hard time including people with disabilities in any true and meaningful way in our society at large? In a recent conversation I (AH) had with adults living with a wide range of disability (physical and mental), they talked about not being able to find work and how frustrating that is. They recognized the impracticality of the employers actually hiring them, because businesses have a bottom line they need to protect and "someone else will always be more qualified and more productive than me." As long as we are expecting people with disabilities to be "as productive as" their able-bodied counterparts, we will never be able to fully include them in society.

There are exceptions, of course, but for the most part, businesses often do not hire people with disabilities, even though businesses with 15 people or more are legally

---

4 James Charlton, *Nothing About Us Without Us*. California University Press, 2000.

required not to discriminate on the basis of disability.[5] Some of the reasons for this are that people with disabilities might need support or accommodations beyond what is already in place and that businesses see it as risky and not cost-effective to hire them, particularly small businesses. In education, where all children are supposed to be guaranteed accommodations that will allow them to access their education, underfunded and overworked school systems often cannot afford to support students with disabilities effectively.[6] Our entire economic system and worldview need to change before we can expect true justice for people living with disability. True justice would allow people with disabilities to be fully integrated into families, schools, community life, and jobs, with the support that they need to participate. In that way, their gifts, talents, and perspectives would be integrated into society.

Capitalism places a high value on productivity. This is true in our working world, and it also has an impact on the ways that we value humans and their inherent worth outside of the workplace. In personal relationships, we tend toward an expectation of reciprocation, which tells me that I'm only going to do X for you if you are going to do X for me. When talking about people with disabilities, many well-intentioned people suggest that people with disabilities have worth because they can "contribute to society" in meaningful ways; and while they can and do contribute economically, artistically, and in many other ways, what that sentiment communicates is that people who don't contribute in ways that are labeled as valuable under capitalism do not have worth. We need to disrupt this concept of contribution in order to achieve true, connected, community, in which people are not going to give and receive equally.

Our capitalist system encourages people to be strong, independent, and not to admit weakness, but the truth is that any of us at any point in our lives could suddenly be in a position where we need help. When we use capitalism as our society standard, people who are more productive are more valuable, and people who are not fully productive are a liability. Having a disability, having children, or caretaking for a family member are all limitations that prevent us from being fully productive working members of society. The need to protect the bottom line makes it very difficult to fully include people with disability in the working world and in public education. This whole setup hurts all of us. It creates a situation in which we worry (consciously or not) about whether we are productive enough, and what will happen to us if we can't contribute in a way that capitalist society values.

Independence is seen as a sign of strength and needing others as a sign of weakness. Disability justice seeks to turn this framework on its head. Theo Yang Copley writes that "ableism depends on maintaining the myth that we can be self-sufficient if we are strong enough—the myth of independence. Disability justice proposes a framework for seeing oneself that is more relational and transformative—interdependence, in which other people are necessary for physical, emotional, and community health

5 U.S. Department of Labor, "Employers' Responsibilities," November 4, 2019, https://www.dol.gov/general/topic/disability/employersresponsibilities.
6 At a gathering I (AH) attended in Massachusetts in 2017 of parents of children with limb differences and congenital amputations, a number of parents were talking about the benefits of having a 504 plan for their child (a 504 plan provides accommodations and modifications that allow the student to better access their education). Several other parents in the room had never even heard of this and had never been told that their child's school district was mandated to provide accommodations.

and well-being. Interdependency values our connection to others and communities."[7] We need each other. In disability justice we let go of productivity and efficiency in favor of community and interdependence. Disability justice allows us to imagine a world in which we can prioritize relationships and community, and in which productivity is not the most important value.

Disability justice is not about securing equal rights and access for people with disabilities. It is about shifting our worldview to one in which disability is not viewed as a tragedy that has to be overcome, but a difference to be honored and celebrated. It is about creating a just world for everyone.

Examining and Evaluating Our Own Thoughts and Actions

You are your child's first and most important teacher. To instill a sense of disability justice in your children, you must first examine your own beliefs and actions. This exploration involves 1) your language, 2) your values, and 3) your actions to create accessible spaces within your own life and work.

1. Language

What are your go-to insults for people? Many people within the social justice movement have already eliminated some ableist language such as "lame" or "retarded," which is great! However, language goes deeper than obviously derogatory words. The words we use make a value statement about the people who are generally associated with those words. Are people who disagree with you "stupid" or "crazy"? What does that reflect about your attitude toward people with intellectual disabilities or mental health issues, or who are neurodivergent? What steps can you take to change your language in ways that center and support disabled people?

In the article "40 Alternatives to These Ableist and Oppressive Words," S.E. Smith writes, "Imagine if a term associated with your identity was considered an insult. It would sting, right? And every time people used it, they would be reinforcing the idea that people like you are bad and unwanted."[8] Smith follows this sentiment with a list of problematic words and some creative and useful words to replace them. For example, Smith suggests replacing "crazy" with intense, awesome, wild, amazing, or fascinating, and "stupid" with frustrating, pointless, annoying, irritating, or obnoxious.

Even when we do our best to watch our language, we will all fall short at some point. The important thing is to correct yourself, and when you do it in front of your children, explain why what you said is not okay. Then, offer a more accurate word or phrase that captures your feelings without having ableist connotations. You can also do this when watching television or reading books with your child: point out the ableist words that are used, talk about why they might be used, and have your child come up with better words to use.

---

7 Theo Yang Copley, "What Disability Justice Has to Offer Social Justice," Grassroots Institute for Fundraising Training website, November 1, 2011, https://resourcegeneration.org/what-disability-justice-has-to-offer-social-justice/.

8 S.E. Smith, "40 Alternatives to These Ableist and Oppressive Words," Jan 6, 2017, Care2 website, redirected to https://www.msvixenmag.com/www.msvixenmag.com//2018/03/40-alternatives-to-these-ableist-and.html. Check out the full guide to recognizing and replacing ableist words you might be using in daily conversation.

2. Values

Tom Hobson, an early childhood educator, says, "[Children] are always listening. Not just to the words we say to them, but those we say in their presence to others. That is their real classroom. When we adults take that seriously, that's when our children begin to make us better people, the kind who think about the words they say and the tones we use with the people in our lives. They make us work to become the people we've always wanted to be, if only because that's the sort of person we want them to be."[9]

Think about the qualities you praise in your children. If you find yourself praising them for what might be considered "innate abilities" such as intelligence, strength, or artistic talent, think about what you are saying about people with and without those abilities. Do you make it clear that you will support them in whatever they do, even if it does not line up with the values *you* were raised with? For example, many college-educated parents expect that their own children will go to college as well, and find this path to be an important part of their identity. What do you expect your child to achieve? How does that affect their view of their abilities? Your children will follow your lead. Not only will your attitudes affect your children's views of themselves, it will affect the way they interact with people in their community.

Tom Drummond, a former professor of early childhood education in Seattle, Washington, suggests not praising your children at all.[10] He suggests that adults should use narration, non-verbal positive communication, and informational feedback on children's activities and accomplishments. Describing valued behavior reinforces a child's choice to perform that behavior, and avoiding the use of praise focuses your child's concentration on their behaviors and choices—which they can control—rather than their innate abilities, which they cannot control.

Here are some examples of informational feedback:

Instead of saying "good job, you're so smart," describe specific behaviors:
"You turned the piece until it fit into the puzzle. You figured it out!"

Instead of saying "what a beautiful picture, you're so talented," describe the artwork:
"I see that you used lots of colors in your painting. There is a red circle and a blue squiggle."

Instead of saying "good job," describe a child's actions:
"When you helped clean up, it made it so much easier to do. Now it is so much easier to find what we're looking for."

Using this practice with your children can make it easier for children to take others as they are and not consider them based on value judgments about their abilities or disabilities.

---

9 Tom Hobson, "Strive to Be the Person You Want Them to Be," Teacher Tom's Blog, Feb. 21, 2019, http://teachertomsblog.blogspot.com/2019/02/strive-to-be-person-you-want-them-to-be.html.
10 Tom Drummond, "Enterprise Talk: A Handrail to Authenticity," retrieved April 9, 2019, https://tomdrummond.com/leading-and-caring-for-children/enterprise-talk.

3. Actions You Take to Advocate for Accessibility

PLAY DATE CHECKLIST

WHEELCHAIR ACCESSIBLE ? ✓

FRAGRANCE-FREE SPACE ?

ACCESIBLE FOR GUESTS WHO DON'T DRIVE ?

INTERPRETATION THERE ?

CAN WE ADJUST SOUND AND LIGHT ?

(P.S. HOW DOES SCHOOL HELP PEOPLE WITH DIFFERING ABILITIES AND NEEDS ? - FOR FOLLOW-UP)

Think about the kinds of events and activities you choose for or plan with your child. Do you have birthday parties? Arrange playdates? Are you active in your local community? These are all great opportunities to talk with your children about accessibility. If your child is old enough, have them help you brainstorm ways to make your activities more accessible. When planning a birthday party, talk about where the child wants to hold it and how that space might impact the ability of others to attend. Remember that you do not always know if a child or their caregiver has a disability or how that will affect them. This exercise is important even for people who do not currently have friends with disabilities; practice making these accommodations will ease the process when the need for accommodations becomes specific and relevant.

For example, a destination such as an arcade might be too loud or bright for a child with sensory processing disorder, and a ropes course might be inaccessible for a child with a mobility disability. Make a list of questions about accessibility and call or email venues with your child before selecting one. Some ideas for questions:

- ❋ Is the event wheelchair accessible? This kind of accessibility includes ramps and/or elevators, wide aisles and doorways, accessible parking, and accessible bathrooms.
- ❋ Is it possible to make the venue fragrance-free? Ask about what soaps and cleaners are used, and about how to inform attendees about fragrance-free spaces.
- ❋ Is the event accessible to those who don't drive? For example, is it located near a bus stop?
- ❋ Will there be a sign language interpreter available?
- ❋ How loud or bright is the venue? How could it be modified to reduce aspects that might be overwhelming for people with sensory processing issues?

Another way to discuss accessibility with your child is to talk about their school. What does their school do to help children and parents with disabilities? What could

Sister pushing younger brother in a wheelchair on an outing. Credit: Shutterstock

they do better? Brainstorm with your child about potential accessibility problems at their school and create a plan with them to bring an issue to the school's attention. If your child has friends with disabilities, talk about what those friends might benefit from in these situations. Using these concrete personal examples will help your child be invested in accessibility advocacy.

Read

❀ "Interdependency (excerpts from several talks)," by Mia Mingus on *Leaving Evidence*[11]
❀ "Intelligence Is an Ableist Concept," by Amy Sequenzia[12]

Reflect

1. What's your first reaction when you think about someone with a disability? Is your reaction negative or positive? (Disability communities consider feelings of pity or inspiration to be negative, because they are distancing and don't engage with people with disabilities as whole people). If they are negative, what needs to happen in your life to shift your mental framework around disability?
2. What kind of interdependence do you cultivate in your own life?
3. In what ways do you observe the presence or absence of disability justice in your workplace and community?
4. What is disability justice's role in social change? What could your role be in being a part of that change?

Talking with our kids about disability justice

For many parents who are nondisabled, the starting place in talking with kids about disability justice is figuring out how to respond in public when children comment or stare in public upon encountering someone with a disability. Children are sometimes scared of people with disabilities and react to that fear with anxiety. Adults are too, but we usually hide it better! Sometimes children are simply curious, and that curiosity leads them to point, stare, or make comments. As parents trying to raise compassionate, polite children, we are embarrassed that our child would respond like that. We might think, "I wish my child didn't say anything," or "My child is being rude to this person with a disability so I need to get them out of here quickly." It is not our job as parents to shush our children in this situation. People who look or act differently than what's expected get stared at a lot; your child is not alone in making their observation about someone's wheelchair, or the way someone flaps their arms, or someone's unusual gait. How can we stave off embarrassing moments in public places, in which a child rudely

---

11 Mia Mingus, "Interdependency (excerpts from several talks)," *Leaving Evidence* blog, Jan. 22, 2010, https://leavingevidence.wordpress.com/2010/01/22/interdependency-exerpts-from-several-talks.
12 Amy Sequenzia, "Intelligence Is an Ableist Concept," on Ollibean website, retrieved Sept. 19, 2019, https://ollibean.com/intelligence-is-an-ableist-concept.

or loudly acknowledges someone's difference? We can't. These moments will happen and although it may be embarrassing, it's the way that we respond that makes an interaction more meaningful and determines whether it is experienced as negative or not.

In her essay "Talking to Kids about Disability (and Voldemort)," Mary Evelyn Smith, mother of a child with spina bifida, talks about what happens when we react negatively to our children's questions.

> Disability *isn't* bad . . . (but) pointing out our differences makes us uncomfortable. We don't know what we're *allowed* or *not allowed* to say about disability. So we prefer to say nothing. The problem is that our children are still learning the rules. They see difference in the world and they *ask* questions. They see difference and they *speak* it. They see difference and they *point their fingers*. All we can do is react. And our reactions send a message to our children. Our reactions tell them how to feel about the differences they see.[13] (emphasis in original)

Talking openly is key to creating a more just and accepting world. Children notice, and parents notice, when people have disabilities. We should notice! People are beautiful, interesting, and important, not in spite of their difference or disability, but because of it.

Often, nondisabled adults take it too far with the admonishment not to point, stare, or comment. As a result, people with disabilities feel unseen and unnoticed, because everyone is so careful not to draw attention to the obvious fact of someone having a disability. We need to be able to talk openly about disability in order to begin undoing the taboo. A community member who is blind told me (AH), "I can hear people very clearly, and I often hear parents telling their children not to point or stare, or I know they are moving so far out of my way to avoid being touched by my cane. I would much rather be asked questions than be invisible. I'd rather people say hi to let me know they are there." Don't let the people in your town feel invisible! Say hello, acknowledge their humanity, and teach your children to do the same.

Everyone wants to be noticed and acknowledged. Teaching our children to acknowledge everyone is important, and that means letting our children notice differences. Physical characteristics do not define a person, but they are part of a person. It's okay that your children notice physical or behavioral disabilities. Honor this.

So what do we do when our children notice difference and point it out inappropriately? What do we do when they make a rude comment? There is no right answer, but often it's very helpful to take a moment to talk *to* the person your child was talking *about*. Instead of shaming your child, bring them into an appropriate conversation in which you greet the other person as a person, not just a curiosity.

The following excerpt is from Rachel Garlinghouse's essay, "7 Things to Do When Your Kid Points Out Someone's Differences."[14] Garlinghouse provides a step-by-step

---

13 Mary Evelyn Smith, "Talking to Kids about Disability (and Voldemort)," https://www.huffpost.com/entry/how-to-talk-to-kids-about-disability-and-voldemort_b_5781970.
14 Rachel Garlinghouse, "7 Things to Do When Your Kid Points Out Someone's Differences," *The Mighty*, April 7, 2015, https://themighty.com/2015/04/what-to-do-when-kids-point-at-someone-in-public. The

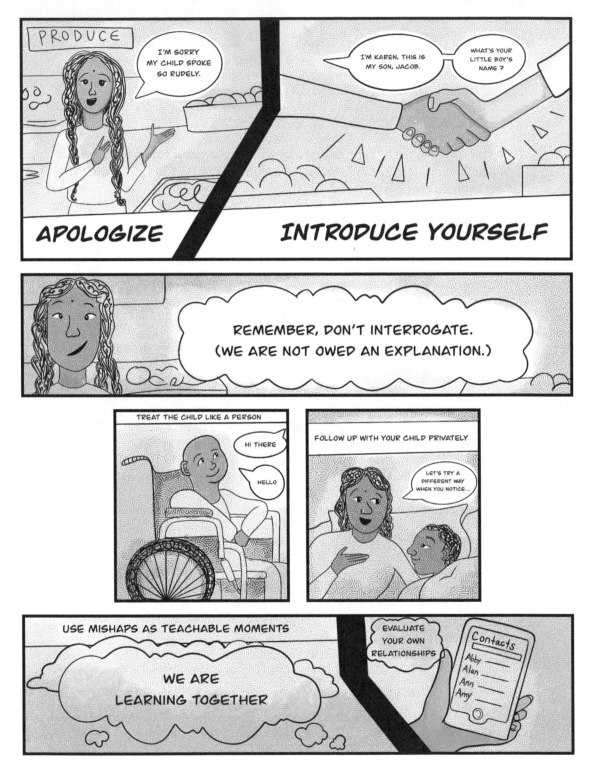

guide to responding in a positive, affirming way to a child's public questions. Here's what she suggests:

> Many of us have been there. We are going about our business when our child notices someone different: the woman with the large backside, the man in the wheelchair who is missing a leg, the child with Down syndrome. Our natural instinct is to shut down the situation as quickly as possible, but doing so sends a powerful message to our children.
>
> Instead of shushing children for stating the obvious, that the person (or family) in front of them appears different, parents can do the following:
>
> **1. Apologize.** When your child behaves rudely, apologize on the child's behalf, immediately and without excuse. Try something like: "I'm sorry my child spoke rudely. He is curious about your son and didn't respond appropriately."
> **2. Introduce yourself.** Follow up your apology with a personal introduction. "I'm Kate, and this is my son Jacob. What is your little boy's name?" Be sure to address the child, as well. He or she shouldn't be ignored. Say something like, "Hi there! How old are you?"
>
> **3. Don't interrogate.** There is no reason to ask what is "wrong" with a child or demand an explanation of the child's condition or the family dynamic. If a parent wishes to share information about his or her child or family, that is their choice. If the child wishes to share, depending on the age and level of maturity and development, that is the child's choice.
>
> **4. Treat the child like a person, because he or she is a person.** Smile, offer a compliment, and make small talk. This is how friendships are formed.
>
> **5. Follow up with your child privately.** Talk to your child about the appropriate way to respond to someone new. This might mean an immediate introduction, offering to share a toy or play together, or even something as simple as a smile or a high-five. Remind your child that it's okay to notice difference, but questions and comments should be reserved for private, family conversations at a later time. You may not have all the right words to explain a situation, but remember that by being open and honest with your child, you are conditioning your child to know that he or she can come to you about any topic and be received with open arms and heart.
>
> **6. Use any mishaps as teachable moments, for both you and your child.** Children will be children. They will say things they shouldn't. If you don't handle a situation well in the moment, admit that to your child and discuss what should be done differently in the future. If you do shush your child, apologize for doing so. And if your child, despite your preparations, responds to a situation inappropriately, talk about how it can be better handled in the future.

7. Evaluate your own relationships. How diverse is your circle of friends? Do you welcome others who are different from you? Do you have true friendships with others who don't share your race, religion, age, or ability? If your child were to look at you and your friends, would they see sameness or acceptance of difference? You cannot expect your child not to be intrigued by someone who looks different when the child is only around those who look and interact just like him or her.

Children are naturally curious and excited when they discover something or someone new. As parents, our job is to demonstrate to our children what empathy, compassion, friendship, and diversity looks like. Shushing is shame-inducing, not inclusion-promoting. Next time, smile, say hello, and give friendship a chance to form.

Here are a few examples of parents we know talking with their kids about disability and disability justice:

Crista is a 47-year-old white middle-class woman who lives in Guilford, Vermont, with her husband and their son, two cats, a dog, and six chickens. She is mom to Nate, who is 11½ and who has Down syndrome. She has been an educator for over 20 years, is an active member of the Vermont Disability Council, and is a fellow in the LEND (Leadership Education in Neurodevelopmental and Related Disabilities) program at the University of Vermont.

Nate is a great reader and started reading all the Black Lives Matter signs in our neighborhood. He decided to make a sign for our house too.

Scene: We've just finished watching a favorite movie of Nate's.

Nate: What is freedom?
[It's clear he has been thinking about this for some time.]
Nate: Is it like getting ice cream whenever you want?

Reflections: Many hours of our day are devoted to answering Nate's questions. It's as if he is working to match the pieces of his life to what he sees in the latest animated box office hit; he wants that mirror of understanding. There are questions that are hard to answer: "What does defeat mean?" and "why no truce?" These questions are big and meaty, and Nate doesn't give up until he gets an answer he is satisfied with. I often think, and have many times observed, how different these conversations are with those who don't understand Nate or believe he is capable of asking these kinds of questions or understanding their answers. And yet even at 11, Nate is showing us that he wants and deserves agency. Every day he communicates his opinions and desires and responses to his life. As parents, we see ourselves as facilitators of that drive. Second to loving him, it is our most important job.

"What is freedom?" Nate came to a fundamental question that I imagine we all wrestle with at some point in our lives. While the answer that worked for him may have been simple and concrete, I so appreciated his effort to try and make sense of that very big word. Freedom. What will that mean for him? And how do we help others value his voice? How do we mirror for him a world with people who see him as part of their story?

Ei Ei Samai is a mixed-identity mama, whose personal politics are shaped by a childhood in post-colonial Burma, adolescent years in Silicon Valley, and adulthood in the six continents in which she has lived, studied, and traveled. She has two boys, three and a half years apart. (In the story, O is four and K is one.) Her primary professional mission is to make the world a safer, kinder, fairer place for children all over the planet.

Scene: O and I are on vacation in London. After getting a little lost in a strip mall, we're helped by a man who notices our confused looks and gives us some information. It is hard to communicate because he speaks only Spanish. Using my broken Spanish and lots of hand gestures, we get what we need. We thank him and part ways.

O: Mama, that guy walks funny. Why?

Me: Hmm, yeah—it's different, isn't it? What do you think about it?
O: I don't know.
Me: Well, you know how you're little and some kids in your class are big?
O: Yeah, I guess sometimes it's different.
Me: Yes. Human bodies can have lots of things that are the same and lots of things that are different. And we can notice things that are different, but we don't ever make fun of people who are different.
[My son accepts this unquestionably as a truth of life, because kids are awesome like that. About an hour later, we're waiting for a bus to take us back to our Airbnb when the same man walks by. I flag him a greeting; he gives me a handshake and O a high five. He wishes us a good day and walks on.]
O: Mama, I'm glad we ran into him! He's a nice guy, right?
Me: Yeah! What a coincidence!

Kristen Elde is a 40-year-old cis white woman who lives in Northampton, Massachusetts, with her husband (36, white) and son (5, white). She loves poetry, running, and working for social change with her family.

Recently my kid has seen a few adults with dwarfism, which has led to discussions about what causes people's bodies to develop in the specific ways they do. I've talked with him about how the most common types of dwarfism are genetic ("information in the cells of the body as a result of the egg and sperm that produced the body") and the fact that, like differences in other physical characteristics, certain body shapes and sizes aren't "better" or "worse" than others. We also talked about how people of all ages are teased and targeted and made to feel bad about their bodies, which is hurtful and something to speak out against.

Some days after, Finn was telling me a story he was making up on the fly. It featured several kids, two of whom had dwarfism and were worried they'd be teased by some of the other kids because of how they looked. The story was cut short, because, well . . . six-year-olds = distraction. Subsequent attempts to get him to pick back up with it have failed, but it's always encouraging to see that some of these conversations we're having as a family are getting through to him.

I picked up a book written by Karalee Braithwaite, whose daughter was born with the most common form of dwarfism, achondroplasia: http://imjustsmall. com. In Braithwaite's words, "I wrote this book to inform other children (from about three to nine years of age) about her condition and to help them understand that despite this difference she is still an ordinary, regular child who likes to play and laugh just like they do." I read the book to Finn the other night and he was into it, so we looked up some short videos on kids with achondroplasia and watched together.

Rowan Parker, chapter coo-author, is a 34-year-old white transgender man who lives in Northampton, Massachusetts. He works as a developmental specialist for an early intervention agency, helping families with children with disabilities and developmental delays to best support their young children. He is also a foster parent who works with teens.

Foster-parenting brings its own set of challenges when it comes to talking with your kids about disability justice. I wrote above about a conversation I had with a 14-year-old foster child, L, about his reluctance to arrive at school in a VanPool (transportation provided by the school, usually for children with mobility disabilities) because he was afraid of being teased (see page 180). If I could do that conversation over again, here is how it might have gone:

Me: Why don't you want to go in the VanPool?
L: Other kids make fun of the VanPool kids, they say they're SPED.
Me: What does SPED mean?
L: You know, special ed.
Me: What do they say about special ed kids that makes that such a bad thing to be associated with?
L: They mean that they're stupid and weird.
Me: Do you think that about kids in special education?
L: No! I mean, my sister is autistic, so I can't think that.

At this point I could have helped L create a script to push back at peers who made fun of him.

Peer: Hah, you're on the VanPool, what are you, SPED?
L: What do you mean by SPED?
Peer: You know, special ed.
L: Is that a bad thing to be?
Peer: Well, you know, weird, stupid . . .
L: My sister is in special ed and she's pretty great.

Reflections: This interaction could have strengthened my child's feelings of pride in his sister as well as improved his ability to talk about disability in a way that centers and upholds the humanity of people with disabilities. When we take the opportunity to talk with our children and help them connect their own experiences to disability justice, we empower them to find their own voice when speaking up against ableism.

Marisa is a Deaf white cisgender woman who lives in the foothills of the Rockies near Santa Fe, New Mexico. She and her partner watch in awe as their two children, 10 and 7, Sierra who is Deafblind and one CODA (child of deaf adult), grow. She runs a forest school program, a school garden, and several other projects at a school for the Deaf.

Scene: Sierra is starting her speech at the capitol. A sign language interpreter voices her words, conveying Sierra's information and tone as accurately as possible.

Sierra: My name is Sierra. This is my name sign [holding name sign depicting "strong/bold"].* Notice that I'm using sign language? I'm Deaf and have several other disabilities, including partial blindness and a brain tumor. Children with disabilities are part of the fight against the climate crisis—we are impacted. We will likely be more affected by climate change [than people without disabilities], and we have a right to clean air and water, same as you.

Reflections: Sierra discusses disability justice within climate activism and offers insight on resilience, interdependence, creativity, adaption, hope, and working together. She knows these lessons through her daily interactions and wishes to offer tools to help people cope with foreboding climate disasters. While watching her numerous speeches, I have observed many different reactions from people. Our experience has often been that the more privilege people have, the more likely they are to have a petrified, deer-in-headlights response. This makes us feel alienated, awkward, and like a spectacle. As Sierra's parent, it's hard because I sometimes deal with people fumbling, saying ignorant things, or avoiding us when we are in public. Sierra is also becoming more aware of how the world views her disabilities as she grows, although she has typically not allowed those views to deter her confidence and desire to be present in this world.

My partner and I work to guide and support Sierra in autonomy and empowerment as a whole person; we pay attention to her needs and follow her lead. This is essential because in many discussions about social issues, disability is left out. And yet our unique perspectives can offer creative solutions to many issues that affect our world. When we advocate for access, it benefits all involved and rarely disadvantages anyone. We are all in this world together, and each one of us is responsible for collective access and liberation.

* "Name signs are a way to identify someone without fully spelling out their name using American Sign Language (ASL). These names often reflect the person's character and are usually devised by someone within the Deaf community." Source: verywellhealth.com/using-name-signs-for-personal-names-1048725

Reflect

The stories above are not meant to demonstrate perfect responses or actions, but rather to encourage us to think about the ways we are communicating with the kids in our care.

1. What thoughts do you have after reading these stories?
2. What could you ask your child to better understand their experience and/or perspective?
3. How did these parents practice an age-appropriate approach to the conversations?
4. What else could these parents have said or done?
5. What could one of the situations/conversations have looked like in your family?
6. What's one way you could be braver in your conversations and actions with your kids?

Your turn:

Read

- "Talking to Kids About Disability (and Voldemort)," by Mary Evelyn Smith[15]
- "7 Things to Do When Your Kids Point Out Someone's Difference," by Rachel Garlinghouse[16]
- "Disability Awareness: 10 Things Parents Should Teach Their Kids About Disabilities,"[17] by Tiffany Carlingson
- "The Spoon Theory," by Christine Miserandino, from the *But You Don't Look Sick* blog[18]

Watch

- "What Is Autism?" by Amythest Schaber[19]

15 Smith "Talking to Kids," https://www.huffpost.com/entry/how-to-talk-to-kids-about-disability-and-voldemort_b_5781970.

16 Garlinghouse, "7 Things," http://themighty.com/2015/04/what-to-do-when-kids-point-at-someone-in-public (and above).

17 Tiffany Carlingson, "Disability Awareness: 10 Things Parents Should Teach Their Kids About Disabilities," Huffington Post, August 2, 2013, huffingtonpost.com/2013/08/02/disability-awareness-parents-teach-kids_n_3696279.

18 Christine Miserandino, "The Spoon Theory," *But You Don't Look Sick* blog, retrieved Sept. 19, 2019, https://butyoudontlooksick.com/articles/written-by-christine/the-spoon-theory.

19 Amythest Schaber, "Ask an Autistic #23—What is Autism?" April 18, 2015. YouTube video, 12:38, https://www.youtube.com/watch?v=Vju1EbVVgP8.

Try this:
Practice asking open-ended and curious questions. There is a difference between hurtful questions and curious questions. When a child sees a person with a physical or mental disability, they might say "what's wrong with . . . ?" or "why does that person . . . ?" or you'll notice your child's lingering stare. Practice curious, polite questions with your child so that they see another way to ask their questions and are ready to engage appropriately with a child or an adult who experiences disability. Tone of voice is also important when learning how to make conversation.

Here's an example. Your child might ask someone, "What's wrong with your legs?" You can help them learn to instead say, "I see you wear braces. Those are interesting. Why do you use them?" The first question implies judgment, and the second is a recognition of the person and an opening for conversation. The first question would be expected from a three- or four-year-old; you can help your child ask the second question while also modeling consent. For example, "My child is curious about your leg braces. Would you mind if he asks you a question? Or would you rather not talk right now?"

It's important that your child understand that people who experience disability have all different personalities and moods, just like anybody else. They may not feel like answering your question the day you ask them; they may have been asked the same question five times that day already. It is not this person's job or responsibility to educate your child.

Show your child some pictures of people with various disabilities, like limited motor function, Down syndrome, limb deficiencies, and blindness. These are easily found through an internet search. Do some role playing with your child in which you each practice an introductory conversation with the person in the photograph.

 Reflect

1. Has your child ever pointed at someone in public and made an inappropriate comment? What was your first reaction? How do you think you would respond if this happened again?
2. Do you tend to ignore people with disabilities in public because the potential interaction makes you nervous or uncomfortable?
3. Does your family have positive interactions with people who experience disability? Is there anything you can do to promote or create these interactions? How do you talk with your kids about the people with disabilities who you know or interact with?
4. What is your family's conversation about disability? Do you talk about what someone's life experience might be in a holistic way, not only focusing on the disability itself?
5. What is your comfort level when thinking about disability or interacting with a person who lives with disability? If you are uncomfortable in these situations, what steps can you take to shift your thinking?

Reading/listening/watching together

As you've experienced in the previous chapters, reading/listening/watching together can be a powerful way for parents to start honest conversations with their kids. It is an effective way to start to normalize the experience of people who are different from you. Include material that features main characters who have disabilities but are not defined by their disabilities.

Remember to pick resources that are **mirrors** of a child's personal experience, **windows** into the experiences of others, and **doors** into whole new worlds of what could be possible.

Sean Stockdale and Alex Strick, authors of *Max the Champion,*[20] write, "We need books which simply include disabled children naturally in the landscape, alongside non-disabled peers. Children also need to see disabled protagonists, without disability necessarily having to be an 'issue' or the central theme of the book. We need books that counter the myths and stereotypes of the past, books which remind us that it's not just pirates who wear eye patches, that 'disability' does not always mean wheelchairs, and that disabled people aren't either bitter and twisted or saintly objects of pity. We need to gently familiarise people with the 'social model' of disability, which explains that people are only disabled by society and its attitudes, not by the impairments. Finally, we also need books by authors who are disabled themselves."[21]

To find great books, movies, and songs, you can talk to your local librarian. If they don't have much to suggest, maybe you can work together to get some good disability justice books into the children's room of the library. You can use the website Goodreads, an online book-review community that allows you to build "bookshelves" and review books. They have specific Disability Justice bookshelves you can browse. And Books For Littles[22] has a handy resource guide and lists of what to look for and what to be wary of when choosing a book about people with disabilities. They encourage choosing books that:

❋ feature a disabled character in their own voice.
❋ are created by makers who are *actually* disabled or who extensively consult with actually disabled adults.

And take care to avoid books that:

❋ give voice to nondisabled characters who talk *about* their weirdo disabled friend/brother/classmate.
❋ feature negative, pathologizing, and condescending language.

---

20 Sean Stockdale and Alex Strick, Max the Champion (Francis Lincoln, London, 2014).
21 Sean Stockdale and Alex Strick, *Top 10 Inclusive Children's Books, The Guardian,* July 19, 2013, https://www.theguardian.com/books/2013/jul/19/alexandra-strick-sean-stockdale-top-10-inclusive-childrens-books.
22 "De-Stigmatizing Disability: Stereotype-Smashing Kids Books," Books for Littles website, retrieved Sept. 19, 2019, https://booksforlittles.com/disability-destigma tization.

Your turn: Choose three resources to read/listen/watch with your kids. Use these questions as a guide for conversations before and after.

Before you read:

❀ What makes you think this book is going to be interesting?

❀ What do you think the book is going to be about?

❀ Does this book remind you of anything you've already read or seen?

After you read:

❀ What is similar to your life or experience? What is different?

❀ Do you know anyone who might have experienced this?

❀ If you were [a specific character], what would you do? What would you feel?

Read

Ages 0–3

Hands and Hearts, by Donna Jo Napoli

I Can, Can You? by Marjorie W. Pitzer

My Friend Isabelle, by Eliza Woloson

Susan Laughs, by Jean Willis

The Animal Boogie, by Debbie Harper

Ages 3–6

King for a Day, by Rukhsana Khan

My Silent World, by Nette Hilton

Max the Champion, by Sean Stockdale and Alex Strick

Not So Different: What You Really Want to Ask About Having a Disability, by Shane Burcaw

Zoom! by Robert Munsch

Ages 6–10

Al Capone Does My Shirts and Al Capone Shines My Shoes, by Gennifer Choldenko

El Deafo, by CeCe Bell

Insignificant Events in the Life of a Cactus, by Dusti Bowling

Joey Pigza Swallowed The Key, by Jack Gantos

The Autism Acceptance Book: Being a Friend to Someone with Autism, by Ellen Sabin

Wonder, by R.J. Palacio

Listen *(see P4SJ playlist on Spotify)*

"Aspera," by Erin McKeown (about overcoming struggle, makes reference to a body changing)

"Whistle While You Wait," by Marian Call (about imposter syndrome/anxiety)

"My Man, by They Might Be Giants" (poetic explanation of paralysis)

"Wonder," by Natalie Merchant

Dragon Tales (ages 2–6; cartoon with a main character who uses a wheelchair)

Steven Universe (ages 6+; on the show, Amethyst represents disabled people. She isn't her "intended" size or as strong as others. And it's clear that the Crystal Gems' Homeworld is deeply intolerant, refusing to accept those who, like Amethyst, don't look a certain "ideal" way. How is this like real life? Can you think of ways that it might be hard for disabled people to participate in/feel a part of our community?)

 Reflect

1. What did you learn about yourself and/or your kids from reading/listening/watching together?
2. What else do you need to know to have conversations with your kids about disability justice?
3. How can you turn this learning into action for disability justice? (Refer back to the experiential learning circle and spheres of influence in Chapter 2.)

Taking action

What can we do to be agents of change? How can we be willing participants in shedding our own ableism in favor of a different perspective that honors everyone?

- ❋ Keep learning.
- ❋ Heal from trauma.
- ❋ Read/listen/watch and have conversations with your kids.
- ❋ Talk with people of similar ability about disability justice—share your story, what you're working on, and why you care about disability justice.
- ❋ Be intentional in spending time with and forming strong relationships with people in your community who are working for disability justice.
- ❋ Get involved in local, state, national, and global work for disability justice.

Keep learning so we can shift our mental and cultural framework around disability from negative to curious and respectful. This requires a big shift. We need to embrace what people have to offer. As in the Annie Segarra quotation in the beginning of the chapter, a true vision of justice is one that accepts people for who they are and what they can truly offer. "The things you are capable of doing matter." All people represent a little piece of humanity and have something to give. All bodies and minds are useful, unique, and whole.

Heal from trauma that results from the ways that oppression related to disability has impacted us—either directly or indirectly. All of us are impacted by a society that believes that only people who are productive matter. Recognizing that harm, and healing from it, is important in shifting our cultural beliefs towards wholeness and interconnectedness.

Read/listen/watch and have conversations with your kids. You've already started doing this!

Talk with people of similar ability about disability justice. Share your story, what you're working on, and why you care about disability justice. Talk openly and honestly about disability and what that means for people in our community and around the world. Let's learn more so that our conversations with our children can be open, honest, truthful, and critical.

Be intentional in spending time with and forming strong relationships with people in your community who are working for disability justice. Form relationships, find out what you can do to support people with disabilities in your community, and create educational opportunities for your kids. My (AH) seven-year-old son recently spent an hour with a man who uses a wheelchair for mobility. After meeting him, without any further discussion from me, he started noticing accessibility issues all over town. "It's cool that the church has a ramp," he observed, "so that Reuben can get in and out by himself. But that shop doesn't have a ramp." Just having relationships with people with disabilities can shift our perspectives dramatically. And you might find out that there are issues in your community that need addressing.

Get involved in local, state, national, and global work for disability justice.

> **Disability Visibility Project** (https://disabilityvisibilityproject.com/about) is amplifying the voices and stories of people with disabilities. Created by Alice Wong, the project gathers stories from people with disabilities. You can visit the website to share your story and hear from people with disabilities.
>
> **Access Is Love** (https://www.disabilityintersectionalitysummit.com/access-is-love) provides resources to support a shift to thinking about access as love, instead of as a burden or an afterthought.
>
> **The National Alliance on Mental Illness** (NAMI, www.nami.org) is a grassroots organization dedicated to mental health education, family support, and advocacy. NAMI hosts walks and conventions, supports people in advocacy work, and more.
>
> **The Buddy Walk** (ndss.org/play/national-buddy-walk-program) is a national event sponsored by the National Down Syndrome Society. It is an annual walk

that happens every October in many communities around the U.S. It is family friendly and easy to attend!

Special Olympics (specialolympics.org) is a sports program started in 1968 that gives people with intellectual disabilities a forum for participating in athletics and competition. Events take place in 170 countries.

Krip-Hop Nation's (kriphopnation.com) mission is to educate the music and media industries and general public about the talents, history, rights, and marketability of hip-hop artists and other musicians with disabilities. Krip-Hop Nation's main objective is to get the musical talents of hip-hop artists with disabilities into the hands of media outlets, educators, journalists, and hip-hop conference coordinators.

Early intervention agencies support children under the age of three who have developmental delays and disabilities. Your local early intervention program likely needs typically developing children to act as peer models in their playgroups. This is a great way to get very young children involved in disability justice. Each state and region has agencies that provide these services—do an online search to locate them.

Disability pride parades happen in cities all over the country, including Madison, Wisconsin; New York City; Los Angeles; and Chicago.

Independent living centers or inclusion centers exist in many towns and cities and offer programming accessible to people with and without disabilities. For example, in Southern Vermont we have an organization called the **Inclusion Center** (inclusioncenter.webs.com). It was started by a mother and son as a gathering place for people with disabilities and their community, and also functions as a mutual support and advocacy organization. The Inclusion Center meets twice a week and the people involved make art together, learn dances, discuss issues affecting their lives, and advocate for people with disabilities. All are welcome to attend. This is a great place to meet people living with disability and participate in their discussions, and find out what we can all do to support their work and struggles. Find something similar where you live.

Your turn:

Spend at least 30 minutes looking through the above organizations and resources and considering ways you and your family could get involved.

 *Reflect*

What else would you like to be doing? Make a SMART goal—specific, measurable, attainable, relevant, and with a time limit. (See page 69 for explanation.)

Examples:

"Our family goal is within the next week to ask our local library to order all of the books on this list that they don't already have. We will read the books as a family and have a conversation about them."

"We have a family friend who has a chemical sensitivity that makes it nearly impossible for them to go out in any public place. I will talk with my kids about this so they are educated and able to ask questions and talk openly with our friend about chemical sensitivity. We will talk about how we as a family can advocate for fragrance-free public places. We will do this in the next two weeks."

"Our school is participating in 'Light It Up Blue Day,' which is sponsored by Autism Speaks, an organization that rejects the opinions and agency of autistic people and perpetuates harmful myths about autism. I will talk with my kids about autism acceptance so that they can make informed choices about whether and how to participate in this activity. We will talk about the autism acceptance movement and other ways to show solidarity with autistic people. We will do this at least a week before the event."

Healing justice practice

Rowan: Group Signing
One of the most healing practices I know is group singing. Whether or not you can vocalize out loud, read music, carry a tune—it doesn't matter. All that matters in group singing is coming together to create something bigger than yourselves. For me, the most healing songs are rounds and voice-braidings. They can be silly or heartfelt, and they all solidify my sense of being in community.

My favorite voice-braiding is a song by Aly Halpert called Loosen, Loosen:[1]

Loosen, loosen baby
You don't have to carry
The weight of the world
In your muscles and bones
Let go, let go, let go

---

1 Aly Halpert, "Loosen, Loosen," available on Soundcloud at https://soundcloud.com/aly-halpert/loosen-loosen.

Holy Breath
And Holy Name
Will you ease,
Will you ease this pain?

Care-Taking Our Emotional Health

We include this practice because of our assumption that everyone has emotions and thought patterns that are sometimes hard and everyone needs support (interdependence not independence). When we understand our unique patterns and needs it can help us address them in a loving community rather than experiencing them as a crisis.

This mental health healing practice comes to you via the *Healing Justice* podcast, hosted by Kate Werning.[1] Links for both the podcast and the practice instructions are at www.healingjustice.org.

First, listen to Augustina Vidal and Rhiana Anthony share the perspective that they and the Icarus Project bring to mental health, or as they call it, "emotional health." The Icarus Project has a grounded and groundbreaking approach to mental health.

Then, do Practice #35: Mad Maps with the Icarus Project's Rhiana Anthony.[2] This involves thinking about what mental health looks like for you personally and making a map of the support you need for emotional health.

We hope this practice nourishes you and your family.

---

1 Augustina Vidal and Rhiana Anthony, "Destigmatizing Mental Health with the Icarus Project," interview by Kate Werning, *Healing Justice* podcast, 1:03, accessed through https://irresistible.org/podcast/35.
2 Ibid.

Community of practice questions

1. What have been your *aha!* moments in this chapter?

2. What have been your successes in talking/reading with your kids?

3. What have been your struggles?

4. What have been your somatic/body sensations and responses throughout this chapter?

5. Share your SMART goals. How can the group support you in achieving them?

6. What else do you want to learn?

Chapter 6

PARENTING FOR GENDER JUSTICE

BY LEILA RAVEN

Research studies have consistently shown that when parents offer repeated, predictable experiences in which they see and sensitively respond to their children's emotions and needs, their children will thrive—socially, emotionally, physically, and even academically. While it's not exactly a revelation that kids do better when they enjoy strong relationships with their parents, what may surprise you is what produces this kind of parent-child connection. It's not how our parents raised us, or how many parenting books we've read. It's actually how well we've made sense of our experiences with our own parents and how sensitive we are to our children that most powerfully influence our relationship with our kids, and therefore how well they thrive.

—DANIEL J. SIEGEL, MD, AND TINA PAYNE BRYSON, PhD, *The Whole-Brain Child: 12 Revolutionary Strategies to Nurture Your Child's Developing Mind*

In a culture of domination everyone is socialized to see violence as an acceptable means of social control. Dominant parties maintain power by the threat (acted upon and not) that abusive punishment, physical or psychological, will be used whenever the hierarchical structures in place are threatened, whether that be in male-female relationships, or parent and child bonds.

—BELL HOOKS, cultural critic and theorist, *Feminism is for Everybody*

Families constitute primary sites of belonging to various groups: to the family as an assumed biological entity; to geographically identifiable, racially segregated neighborhoods conceptualized as imagined families; to so-called racial families codified in science and law; and to the U.S. nation-state conceptualized as a national family . . . Because the family functions as privileged exemplar of intersectionality in structuring hierarchy, it potentially can serve a similar function in challenging the hierarchy. Just as the traditional family ideal provides a rich site for understanding intersectional inequalities, reclaiming notions of family that reject hierarchical thinking may provide an intriguing and important site of resistance.

—PATRICIA HILL COLLINS, Black feminist theorist

Sha Grogan-Brown (in middle), anti-racist, white, queer, trans dad of a 5-year-old in Washington DC. (Sha's artwork appears on page 275.)

 *Reflect*

Use the following questions as a guide to reflect on the quotations above. You can write or paint, and share your responses with someone or just think quietly, whatever works best for your learning style.

1. How does the gender of the child or children in your care impact the way you parent them? Think specifically about how you respond to their big emotions, how you address harmful or unhealthy behaviors, and how you support their creativity.

2. How does your gender impact the way you provide care? Think about how your gender intersects with other identities you hold. How do expectations or norms about your gender and other identities impact the way you provide care?

3. What are some of the messages that the child or children in your care are getting about gender and families? What and who is influencing these messages? How do you feel about the messages?

4. How can we "rewrite" these narratives for ourselves and the kids in our care?

Story

Leila

From the Caribbean Islands to New York City, my grandparents moved to the colonized land known as the United States to pursue the "American Dream"—a dream my Bronx-bred Puerto Rican mother instilled in me, my older sister, and younger brother as the path to our safety and well-being. A dream that was never meant to include us—and certainly not meant to include me, a Puerto Rican, Dominican, and Lebanese queer girl several shades darker than my mother and siblings and often perceived as racially ambiguous or Black.

But I bought into it. I was taught to blend in, "don't be fresh," and take responsibility for myself. My brown skin never allowed me to blend in, so I overcompensated in the way that I could: I learned to take responsibility for everything.

Fourth-grade teacher singled you out as a problem child in an otherwise all-white class? Take responsibility, say you're sorry. Men on the street are whistling at you and telling you what they want to do to your 12-year-old body? Take responsibility, cover up. Moving back and forth between New York and New Jersey, I found myself navigating sexism and homophobia in urban communities, and racism on top of that in mostly white suburban communities.

When I was 13, the state separated me and my siblings from our mother, and worse, from each other. The abuse we had been experiencing was severe and escalating, and an intervention was needed. And yet, tearing siblings apart at a time when we needed each other most was in itself an act of violence that exacerbated my trauma and sense of isolation. Over the next two years, I moved to several homes and two new schools. After I was sexually assaulted and found no recourse, I ran away.

If there was no one left to care for me then I'd have to find a way to care for myself.

Racial capitalism had instilled in me the belief that my experiences with violence, poverty, and homelessness were not social problems but moral failings. It followed, then, that if bad things were happening to me then *I* was bad. And when being bad became a part of my identity, it felt unchangeable. If I couldn't change it, I'd embrace it. I learned to steal, cheat, and lie to survive. Suddenly, my sexuality was not a source of shame but a resource: I traded sex and used romance to access the things I needed to survive in the years until I had stable housing, and even then, I used sex work to make ends meet when I was short on rent.

Even despite my lived experiences, I swallowed up the American dream. I thought: if it worked for everyone else, the problem must be me. So I hid the parts of myself that betrayed my inability to assimilate. I contorted my life story to fit into a cookie cutter mold that had never been built for me. I left out my experiences with stealing and survival sex work. Instead, I told myself and anyone who would listen that hard work and personal responsibility were all I needed. I didn't want people to know the truth, because I was afraid of what it meant about me: that I was a *street kid*, that I was *bad*, that I *deserved abuse and homelessness*.

Later on, I learned that I am so much more than the worst things that have happened to me. I learned to draw on my experiences as a street kid to build a lifestyle that subverted systems of oppression and moved me toward the world I wanted to create.

As an adult, and as a parent myself now, I've learned to separate the people we are from the things we do. I often tell my child, "There are no bad people, only bad behaviors. *You* are not what you *do*." I pair this lesson with one about accountability: we all do bad things sometimes; that doesn't make us bad people. What's important is that, when we do something that hurts someone, we apologize, we ask them how we can make it right, and we follow through with our actions. And when someone does something that hurts us, we can tell them, "Stop. That's not OK." My child and I practice this line together, sometimes with one hand out in front of us in the form of a stop sign, and sometimes we also include words that tell others how we feel about their behavior, something like "stop, I don't like it when you hit me. It's not OK."

It has been a long journey for me, from apologizing for my existence to learning how to set boundaries. I don't put the blame entirely on the people who brought me into this world for seeking to assimilate. It wasn't my mother or my mother's mother who created the binary checkboxes for "male" and "female" that many of us have tried to contort our lives and experiences to fit. They made their best guesses about what they needed to do to survive within those bounds, internalized a logic that rationalized their survival strategies, and passed it on. But not all of us fit within those boxes, and the choice to assimilate depends on our willingness to discard those who can't or won't conform.

I was one of those who wouldn't, or couldn't.

In the year before I became pregnant, the narrative I had constructed about my life came crumbling down. I had tried to conform to the norms and the kind of life that I was taught would earn me safety: a full-time salaried job and a monogamous life partner. My partner and I were together for a year before he hit me. I'd brushed off the ways that abuse showed up in our daily life: the name calling, the condescension, the restrictions on my communication with friends. When he finally hit me, he struck a blow to a version of reality that I had clung to as a coping mechanism to survive: the idea that I was in control of anything that happened to me and that by working hard and trying to assimilate, I could keep myself safe.

Recognizing the abuse in my relationship was difficult, but I found resources and support to guide me through it. It was much more difficult to accept a new world-view—a framework that acknowledged the role of systems beyond my control in shaping my life experiences. But time and time again, the experiences I had in my daily life kept chipping away at the smokescreen. One night, I had gathered the energy to fight back against my partner, picking up a knife to scare him off. When the police arrived at our home, my partner was arrested for "simple assault" and I was arrested, too, for "assault with a deadly weapon." I was placed in a jail cell right next to my abuser's cell. I didn't know then, but I know now: For Black women and women of color, protecting ourselves from abuse is a crime.

When the state becomes a second abuser, it reinforces the abuse at home and upholds the idea that those of us experiencing abuse are to blame. At the time, mainstream domestic violence organizations had little to say about the criminalization of survivors. I remember being told, "Sometimes the cops get it wrong." I felt isolated in an experience that I later learned was shared among many survivors of color, and especially those who are Black, trans, and queer.

Unsure about whether the abuse was my fault, I spent two years wavering back and forth between attempts to untangle myself from my abusive partner and attempts to make our relationship safer. I had doubts that leaving would make me safe. Still holding myself responsible for my experiences with abuse, I thought: *What is it about me that brings out violence in others?* Finding a way to please my partner, to conform to the expectations that others had of me, was the path I'd always been taught would lead to safety. Not knowing any other way, I stayed on the path.

Knowing that my partner's alcohol addiction played a role in the abuse in our relationship, I believed that if I could keep him sober then I could keep us safe. I didn't know back then that alcohol doesn't *cause* abusive behavior, that it's more often used instead as an excuse to conceal the factors that actually drive abusive behavior, like a belief in rigid gender norms. He said he wanted to be sober and he wanted us to be safe. I took him at his word. But I saw myself as ultimately responsible for making our relationship safe.

So I tried something new. I drew a thermometer on a long sheet of paper and taped it onto the wall of the bedroom we shared. I drew marks along the thermometer, each line representing a new day. For every day he stayed sober, I'd color in a space; he'd earn a point. If he could go somewhere besides work without me and stay sober, he'd get a point and a half. I wanted to incentivize him to stay sober without me, to see his sobriety as an end in itself, and I also wanted to negotiate space away from him.

I came up with rewards to encourage him to hit benchmarks. If he could earn some number of points, we'd take a trip together. If we filled in the whole thermometer, we'd move back in together. I built in room for error. I established reliable, consistent consequences to reinforce my boundaries. I wanted to support him, I wanted to stay in the relationship, and I wanted to be safe.

I didn't realize it then, but I was learning the most important lessons about parenting and about anti-carceral strategies for promoting safety and justice, by seeking to reduce harm in my abusive relationship. I learned that I needed to let go of my urge to control him and that I could only control my own behavior. I learned to respect his autonomy: only he could make the choice to change behaviors.

The thermometer represented a new approach that I have carried over to my caregiving practice. Behavior is communication, and when children are behaving in ways we don't want to encourage, it is because they are using every strategy at their disposal to get the support they need. If we are intervening at the stage when bad behavior has escalated then we might be intervening too late. Often we can prevent bad behaviors by giving attention to, and positively reinforcing, good behaviors. It is common for caregivers and adults to comment only on children's bad behaviors, and in doing so, we communicate that these are the behaviors that will get our attention. We may then become frustrated and exasperated when the behaviors continue, not realizing that we may have been feeding only the negative behaviors and neglecting positive behaviors along the way.

That said, adult men are not children, though this isn't always immediately clear. This sounds like a joke, but it's a reality. Caretaking is a form of feminized labor, and in Western culture, mainstream gender norms impose a disproportionate expectation of care work on gender-oppressed people—including cisgender women, transgender people, gender nonconforming people, queer people, and especially those who are marginalized by multiple forms of oppression. While we can apply many of the same strategies to adults who are causing harm to encourage them to take accountability, it's important to distinguish between harm and abuse. Abuse is a repetitive pattern of seeking power and control over another person, and abusive behavior is often rewarded in a culture and society built on oppression. Incentivizing positive behaviors won't solve abuse; a community-based response, involving consequences and boundaries, can create safety from abuse. Still, many of us learn caretaking skills in relationships with patriarchal partners.

I became pregnant weeks after ending my abusive relationship. In January 2014, the birth of my child propelled me into a new way of living and loving. As a new, young, solo mama, I built a caregiving village out of necessity. I left the nonprofit job that took me away from home too many hours of the day, and I jumped into grassroots organizing. Slowly I began to strip away the many layers I had hid behind to conform, and I tapped back into the strategies that helped me survive as a street kid.

"It's a boy!" a nurse told me. I thought about what it meant to raise a boy in the context of rape culture. I knew it would be important to me to teach my child about setting and respecting boundaries, the meaning of consent, and how to use our words to communicate our needs and feelings. It felt like the whole world was working against me at all times. I saw the ways that even infants and toddlers who are perceived as boys experience everyday violence.

When my child would fall, strangers would say, "You're OK! You're a tough guy!" When my child wore a fedora, people commented, "He looks like a *little pimp*!" When the cashier at the supermarket had only flower and flag stickers to offer, she assured my child, "You want the flags." And when my two-year-old was offered a choice of many colored straws and chose pink, the server told us, "Pink is for pimps!"

Maybe they all meant well. But what kinds of messages was my child receiving, and internalizing, about gender before I even realized I needed strategies to counter those messages?

Around this time I became deeply immersed in the movement to end patriarchal violence, understanding the state as both an instrument of violence and as a set of systems perpetuating interpersonal violence against Black people and people of color, especially those who are trans, gender nonconforming, and queer. I became the executive director of Collective Action for Safe Spaces, a DC-based grassroots organization seeking to build safer public spaces for everyone. This chapter contains some of the lessons I've learned from this work and applied to my caregiving approach, while better coming to understand my own experiences with gender, sexuality, consent, and boundaries.

Gender oppression is upheld by a culture based on hierarchical domination, and the key to disrupting oppression is creating and promoting a new set of values. Instead of using our power to impose our will on others, we have to leverage our power to lift up voices that are often marginalized and silenced. And that work starts at home: We have to listen and believe children when they tell us who they are, what they need, and where their boundaries lie. Applying a consent framework to our caregiving allows us to see our children not as carbon copies of ourselves, but as individual people with their own autonomy, needs, and boundaries.

In our family, this approach created space for the child I'm raising to define her gender identity and expression for herself instead of accepting the boxes checked for her. Early on that meant kids would ask, "Are you a boy or a girl?" and my three-year-old would say, "No." Later she firmly expressed that she identified as a girl, and just like I had done when I first gave her what I now refer to as her placeholder name, she used cultural influences to come up with a name for herself. She is clear about her identity; it is up to the rest of us to listen.

The dominant culture stigmatizes parents like me, who reject the hierarchical nuclear family model. "You're her mother, not her friend," I've been told by parents who have seen my child run away from the dinner table while I strongly encourage, but do not demand or force, that she come back and eat. And what if I am her friend? What if I have let go of any desire to control or dominate her, and what if I believe a good friend is a good caregiver who does everything in their power to listen and ensure that those in their care are heard and affirmed, kept safe and supported in being accountable to their values and their community? What if I have accepted that the child I raise is not my property, that I do not own her and cannot control her?

Nonhierarchical family structures aren't new; in fact, this model has been necessary for the survival of many communities impacted by structural oppression. You don't read about people like us in parenting books. We are street kids who have become caregivers. We are trans and queer people who have experienced family rejection and homelessness. We are the ones who were separated from those who birthed us by police brutality, incarceration, harmful immigration policies, and intervention by the foster system. We worried that we could never become parents or caregivers because, through a sort of collective gaslighting by the dominant culture, the lack of experience in the nuclear family structure has become a source of shame. Now I understand that my experience as a street kid is no longer a source of shame but a resource; I draw from my experiences surviving outside the bounds of Western capitalist, imperialist, white supremacist, and patriarchal cultural norms to build a society that promotes values like empathy, accountability, integrity, cooperation, and respect.

As Saidiya Hartman writes in her 2019 book *Wayward Lives, Beautiful Experiments,* "The mutuality and creativity necessary to sustain living in the context of intermittent wages, controlled depletion, economic exclusion, coercion, and antiblack violence often bordered on the extralegal and criminal." Social and economic exclusion has led many of us to turn to criminalized survival strategies like working in the street economies to meet our needs.

Our alternative lifestyles are not signs of our brokenness but rather symbols of our resistance against oppression and signs of our survival against all odds. Just as Hartman's book documents the ways that Black communities used fluid family relationships and creative survival strategies in the early 20th century to navigate social and economic exclusion, those alternative models of surviving and caring for each other show up in many communities navigating oppression for whom the nuclear family structure wasn't built. Then and now, we have forged networks of kinship not rooted in blood relations or entitlement to power based on age or status, but rooted in mutual respect and care.

Power doesn't have to be expressed through dominance. Power can be about listening, learning, and leveraging privileged positions to support and amplify the voices of others. We have to cede the desire to dominate in order to build up the capacity of young people to be autonomous, resist oppression, and create a culture of care.

As Patricia Hill Collins wrote, the family is an important site of resistance against oppression because it's a space where violence to maintain hierarchy has been normalized.[1] The model we need exists in the histories of Black trans and queer resistance. It exists already among street kids who have redefined family and built networks of community care. And it's a practice that I work to build and nurture in my own family. As conveyed via the title of the book of Ching-In Chen, Jai Dulani, and Leah Lakshmi Piepzna-Samarasinha about interrupting abuse in activist communities, *the revolution starts at home.*

---

1 Patricia Hill Collins. "It's All in the Family: Intersections of Gender, Race, and Nation." Hypatia 13 (3):62-82. 1998.

Marching in Washington D.C. Pride Parade, 2016.

 Reflect

We all have a story that shapes the way we experience and understand the world. What's your story? Fill out the "Childhood Memories" worksheet *(see Appendix L: https://www.parenting4socialjustice.com/)*, then respond to these reflection questions:

1. What are the key moments, relationships, and experiences that have shaped the way you understand your gender? Draw a river, and along the river create visual representations of those influences.
2. What are some of the ways that other identities you hold (such as your class, race, and sexual orientation) have impacted your gender experience?
3. What are some privileges you hold? Start your self-assessment by thinking about gender, remembering that gender cannot be separated from any of the other ways that you may be either privileged or oppressed by systems of domination.

4. What are some ways you can use those privileges to support people who are more marginalized than you? Again, start with gender and then think about how your gender intersects with other privileged or oppressed identities you hold.

5. What is your family structure? How is this family structure represented or characterized in the mainstream media, if at all? How does this structure help promote, or hinder, the values you seek to impart to the children in your care?

The stories we are told are the stories we tell

Before we can practice caregiving in a way that promotes respect for consent and boundaries, we have to understand the systems and structures we're navigating.

Gender and the system of cisheteropatriarchy

We are all at different points on our journey toward understanding gender and the ways it impacts our lives. This chapter is written with the intention of bringing all of our diverse experiences to the table to support learning.

Before we dive into navigating gender oppression as caregivers, let's break down some key concepts that will be used throughout this chapter:

❀ **Cisgender:** A term for someone who identifies with the gender associated with their sex assigned at birth.

❀ **Consent:** An agreement between people made verbally or nonverbally. Respecting consent means demonstrating care for the needs, boundaries, and autonomy of others.

❀ **Gender:** Something we feel on the inside that we can express on the outside through things we wear, things we like to do, and ways we act.

❀ **Gender binary system:** The system of beliefs, structures, policies, and practices that assume and assert that there are exactly two genders ("male" and "female"), where gender and sex are assumed to be interchangeable. This system, reinforced by mainstream media and cultural norms, informs our understanding of our bodies and our assigned and acceptable "roles" in society.

❀ **Gender nonconforming** or **nonbinary:** Terms to describe people whose gender does not fit into binary expectations. Some people who are gender nonconforming or nonbinary identify as transgender.

❀ **Gender norms:** Social expectations about how to dress, what kinds of activities to participate in, and how to act imposed on us based on our real or perceived gender.

❀ **Heteropatriarchy:** A colonial construct and concept that defines both masculinity and femininity in narrow and limiting ways in order to maintain a binary distinction between male and female, dominant and subordinate.

Heteropatriarchy serves to naturalize all other social hierarchies, such as white supremacy and settler colonialism.

- ❊ **Intersectionality:** A theory that attends to the complexity of identity and experience as constructed by multiple, interlocking systems of oppression (such as racism, classism, and sexism) for the purpose of understanding and shifting those systems of oppression

- ❊ **Patriarchal violence:** An interconnected system of institutions, practices, policies, beliefs, and behaviors that harm, undervalue, and terrorize girls, women, intersex, gender nonconforming, LGBTQ, and other gender-oppressed people in our communities.[2]

- ❊ **Sex:** Usually used to describe one of two things: (1) bodies, (2) something people do to feel good in their bodies and/or in some cases to reproduce.

- ❊ **Sex work:** The exchange of money or resources for sexual labor.

- ❊ **Transgender:** A term for people whose gender identity, expression, or behavior is different from those typically associated with their assigned sex at birth.

Gender oppression is primarily characterized by patriarchal violence—an interconnected system of institutions, practices, policies, beliefs, and behaviors that harm gender-oppressed people. While this chapter does not attempt to cover all of the ways and structures that uphold gender oppression, it addresses some of the ways that gender oppression is upheld by schools, families, and the state. Patriarchal violence is used to coerce conformity with patriarchal gender norms that align with the gender binary system. As defined above, the gender binary system is the system of beliefs, structures, policies, and practices that assume and assert that there are exactly two genders ("male" and "female"), where gender and sex are assumed to be interchangeable. This system, reinforced by mainstream media and cultural norms, informs our understanding of our bodies and our assigned and acceptable "roles" in society. It is enforced by patriarchal violence, and it is one of the mechanisms that upholds the cisheteropatriarchal system.

What is the cisheteropatriarchal system? The Anti-Violence Project (AVP) defines heteropatriarchy as "a colonial construct and concept that defines both masculinity and femininity in narrow and limiting ways in order to maintain a binary distinction between male and female, dominant and subordinate."[3] Multiple systems of oppression—including cissexism, heterosexism, and patriarchy—work together to marginalize people who are women and girls (especially those who are trans) as well as queer, transgender, and gender nonconforming people more broadly. Referring to the system as *cis*heteropatriarchy helps us move away from an analysis that is gender essentialist

---

2"What Is Patriarchal Violence?" Abolishing Patriachal Violence Innovation Lab by Black Feminist Future, Collective Action for Safe Spaces, and Freedom, Inc., https://issuu.com/blackfeministfuture/docs/understanding_patriarchal_violence.

3 The Anti-Violence Project. Glossary. https://www.antiviolenceproject.org/glossary/#heteropatriarchy.

(or rooted in the gender binary) and trans-exclusionary (or failing to be inclusive of trans and gender nonconforming people).

Cisheteropatriarchy works with other oppressive systems, like capitalism and white supremacy, to create hierarchies of oppression that put those who are marginalized by multiple systems of oppression—such as Black, disabled, trans women who are oppressed by racism, ableism, and cisheteropatriarchy simultaneously—at the bottom. This chapter focuses on the experiences of people who are marginalized by multiple, interlocking systems of oppression—a theory with its roots in the organizing work of groups like the Combahee River Collective and later referred to as intersectionality by Kimberle Crenshaw. By placing those who are marginalized by multiple systems of oppression at the center of our analysis, we are able to develop a deeper and more comprehensive understanding of how those systems operate and what's needed to dismantle all systems of oppression.

How did the cisheteropatriarchal system become normalized in Western culture? People around the world have not always thought about gender through the lens of the gender binary system! In fact, these systems were invented by European colonizers that created the oppressive hierarchical categories of race and gender and then used faulty biological science to justify this system of domination and exploitation for their own gains. Unlike precolonial societies in places like Africa and Asia that relied on cooperative ways of living, Western colonization imposed hierarchies on communities and replaced communal relations with "relations of domination and submission."[4] The reliance on the gender binary in modern mainstream Western culture reinforces gender norms that are harmful for everyone. Beyond confining children (and adults) to restrictive ideas of gender that don't accurately represent our internal experiences, studies have shown that exposure to rigid gender norms increases young people's risk of poor mental and behavioral health.[5] And worse, gender-oppressed people face high rates of interpersonal and institutional violence in a cisheteropatriarchal society.

Patriarchal violence as a tool of cisheteropatriarchy

> "While male supremacy encourages the use of abusive force to maintain male domination of women, it is the Western philosophical notion of hierarchical rule and coercive authority that is the root cause of violence against women, of adult violence against children, of all violence between those who dominate and those who are dominated. It is this belief system that is the foundation on which sexist ideology and other ideologies of group oppression are based; they can be eliminated only when this foundation is eliminated."
>
> —bell hooks, *Feminism is for Everybody*

When our bodies, and our inner experiences, don't perfectly conform to the gender binary system, there are large and small ways that the dominant culture strikes

---

4 Césaire, Aimé. "Discourse on Colonialism." New York: MR, 1972. Print.
5 Brian Heilman with Gary Barker. "Masculine Norms and Violence: Making the Connections." Washington, DC: Promundo-U.S. (2018).

back, and for many queer, trans, and gender nonconforming young people, patriarchal violence starts at home. In the U.S. more than half of youth experiencing homelessness were asked to leave home by a parent or caregiver. Nearly 40% of homeless youth identify as gay, bisexual, or transgender.[6] More than 60% of young people experiencing homelessness have experienced physical or sexual assault on the street.

High rates of homelessness among trans, queer, and gender nonconforming youth lead many young people to trade sex to access housing, food, and basic resources. Federal law defines all young people in the sex trades as child sex-trafficking victims, although the vast majority of young people do not have a trafficker or third-party exploiter. The response to young people in the sex trades has overwhelmingly involved increased criminalization and state surveillance. However, increased policing has failed to meet the material needs of young people in the sex trades, and it has failed to prevent or address sexual exploitation of youth. The most effective way to prevent youth homelessness and end the exploitation of young people is to ensure that trans, gender nonconforming, and queer youth are affirmed, safe, and supported at home.

As adults, trans, and gender nonconforming people face similarly high rates of violence and marginalization. In Washington, DC, 48% of employers preferred a less qualified cisgender applicant over a more qualified transgender applicant,[7] leaving 55% of Black transgender adults in the city unemployed.[8] This pattern also plays out on a national scale: more than three-quarters of transgender adults have experienced some form of employment discrimination, with higher rates for trans people of color.[9] High rates of discrimination in accessing employment also translates to high rates of homelessness for trans people: one in five transgender people have experienced homelessness at some point in their lives.[10] One in five trans people have been discriminated against when seeking to access housing, and one in ten have been evicted because of their gender identity.[11] Through interpersonal and systemic violence, trans people—especially Black trans people and trans people of color—are marginalized in U.S. society.

Patriarchal violence also specifically targets trans and cis women. One in five women will experience sexual assault and one in four women will experience intimate partner abuse in their lifetime. Everyday incidents of interpersonal violence, including sexist comments and unwanted sexual advances, work to reinforce gender oppression backed by the threat of further violence. Fifty percent of women's murders are done by a current or former intimate partner, and Black women experience the highest rates of murder of any racial group.[12] Interpersonal violence against people

6 Street Outreach Program Data Collection Study Final Report. Administration for Children and Families Family and Youth Services Bureau. https://www.acf.hhs.gov/archive/fysb/report/final-report-street-outreach-program-data-collection-study.
7 Imse, E. and Rainey, T. *Qualified and Transgender*, DC Office of Human Rights, 2015.
8 Access Denied: Washington, DC Trans Needs Assessment Report, November 2015.
9 National Center for Transgender Equality, https://transequality.org/issues/employment.
10 National Center for Transgender Equality, https://transequality.org/issues/housing-homelessness.
11 Ibid.
12 "Racial and Ethnic Differences in Homicides of Adult Women and the Role of Intimate Partner Violence—United States, 2003–2014." Center for Disease Prevention and Control.

marginalized by gender oppression occurs in both private and public spaces, by state and nonstate actors—and in all of these settings, the risk of violence is higher for Black and Indigenous women, women of color, people who are transgender, disabled people, and especially people who hold identities that are marginalized by multiple layers of structural oppression.

Marginalization further contributes to the high rates of physical violence against trans people. Twenty-six percent of respondents to the National Transgender Discrimination Survey have been physically assaulted on at least one occasion because of anti-trans bias. Transgender people of color and transgender women are disproportionately affected, with nearly three out of four deadly acts of anti-LGBTQ hate violence targeting trans women and girls.[13] As of this writing in August 2020, 26 trans and gender nonconforming people had been killed in the U.S. and Puerto Rico so far that year. More than half of those killed were Black.

Using systems of punishment to police gender and families

Patriarchal violence is reinforced by state institutions that seek to maintain oppressive hierarchies and norms. While it is important to change behaviors and interrupt abuse on the individual level, it isn't enough. Oppressive hierarchies are deeply entrenched in, and reinforced by, state structures that promote punishment and control instead of safety and accountability.

Discipline is teaching, not punishment, and yet Western society is structured in a way that conflates punishment with discipline and safety. The word *discipline* derives from the Latin root word *discere* meaning "to learn." Research on childhood education shows that children thrive in environments where the approach to discipline involves teaching positive behaviors rather than punishing negative behaviors. However, the criminal punishment system and child welfare system function in the opposite way: oppressive norms are reinforced by state institutions that use surveillance, control, and punishment to coerce conformity, rewarding behavior that aligns with oppressive norms and punishing behaviors that defy norms.

The modern prison system has its historical roots in U.S. slavery: the 13th Amendment to the U.S. Constitution abolished slavery "except as a punishment for crime." In the context of a capitalist, white supremacist, cisheteropatriarchal system, crime came to be defined by the ways that Black people, immigrants, and even poor whites survived. A refusal, or inability, to assimilate was and continues to be criminalized. For example, the earliest juvenile detention centers in the U.S. were created to uphold gender norms and punish young people—especially girls, trans, and gender nonconforming youth—who did not conform. Much like today, conformity was enforced through policing, whether directly by law enforcement agents or by everyday people performing the work of the state to uphold racist, patriarchal oppression.

As Saidiya Hartman documents in the book *Wayward Lives, Beautiful Experiments: Intimate Histories of Riotous Black Girls, Troublesome Women and Queer Radicals*, police officers and even neighbors have participated in the policing of Black women and girls occupying public spaces. "Being too loud or loitering in the hallway of your

---

13 James, Sandy E., Herman, Jody, Keisling, Mara, Mottet, Lisa, and Anafi, Ma'ayan. 2015 U.S. Transgender Survey (USTS). https://www.transequality.org/sites/default/files/docs/USTS-Full-Report-FINAL.PDF.

building or on the front stoop was a violation of the law; making a date with someone you met at the club, or arranging a casual hook up, or running the streets was prostitution. The mere willingness to have a good time with a stranger was sufficient evidence of wrongdoing. The court, like the police, discerned in this exercise of will 'a struggle to transform one's existence,' to stand against or defy the norms of social order, and anticipated that this noncompliance and disobedience easily yielded to crime."

Black women, girls, and poor people are targeted by laws against vagrancy and loitering for being unwilling, or unable, to participate in the mainstream capitalist economy or the patriarchal nuclear family. As Hartman writes, "Vagrancy was a status, not a crime. It was *not* doing, withholding, nonparticipation, the refusal to be settled or bound by contract to employer (or husband)." Then and now people have been surveilled and criminalized for being Black, queer, trans, poor, disabled, and/or housing insecure, and for finding ways to survive outside of capitalist, white supremacist, cisheteropatriarchal norms.

High rates of employment discrimination and housing discrimination against trans people, and especially Black trans people and trans people of color, have led trans communities to rely heavily on criminalized labor like sex work to survive. Trans sex workers, and trans people profiled as sex workers, are at increased risk of police harassment and state violence. In New York, sex workers' rights groups are working to repeal a statute against "loitering for the purposes of prostitution," known colloquially as the "Walking While Trans" ban or as a "stop and frisk" policy targeting Black and Latinx women. In 2018, 49% of people arrested under this statute were Black and 42% were Latinx; more than 80% were trans and cis women. Rooted in the same racist and sexist logic that led to the creation of anti-vagrancy laws that have targeted Black women since the early 20th century, laws against loitering and sex work are used to police the gender, sexuality, and autonomy of Black women today. Shut out of housing and employment options, Black people and people of color who are gender oppressed are then once again criminalized for any refusal or inability to conform to gender norms.

Gender oppression is also upheld in schools through oppressive policies enforced by punishment, particularly for Black students and students of color. In the U.S., access to education has historically been criminalized for Black people, starting with South Carolina's Negro Act of 1740 banning literacy for enslaved Black people and continuing through the 19th century with laws criminalizing education for Black people in nearly every state by the time of the Civil War.

Even as Black people gained access to public schools in the 20th century, criminalization evolved into what's now known as the school-to-prison pipeline. School dress codes are an example of a policy used to enforce gender norms and police the sexuality of young girls, especially Black girls, in schools. Girls are sent to detention for wearing short skirts, spaghetti strap shirts, and even open-toed shoes. And race plays a significant role in the ways that girls are policed and punished. As Victoria Law and Maya Schenwar write in their 2020 book *Prison by Any Other Name*, "School authority figures often perceive Black girls as more adult than their peers, and that perception translates into attempts at control and harsh discipline."[14] A 2015 report showed that

14 Schenwar, Maya and Victoria Law. *Prison by Any Other Name: The Harmful Consequences of Popular Reforms.* The New Press. 2020.

Black girls are six times more likely to receive an out-of-school suspension than their white counterparts.[15] In 2019, six-year-old Kaia Rolle was arrested by a "school resource officer" in her Orlando, Florida, elementary school for throwing a temper tantrum.[16] While white girls tend to be encouraged to display emotions, Black girls and gender nonconforming children are punished just for behaving like children. To date, Black people and people of color have never had access to the same quality of education or educational resources as white people in the U.S., and yet even refusal or failure to attend schools is criminalized through truancy laws. By policing Black girls and students of color more broadly, schools act as a site of patriarchal violence that upholds racial capitalism and cisheteropatriarchy.

The cisheteropatriarchal system is further reinforced in the patriarchal nuclear family—a microcosm of the capitalist system. In the patriarchal nuclear family, there is a married couple and children, with the father/husband typically as breadwinner and head of household while a wife and children play subordinate roles and manage unpaid housework. However, the patriarchal nuclear family model was nearly impossible for Black communities to adopt under slavery and the ensuing Jim Crow era, involving widespread housing and employment discrimination against Black people as well as systematic family separation.

In the mid-20th century, as white women sought greater equality with men by increasingly taking work outside of the home and assimilating into the same systems that depended on hierarchies of oppression, Black women and women of color continued to be unpaid or underpaid to take on domestic labor including childcare and housework. Despite needing to navigate completely different hurdles to survive in the context of racial capitalism, Black people have been stigmatized and criminalized for any refusal or inability to assimilate to patriarchal nuclear family norms. For example, advisor to President Lyndon Johnson, Daniel Patrick Moynihan, wrote a report called *The Negro Family: The Case for National Action*, known more widely as the *Moynihan Report* of 1965. In the report, Moynihan blamed poverty in Black communities on Black families' lack of conformity to the nuclear family model. The report, reinforced through mainstream media and political rhetoric, has been used to justify and perpetuate policies that further ingrained the idea that social problems are a product of individual moral failures, while defining moral failures as nonconformity with oppressive norms. While mainstream narratives and faulty data blamed poverty in Black communities on family structure, the reality is that Black communities, and especially trans and queer people who also face family rejection, have developed family structures that enabled survival against anti-Black racism and capitalist oppression.

The state has expanded its power to surveill, regulate, and punish nonconformity to family life through the creation of the "child welfare" system—more aptly referred to as the family policing system by the acclaimed scholar and lawyer Dorothy Roberts. The system invests heavily in punitive, rather than supportive, measures to address

15 Crenshaw, Kimberlé Williams. "Black Girls Matter: Pushed Out, Overpoliced, and Underprotected." Center for Intersectionality and Social Policy Studies and the African American Policy Forum. 2015.
16 Darby, Luke. "Florida Police Officer Arrested and Handcuffed a 6-Year-Old Black Girl for a Tantrum in Class." GQ, September 23, 2019. https://www.gq.com/story/six-year-old-black-girl-arrested-for-a-tantrum.

family hardship and violence. As Victoria Law and Maya Schenwar write in their 2020 book *Prison by Any Other Name*, "Contrary to public opinion, most of the time, when children are removed from the home, it's not because of abuse; the allegation is usually neglect. Neglect is an allegation that encompasses a range of problems—in addition to leaving a child alone for periods of time, it can refer to homelessness or substandard housing, a lack of weather-appropriate or clean clothing, and chronic latenesses or absences from school." A full 74.9% of cases of child maltreatment are for "neglect" and most of these cases of neglect are directly connected to poverty.[17]

Consistent with the norms of the dominant culture, the family policing system individualizes the problems of child abuse and neglect. Rather than addressing root causes by ensuring that families have the resources needed to survive, the system uses the threat of family separation to punish parents for being unable to care for their children, or even for replicating the behaviors that have been normalized by state institutions. In circumstances where physical or sexual abuse is present, the system has little to offer. In fact, the patriarchal nuclear family creates an isolated context where oppressive norms and abuse can thrive. In other words, the state creates a context that promotes and perpetuates abuse and hardship, especially for Black people and people of color—and then punishes people for being unable to survive within that context.

Family separation, or removing children from their parents or caregivers and placing them in alternate homes, is a practice of the family policing system that also finds its historical roots in the brutalities of colonization and chattel slavery. As Hortense Spillers has written, enslaved people were dehumanized and considered property. While the patriarchal nuclear family promotes the idea of children as the property of parents (and particularly fathers), all enslaved Black people were considered property, and children were systematically separated from their mothers and sold. "Certainly, if 'kinship' were possible, the property relations would be undermined, since the offspring would then 'belong' to a mother and a father."[18] Forced separation of mother from child reinforced the state of Black people as not human but as property under racial capitalism. The practice of family separation happens today in multiple forms, such as through incarceration, deportation, and child removal and displacement by the foster system. These punitive approaches fail to address root causes of hardship and even violence in families and most severely impact those who are already marginalized by mainstream capitalist society: poor communities of color, immigrants, disabled people, and especially poor Black mothers.

Terrorized in their homes, streets, and schools, women of color are the fastest growing population in U.S. prisons.[19] There are many cases of Black women in particular who have been incarcerated for actions taken to resist patriarchal violence. This reality has led to freedom campaigns for survivors of violence like Marissa Alexander,

---

17 "Abolish Policing, Not Just the Police." Haymarket Books event on July 2, 2020. https://www.youtube.com/watch?v=qt-JDtLoOnE&ab_channel=HaymarketBooks.

18 Spillers, Hortense J. "Mama's Baby, Papa's Maybe: An American Grammar Book." Diacritics 17.2 (1987): 65-81. Print.

19 "Invisible no more: police violence against black women and women of color." Andrea Ritchie, Boston: Beacon Press, 2017.

Bresha Meadows, Cyntoia Brown, and CeCe McDonald, as well as current campaigns for GiGi Thomas, Alisha Walker, Liyah Birru, and Tracy McCarter.[20] Black women and women of color are also criminalized for actions taken to protect their children from violence by intimate partners. In 2014, a BuzzFeed news investigation found 73 cases of mothers who were sentenced to ten or more years in prison between 2004 and 2014; 38% of these mothers were domestic violence survivors.[21] In 2017, Danielle Whyte was charged with manslaughter when her boyfriend murdered her infant son and then threatened to kill her if she called police. Resisting patriarchal violence, especially for Black women, is frequently considered a crime.

Rather than addressing the root causes of violence and working to increase safety, state institutions use surveillance and punishment to coerce people to conform to oppressive norms. Trans and queer people of color have out of necessity needed to create new norms to survive within a system that was not created for us. Within the context of racial capitalism, all ways of being that don't conform to white supremacist cisheteropatriarchal norms are surveilled, policed, punished, and criminalized. When punishment is the approach that state structures like the criminal punishment system and the child welfare system have normalized, particularly in the lives of poor communities and communities of color, it becomes difficult to practice a different way of relating to each other in our everyday lives—to resist the use of punishment in our caregiving and instead embrace a model of discipline that promotes education, support, and resources. And yet this is exactly what is needed to build safer families and communities. While changing the way we live our daily lives is not enough to dismantle systems of oppression, we can embrace a new framework as a prefigurative politics, creating the world we want to live in as an everyday practice.

 Reflect

Pause, and breathe. You've taken in a lot of information in this section that might challenge the way you've been taught to think about Western culture and state institutions. Check in with your body: are you shutting down? Glazing over? Energized and motivated to create change?

Embracing an entirely new worldview won't happen overnight. Move slowly, come back to this section later if needed, and keep up your political education.

Key resources for further learning:

　❋ *Women, Race, and Class*, by Angela Davis
　❋ *Feminism Is for Everybody*, by bell hooks

---

20 Survived and Punished. https://survivedandpunished.org/.
21 "These mothers were sentenced to at least 10 years for failing to protect their children from a violent partner." BuzzFeed News, October 2, 2014. https://www.buzzfeed.com/alexcampbell/these-mothers-were-sentenced-to-at-least-10-years-for-failin.

❀ *Combahee River Collective Statement:* https://www.blackpast.org/african-american-history/combahee-river-collective-statement-1977
❀ *Prison by Any Other Name,* by Victoria Law and Maya Schenwar

Interrupting everyday gender oppression

As we work to dismantle systems that promote punishment and uphold oppression, we also have to work to interrupt oppression and build safety into our communities.

Ashley Fairbanks / @ziibiing / ziibiing.com

As this chart by Ashley Fairbanks demonstrates, everyday comments and behaviors that harm gender-oppressed people are backed by the threat of even more severe forms of violence. We cannot address the rates of violence against gender-oppressed people without taking action to address oppressive language and behaviors we encounter in our everyday lives.

There are a lot of ways we can intervene to challenge oppressive norms. Collective Action for Safe Spaces draws from the Green Dot system of bystander intervention to respond to harassment and microaggressions. This model divides bystander intervention into the five D's: **direct** (directly intervening to respond to either the person being targeted, or the person engaging in an oppressive behavior), **distract** (drawing attention away from the behavior or situation, usually with the goal of stopping the immediate situation before moving to another strategy), **delegate** (involving others in an intervention), **document** (taking notes or recording an incident), and **delay** (pausing to assess the situation, usually before moving into another strategy such as directly checking in with the person harmed). Below are some examples of direct interventions.

Here are some tips for speaking up directly when we hear a comment that promotes a harmful stereotype or oppressive norm about a marginalized identity, person, or group:

- ❀ "Can you help me understand what you meant by that?"
- ❀ "I wonder if you realize how that comes across."

In some situations, we may need to be more assertive. Here are some assertive statements we can use:

- ❀ "That's not OK."
- ❀ "That's disrespectful."

We can also turn to the people being targeted and ask questions that affirm their experience and create space for their own intervention:

- ❀ "Are you OK?"
- ❀ "Is there anything I can do to support you?"

The vast majority of incidents of patriarchal violence are perpetrated by people who are in a close relationship with the person targeted. That means it's crucial to speak up to interrupt harmful and oppressive language that we hear from people in our lives: our neighbors, our friends, our families, our partners, and even our kids and ourselves.

Here's a story from a friend of ours whose daughter is learning to interrupt oppressive behaviors:

Romina Pacheco, pronouns she/her/ella, is a Black Latina born and raised in the Caribbean city of Maracay, Venezuela, who now lives in Bridgeport, Connecticut. Her light and joy are her two children, Asha, age 11, and Pierre Arisitides, age 2. Romina is a social justice and equity specialist at an education nonprofit in western Massachusetts. She looks forward every day to a delicious cup of coffee (or two or three!), sharing stories with friends, and co-constructing a world where healing, justice, laughter, and connection are at the core of everyday experiences.

Scene: My daughter, age 10 at the time, is wearing a T-shirt one of my dear friends gifted her that says "Female Athlete" but with the word "Female" crossed out: Female Athlete. On reading the shirt's message, her dad responds with what sounds like a lecture about its meaning.

Asha, interrupting him: Dad, you're mansplaining me. Stop doing that.

Asha's dad: What is mansplaining? I was just trying to tell you what your shirt means.

Asha: That! You just did it again.

[A little spark of joy lights up inside me on overhearing the conversation.]

Reflect

The above is an example of a real conversation and is not meant to be perfect (none of them are!).

1. What do you wonder about after reading this story? What questions come up for you?

2. What could you ask your child to better understand their experience and/or perspective?

3. Can you imagine having this conversation in your family?

4. How might your conversation be similar? How might it be different?

What would it mean to achieve gender justice?

Interrupting oppression in our caregiving and our interpersonal relationships can be a great place to start—though to reiterate, it's not enough without systems change.

Patriarchal state violence and interpersonal violence are interconnected and mutually reinforcing. The state enacts patriarchal violence against us, and criminalizes many of us for surviving, and at the same time, those who use patriarchal violence are carrying out the work of the state to uphold patriarchal oppression. That means that any strategy to eradicate patriarchal violence must seek to eradicate both interpersonal and state violence. An analysis informed by intersectionality—a theory that attends to the complexity of identity and experience as constructed by multiple, interlocking systems of oppression (such as racism, classism, and sexism) for the purpose of understanding and shifting those systems of oppression—allows us to develop comprehensive strategies for building safety. This analysis helps us recognize that different communities have different experiences and, accordingly, different and specific needs. For example, one of the only pathways to freedom for many criminalized survivors of intimate partner violence is clemency from governors. Without an analysis of gender and other forms of oppression in addressing state violence, the unique needs of criminalized survivors may be overlooked. Similarly, an analysis of gender, race, and class in addressing state violence informs campaigns to repeal laws criminalizing sex work or even a mother's "failure to protect" her child from her abuser, recognizing that these laws specifically target Black trans and cis women. As has been practiced by Black feminist revolutionaries throughout history like Sojourner Truth and the Combahee River Collective, placing those who live at the intersections of multiple layers of oppression at the center of our advocacy allows us to challenge multiple forms of oppression simultaneously.

Gender justice means creating a world where all gender-oppressed people—cisgender women, transgender people, gender nonconforming people, queer people, and especially those who are marginalized by multiple forms of oppression—can feel safe in public spaces, our intimate relationships, and our everyday lives. Safety for gender-oppressed people not only means freedom from interpersonal violence and state violence, but also access to the resources needed to survive and live well. Many mainstream feminist and queer organizations, primarily those led and made up of middle-class white people, have sought progress by advocating for access into many of the same oppressive roles in society historically held by cisgender hetereosexual white men, However, most radical Black trans and queer feminist organizations seek not assimilation and inclusion in an oppressive society, but rather freedom from oppression.

Cisheteropatriarchy is challenged and subverted by the everyday resistance of trans, queer, and gender nonconforming people, including the community organizing efforts of trans and queer-led groups like the Transgender, Gender-variant and Intersex Justice Project (TGIJP) in California, Black Trans Media in New York, and Collective Action for Safe Spaces (CASS) in Washington, DC. For example, during the 2020 uprisings sparked by the Minneapolis police murder of George Floyd, Black trans and queer organizers drew thousands at an action in front of the Stonewall Inn in New York, uplifting the ways that state violence and interpersonal violence intersect for Black trans people killed by state and nonstate actors, such as Tony McDade (a Black trans man murdered by police in Tallahassee, Florida) and Nina Pop (a Black trans woman stabbed to death in Missouri).

There are also more liberal reforms that have demonstrated a shift in the way gender is discussed in U.S. mainstream culture. A growing number of cities and states are adding a "nonbinary" option on birth certificates, identification cards, and school application forms, and in some states it is now easier to change the gender marker on identification cards. However, many liberal reforms further assimilate some communities while neglecting the housing, resource, and safety needs of those who are most marginalized by multiple layers of oppression. By centering the needs, experiences, and voices of those marginalized by multiple interlocking systems of oppression, we can build solutions that keep everyone safe.

Progress toward gender justice cannot be measured based on the experiences of those who have broken through glass ceilings, but instead by those who have been relegated to the floor. What are the living conditions of Black, Indigenous, Muslim, immigrant, transgender, queer, and disabled communities? Specifically, what are the conditions of people who live at the intersections of multiple oppressed identities? Do we have access to all of the resources we need to survive? Can we access public spaces without fear of patriarchal violence, hate violence, and state violence? Are our identities and experiences accepted and affirmed by our families and communities? Are our family structures, sexualities, and lifestyles policed, or are we affirmed?

As Black feminist theorist Patricia Hill Collins has written, the family is a crucial site of resistance against hierarchy. The nuclear family model normalizes and legitimizes hierarchical relationships and the conceptualization of power as dominance in our everyday lives and our society. Through nonhierarchical family structures, we can disrupt dominance culture in our everyday lives. Family can offer the opportunity to build, in microcosm, the world we want.

 Reflect

1. What are ways that you have observed oppressive gender norms showing up in your daily life?

2. How are those norms embedded in systems and structures that you and your family navigate? (Think about school, healthcare settings, etc.)

3. Name a few initiatives and policies that seek to further assimilate gender-oppressed people into oppressive structures. Name a few initiatives that can move us closer to eradicating those oppressive structures. What are some ways you can contribute to resisting the former, and assisting the later?

Talking with kids about gender justice

How do we reconcile our hope to raise children who are empathetic, respectful, and resilient with the reality of a culture that promotes hierarchies, binaries, and abuse? While we must actively work to change the world around us and dismantle the systems that uphold oppression, the revolution starts at home: we need to create an environment that rejects oppressive norms and teaches us a new way of relating to each other.

Gender norms were seeping into my family's life before I realized I needed to be working to counter them. One day as I was dropping off my then-one-year-old at daycare, I lingered to listen to the group sing songs in their morning meeting. The teachers led them in singing "The Wheels on the Bus," and while most of the children were not yet verbal, they were able to follow the hand motions of the teachers demonstrating the wheels going round, the wipers going swish, and the horn going beep. To my surprise, the class had added two new lines: "The girls on the bus say, 'Look at my hair,'" and "The boys on the bus say, 'Look at my muscles.'" I saw my one-year-old flexing, subtly being taught that physical strength was valued in boys while physical appearance was valued in girls.

The teachers giggled, as though the lines were just a joke, but for me the incident was emblematic of a larger problem: it was one of many intrusions of oppressive gender norms being reinforced in our lives before my child could even speak. After speaking to friends and other parents about the incident and hearing about some of their own experiences navigating gender norms, I came to understand something important: young people are consistently exposed to cultural messages promoting oppressive ideas about gender, race, class, disability, and other systems of oppression in every aspect of their lives. And although we won't be able to protect them from exposure to oppressive norms, we can engage in dialogue with kids—and with other parents, caregivers, and community members—to offer alternative ideas that promote our values.

Soon after the incident at daycare, I bought a pack of index cards and started sketching. A is for *Abolition*, B is for *Black Lives Matter*, C is for *Consent*. I continued until I had words and art for the whole alphabet. When my child and I flipped through the cards together, we practiced making the sounds of the letters without spending too much time on the meanings of the words. The goal at that point was simply to expose my child to a framework that undermined the oppressive ideologies promoted by the dominant culture. When we equip young people, and ourselves, with the tools to disrupt oppressive norms, we give them context to promote the values we want to see reflected in our communities, like respect and empathy.

The following year I took it further: using my daughter's classroom assignments as a template, I turned the flashcards into a matching game. I listed words like "consent" and "patriarchy" on the left side on a piece of paper and drew associated pictures out of order on the right. The game involved drawing a line from the word to the correct picture, encouraging my child to form associations in a way she might not be taught to think in school.

Making sure our kids have the language to describe the values we want to instill and behaviors we want to promote is just a starting point. After we build a foundation with vocabulary, we have to help kids put these words and concepts into practice.

For one, how can we use our caregiving approach to counter the ways that children, and especially those read as boys, are socialized to suppress their feelings and engage in harmful behaviors? As Daniel J. Siegel and Tina Payne Bryson write in their book, *The Yes Brain: How to Cultivate Courage, Curiosity, and Resilience in Your Child*:

> We often fail to realize the harm we're doing when we condemn and disparage our kids and their feelings. When we distract, deny, or degrade; when we blame or deliver a bootstrap lecture; when we remove ourselves or shut them down and embarrass them for their feelings—when we respond to their emotions with any of these responses, we effectively punish them for feeling healthy, human sentiments and for expressing what's going on inside. This can lead to the numbing of all emotions, teaching kids that feelings and experiences should not be shared.

Kids need to know it's safe to feel their feelings, and we can support them in navigating big emotions using the framework of consent, which we'll discuss more in the next section. We have to **ask** kids how they feel, then **listen** and **believe** them about their inner experiences. Children need to be reminded that their feelings are valid,

including their anger, sadness, and frustration. Although they might be frustrated about things we don't feel are worthy of frustration (like that "no dessert for dinner" rule), it's OK for them to feel their feelings. Before children's brains can be receptive to a lesson about how lollipops are not a healthy dinner food, kids need to know that we *empathize* with their inner experiences. We have to teach our kids empathy by modeling empathy: validating their pain when they are hurt and giving them space to talk about what they feel inside.

Siegel and Bryson describe the needs of children using the 4 S's: children need to be **safe**, **secure**, **soothed**, and **seen**.

Sometimes when children are engaging in bad behaviors we jump to teaching them lessons about why the behaviors are bad and what to do instead. But the research has taught us that our brains don't work that way! Young people, and adults, are less likely to be receptive to lessons taught while they're experiencing big emotions. Just like adults who become defensive when we're told we've done something harmful, kids need to have their internal experiences seen and soothed before they can feel safe and secure in being accountable for their actions.

In *The Whole-Brain Child: 12 Revolutionary Strategies to Nurture Your Child's Developing Mind*, Siegel and Bryson offer 12 strategies for healthy communication. One of the strategies I use often in interactions with adults and children is "connect and redirect"—to help parents and caregivers remember to connect with kids emotionally, right brain to right brain, by validating their feelings before helping redirect them to logic and lessons. Siegel and Bryson expand on this strategy in *The Yes Brain*. "Connecting means offering empathy and a soothing presence through physical affection, empathic facial expressions, and loving, understanding words."[22] Before kids can be receptive to lessons about behavior change, they need to feel safe, secure, soothed, and seen. After their feelings are honored, their brains become better able to let down their defenses and receive new information.

It's also important to remember that being compassionate and empathetic with our kids' big emotions isn't the same as letting them off the hook for bad behaviors. While we must meet kids where they are, and offer patience and understanding as they learn the world, we must also learn to practice setting boundaries and establishing consequences for hurtful and harmful behaviors.

This lesson is especially important for people who are raising white and non-Black kids, and boys of all backgrounds. The dominant culture teaches white kids and boys that the world belongs to them, that they are entitled to what they want, and that they can get what they want through aggressive and dominating behavior. These messages are communicated in many ways, and it's important for caregivers to respond by setting and reinforcing boundaries and consequences for oppressive behavior when it manifests in our kids and our peers.

In her book *Turn This World Inside Out: The Emergence of Nurturance Culture*, Nora Samaran shares an anecdote about her six-year-old godson, Kyle, who has been taught to take accountability and sometimes uses the language of accountability to

---

22 Siegel, Daniel J., and Tina Payne Bryson. *The Yes Brain: How to Cultivate Courage, Curiosity, and Resilience in Your Child*. First edition. New York: Bantam, 2018.

evade it. She writes, "He knows, at age six, that when you hurt someone, you go back right away to own, apologize, and repair the harm. If he hurts his friend while playing, he (ideally under his own initiative) is expected to promptly name what he did, apologize sincerely and lovingly, and ask his friend what he needs or how he can help make things right between them: a hug, a high five, or an offer to play. He is taught to listen to the needs and feelings of others and act in a responsive way."[23] This is a good start, but what happens when we validate feelings that are rooted in oppressive beliefs and values? "Sometimes Kyle can't tell the difference between feeling bad because he hurt somebody and feeling bad because someone hurt him," shares Nora, who recounts the below story.

Scene: Kyle and his dad are at the table. Kyle is restless and grouchy about having fruit for dessert when he wanted ice cream. He is kicking. He is six; he has a lot of energy. When he gets frustrated he still sometimes flails and needs help knowing how to express his anger in good ways.

Kyle's mother: Are you feeling angry because you wanted ice cream? It's OK to feel angry. I hear you. All of your feelings are good. It's not OK to kick people, though. If you feel angry you can say, "I feel angry!" You're always allowed to feel anything you want, but kicking is not OK.

[Kyle, still flailing, kicks his dad on the shin.]

Kyle's dad: You know what, Kyle, my feelings are hurt because you kicked me. I don't want to sit next to you right now.

[Kyle's dad goes to a different room. Because this is a securely attached family, he is still available if Kyle wants him, and he is not going far and not going for long. Kyle runs off to his room.]

Kyle's mother: Kyle, you kicked Dad. Come back and say sorry and make it right.

[Kyle comes back to his mum, crying.]

Kyle, using precisely the language he was taught to use (name hurtful action, name your feelings, ask for repair): You said I kicked Dad! You're saying I'm bad! That hurts my feelings! You have to say sorry!

Kyle's mother, *suppressing a mix of bemused laughter and exasperation and hugging Kyle*: Kyle, it's true that we teach you that no one is bad. I love you and you are good. But you did kick Dad. It's OK for you to hear that, and I do not need to apologize. Now go say sorry and make it right.

Reflections: Kyle actually thought his bad feeling at being told he kicked his father was the same thing as the kick itself—and he was absolutely genuine in his distress, upset and crying. He really meant what he was saying; he hasn't made this connection yet and we have to make it for him. He is growing, and we guide him like a young tree.

23 Samaran, Nora. Turn *This World Inside Out: The Emergence of Nurturance Culture*. AK Press, 2019.

Young people are growing up within the context of structural oppression and a culture that reinforces cisheteropatriarchy and white supremacy; we have to be prepared to respond to the entitled and oppressive behaviors that may manifest as a result of social conditioning. While principles like "all feelings are valid" can provide a helpful roadmap that applies to most situations, there are exceptions to every rule. When we adopt validation as doctrine without nuance, we run the risk of enabling abuse and upholding oppression.

Raising children and being prepared to respond to entitled and oppressive behaviors. Credit: Shutterstock

None of us are immune to the ways that systems of oppression manifest in our everyday lives. We all breathe in air polluted by rape culture, white supremacy, cisheteropatriarchy, ableism, ageism, and capitalism. If we don't consciously, and constantly, struggle against the messages of the dominant culture, we are bound to internalize oppression. That's why it's important for us to learn both to intervene *and* to take accountability when we are told that we have said or done something that has harmed others.

The best way to teach kids to be accountable is to model accountability. It's our responsibility to apologize when we make comments or engage in behaviors that have harmed others. When we've done something wrong, we are responsible for working through our own feelings of shame or defensiveness and making it right. That includes apologizing to our kids and helping them see that no one is above accountability.

It's normal to feel defensive when we are told that we've hurt someone. Often, we fear that doing something bad makes us a bad person. As I shared in my story, I've learned to separate the people we are from the things we do. There are no bad people, only bad behaviors. The question isn't whether we'll make mistakes but how we respond when we do: own and repair, or dismiss and deny? What's important is that, when we do something that hurts someone, we apologize, ask them how we can make it right, and follow through with our actions.

Accountability isn't about determining whose truth is the *real* truth. Your boundaries are different from other people's boundaries. Something someone said or did may not be a violation of your boundaries, and the same comment or action may have been a violation to someone else. You don't have to know what it's like to experience what they have experienced to believe that their experience is real. Embracing accountability requires us to dispel the myth of the binary of good/bad, acknowledging that all of our feelings and experiences are valid and real and may contradict each other. Seeking accountability instead of punishment changes everything that we've been taught about safety and justice. It means we don't need one person to be right and one person to be wrong, or one person to be punished and the other to be vindicated. It means we're willing to hear and empathize with the experiences of others and take responsibility for the ways our words and actions have impacted others.

So remember: **ask**, **listen**, **believe**, and *act accordingly.*

A colleague from Collective Action for Safe Spaces, Krystal Atha, and I collaborated to develop what we refer to as the Four A's of taking accountability:

❀ **Apologize!** Name the behavior, and say you're sorry. No excuses or qualifiers. If you're not ready to take full responsibility, take as much responsibility as you feel comfortable with in the moment.

❀ **Acknowledge** and own the impact of your behavior, not your intentions. ("I'm sorry that I . . . " and not "I'm sorry you felt . . . ")

❀ **Ask** how you can make it right.

❀ **Action!** Follow through on your commitment to setting things right, and work to prevent the harm from happening again.

We're going to make mistakes sometimes. That's OK! Practicing this framework helps us interrupt and address the ways we perpetuate gender oppression in our every-day lives. If our goal is safety and healing, rather than shame and punishment, accountability moves us forward.

 Reflect

1. Have you heard language that might fall into the category at the bottom of the pyramid? What are some examples, and how have you responded?

2. What are some ways you've seen oppressive norms formalized in structures or policies in your neighborhood, school, or other communities in which you participate?

3. Have you ever worked to change a structure or policy that seemed to promote harmful ideas about gender or sexuality? If so, how? If not, how could you start?

Talking with kids about consent

Hierarchy is baked into the way U.S. institutions and mainstream culture structures our society, our schools, and, most disconcertingly, our families. Many young children are taught that respect means obedience and that it is owed to people who are older, physically stronger, or in positions of authority. This widespread dismissal of young people's autonomy is at odds with the movement to build a culture that promotes consent, respect, care, and empathy.

Consent is about respect, not defined as obedience but as demonstrating care for the needs, boundaries, and autonomy of others. Sometimes as caregivers, as parents, as people with positions of power or status, we assume we know everything rather than accepting that people are experts in their own experiences. In practice, respecting consent means that when people tell us what they need, we believe them. We can offer our perspective and share information and resources; then, we need to give people space to make their own decisions. One strategy to help with listening is to repeat back what we've heard. We can acknowledge the need that's being communicated and respond directly to it, before jumping to suggest alternatives or teaching lessons.

In the kid domain, I often say things like, "I know you want to stay at the park longer. You're having so much fun here! We have to leave to eat dinner though. Do you want to come back to the park again tomorrow?" Acknowledging a child's feelings when it comes to everyday disagreements can show kids that we respect and care about their feelings and needs, even though they can't always get their way.

It's not enough to talk to kids about consent; we have to practice it. More than anything, kids learn from what we *do*, not from what we say. If we want our kids to be able to set boundaries; take responsibility for their actions; communicate their feelings, needs, and boundaries; and respect the consent and boundaries of others, we have to start that work with ourselves, in our interactions with kids.

To recap: respecting consent means demonstrating care for the needs, boundaries, and autonomy of others. It involves three main actions: ask, listen, and believe. The only way to be sure about a person's needs and boundaries is to ask. If you don't know someone's pronouns or you're not sure if they'd like to be hugged, it's better to check in than to assume. That said, body language is a valid and important way that people communicate, and sometimes people let us know with their body language if they want to be hugged or touched. Pay attention to whether someone is leaning in and outstretching their arms or backing away and turning inward. Next, listen: if the person has communicated that they use they/them pronouns or that they don't want to be hugged, then respecting consent means believing that they know best about their needs and boundaries. We can then demonstrate respect for their autonomy through our actions by attending to those needs and boundaries as we interact with the person.

Here's an example of an interaction that shows how an adult can ask, listen, and believe a child about their feelings, needs, and boundaries in order to respect consent:

Adult: Do you want a hug?
Child: No.
Adult: Thanks for letting me know! How about a high five?
Child: Sure!

Caregiving through the framework of consent means demonstrating respect and support for the autonomy, boundaries, feelings, and experiences of someone in our care; understanding and recognizing that those boundaries, feelings, and experiences are not static and can always change; and being accountable to listening and believing young people when they tell us who they are, what they need, and where their boundaries lie.

Consent can get tricky

When it comes to most things related to caregiving, we often find ourselves making the best guesses we can in a given moment and then adjusting accordingly when we have more information. Navigating consent is particularly tricky before kids become verbal: we want to respect our very young children's autonomy, but when infants and toddlers are not able to tell us what they want and don't want, we find ourselves learning through trial and error. We become attuned to body language. *Do you want to be changed? Fed? Held?* Not to mention questions about identity and expression. *What pronouns do you want me to use for you? What do you want to wear?* We make a lot of guesses, and sometimes we get it wrong.

Even when young people are able to communicate beyond nonverbal cues, we have to make decisions to promote the health, well-being, and safety of our children that might conflict with their autonomy. Some forms of physical touch are necessary to keep the kids we're caring for healthy and safe (and, well, alive). A baby might resist a diaper change, and we are still responsible for doing our best to keep them clean and safe.

Respecting the consent of very young children starts by recognizing that they have very little power in the world, and their caregivers have a lot of power. This power imbalance is not inherently bad; some power imbalances are inevitable. It's how we use our power that matters. Abuse involves leveraging a power imbalance to exploit or control someone else. Alternatively, we can use power in a way that emphasizes the autonomy of people in our care and builds up their capacity. Remembering the power imbalance will help us make sense of moments when their eyes well up with tears because they wanted to be the one to flip a light switch or push the button to call an elevator. We make so many decisions every day without giving kids much of a choice about where they're going, when we're leaving, and how we're getting there. Even when we do ask for kids' input, we tend to reserve our veto power and make the final decision. Often this is appropriate because we may have more information about the world and the way it works. When we communicate the information we have and ask for input (or offer options), we build up young people's capacity to make good decisions and model through our actions that consent matters.

Talking with kids about gender, bodies, and sex

Consent is an important framework for understanding and respecting our children's gender identity and expression. Just as we can ask whether kids want to be greeted with a hug, high five, or wave, and listen and believe kids when they tell us to stop tickling them, we can apply these guidelines to understanding and respecting a child's gender identity and expression: ask, or let a child tell you, how they identify and which pronouns to use. Then listen and believe them, and respect their gender!

People often ask me, "But don't kids change their minds all the time?" And the answer is yes! We can believe them every time, knowing that gender identity, expression, and pronouns may change. Respecting consent involves recognizing that boundaries, feelings, and needs may change, even in the course of one interaction, and we have to respond accordingly when those changes are communicated, verbally or nonverbally. Just like gender, boundaries are always subject to change, and respecting consent means accepting those changes when they occur.

Gender is not binary, and it is not the same as sex assigned at birth. Before children are born we're often asked questions like "are you having a boy or a girl?" ("I'm having a baby!" you might respond.) We're asked to fill out forms checking one box, male or female, to access birth certificates and healthcare, and body parts are often used to determine which box to check. This is referred to as *sex assigned at birth*: kids are assigned the "male" sex at birth if they have a penis and the "female" sex if they have a vulva.

People whose body parts cannot be clearly defined as either a vulva or a penis are considered "intersex." Often, the idea that gender is binary has led to forcible surgeries for people whose bodies were born with bodies perceived as neither male nor female. There is a growing movement against medically unnecessary and nonconsensual surgeries on intersex people, and in recent years legislation has been introduced in states like California to ban medically unnecessary surgeries on intersex people (though the legislation failed to pass as of January 2020).[24] Intersex surgery on infants is one of many ways that gender conformity is coerced, and reinforced by violence, starting at birth.

When we talk about bodies, remember: body parts don't define gender! Sex is a word that people usually use to refer to one of three things: (1) bodies, (2) something people do to feel good in their bodies, and (3) a way to make babies.[25] Although sex is generally assigned at birth based on body parts, gender is more complicated than that. Sex is not the same as gender.

Gender identity can be defined as "our deeply held, internal sense of self as masculine, feminine, a blend of both, neither, or something else. Identity also includes the name we use to convey our gender. Gender identity can correspond to or differ from the sex we are assigned at birth."[26] (Also, see image on page 246.)

Apart from supporting young people in defining their gender identity and expression, talking to kids about their body parts without shame or secrecy can help promote their self-esteem and allow them to be better advocates for their healthcare. Educating

---

24 Refer to InterACT for more information.
25 Cory Silverberg and Fiona Smyth. *Sex Is a Funny Word: A Book About Bodies, Feelings, and YOU.* New York: Seven Stories Press, 2015. Print.
26 "The Language of Gender," Gender Spectrum, retrieved September 20, 2019, https://www.gender spectrum.org/the-language-of-gender.

young people about their bodies is also important in preventing and addressing sexual violence. If young people have names for their body parts and know what the words mean, they will feel more comfortable using this language to talk to someone about their experiences, needs, and desires.

How can we talk about our bodies without reinforcing binary gender? We can use gender neutral language. Instead of "boys have penises" and "girls have vulvas," we can say: some people have penises, and some people have vulvas. Some bodies have sperm, and some bodies have eggs. Because many forms of patriarchal violence have been normalized in Western culture, it can be difficult to learn more affirming and comprehensive ways of thinking and talking about gender. It will take practice; expect bumps along the way.

One day when my daughter was five, she came home and angrily told me, "Grandma says that only *boys* have penises!" I sighed, exasperated. I had only recently reconnected with my mother, and I had set boundaries with her when she had previously made comments and took actions that invalidated my child's gender identity and expression. We had already come so far: she finally had come to accept my daughter's gender, name, and pronouns. So what went wrong?

My daughter insisted that I call my mother and explain that girls can have penises too. "She has to say sorry," said my daughter. Understanding my role as a parent and ally, I made the call.

Me: I hear you said that only boys have penises. I know you know that girls can have penises too. What happened?

Grandma: I knew I was going to be in trouble. She asked me how I knew Barney [Grandma's dog] was a boy. I said "because he has a penis." I wasn't thinking! But I knew right when I said it that I had said something wrong.

Ahhh, I thought. This was tricky! How could I explain to my mother that she didn't really know the gender of her dog without the dog ever communicating their gender, while also explaining to my daughter that *most people* assign a gender to their pets based on genitals?

Well, I tried by saying just that. Neither party was content. My mother insisted that her dog was a boy and my daughter insisted that a penis didn't make someone a boy. Sometimes we have to live with multiple contradictory truths.

In the end, what mattered was that my mother had said something hurtful and my daughter needed an apology. Even if she continued to insist her dog was a boy, my mother needed to demonstrate accountability for making a comment that undermined trans identities. Thankfully, she made an apology that satisfied my daughter (and my daughter continues to insist that Barney's gender is yet to be determined).

We can use the **ask, listen, believe** framework to support trans and gender non-conforming kids who are facing questions from other kids and adults.

Here's an example of a conversation I participated in on a playground when my daughter got questions about her gender at a time when she was not conforming to binary gender:

Child 1: Are you a boy or are you a girl?

Josefine[27]: No.

Me: Some people aren't a boy or a girl.

Child 1: Then why is he wearing a dress?

Josefine: I like dresses!

Me: Anyone can wear a dress!

Trans and gender nonconforming kids can often speak up for themselves in responding to questions from their peers. As adults and caregivers, it's our responsibility to back them up in these interactions and take the lead in educating ourselves and other adults about the experiences of trans and gender nonconforming people.

Here are examples from parents we know talking with their kids about consent, gender, sex, and bodies:

Rachael Koeson is a 38-year-old cisgender white woman who lives on Anishinaabe land now called Grand Rapids, Michigan, with her husband (40, white cisgender man), 10-year-old white cisgender daughter, and 5-year-old white transgender daughter. She has a somatic healing practice called A Midwife for Collective Liberation, where she works with supporting people to explore how the values of systems of oppression live in our bodies so that we can heal and begin to embody chosen values and then bring into being new worlds where we are all free and supported.

Scene: I'm at the top of the stairs sitting on the floor with my (then) four-year-old.

Kid, sadly: I have to be a boy because I have a penis, but I really like to wear dresses.

Me: You know you can be a boy and wear dresses. You wear dresses all the time.

Kid: But I have to be a boy because I have a penis.

Me: Actually your body parts don't have anything to do with being a boy or a girl. Some boys have a vulva and some girls have a penis, and there are lots of people who are a boy and a girl at the same time or are neither a boy or a girl.

Kid: Could I be a boy and a girl at the same time?

Me: Of course! If that is how you feel, that is who you are!

Kid, bursting into a huge smile and giving me a giant hug: I love you so much Mommy!

Me: I love you too honey—no matter what!

Kid: I am a boy and a girl at the same time!

Me: Yay! I am so happy for you. I know about someone else who is nonbinary. That's a word some people use to mean that they are a boy and a girl at the same time or not a boy or a girl. Their name is Alok, can I show you some pictures of them?

---

27 Name changed.

Kid: Yes please.
[We look at pictures of Alok Menon on Instagram (@alokvmenon) together and my child happily points out their favorite outfits that Alok is wearing.]

Reflections: This conversation was important in my child's gender journey and I felt good about how I handled it. I was glad that I already had some knowledge about people who are gender nonconforming, nonbinary, and transgender. I was grateful that I knew of someone who I could show her as one representation of a nonbinary person. This wasn't our first conversation along these lines but I remember this one vividly because 1) I was surprised she didn't already know she didn't have to be a boy because of her body parts and 2) she was so happy when she did understand that her body parts didn't have to dictate her gender. Since then she has shifted to identifying as a girl and uses a new name and she/her(s) pronouns. I am glad I was able to stay present and positive in this conversation because of work and learning I had already done.

Shela Linton, pronouns she/her/hers, is a Black-Indigenous queer femme who identifies as working poor. She is "Gma" to Anayah, age three, and parent to Z. Shela and her family live in Brattleboro, Vermont. When she's not working as a community organizer and activist, she enjoys river days, hiking, and exploring ways to heal through ancestral practices. (Shela is holding the megaphone on this book's cover photo.)

Scene: In 2019 my almost three-year-old grandbaby and I are at the library to get some books. We're together for our weekly visit, as we have done since she was born. I recently noticed a shift in A; she has started to really identify as a girl. A, who has been commenting when she sees people with long hair or dresses that they are girls like her, picks out My Princess Boy by Cheryl Kilodavis (not her first time reading this book).

[Right away A points out that the princess boy is a girl and the brother is a boy.]
Shela: Why do you think that?
A: They're wearing a dress.
[A is adamant that the princess boy is a girl. We talk through why she thinks this—the dress, tiara, dancing. Then we talk about who else wears dresses and tiaras and likes to dance, and how these people are not all girls.]
Shela: So your friend who is a boy likes to dance?
A: Yup, Gma.
Shela: Do you think he'd like to play with dresses and tiaras?
A: Maybe.
Shela: So when boys wear dresses it doesn't necessarily mean they are girls, and in this book boys can be princesses.

[A is still stuck on thinking the princess boy is a girl and the brother is a boy. We talk more about how some people express themselves in ways that have people thinking "this is a boy" or "this is a girl." I share with her that I believe you can wear what you want and express yourself how you want and it doesn't make you a boy or girl, it makes you someone who likes, in some cases, dresses and tiaras. I can see in A's eyes that she is taking it all in.]

 Reflect

These are examples of how these conversations could have gone and are not meant to be perfect examples (none of them are!).

1. What thoughts do you have after reading these stories?
2. What could you ask your child to better understand their experience and/or perspective?
3. How did these parents practice an age-appropriate approach to the conversations?
4. What else could these parents have said or done?
5. What could the situation/conversation have looked like in your family?
6. What's one way you could be braver in your conversations and actions with your kids?

Key resources for further learning:

- The Gender Unicorn: http://www.transhealthsa.com/wp-content/uploads/2017/05/The-Gender-Unicorn.pdf
- The Gender Wheel, by Maya Gonzalez, draws inspiration from Mayan and Aztec calendrical wheels to demonstrate the infinite and dynamic nature of gender: http://www.genderwheel.com/about-the-gender-wheel/
- "How to Talk to Young Kids About Gender" by Nadine Thornhill: https://www.talkwithyourkids.org/lets-talk-about/how-talk-young-kids-about-gender.htm
- The organization Gender Spectrum has a lot of great resources for parents working and talking with their children about gender: genderspectrum.org
- Parenting for Liberation Podcast Episode 19: "Let's Talk About Sex," by Trina Greene Brown, an interview with Ignacio and Amanda Rivera: https://anchor.fm/parentingforliberation/episodes/Episode-19-Lets-Talk-About-Sex-Interview-with-Ignacio-Amanda-Rivera-The-HEAL-Project-ebdm21

1. How do you talk to the children in your care about their bodies? Think about conversations you've had about bathing, body parts, and hugs from relatives.
2. How do the school systems you interact with reinforce the gender binary? How can we as parents advocate for safer schools that reject racialized gender policing and promote real safety?
3. What was your learning like around gender, sex, sexual orientation, and gender expression? What are the messages you would like your kids to have about the gender spectrum?
4. Think of a time your child has said something about gender or sex. How did you respond? How would you like to respond if you had the opportunity again?

Ariel and Anne (who share a conversation in Chapter 2 and 7) reading together.

Reading/listening/watching together
There are many great books out there about gender justice that can help us talk with our kids about consent, gender, sex, and bodies. These books create a whole different message around gender—one that is fluid, accepting, expansive, and encouraging of young people to be who they are. These books can both validate your own child's experience and illustrate for them all of the ways they can be in this world.

One favorite is *Sex Is a Funny Word: A Book About Bodies, Feelings and YOU* by Cory Silverberg and Fiona Smyth. This book uses comic strips and simple, inclusive language to help kids learn important concepts, covering everything from sex and gender to respect and relationships.

Another good read is *I Am Jazz* by Jazz Jennings, a young trans girl. This is a story of how a trans kid came to define her gender. One flag about this book is that it refers to having a "girl brain but a boy body." While it's important to support trans folks in telling their own stories, it's also important to talk with our kids about the distinction between gender and bodies. How would yoou do that? More recently, *When Aidan Became a Brother* by Kyle Lukoff tells the story of a trans boy who helped his parents prepare for the arrival of his new sibling and encountered questions and expectations about gender even during the pregnancy stage.

There are also some fantastic coloring books that challenge mainstream messages about gender and sexual orientation. Check out Jacinta Bunnell's *Girls Will Be Boys Will Be Girls* and *Sometimes the Spoon Runs Away with the Other Spoon Coloring Book*—these radical activity books celebrate trans, queer, and gender nonconforming people. Another good coloring book is *A Not So Typical Night Out* (https://batjc.files.wordpress.com/2019/06/comic-book-final.pdf) by the Bay Area Transformative Justice Collective, about taking accountability for sexual violence.

Your turn:

Choose three books from the book list below (or other similar books) to read with your kids, and practice asking questions like those above. Refer to pages 114–115 for questions to ask your kids before and after reading/listening/watching together.

Read

Ages 0–3
   Neither, by Airle Anderson
   C Is for Consent, by Eleanor Morrison
   How Mamas Love Their Babies, by Juniper Fitz and Elise Peterson
   My Body! What I Say Goes! by Jayneen Sanders

Ages 3–6 (many of these can be read with your toddlers too—they'll like the pictures!)
   Tell Me About Sex, Grandma, by Anastasia Higginbotham
   Julian Is a Mermaid, by Jessica Love
   Sparkle Boy, by Leslea Newman
   The Paper Bag Princess, by Robert Munsch
   What Makes a Baby, by Cory Silverberg
   When Aidan Became a Brother, by Kyle Lukoff

Ages 6–10
   Drum Dream Girl, by Margarita Engle
   Sex Is a Funny Word, by Cory Silverberg and Fiona Smyth
   The Gender Wheel, by Maya Christina Gonzales

Let's Talk About Body Boundaries, Consent and Respect, by Jayneen Sanders
What Does Consent Really Mean? by Pete Wallis and Thalia Wallis

"Don't Touch My Hair," by Solange
"Like a Girl," by Lizzo
"How Far I'll Go," from the movie *Moana*
"Reflection," from the movie *Mulan*
"Brown Skin Girl" by Beyoncé, Blue Ivy, SAINt JHN, and Whizkid

Woke Kindergarten Read Aloud: They, She, He, Easy as ABC https://www.youtube.com/watch?v=oxzo9O9KDkM

Steven Universe (ages 6+); This show uplifts queer and gender nonconforming characters and offers healthier representations of masculinity.

Frozen (all ages): Research shows that the vast majority of attacks on women and girls are perpetrated by people we know, and especially intimate partners. And yet children's movies often feature villains who announce their evil plans and are known for their evil deeds. When we draw a false binary between good and evil characters, it becomes more difficult to understand and address harmful behaviors in people that are trusted. A favorite among young people born in the 2010s, *Frozen* is a story about two sisters, Anna and Elsa, who are working to save their kingdom and restore their relationship after the loss of their parents. Rather than centering a romantic love story, the movie focuses on the strength of sisterhood and sisterly love. When the movie does discuss romantic love, it breaks down one of the most prevalent myths in children's media about "bad guys" or "evil villains." In *Frozen*, Prince Hans preys on Anna's vulnerability, builds her trust, leads her to believe that he loves and cares for her, and seeks to move quickly in the relationship—much like abusive intimate partners do in real life. It's not until later in the film that it becomes clear that Prince Hans has an ulterior motive. Bonus: when Kristof wants to kiss Princess Anna, he asks first! This creates a great opportunity to talk to kids about consent.

Moana (all ages): *Moana* is a quintessential feminist tale of friendship and transformative justice, featuring complex characters and a fierce young woman of color in a heroic lead role. In it, Te Ka is depicted as a whole person who has been harmed, having had her heart stolen, leading her to engage in harmful and destructive behavior. The harm reverberates across an entire community, leading to damaged land and water that makes it difficult for the community to survive. The only way to repair the community is to repair the harm. Moana embraces Te Ka with care, empathy, and compassion. "This is not who you are," she sings as she confronts the destructive force and works to restore the stolen heart. Te Ka transforms back into the beautiful goddess Tefiti. With actions taken toward repairing the harm, including consequences for the demigod Maui who stole the heart, the community is able to be restored.

The Owl House (ages 6+): Featuring bisexual Afro-Dominican teen Luz Noceda as the main character, *The Owl House* tells the story of a 14-year-old girl who always finds herself in trouble because she is seen as too weird and too different from her peers. When her mother decides to send Luz to a camp meant to encourage her to conform, Luz ends up wandering away into an alternate universe of witches and weirdos where she soon becomes a witch's apprentice. In the very first episode, people who are incarcerated are portrayed as protagonists who have been punished for being different, while a warden is seen as the villain. Luz helps to free those who are incarcerated, declaring "nobody should be punished for who they are." This challenges the legitimacy of punishment and prisons while celebrating nonconforming identities and forms of self-expression.

It's important to ask questions and engage in dialogue about the media we consume that impart messages and lessons about consent, gender, sex, and relationships, whether or not those messages and lessons were intended.

Here are some ideas for starting these conversations:

❋ Did you see how that character asked for consent before kissing someone? That's so important. Do you remember what it means to ask for consent?
❋ Did you notice how Maui apologized to Te Fiti? What made that a good apology?

For other recommendations of gender justice books and films, see the resource list on page 335.

 Reflect

1. What did you learn about yourself and/or your kids from reading/listening/watching together?
2. What feelings and body sensations came up for you while reading/watching/listening?
3. What else do you need to know to have conversations with your kids about gender and gender justice?
4. What are you wondering about?

Taking action

There is always work to do to build gender justice. In our everyday lives, we can interrupt patriarchal violence and gender oppression wherever it shows up—whether it's in our schools, our communities, or our homes. This means actively resisting the urge to replicate punitive approaches modeled by state institutions and cultivating behaviors associated with the values we want to promote: respect, empathy, nurturance, and accountability. In this chapter, we covered strategies for interrupting oppression like taking accountability using the Four A's (acknowledge, apologize, ask, and action) and having conversations with people in our lives (including children and young people in our care) about gender oppression. And as emphasized throughout the chapter, making change at the individual level is important, but it's not enough. We have to root out the ways that gender oppression and intersecting oppressions are upheld by state institutions. This means challenging the presence of police in our schools and communities and joining the call of radical movements to defund and abolish the systems of prisons and policing, in all their forms. Read more on 8toAbolition.com about specific, actionable policies you can support in your local community to dismantle systems of punishment and move toward building a culture of care, safety, and accountability. Defund police, demilitarize communities, remove police from schools, free people who are incarcerated.. and invest in care not cops.

So how can you turn all this learning into action?

❁ Examine your own experiences with gender and sex. Learning is action.

❁ Speak out! Have more gender justice conversations.

❁ Read/listen/watch with your kids.

❁ Get involved in local, national, and global work for gender justice.

Examine your own experiences with gender and sex. Learning is action. You've already started! By reading and engaging with this chapter, you're taking action for gender justice. A big part of it is examining the things we've learned about gender and sex and how that learning has impacted us. With the "Childhood Memories" worksheet (Appendix L), you can talk about the ways that gender norms and messages about gender have informed and impacted your own experiences. And check out the resource lists toward the end of the book for recommended articles, films, and books you can plug into to learn more.

Speak out! Have more gender justice conversations. Your kids will get ideas outside the home about gender and sex—often messages that counter what you want them to learn. When and where you can, speak out! If your kid comes home saying their coach told them they were "throwing like a girl," talk to both the coach and your kid about it. If your child doesn't identify as a boy and wants their classmates and school to respect that, talk to your school. When you hear your child making generalizations about what people of a given gender can do or wear, ask them where they're getting these ideas. There are so many ways and times to speak out and continue the conversation with both your kids and those who impact their lives.

Read/listen/watch with your kids. This is action!

Get involved in local, national, and global work for gender justice. Wherever you are there are always organizations doing great work around gender justice. Here are a few that are involved in action, education, and research across the country:

Collective Action for Safe Spaces (collectiveactiondc.org) is a Washington, DC-based grassroots organization that applies comprehensive, community-based solutions using an intersectional lens to eliminate public gendered harassment and assault in the DC metropolitan area. Bystander intervention, healthy masculinities, consent, transformative justice, and public health approaches to gendered violence and gendered state violence are all addressed.

Gender Spectrum (genderspectrum.org) offers a wide range of materials and trainings on gender inclusivity and creating safe environments for youth.

Rethink Masculinity (collectiveactiondc.org/our-work/rethink-masculinity) is a program of Collective Action for Safe Spaces, ReThink, and the DC Rape Crisis Center that seeks to address gendered violence by engaging masculine-identifying people in work to promote healthy masculinities. The program aims to build nurturance culture, make connections between gender norms and gendered violence, and create an environment where everyone feels responsible for making our communities safe.

Survived & Punished (survivedandpunished.org) is an organization with chapters in Chicago, New York City, and Oakland that aims to bring freedom and support to criminalized, incarcerated survivors of gendered violence through defense campaigns, fundraisers, letter writing, and other forms of advocacy.

Your turn:

Spend some time exploring the above resources and considering ways you and your family could get involved.

 Reflect

1. What are ways that you're working for gender justice in your community? How do you involve your kids?
2. What else would you like to be doing? Make a SMART goal—one that is specific, measurable, attainable, relevant, and with a time limit. Examples (see page 69 for explanation):

> "My SMART goal is to have conversations with my child about the media they consume and even assignments they receive from school. I will have at least one intentional conversation a week."

> "My SMART goal is to next month attend the parent support group for parents and caregivers of LGBTQ youth in my community so that I can learn more, ask questions, share my experiences, meet parents, and support my queer/trans/gender nonconforming child."

Healing justice practice

Storytelling and creating public art are practices that help us heal ourselves and our communities. With the 2020 global pandemic and mass uprisings in defense of Black lives, my daughter and I have found ways to participate in social distancing while still engaging in community-based actions. For example, I have taught my daughter to wheatpaste messages, like the #8toAbolition platform that outlines eight measures we can take to move toward a world without prisons or policing.

Wheatpasting is simple! You can find recipes online for homemade wheat paste using everyday household items, or you can go to an art store to pick up wheat paste powder and then just add water. You'll also need a paintbrush and the message or art piece you want to post, ideally on printer paper or another thin paper. After you have your mixture, use your brush to spread the paste over an outdoor surface, like the base of a light pole, then place the piece of paper over the area with paste and paint another layer of paste over the art.

We also use sidewalk chalk to spread positive messages through public art.

Community of practice questions

1. What have been your *aha!* moments in this chapter?
2. What have been your successes in talking/reading with your kids?
3. What have been your struggles?
4. What have been your somatic/body sensations and responses throughout this chapter?
5. What do you want to know more about?
6. Share your SMART goals. How can the group support you in achieving your goals?

Chapter 7

PARENTING FOR COLLECTIVE LIBERATION

BY ANGELA BERKFIELD

There is no such thing as a single-issue struggle because we do not live single-issue lives.
—AUDRE LORDE, Black feminist, lesbian, poet, warrior, mother;
from the address "Learning from the 60s"

We are all carrying grief, a deep unimaginable grief that impacts how we receive and connect with one another. It is a cumulative emotional and spiritual wound that results from the history of violence that we all share. It doesn't matter if we come from an oppressor population, an oppressed population, or if our ancestors simply witnessed the violence and destruction of oppression: we all carry the imprint of that wound in our souls. This creates a barrier that prevents us from being able to truly see one other, meet one other, and connect with one other.[1]
—SHERRI MITCHELL, Weh'na Ha'mu Kwasset, an Indigenous rights activist,
spiritual teacher, and transformational change maker

It is the people who are most marginalized, the people who have most been bound by societies, who most deeply understand what it is to be free.[2]
—REV. ANGEL KYODO WILLIAMS

If you have come here to help me, you are wasting your time. But if you have come because your liberation is bound up with mine, then let us work together.[3]
—LILLA WATSON, Aboriginal activist group, Queensland, Australia

---

1 Sherri Mitchell, *Sacred Instructions: Indigenous Wisdom for Living Spirit-Based Change* (Berkeley, North Atlantic Books, 2018), pg. 55. *Sacred Instructions* is a powerful weaving of how centuries of violence are impacting our lives, and what we can do for healing.
2 "Your Liberation Is on the Line," *Buddhadharma: The Practitioner's Quarterly,* Spring 2019, pg. 78.
3 Lilla Watson, as part of Aboriginal activist group, Queensland, Australia, 1970s, https://lillanetwork. wordpress.com/about.

Youth Climate March, 2019, Brattleboro, VT. Photo credit: Marco Yunga Tacuri

 Reflect

Use the following questions as a guide to reflect on the quotes above. You can write or paint, and share your responses with someone or just think quietly, whatever works best for your learning style.

1. What is a social justice-related issue that you feel passionate about? How is it connected to other social justice issues? It might be helpful to brainstorm connections to other issues that you might not think of at first. For example: I care deeply about the climate crisis. Questions I ask myself: In what ways are the impacts of the climate crisis experienced disproportionately? Whose voices are dominant in the climate justice movement?

2. What is the grief you carry? How does it impact your ability to connect with others?

3. Do you feel the need for liberation? How do you think about your liberation as connected to the liberation of others?

Story

Waking up

I am white. I benefit from whiteness.
AND I am more than white.
I am descended from mother, father, ancestors, immigrants, Irish,
Danish, from boats, ocean, tears, original people, roots, herbs, soil, stars,
universe.
As a woman I carry the pain of mother, grandmother, seven generations
back, bodies who know violence.
My wrists hurt—phantom pain.
In past lives they have been cuffed, imprisoned. My soul hurts—
phantom pain. From past lives until today she has believed she doesn't
matter, isn't worthy, isn't as beautiful as . . . or as smart as . . .
As a Christian I was taught to love the other as myself; I was also taught
there is only one way. Contradictory messages. Wading through to find
the essence of truth.
In school I was taught dates, famous people (mostly white men),
a reigning conquerors trope.
Narratives challenged by mentors and teachers, traveling by bus
and on foot, volunteering all night long, deep and true friendships.
Waking up.
Listening to mother earth I receive messages of the past, the future,
of truth, of abundance. I am healing the imprint of trauma.
Waking up.
I am love. I am friend. I am music. I am creation. I am you. I am us.
I am change.
Waking up.
Liberation. Collective liberation.

I wrote this poem after a two-day workshop with Sherri Mitchell on trauma and decolonization. Even though I think of myself as not having trauma, she very easily read the imprint of trauma on my body. I am realizing that just because I haven't had specific trauma in this lifetime doesn't mean that I don't carry the imprint of trauma from all of the harm and violence that is happening around me, that has happened to my ancestors, and that I am receiving benefit from. I also carry secondary trauma from having supported many hundreds of people who have experienced complex trauma, including some of the people closest to me. Lately I have been learning more about historical trauma from slavery, war, land theft, genocide, and poverty. I am learning that trauma gets passed from generation to generation at a soul level, and a cellular level, and it impacts our communities and our efforts toward justice. It contributes to the separation we are already steeped in.

When Sherri was sitting with each person in the workshop, hearing their trauma, shifting the energy of their trauma, I could see clearly how all of these traumas are connected. The great monster of colonization has been killing the souls and squashing the hearts of humans, and pillaging the gifts of Mother Earth for century upon century. That trauma lives in our bodies and sometimes causes us to hurt others, to reenact the pain and hurt. We see it over and over again, oppressed becomes oppressor. It's a vicious cycle. Without true healing we get stuck in a cycle of violence. Yet when oppressive systems don't change, humans have a hard time actually healing. The trauma of being enslaved is connected to the trauma of being abandoned or emotionally abused by parents. The trauma of enslaving, of being the slave master, is connected to continued abuse of self and others, even the ones we love most. It is all connected.

To free ourselves from that cycle of violence and the resulting trauma and the separation we feel, we all need to get free. That is collective liberation. Catalyst Project[4] defines collective liberation as "a recognition that each person's liberation is tied up in the liberation of all people, and that racism and white supremacy, along with all other forms of oppression, dehumanize both those they oppress and those who (at least in the short term) profit or are privileged by them."

I've been working on getting clearer about what collective liberation means and how to weave it into my parenting. This chapter may feel different than the other chapters because it is a place of active learning for me. There are more questions than answers in this chapter. I invite you into that learning with me.

Here's one way that learning edge shows up and how I am engaging with it. A few years ago a friend and colleague reflected back to me that when I tell my story about class and race I so often tell the stories of oppressed people. I need to learn and tell my own story. This is hard to do. Having lived a life of privilege and not having experienced specific trauma in this life, it is easier to think and talk about the "other," which inevitably means telling someone else's story. My social justice story has been one of working to end oppression of other people. Yet I now know that I am also impacted by that oppression. I benefit from a system of oppression and need to name that in my story. And I'm harmed by it and I need to name that too. I've been working on doing that, and I notice a powerful and important shift in my story, and in the way that people receive it. I am committed to continually uncovering my own story, so that I can show up more authentically and accountably for social justice work, including visioning a just future.

I continue to find resources that support me in doing the work of uncovering my story. A friend passed along a resource, the Healing Justice podcast,[5] and encouraged me to listen to the episode on ancestral healing for racial justice (mentioned on page 120). The episode comes with a practice activity that involves envisioning one's ancestors. For the first time in my life, one of my ancestors appeared to me. My great-great-great grandmother, five generations back, appeared to me in this vision. She immigrated to the U.S. from Ireland sometime before 1860. During a subsequent meditation she took me to visit her grandmother, seven generations back, in the late 1700s. I'm sure they

4 Catalyst Project, Anti-Racism for Collective Liberation, From handout at workshop, October 2008. Catalyst Project is an organization in Oakland, CA, that builds multiracial movements for collective liberation. http://collectiveliberation.org.
5 There are so many powerful interviews and practices on this podcast (https://www.healingjustice.org).

have been there all along and this was just the first time I was paying attention. I was finally able to understand that my ancestors are real people and still a part of me. This visioning and reconnecting practice has allowed me to begin a relationship with my ancestors that is healing my ancestral trauma of separation.

That practice has opened up the possibility for me to make more connections, to dig beneath the top layer of my experience to think about what else is happening around me. Here's one example of that increasing awareness. Growing up I thought I was free and my life had many characteristics of freedom. However, ten miles away were neighborhoods with substandard housing and not enough jobs. This is where poor and working-class folks lived, many who were Black, Latinx, and Native American. In the 80s and 90s those neighborhoods were flooded with drugs, were heavily policed, and men were being ripped from their families and thrown in jail. These neighborhoods are often described as having one of the highest homicide rates in the country. We could also describe the area as being on the frontlines of an economic and white supremacist catastrophe, but growing up, I never heard it described that way. The root causes of the homicide rate were not talked about by the media, legislators, or my social work professors, nor by the social service organizations serving the area. All of that injustice was occurring right around me, in my energy field, and I had no idea. Which doesn't mean it wasn't impacting me.

I served food at soup kitchens in those hurting neighborhoods and tutored kids in the local schools. I was taught that we are all one human race and that sharing what we have with others is fundamental to being human. But I was not taught to name the systems of power and privilege that were making our life experiences so different and disparate. I was taught to love others, but not that our material circumstances were interconnected.

Applying systems of oppression thinking, I now recognize that economic structures, policies, and cultural beliefs contributed to the disparity between those neighborhoods and the ones where I grew up. Drug policy was written and enforced such that there was an excuse to lock up Black, Latinx, and Native Americans.[6] School funding was (and still is in many places) tied to property taxes. This policy makes schools in poor neighborhoods substandard while schools in high-tax bracket areas can thrive. Capitalism requires profit and growth, which during the 70s through 90s led companies to move factories and jobs out of the country. This left neighborhoods and cities without jobs for the working class, impoverishing many while putting more money in corporate coffers.

Collective liberation thinking compels me to ask how I am connected to these patterns of inequality and violence. What was my experience, living adjacent to those neighborhoods? How did my neighborhood benefit from the policies that hurt nearby areas? Well, I didn't personally know anyone who had gone to prison. We had good schools, job opportunities, high property values, parks, sidewalks, and grocery stores. So how was I hurt by that situation? One answer is that it caused me to feel separate from people who were having a different experience than me. It gave me an unhealthy feeling of being right or better than others, otherwise known as internalized superiority.

6 To learn more about racialized drug policy, watch the movie *13th* by Ava DuVernay or read *The New Jim Crow* by Michelle Alexander.

It caused me to pity others instead of placing responsibility on systems. In some cases I had the opportunity to build relationships with people who were suffering, but it was unbalanced because I had unknowingly more power in the relationship. As I gained knowledge and perspective, I came to realize that I was connected to that pain and oppression, so I wasn't really free.

The oppressive systems we live in are not inevitable! It can feel overwhelming to realize that larger structures and policies must change for these disparities to change. Naming what exists is painful and heartbreaking; it brings feelings of rage, depression, guilt, shame, and deep sorrow. Those feelings are part of the healing process, and they are absolutely necessary if we are going to be personally liberated and if we are going to be able to join the struggle for the liberation of everyone. This process of naming makes it possible to activate just and equitable systems.

The way these feelings show up in me is through crying. Tears flow easily when I am sad, enraged, or joyful. Crying runs in my family, we feel things deeply. When my dad or aunt tell a good story, they get tears in their eyes and my grandpa was the same way. Both my dad and my grandpa were Baptist pastors, and they often cried while they preached. I'm thankful for that family legacy, which has allowed me to accept my feelings and be okay with showing my feelings publicly. As a social justice facilitator I certainly have many opportunities to cry in public. My kids also get to see me cry a lot, especially when reading social justice kid's books. I'm laughing as I write this because when I pause while reading a storybook, my kids look at me to see if I'm crying. I often am. "C'mon, Mom, keep reading," they say. But I know that it is important that they see how deeply the story touches me, enough that emotion is all over my face.

Even while it is important for me to activate the emotions that have been intentionally suppressed, I must recognize when my emotions, and especially tears, are a result of white fragility. Tears are sometimes used by white people as a defense mechanism to avoid attending to how we have impacted people of color. They can take attention away from the real issues and create a situation in which people in the room have to provide emotional support for the white person who is crying, a replication of a very old pattern of white people extracting emotional labor from people of color. It is also true that emotions are perceived differently based on who is expressing them and how much power the person has in that context. For example, when I cry in a training, the white participants often empathize with me and can connect more with my story, whereas when my co-facilitator, a Black woman, cries in a training, she is perceived as manipulative or her crying evokes a pity response. I am learning to know the difference between when expressing emotion is essential to connecting with the issues and each other, and when it is distracting and diverting.

Each of us have our own ways of showing emotion. Mine is crying, yours might be raging or withdrawing or humor. While we need to be aware of and address the issues connected to expressing our emotions, it is still very important, essential even, that we let ourselves feel. We need to feel the pain, feel the heartbreak, feel the rage, the hopelessness, the sorrow, the fear, feel the feelings that have been covered up for so long by lies. If we can let ourselves feel again, it will be much easier to feel connection, solidarity, hope, beauty, freedom, and the liberation that can be ours in the truth-telling.

This transformation does not happen overnight; the journey from despair and rage to liberation takes time and happens over and over again.

One of the precious gifts that parenting has given me is the gift of holding multiple truths at once. This is an important skill for collective liberation: recognizing that liberation isn't about one or the other, but instead multifaceted. In my house we are laughing our heads off one moment, arguing the next, and calmly reading the moment after that. We go through so many emotions together all day long that I can't keep up. This emotional roller coaster is one of the aspects of parenting that has been really frustrating for me. But now, as I'm waking up to how tumultuous the world really is, I can see how this lesson of parenting is useful for adults as well as kids. I have been building my skill of holding anger and love at the same time, pain and beauty simultaneously, holding deep grief and also moving through that grief to take action, and holding a vision for justice, even while the world seems to become more unjust by the minute.

I'm early in my journey of understanding collective liberation and it has already opened up a much deeper well of commitment to the struggle for justice, to learning about my own healing, and to supporting others in their process of healing. It has strengthened my relationships in the struggle for justice and has made it easier for me to talk with others who have not yet joined the struggle that acknowledges how collective liberation is so important for all of us.

 Reflect

1. What is your collective liberation story? Where are you at in the journey of knowing where you come from and where you want to go?
2. Do you believe in collective liberation? Is some part of you holding onto your own freedom at someone else's expense, or holding onto the "savior" idea of liberating someone else? What response does your body have to this question?
3. Where do you feel that wound from centuries of violence imprinted in your body and in your soul?
   a. If you do feel the wound, what are you doing for your own healing? Is your healing connected to collective healing?
   b. If you don't feel the wound, why is that? Is there something blocking you from feeling it? What lessons and structures have conspired to prevent you from feeling it? Who/what is invested in your continuing to not feel it?

Collective liberation, intersectionality, and emergent strategy

According to the Merriam-Webster dictionary, liberation is the act of setting free, or the state of being free, or a movement seeking equal rights and status for a group.[7]

---

7 Liberation, Merriam-Webster website, retrieved August 20, 2019, www.merriam-webster.com/dictionary/liberation.

Liberation movements sometimes refer to armed or nonviolent struggles against colonizing forces, such as the National Liberation Movement in India to end British rule, and the Palestinian liberation movement to end Israel's occupation of Palestine. Well-known liberation movements include Black liberation (e.g., Black Panthers, Movement for Black Lives), Native American liberation (e.g., American Indian Movement), gay liberation, queer liberation, trans liberation, disability liberation, women's liberation, and liberation theology (a Latin American movement for liberation of the poor that grew out of some Catholic parishes).

Collective liberation does not take precedence over these other, more specific liberation movements. It provides a framework for seeing how all liberation is connected. It also makes clear that people with privileged identities have a stake in liberation and need to join the struggle along with the oppressed people of the world. Our suffering is connected and if we can't get to how deeply it is interconnected we can fall short in our healing and in our solutions. Colonial capitalism has trained us away from that way of thinking, and we desperately need to return to it, for our mental health and for our actual survival as a species.

How do we apply collective liberation to our lives? It's not all or nothing. Activist Chris Crass (who also wrote one of the Forewords for this book), a co-founder of Catalyst Project and author of *Towards Collective Liberation: Anti-Racist Organizing, Feminist Praxis, Movement Building Strategy,*[8] suggests asking: **How can we maximize what is liberatory and minimize that which is oppressive—in ourselves, in our movements, and in society?** This question is a way to examine how we are and aren't doing collective liberation in any given part of our lives.

I'll start by applying this question to my organizing work with The Root Social Justice Center in Brattlelboro, VT:

> At The Root we are growing a movement for racial justice. We are a multiracial leadership collective and we have five programs that all contribute to the racial justice movement. To maximize what is liberatory, we are prioritizing healing from white supremacy and injustice through a culture shift: practicing somatic abolitionism,[9] offering classes for BIPOC (Black, Indigenous, people of color) on natural herbs from a decolonized lens, and hosting monthly gatherings to connect and have fun. We also purposefully take time off from our busy organizing schedules to spend time with our families and our own healing practices. We minimize what is oppressive by being clear about what our capacity is as organizers, instead of being pulled into a white supremacist culture of urgency. We take intentional time in our meetings to give each other positive and constructive feedback, which allows us all to recognize and minimize the ways we might be oppressing others. We also take action in

---

8 Chris Crass, *Towards Collective Liberation: Anti-racist organizing, Feminist Praxis, and Movement Building Strategy* (Oakland, CA: PM Press, 2013). You can read a chapter from Towards Collective Liberation here: https://collectiveliberation.org/wp-content/uploads/2013/01/Catalyst-Project-From-a-Place-of-Love.pdf.
9 Resmaa Menakem, "Mending Racialized Trauma: A Body Centered Approach with Resmaa Menakem," July 2019, https://connectfulness.com/episode/010-resmaa-menakem-racialized-trauma.

restorative ways when any harm has been done, using facilitated accountability circles to address harm.

I will also apply this question to my parenting:

In my parenting I maximize what is liberatory by openly naming and celebrating the strengths and the unique gifts my children have to offer the world. I celebrate my oldest son's tears as his beautiful ability to express deep emotion. I celebrate my youngest son's ability to give gifts in a way that reflects his acute awareness of what brings people joy. I minimize what is oppressive by giving them information about historical oppression so that they have the knowledge needed to not repeat the past. I talk with them daily about their feelings to avoid the trap of toxic masculinity. I provide avenues for them to develop friendships outside of their comfort zones.

 Reflect

1. How do you maximize what is liberatory and minimize that which is oppressive—in yourself, in your parenting, in movements you are part of, and in society?
2. Two concepts that help me better understand how to go about working for collective liberation are intersectionality and emergent strategy.

Intersectionality

When we think about race, class, gender, and ability (as well as other categories like age, religion, sexuality, and nationality, and related issues like climate change, homelessness, addiction, hunger, drug abuse, incarceration, and immigration) as separate issues/problems it can feel overwhelming. There are so many problems, what can we really do? When we feel overwhelmed, normal reactions are panic responses—fight, flight, freeze, or fawn (complying so as to make things easier or to survive).

On the other hand, drawing the connections among all of these issues can be very motivating. A connected understanding helps us to know that when we are working on one issue, our actions will have an impact on broader movements for social justice. And it helps us to articulate to others what the problems and solutions are and how movements are connected.

An important concept in explaining the connection of systems of oppression is intersectionality, which we define as the complexity of identity and experience as constructed by multiple, interlocking systems of power (such as racism, classism, sexism . . .), articulated for the purpose of understanding and shifting those systems of power.[10] Identity is complex, and the way each of us experiences identity has to do with those systems of power we have been talking about. Our class, race, ability, and

---

10 Davey Shlasko (2015), "Using the Five Faces of Oppression to Teach About Interlocking Systems of Oppression, Equity & Excellence in Education," 48:3, 349–360, DOI: 10.1080/10665684.2015.1057061.

gender are all connected and we experience the world through them all simultaneously, even though we often aren't aware of it. The second part of the definition is really key here, it states that the purpose of understanding intersectionality is to shift power imbalances.

I'll start with myself as an example. Some of my salient identities are: white, middle class and married into owning-class privilege, able bodied (for my whole life so far, yet as this book goes to press, dealing with metastatic breast cancer), cisgender, woman. These identities are interlocked and have caused me to have a specific experience in the world. For example, as a cisgender female, in many work settings I feel oppressed. My ideas are not listened to in the same way that male coworkers' ideas are considered, and I am hypervigilant about not being sexually harassed. Both patterns lead to emotional distress at times, and also an overloaded nervous system. However, the privileges I have because of race, class, and ability mean that I am still able to meet my basic needs. When a particular work situation has not been good for my mental and physical health, I have been able to get a different job. I own a car, so I am able to leave a dangerous situation when I need to, instead of relying on public transportation or catching rides with friends. I have access to health care and some disposable income that makes it possible for me to address physical and mental health concerns that are connected to the oppression I experience as a woman. The way that I experience the world as a woman is inseparable from my whiteness, my class, and my ability. Being able to name that has made it possible for me to challenge power imbalances because of gender, and also to be in solidarity with people who experience additional oppression because of race, class, ability, or other identities.

Let's go back to the example of why I am able to cry in public in a way that, for the most part, adds to my legitimacy as a professional rather than detracts from it. I am crying in a way that's considered appropriate for a white woman, because of sexism and because of racism. Often this allows me to get what I need (even though that is not at all why I feel like I am crying): to get out of a speeding ticket, to get a pay raise, to gain sympathy from the people I am working with. At other times it provides an excuse to not take me seriously, because showing emotion is not considered appropriate for people in leadership positions. If I can see how oppression is playing out in the moment, I can begin to interrupt the oppressive pattern by naming what is happening both to myself and others around me.

Quite honestly, intersectionality is a learning edge for me. I continue to recognize how intersectionality works and how I play a role in it, sometimes to my benefit and other times to my detriment. I'm working on recognizing where I can maximize what is liberatory and minimize what is oppressive.

 Reflect

1. What is your intersectional experience of the world? Can you think of at least one example? And another?

When we share our experiences with each other, we can better understand how the larger system of oppression functions. The lens of intersectionality is important because it helps us to more accurately understand and more effectively shift those systems of power that are hurting all of us (even though some of us are much more aware of that pain than others).

To better understand intersectionality I recommend you watch the TEDx talk by Kimberlé Crenshaw in which she explains the urgency of intersectionality in addressing police violence against women of color.[11] She describes how the media reports on Black men who are killed by police and mostly ignores the women who are being killed. She talks about racism and sexism at work together, inseparable from each other—though I was disappointed that she didn't bring in class or disability, which often get left out in conversations about intersectionality. When we don't recognize the interlocking nature of systems of oppression, people get left out and we can't get to the root of the problem.

Let's think about intersectionality in our own lives, both in the work we are doing and how we are talking about issues with our kids. To get at intersectionality it can be helpful to ask the following questions:

1. Who is impacted by a particular issue? Who else? (For example, I might think about an issue, and it might be immediately obvious to me that it's related to sexism and negatively impacts women. So I ask myself, is it also related to racism? Classism? Ableism? Something else?)
    a. Within the groups that are impacted, which subgroups are *most* impacted? (For example, an issue might impact all/most women, but it might have an especially severe impact on women of color who are single mothers.)
    b. What would it look like to put the folks who are most impacted in the center of our analysis and strategy?
2. How is this issue impacting me? (Even people who are privileged by an issue are impacted. If you can't think of a specific way you're impacted, think about who you are disconnected or distanced from as a result of the issue.)
3. Why is it this way? How did it get to be this way? Who benefits from it staying this way?
4. How could it be different?
5. Who needs to be at the decision-making table and organizing for solutions?

I'll apply these intersectionality questions to the lack of affordable housing.

1. **Who has been impacted by the lack of affordable housing (a major issue in the area where I live)? And who are the *most* impacted? Which of the groups impacted by housing instability are least likely to find the resources they need for stability?** I know that the lack of affordable housing in my area impacts poor people and often working class people as well. It is impacting

---

11 Kimberlé Crenshaw, "The Urgency of Intersectionality," uploaded October 2016. TED talk, https://www.ted.com/talks/kimberle_crenshaw_the_urgency_of_intersectionality. Be advised: this talk is a tear-jerker.

people of color and especially single mothers and trans and genderqueer people. It is also extremely hard for people with disabilities to find housing that is accessible that they can afford. So the most impacted are poor, Black and Indigenous, women/queer/trans, single parents with disabilities. This isn't going to be true in every situation, but it holds true in general and statistically.

2. **How is this impacting me?** I have never been without dignified housing. My race, class, and ability identities have ensured housing. Even in those times when my budget was tight (by choice because I was traveling or volunteering or staying at home with my kids for the first year of their lives), I was able to use my social capital to find affordable and nice off-the-market housing options.

3. **Why is it this way?** The housing industry is connected to individualistic and merit-based ways of thinking that are inherent to capitalism. Housing and real estate are profit-based industries, meaning housing is only built when the developer can make a profit from it, and usually only in the way that is the *most* profitable. This holds true even if an only somewhat profitable project would benefit many more people. The dominant values/beliefs of our society shape the policies we make. A few examples of underlying beliefs that have contributed to current housing policy are: you deserve what you get, housing is only for those who "deserve" it, only able-bodied people matter, poor people are lazy, Black people are criminals, and single moms are promiscuous and therefore undeserving. These beliefs have shaped policies around development, housing assistance programs, and more that have contributed to the current affordable housing crisis.

4. **How could it be different?** Housing could be built based on need or the well-being of the community, rather than profit for a few. We could think about housing as a human right for everybody. We could recognize that there is enough for everyone, or to put it another way, that no one should take seconds (have a second home) until everyone has gotten firsts (a dignified place to live). We could connect the issue of homelessness to the issue of hunger, to the lack of health care, to war, to out-of-control incarceration, and so on. We could ensure that the people at the planning table for future housing policy are those who have been the most impacted by the affordable housing crisis. We could recognize that when all people have dignified housing it actually benefits everyone.

5. **Who needs to be at the table for decision-making and organizing for solutions?** The people at the table must include those most impacted by the lack of affordable housing, such as poor people, people with disabilities, people of color, migrant workers, veterans, and single mothers. It is not a small or easy task to change who is at the table, and to do so in a way that people are truly listened to and not just tokenized. I'm writing about this leadership shift from a very practical place. I'm currently part of a training and consulting team that is actively working with all kinds of groups, including organizations,

businesses, and local governments, to bring about this shift in leadership and decision-making and the culture change needed for the shift to be equitable.

When we apply intersectionality to the issues we are working on, it is more likely that our efforts will be led by the people who are most impacted. The solutions that emerge from their leadership will be more likely to get at the root causes of problems, and these solutions will benefit everyone—collective liberation!

 *Reflect*

Apply the five intersectionality questions to something you're working on or a movement you're a part of.

Emergent Strategy

Another framework that can help us shift our thinking and action toward collective liberation is emergent strategy. This is a relatively new theory coined by adrienne maree brown in her book *Emergent Strategy: Shaping Change, Shaping Worlds.*[12] brown's work is built on foundations inherited from many leaders and elders of the past and present whose ideas and practices come together to form the strategy. One of the key people brown received mentorship from was Grace Lee Boggs, a leader in the civil rights movement who organized in Detroit up until her death at age 100 in 2015. brown dedicates the book to Grace Lee Boggs and quotes her as saying, "Transform yourself to transform the world."[13]

brown describes six main elements of social change taking place in the current moment and gives examples for how these elements are playing out in a transformational way. She outlines the core principles that interact with these elements. These elements and principles provide a blueprint for collective liberation in action, and an antidote to many of the characteristics of white supremacy culture. *(see Appendix H: https://www.parenting4socialjustice.com/)* It is more than a strategy; it is a culture shift.

Elements with their principles:
1. Fractal—the relationship between small and large.
   ❋ Small is good. Small is all.
2. Adaptive—how we change.
   ❋ Change is constant, be like water.
   ❋ There is always enough time for the right work.
3. Interdependence and decentralized—who we are and how we share.

---

12 adrienne maree brown, *Emergent Strategy: Shaping Change, Changing Worlds* (Berkeley, CA, AK Press, 2017).
13 brown, *Emergent Strategy*, pg. 53.

- There is a conversation in the room that only these people at this moment can have. Find it!
- Trust the people. If you trust the people, they become trustworthy.
4. **Non-linear and iterative**—the pace and pathways of change.
   - Never a failure, always a lesson.
   - Move at the speed of trust. Focus on critical connections more than critical mass.
5. **Resilience and transformative**—how we recover and transform.
   - Less prep, more presence.
   - Build resilience by building relationships.
6. **Creating more possibilities**—how we move towards life
   - What you pay attention to grows.

I'll go through each of the elements, giving personal examples of emergent strategy related to my parenting. As you read, consider how you might apply the elements in your family.

> **Element:** *Fractal—the relationship between small and large*
> **Principle:** *Small is good. Small is all.*
> "I have to use my life to leverage a shift in the system by *how* I am, as much as with the things I do." ~adrienne maree brown[14]

This element challenges the capitalist notions that bigger is better *(throughout this section, see Appendix H: https://www.parenting4socialjustice.com/)* and the white supremacy culture characteristic of quantity over quality and having more progress.

For much of my life I've felt like I'm not doing enough, and this has led to me to say yes to too many things, which has often led to overwhelm and burnout. It sometimes frustrates me to have to be at home putting my kids to bed when I would rather be at an organizing meeting. This element reminds me that my relationship with my kids is everything and impacts the whole. The time spent putting my kids to bed in a loving, connected way has a ripple effect. This principle reminds me to be present in every moment, and especially in my parenting. Small is all.

> **Element:** *Adaptive—how we change*
> **Principle:** *Change is constant, be like water.*
> **Principle:** *There is always enough time for the right work.*

This element challenges our resistance to change and the lie we've been told: that things have always been this way and will always be this way. The element is an antidote for the white supremacy culture characteristics of urgency, perfectionism, and right to comfort.

My son put multi-colored clay under the door to his room. When I opened the door the clay rubbed all over the carpet, creating rainbow carpet. I was furious. I yelled.

---

14 brown, *Emergent Strategy,* pg. 54.

I sent him to timeout. Within ten minutes, and after lots of deep breathing, I was able to shift my thinking. I recognized it was more important to connect with him than to send him into isolation. I found him, gave him a big hug and kiss (with his consent), and apologized for yelling. I told him that even when I am angry with him I will always love him. I chose to use this hard moment as a time for connecting and learning, instead of shaming and isolation. This situation helped me to see how I've been able to adapt and upgrade my parenting tools, instead of my old pattern of seeing myself as a bad mom because I yell. Change is constant. In this situation, both my son and I are doing the right work.

❀ **Element:** *Interdependence and decentralized—who we are and how we share*
❀ **Principle:** *There is a conversation in the room that only these people at this moment can have. Find it!*
❀ **Principle:** *Trust the people. If you trust the people, they become trustworthy.*

This element challenges individualism and also challenges the concentration of wealth and power. It is an antidote for the white supremacy culture characteristics of power hoarding and individualism.

We were on vacation for a week with Abigail Healey and her family, who are also white. Across the two families we have a mix of class backgrounds, from working poor to access to owning-class wealth. The four boys, who at that time ranged in age from five to nine, started playing a game of cops and robbers, zooming around right underfoot of the four adults who were hanging out chatting. Instead of saying "go play in the other room," we engaged with them in their game. The older boys said, "We are the police, we make the rules, you are going to jail." We complained that they were cheating because we hadn't done anything wrong and that they were just trying to get us off the couch because they wanted it. They said, "We can cheat if we want to, we are the police." This gave us an opportunity to talk about how policing works in real life, and about how people with power abuse their power to get what they want or to stay in control. We asked the kids how it could be different. Of course the boys weren't interested in having that conversation; they were having too much fun feeling powerful. But they had the chance to hear our questions.

Remember the Paulo Freire quote on page 49? *"Education either functions as an instrument which is used to facilitate the integration of the younger generation into the logic of the present system and bring about conformity, or it becomes the practice of freedom, the means by which men and women deal critically and creatively with reality and discover how to participate in the transformation of their world."*[15] In the above example, we had interrupted the patterns of thinking and acting through the questions we asked our kids. I'm sure there are plenty of times we don't interrupt status quo thinking, probably because we don't even notice it, but as we continue to learn, we also bring our kids on the journey of our learning and growing awareness. Learning in this way becomes decentralized, instead of something the kids think just happens at school.

---

15 Paulo Freire, *Pedagogy of the Oppressed* (New York: Herder and Herder, 1972).

> ❊ **Element:** *Non-linear and iterative—the pace and pathways of change*
> ❊ **Principle:** *Never a failure, always a lesson.*
> ❊ **Principle:** *Move at the speed of trust. Focus on critical connections more than critical mass.*

This element challenges the capitalist worship of success and the definition of success as measured by having more. It is an antidote for the white supremacy culture characteristics of either/or thinking, perfectionism, only one right way, and progress is bigger/more.

In most public schools our children have very little time for creative play. Even at a very young age they are trained to sit still and fill out worksheets. This teaches them that reading and writing are more important than make-believe and making messes and complex problem-solving in a group. My lifestyle makes it challenging to counteract those messages with my kids. My kids have to do lots of sitting quietly and filling out worksheets. I'm not able to homeschool and I can't afford private school that might (or might not!) take a different approach. Because I'm working full-time, I have limited time for critical conversations and creative messes at home. This makes me feel like a failure. I'll be honest, I freak out weekly over the creative messes that my kids make because it is getting in the way of my productive day which makes me feel like I've failed even more.

I am now conscious about shifting my failure narrative to one of learning. I recognize my own limitations and I recognize that my kids' messes are helping me interrupt the white supremacy characteristic of perfectionism. Also, my minor temper tantrums give me the opportunity to repair harm, to admit that I was the one at fault, to apologize, and to take time to create with my kids or to clean up with them. This builds critical connection.

> ❊ **Element:** *Resilience and transformative—how we recover and transform*
> ❊ **Principle:** *Less prep, more presence.*
> ❊ **Principle:** *Build resilience by building relationships.*

This element challenges capitalist and colonized thinking about punishment and "pull yourself up by your bootstraps" mentality. It is an antidote for the white supremacy culture characteristics of defensiveness, fear of open conflict, and only one right way.

I often feel guilty because I'm not doing structured activities with my kids, like a fun art project or baking or playing a game. This guilt is connected to my class privilege. Growing up I had a stay-at-home mom and we did all kinds of activities that fit into a version of middle-class norms of play. My guilt is also connected to the class privilege of working full-time. When I shift this guilt to thinking about resilience and transformation, I recognize that I am meeting my kids' deeper needs. They need a strong relationship with me and with people around them, and they need tools and skills for changing the world. I do "less prep" of structured activities and spend more of my parenting time just being present with my kids—loving them, reading to them,

Brattleboro VT, Parenting for Social Justice Community of Practice picnic in 2016.

being in relationship with people in the community with them, and going to community events for change. We are building all of our resilience by building relationships with each other, with the earth, and with the community around us.

In the above photo you can see a fun family gathering that happened in 2016. This was an intentional gathering for families working on social justice issues. We wanted our kids to know they are an important part of this social justice community and to have a chance to build friendships with the other kids. My kids are on the ground under the canopy, having a blast. These kinds of activities are good ways to build resilience by building relationship.

> ❀ **Element:** *Creating more possibilities—how we move towards life*
> ❀ **Principle:** *What you pay attention to grows.*

This challenges the deficit narrative that is so prevalent in U.S. culture. It is an antidote for the white supremacy culture characteristics of power hoarding, I'm the only one, and individualism.

My kids are awesome. They give big hugs. The love all kinds of sports and games, and they have so much fun playing with friends. They leave wet towels on the floor, forget to flush the toilet, and pretend to wash their hands but don't. Sometimes I focus more on what is going wrong than what is going well. When I notice this pattern and shift my attention to their strengths, I enjoy my time with them much more. A few years ago I described to my therapist how frustrated I was with my youngest child. My therapist asked if there were times when it didn't feel like that. I thought for a while and said, "Yes, when we are on a hike together." She suggested we go hiking more. And just like that, I shifted my relationship with him. We went hiking more. We were happy together more often. When we got back to the house the challenges were still there, but they didn't feel as hard because we had just had a good time together. Ever since then, whenever things start to feel hard again I remember that we need to get out and hike. This creates more possibilities in our relationship and shifts the power imbalances.

This element is parallel to the 10-10-80 rule from Sherri Mitchell we talked about (on page 11) in the Introduction.[16] It is worth repeating here: Mitchell advises us to spend 10% of our time understanding the problem, 10% of our time in resistance to the root of the problem, and 80% of our time creating the world we want to live in. What we pay attention to grows.

Emergent strategy is a blueprint for reconditioning our thinking and action that helps us move beyond the confines of capitalism, patriarchy, white supremacy, and interlocking systems of oppression. This strategy is being applied in current movements for social justice all over the U.S. and the world. And it can also be applied in the small everyday ways that we interact in our families and communities. Emergent strategy gets us closer to collective liberation!

 Reflect

1. Pick two emergent strategy elements and come up with examples of how you are applying them in your parenting or in social justice work you are involved in.
2. What limitations are you bumping up against in your parenting? Try applying the emergent strategy elements. What happens?

Examples of movements using a collective liberation framework

Collective liberation is motivating many of the social justice struggles of these times. It is bringing many groups together who have worked separately before. In this section we'll look to the climate justice movement and the #MeToo movement to better understand what collective liberation means and how it works in practice.

First, let's look to the Climate Justice Movement

The symptoms of climate upheaval are intensifying: record-breaking natural disasters, rising global average temperatures, wildly fluctuating local temperatures, species extinction, and rising sea levels. We must stop burning fossil fuels and consuming unsustainably. We must address the root causes: an extractive economy that requires growth and an ideology that says humans are separate from the earth. Climate upheaval is an issue that impacts all of us, yet it hits poor and working class people, people of color, Indigenous people, and underdeveloped nations first and the hardest.

Mainstream discourse has been either ignoring the crisis or asking for business-as-usual solutions like the carbon emissions tax. On the other hand, the climate justice

---

16 Sherri Mitchell, *Sacred Instructions: Indigenous Wisdom for Living Spirit Based Change* (Berkeley, North Atlantic Books, 2018).

movement has centered the voices and solutions of the people most impacted, and is bringing together diverse groups and organizations. The difference in solutions is radical. One of the leaders in the climate justice movement work is the Climate Justice Alliance[17] (CJA), which has a "translocal organizing strategy and mobilizing capacity that is building a Just Transition away from extractive systems of production, consumption and political oppression, and towards resilient, regenerative and equitable econ-omies. We believe that the process of transition must place race, gender and class at the center of the solutions equation in order to make it a truly Just Transition." Because of CJA's strategy to prioritize people who are most impacted, they are able to clearly articulate why a carbon tax is a false solution.[18] The policy and grassroots actions they put forward include a ban on all new oil and gas exploration and keep-

photo credit: Sha Grogan-Brown, Grassroots Global Justice Alliance

ing 80% of all known remaining fossil fuels in the ground!

You can learn more about ways that the people most impacted are leading the movement—through the Grassroots Global Justice Alliance,[19] Rising Tide,[20] and the Indigenous Environmental Network.[21]

Even though the climate justice movement is doing really important work, there is still room for constructive criticism of or within the movement. All of our organizations and movements are located within the white supremacist, capitalist, patriarchial system. We need to watch out for where we are competing when we should be collaborating, and where we are making concessions that will benefit some people but not the most impacted. We must continue to hold movement leaders accountable to social justice principles and collective liberation. And when we ourselves are in positions of leadership, we must be willing to be held accountable.

---

17 Climate Justice Alliance was founded in 2013 and is made up of over 70 urban and rural organizations: https://climatejusticealliance.org/about.
18 "Carbon Pricing: A Critical Perspective Community Resistance", Climate Justice Alliance and Indigenous Environmental Network, October 2017, https://drive.google.com/file/d/18bfpaO4f8l4e9Cm JPRL99FstaYqKthxV/view.
19 http://ggjalliance.org.
20 https://risingtidenorthamerica.org/features/principles.
21 http://www.ienearth.org.

Now let's look at the #MeToo Movement

The #MeToo movement was started by Tarana Burke a decade ago with the goal of ending sexual violence. Violence is a cornerstone of colonial, corporate capitalism as you read about so clearly in Chapter 6. This violence impacts everyone. We can see that in how it shows up in our homes. According to the National Coalition Against Domestic Violence (NCADV), one in five women and one in seventy-one men in the United States have been raped in their lifetime.[22] No one is exempt from being exposed to this kind of violence. It cuts across all identities, although it is more pronounced for BIPOC, women, LGBTQIA, people who are disabled, and who are poor. NCADV also reports that American Indians are three times more likely to experience sexual violence than any other ethnic group. Over half of American Indian women report being sexually assaulted.[23]

One of the mainstream responses to sexual violence has been to put laws into place that make sexual harrassment in the workplace illegal. Workplaces then provide training for their staff about sexual harassment. That has been in place for decades. Enter: the #MeToo movement, which is really a movement of truth telling, of coming forward to share where sexual abuse and harrassment have continued unabated. This movement has given our country an inside look at how those policies and trainings haven't had the hoped-for impact, or haven't gone far enough. Patriarchy, and the violence that comes along with it, is still intact.

In a 2018 TEDWomen talk Tarana Burke says, "Trauma halts possibility. Movement activates it."[24] She says, "We have to re-educate ourselves and our children that power and privilege don't always have to destroy and take, they can be used to serve and to build." Her vision and actions helped launch an intersectional and decentralized movement that is working to end sexual violence. As a Black woman she is a powerful leader and spokesperson because she has been on the frontlines of this violence in the communities she has been living and working in.

The movement is so powerful because it creates a space for survivors to stand up and be heard. With the multitudes of people coming forward it has been possible to bring many perpetrators down from their positions of power. One statistic that shows concrete success of the movement is that as of October 2018, #MeToo had brought down 201 men from positions of revered leadership and power. These men had used their positions to harm women.[25] The movement is also about ending policies that protect violators (such as nondisclosure agreements) and putting in place policies that

---

22 National Coalition Against Domestic Violence website, retrieved July 14, 2019, https://ncadv.org/statistics.

23 National Coalition Against Domestic Violence, "Domestic Violence Against American Indian and Alaska Native Women," NCADV website, retrieved July 14, 2019, https://www.speakcdn.com/assets/2497/american_indian_and_alaskan_native_women__dv.pdf.

24 Tarana Burke, "Me too is a movement not a moment," November 2018, TED talk, 16:07, https://www.ted.com/talks/tarana_burke_me_too_is_a_movement_not_a_moment?language=en#t-557171. This is a TED talk worth watching!

25 Audrey Carlsen, Maya Salam, Claire Cain Miller, Denise Lu, Ash Ngu, Jugal K. Patel, Zach Wichter, "#MeToo Brought Down 201 Powerful Men. Nearly Half of Their Replacements Are Women," New York Times, Oct. 23, 2018, https://www.nytimes.com/interactive/2018/10/23/us/metoo-replacements.html.

protect workers who are not currently protected, such as farm workers, domestic workers, and independent contractors.[26]

The movement has had a profound impact on consciousness in the U.S. One person interviewed for the article said, "Americans are thinking more than ever about power: who has it, who doesn't, and how those with more power are trying to control those with less. There are a lot of reasons for that, including the election of Donald Trump, but #MeToo has been a significant driving force behind the change."[27]

There is much critique of this movement, as one would expect of a movement that is challenging patriarchy in such a powerful way. One of the critiques from a collective liberation viewpoint is that there are not enough people from the front lines (the people who are the most impacted by sexual violence; think back to our questions about intersectionality) who are leading the movement. We can hold movement leaders accountable, asking for more leadership from people who are the most impacted by sexual violence.

 Reflect

1. Think of a social change movement that you have been involved in or paying attention to. How is a collective liberation framework being used? If it isn't, why not?
2. Write/make art/make music to express your reflections on collective liberation.
3. What else do you need to do to more fully understand or embody collective liberation?

Talking with kids about collective liberation

In my parenting I strive to give my kids the tools for recognizing how they are harmed when others are harmed, and for embodying that belief. I am teaching my kids that:

※ each human being is valuable.
※ each human being has struggles.
※ our struggles are connected.
※ some people have been and are being harmed more than others.
※ sometimes we contribute to that harm even when we don't mean to.
※ we can apologize and transform the pain and separation into love and connection.
※ Black and Native American liberation, queer and trans liberation, disability liberation, and poor liberation is essential and prioritized in collective liberation.
※ there's never a better time than now to work for liberation in small and big ways.

---

26 Anna North, "7 Positive Changes That Have Come from the #MeToo Movement", Vox.com, October 4, 2019, https://www.vox.com/identities/2019/10/4/20852639/me-too-movement-sexual-harassment-law-2019.
27 Ibid.

The reality is I'm not sure I've done a very good job of talking with my kids about collective liberation. I'm wondering if my actions and words are conveying to my kids that social justice is about helping people who are oppressed, because we are often helping people. When I help others I am doing so from a place of mutual aid, not pity or scorn or guilt. But do my kids know that? At the same time, we are also in deep connection with a diverse community of people who are practicing collective liberation. I wonder how my kids perceive it all. I'm continuing to pay attention and ask questions.

In all of my work to gather good social justice kid's books I've found so few that do a good job of conveying the concept of collective liberation. When our storybooks don't convey the concept, we have to understand the concept ourselves and bring it into our conversations about our kids' books, as well as in other moments with our kids.

For example, when I am reading the book *Sitting Bull*[28] with my kids I talk about how our ancestors were some of the settler-colonizers who stole land in the Midwest from the native people which benfitted our family directly. My family farmed the land and made enough money to have a house and go to college, all while not even acknowledging the existence of the people native to that place, nor our connection to the issues that the tribes in the Midwest face today. Our ancestors hurt people; we are still benefitting, and those people are still hurting. Since we are all connected, we are really still hurting too, even though we often ignore it. I compare it to something they can understand . . . "Remember how you hit your brother and stole his money yesterday? And then you didn't apologize and he was still crying? What if that went on for days and weeks and years? What if you never apologized and never gave back the money? He would stay mad and he might not play with you anymore. It wouldn't be that fun in our house anymore. It would make all of us hurt."

I talk about history, I relate it to my kids' lives, I ask if they have questions. I can hear you thinking, "This is too advanced for my kids." But you better believe that a five- or six-year-old Lakota kid already knows the story of how their land was stolen, their ancestors who were massacred and their ancestors who resisted. Many of those kids are learning how to resist colonization through learning ancestral languages, cultural knowledge, and stories, as well as showing up to protests to protect the water. It is only right that my white kids who benefited from that oppression also know the story—because it's true, so they don't repeat it, and so they can understand and make reparations a reality.

I recently found the book *Not My Idea: A Book About Whiteness* by Anastasia Higginbotham.[29] It is the first children's book I've found that clearly lays out how whiteness is hurting everyone, including white folks, and how we as white folks can and must work for change. My seven-year-old really liked the page that shows a contract with a photo of a $20 bill on it where you can sign on the dotted line to bind yourself to whiteness. He really wanted to sign for $20; it is such a tempting page for a kid like him. When we finished reading he went to get his markers and I thought

---

28 S.D. Nelson, *Sitting Bull: Lakota Warrior and Defender of His People* (New York: Abrams, 2015). [*Ed. note:* This is appropriate for ages 6+]

29 Anastasia Higginbotham, *Not My Idea: A Book About Whiteness* (NY, Dottir Press, 2018). I would read this book to kids as young as 4.

for sure he was going to sign the contract binding him to whiteness, but instead he started coloring in the illustration of "knowledge is power." This coloring page in the book is a challenge to that contract. It gives kids a chance to say yes to knowledge, which is needed to challenge white supremacy, rather than saying yes to the privileges and immunity that come from white supremacy. What a relief that he chose knowledge over signing his life away. And to think I had doubted him!

I'm on the lifelong journey toward parenting for social justice from the perspective of collective liberation. I have a good handle on some concepts and can even provide stories to support those concepts, and I'm expanding my vision for liberation. However, it is taking longer to shift my actions than I would like. I've got centuries of conditioning from colonization to undo. It is no small task to shift a helping mentality to one of mutual aid and collective change, in which I recognize that I need liberation as much as anyone. My parenting is a reflection of what I learned from my parents. I have to work hard to interrupt my initial response to protect my kids from the realities of injustice, to spare them from hardship, heartbreak, and pain. I have to remember that not only is it good for them to know the truth, but that it is imperative for the survival of humans and of Mother Earth.

Let's hear from some other parents about collective liberation conversations and action with their kids.

You don't get to not engage. You don't get to decide on your own that this is just how it is, because you cannot possibly understand the nature of your mind without understanding the nature of the collective mind. And in this country, the nature of the collective mind is oppression. It is white supremacy. It is patriarchy. That is what we were born into. If we do not understand the nature of it, how it unfolds, then we can't see how it lives in us. We can't understand how we push the gears of it every single day. Are you one day going to extract yourself from it completely? I have no idea. That's not an interesting question. Just get started.

—Rev. angel Kyodo williams,
"Your Liberation Is on the Line," *Buddhadharma:*
The Practitioner's Quarterly, Spring 2019, pg. 80.

My name is Amber Arnold and I am grateful to be part of this project and to be able to share some of my experience as a multiracial momma and anti-racist healing justice activist in Vermont. I have three children: Layla (8), Elijah (4), and Laylani (2). I am co-founder of SUSU CommUNITY Farm.

I believe in collective care and collective community. I believe that I am responsible for the care and love of all children on this earth. I do my best to remind myself that how I show up in the world isn't just about me, it's

Amber's kids, Layla and Laylani, with some garden vegetables.

about all of you and your babies too. When you hurt, I hurt, and when I hurt, you hurt. None of us will be fully liberated when the other beings in our communities are still experiencing pain, oppression, and marginalization. I believe that though I can't change the whole world, I am responsible for deeply loving, nourishing, and caring for my own body. By taking that seriously and practicing my own care, I am embodying what I wish for my children and those around me and I am sharing that care with others.

When I think about a collective liberation framework, what I want my kids to experience is self-care as collective care. In white supremacy culture (sometimes referred to as American culture) when we talk about self-care it is very individualistic. I'm doing something for me, and it is generally not focused on the collective community.

I'm not into binaries and black and white boxes but I do believe there are only two options here: either we are anti-racist or we are racist. There is no in between. Our children learn not just by our words, but by our bodies and our energetic presence in spaces. I believe that unraveling the white supremacy that lives in my body allows me to show up physically, emotionally, and spiritually aligned with my values and what I teach my children. My children's bodies naturally absorb this anti-racist way of being in the world, that is then shared with those they are in community with. Anti-racist somatics and precolonial body movements are something I am passionate about doing and teaching others.

How do I embody that feeling of freedom, feeling of liberation, and feeling of community and interconnectedness? How do I embody that and share that with my children? It can't be learned through books, it has to be learned through the body. It has to be something they experience. It doesn't have to be complicated.

One of the most transformative things I do with my children is have sporadic dance parties. In white supremacy culture we are told to be still, to listen, to be quiet, to be stiff and paralyzed. This stiffness keeps us detached from our bodies. Dance parties challenge those narratives. We scream, laugh, and feel connected and free. It creates looseness and connection between us, a feeling of freedom. Through movement and just being, there is a release of energy and a release of trauma. We hold a lot of trauma in our joints and pelvis, so when we have those movement practices where we are freely moving it is a way to release that trauma and oppression. This isn't an idea that I created, this is how our ancestors moved through these experiences and released them in their bodies. This is a practice that anyone at any age can do. It allows my children to physically embody anti-racism and connect with the lineages they come from that passed these practices down to us, through our bodies, and in this way we are honoring our ancestors and their revolutionary collective healing.

The other thing I do with my kids is ritual. I go outside with them and we sit with the plants that surround us. We sit for a moment and feel the energy of the plants, and they know to ask for permission before taking from the plant. I teach them about reciprocity and that for everything we take (with permission), we must also give back. They leave offerings of corn meal, rose petals, or other items that feel meaningful to them. Then we come inside and take a bath together. We put the plants into the water and take turns pouring the plants and water over each other's bodies. It's a way to connect with the energy of the plants. They experience the release of whatever they are ready to let go of and bring in whatever they are ready to bring in.

White supremacy turns things into objects that humans have power over. These simple practices are opportunities to live in a way that challenges the narrative of white supremacy. It is a way to embody a very simple yet complex relationship with the land that holds them. We are practicing reciprocity, giving, and receiving. It challenges the relationship of dominance/ownership over plants and over the earth and creates a relationship of stewardship.

Abby Mnookin is a middle class, white, queer, cisgender, Jewish woman who lives in Vermont with her wife and their kids (ages seven and three). She is a climate justice organizer, an outdoor educator, a writer, and a birth doula.

Scene: My older child, six at the time, has shared with us a manifesto she created while out playing with a friend.

Water is life.
Feed Life.
Love is life.
Do not Grab.
You need love.
No hunting people.
Do not pollute.
Tell the truth.

Reflections: Our whole family often goes to rallies and vigils together, standing up for trans rights, racial justice, and victims of mass shootings.

Lucy's Manifesto.

My older child, then four, traveled with me and other Vermont families to the Pennsylvania shale fields to witness firsthand the effects of fracking; I traveled to Standing Rock to join Indigenous Water Protectors resisting the Dakota Access Pipeline and came home with photos and stories. Still, I'm not always sure these conversations and actions strike a chord or make sense to my kids. I sometimes find myself overthinking the conversations, trying to find exactly the right words to explain what can be a violent and unjust world.

My family doesn't remember what our child's specific motivation was with the manifesto, but it was clear that our actions and discussions were having lasting impact, which she'd distilled into pictures and words that she and her friend could understand. Sometimes kids say it best. What a better world this would be if we'd all follow these seemingly simple guidelines, rooted in justice and love.

Ariel Brooks is from Santa Fe, New Mexico, and now lives in Boston. After many years as an educator, she is now working to advance sharing economies and economic democracy.

Scene: On our walk to school, a few days after reading together from Little House on the Prairie (I can't believe I completely glossed over the pointed and casual racism and land theft in my memories of the books), my six-year-old daughter Anne is outraged on behalf of Indigenous Americans.

Anne: Why don't we just give it all back?! Why isn't anyone working on this?!

Me: Well, there are a lot of people working on this, many First Nations are advocating for themselves and there are many people who are supporting their work.

Anne: I help in all the ways I can! I talk to people about how Donald Trump is so bad for thinking that white people are better than black people. And I always give money when I see someone on the street who needs it. Why don't other people help like me?

[My brain races; we're a block away from school. I want Anne to understand that talking about 'helping' others in this tone is part of white supremacy culture.]

Me: I think it's really great that you work so hard to think of others, but sometimes when you offer to help people in that way, it can cause them to feel embarrassed, because they want to be able to have the power to help themselves.

Anne: [Responding how she usually does when we get to school in the middle of an intense conversation and she becomes suddenly self-conscious] OK Mama. Can we stop talking about it now?

Reflections: As I struggled to respond to Anne's 'good helper' remarks, I thought about how every time I talk to my child about hard truths I'm worried that I'm setting her up for paralyzing stress that shouldn't be hers to internalize. About whether I have the resilience to keep hard conversations going at 8:15 in the morning when I'm trying to get myself organized internally for my own busy day. Then about how that thinking is itself only possible because of our white privilege and class privilege and how it's my responsibility to say something. And then around to my child's gender and how I want her to be confident and strong and so worry about correcting her too much.

Rachael Koeson is a 38-year-old cisgender white woman who lives on An-ishinaabe land now called Grand Rapids, Michigan, with her husband (40, white cisgender man), 10-year-old white cisgender daughter, and 5-year-old white transgender daughter. She has a somatic healing practice called A Midwife for Collective Liberation, through which she supports people exploring how the values of systems of oppression live in our bodies so we can heal and begin to embody chosen values and bring into being new worlds where we are all free and supported.

Scene: My older child's bedroom

Kid: I hate myself. There is nothing good about being a white person.
Me *(feeling heartbroken, pausing to breathe and offer myself compassion)*: It is really hard to feel that way, huh?
Kid: Yeah.
[I pause, wait, and remind myself there is "nothing to do, nothing to fix, nothing to figure out, just be with."* Feeling into my feet and grounding into the places where my body meets the support of the bed helps me do this.]
Kid: I don't like myself at all! White people only do bad things.
Me *(feeling into my feet, with my hand over my heart to offer myself kindness)*: Oh honey, that's a really hard way to feel. I feel that way sometimes too.
[After a long pause, I offer her a hug, which she accepts.]
Kid: Do I even get to be a leader? Do I get to do what I want to do?
Me: What do you mean?
Kid: I just don't know what I get to do and what I can't do, because I am white.
Me: I hear you. That can be really complicated to figure out.
Kid: Yeah, I wish I was a Black girl.
Me: I have felt like that too sometimes. It feels like there would be more to be proud of, huh?
Kid: Yeah. All our ancestors were terrible racists.
Me: They were racists and they did do some bad things. I think I understand a little how you feel. I wish I had more white people I could look up to for being anti-racist. I was thinking we could do some research and learn more about that so we could feel connected to some white people we can feel proud of. What do you think about that idea?
Kid: Sure. I still feel bad about being white though.
Me *(pausing)*: I do too sometimes and I also know that I am really trying to learn and do better. I think that we can both learn and do better than our ancestors. We want a world where everyone can feel good about themselves no matter what, right?
Kid: Right.
Me: So let's keep practicing being kind to ourselves no matter what, okay?
Kid: Okay.
Me *(holding and rocking her while hugging)*: I love you honey.

Reflections: I am really grateful that I have an embodied self-compassion practice so that I could stay with this hard conversation. I was trying to hold the space for her to not run away from the hard feelings that come with a legacy of white violence and also not get stuck in the idea that she should feel bad about herself because she is white. I know I still have a lot to learn about how to help her navigate her identity as a white person; I am struggling with many of the same questions she is grappling with. I felt good about being transparent with her about that and also wished I had been more prepared for this conversation with stories of anti-racist white folks we could connect to and feel proud of. We later had a conversation about how it's not really a full picture to say we wish we were someone from an oppressed group because those folks have suffered so much and if we really were from that group we would have things to be proud of and also a lot of hardships, discrimination, and pain. I am glad I saved that for another conversation instead of "correcting" her in this one.

*This internal mantra is one I learned from Lorena Monda and the "Hakomi" training I attended, which I use as a practitioner with clients and as often as possible in my parenting when my kids are feeling big things. This allows spaciousness into my system so I can be more regulated. My kids often co-regulate with me when I can do this.

 Reflect

After reading through these conversations and stories, we invite you to spend some time reflecting. These examples are not meant to demonstrate perfect responses or actions, but rather to encourage us to think about the ways we are talking with the kids in our care. The stories also invite us to think about how we are taking action for collective liberation, both at home and in the community.

1. What felt familiar to you?
2. What surprised you?
3. What could you ask your child to better understand their experience and/or perspective?
4. How might you have responded in similar circumstances?
5. What are you wondering now?

Reading/listening/watching together

Finding resources that illustrate and embody collective liberation is certainly not as easy as finding materials specific to race, class, disability, and gender. Bringing the collective liberation theme into our shared media requires reading many books and being intentional about connecting the issues to each other and to our own lives. As you saw in the parents' stories, there are many ways to do this, from dance parties to writing manifestos to breathing deeply. Here are a few ideas for books/music/videos you can bring into your parenting, followed by questions you can ask to encourage conversation.

Read

Ages 0–3
C is for Consent, by Eleanor Morrison
Feast for 10, by Cathryn Falwell
Feminist Baby, by Loryn Brantz
My Friends, Mis Amigos, by Taro Gomi

Ages 3–6
A Is for Activist, by Innosanto Nagara
Dreamers, by Yuyi Morales
Mr. Lincoln's Way, by Patricia Polacco
Not My Idea, by Anastasia Higginbotham
Sila and the Land, by Shelby Angalik, Ariana Roundpoint, and Lindsay DuPré
The Other Side, by Jacqueline Woodson

Ages 6–10
A Young People's History of the United States, by Howard Zinn
Mighty Miss Malone, by Christopher Paul Curtis
RAD Women Worldwide, by Kate Schatz
The Benefits of Being an Octopus, by Ann Braden
The Birchbark House, by Louise Erdrich
Young Water Protectors: A Story About Standing Rock, by 8-year-old Aslan Tudor and Kelly Tudor (birchbarkbooks.com/all-online-titles/young-water-protectors)

Listen *(see P4SJ playlist on Spotify)*

"Liberated," by DeJ Loaf and Leon Bridges
"Resilient," by Rising Appalachia

"Ripple," by the Grateful Dead

"Solidarity Forever," by Ralph Chaplin and recorded by many artists; I like Pete Seeger's rendition.

"Which Side Are You On?" written by Florence Reese and recorded by many artists

"Your Pain Is Mine," by Ziggy Marley

Watch

"A Message from the Future with Alexandria Ocasio-Cortez"[30] (all ages)

The Story of Stuff: https://storyofstuff.org/movies. These short videos highlight our addiction to stuff and how that addiction is connected to other social and environmental issues. If you apply a collective liberation lens you can connect these videos to many other issues we are talking about in this book.

There are many films on the ZinnEd Project's website recommended for sixth grade and up: https://www.zinnedproject.org/materials/?cond[0]=media_types_str:Films&cond[1]=levels_str:Grades+6-8. Use your discretion in showing younger kids. For example, I showed my third grader the film "The People Speak."

Questions to ask while reading/listening/watching:

1. Do you see yourself in this story?
2. Does this remind you of any other stories we have read? Or of something that has happened where we live?
3. What would you do in this situation?
4. How does this make you feel? What sensations do you notice in your body?
5. What's another ending for this story?

 Reflect

1. What did you learn about yourself and/or your kids from reading together?
2. What else do you need to know to have these conversations with your kids?
3. What other resources would you add to this list?

Taking action

How can you turn all this learning into action? Just like in all the other chapters . . .

❀ Keep learning.

❀ Heal for self and community.

❀ Read/listen/watch and have conversations with your kids.

---

30 "A Message from the Future with Alexandria Ocasio-Cortez," The Intercept, Retrieved October 22, 2019, https://theintercept.com/2019/04/17/green-new-deal-short-film-alexandria-ocasio-cortez. There are other related resources on this page for talking about climate change.

❋ Be intentional in talking with your peers about collective liberation and why it is important to you.

❋ Be intentional in spending time with and forming strong relationships with people in your community who are prioritizing collective liberation.

❋ Get involved in local work that uses a collective liberation lens.

❋ Support national and global campaigns that have a collective liberation framework.

Keep learning. Learning is action.

Heal for self and community. Healing is essential to collective liberation. As Reverend angel Kyodo williams says, "Love and justice are not two. Without inner change, there can be no outer change; without collective change, no change matters."[31]

Read/listen/watch and have conversations with your kids. While you are reading, notice aloud where the issues are connected. Weave themes together by thinking about how your life impacts the lives of others, and how the lives of others impact your life. Name who is the most impacted by an issue. Come up with ideas for addressing that issue as a family.

Be intentional in talking with your peers about collective liberation and why it is important to you. These conversations help us get out of our theoretical heads and into reality and practice. The concept of collective liberation can begin to make sense. We can connect our story to the stories of others. We can be held accountable for the places where we are not going far enough or being truthful. In other words, this can't just be about reading and conversation within our families. It needs to be conversation with others around us.

Be intentional in spending time with and forming strong relationships with people in your community who are prioritizing collective liberation. Collective liberation will become more real as you are around others who are already practicing with this lens.

Get involved in local work that uses a collective liberation lens. I've already shared the organizing I'm a part of at The Root Social Justice Center (www.therootjc.org) and Migrant Justice (www.migrantjustice.net). Two more local organizations I'm involved with that use a collective liberation framework are Out in the Open (https://www.weareoutintheopen.org), which connects rural LGBTQ+ people to build power, and The Vermont Workers' Center (https://www.workerscenter.org), a grassroots membership organization that works to protect workers' rights, including rights to health care.

You can also support national and global campaigns that use a collective liberation framework. Check out:

❋ Grassroots Global Justice Alliance—ggjalliance.org.

❋ Catalyst Project—collectiveliberation.org.

❋ Movement for Black Lives—policy.m4bl.org/platform.

31 Rev. angel Kyodo williams, webpage, retrieved October 22, 2019, https://angelkyodowilliams.com.

- ❀ Sylvia Rivera Law Project—srlp.org.
- ❀ Southerners on New Ground—southernersonnewground.org.
- ❀ Black and Pink—blackandpink.org.
- ❀ United Students Against Sweatshops—usas.org/about/#about-whatisusas.
- ❀ Beautiful Solutions—solutions.thischangeseverything.org.
- ❀ Rising Tide—risingtidenorthamerica.org/features/principles.

And check out kids who are using a collective liberation frame!
- ❀ Earth Guardians are taking action for social and climate justice: www.earthguardians.org.
- ❀ Greta Thromberg speaks at the UN Climate Summit in 2018: http://www.youtube.com/watch?v=VFkQSGyeCWg.
- ❀ 15 youth climate activists to follow on social media: https://www.earthday.org/2019/06/14/15-youth-climate-activists-you-should-be-following-on-social-media.

Reflect

1. How are you working for collective liberation in your community? How do you involve your kids?
2. What else would you like to be doing? Make a SMART goal (specific, measurable, attainable, relevant, and with a time limit). See page 69 for an explanation.

Examples:

"My SMART goal is to learn about the Indigenous struggle related to the land we are living on right now. Within the next month we will go to the local library as a family to see if there are any resources on this topic. We will ask leaders in our town if there are any local people who have direct knowledge on this topic."

"My SMART goal is to start reading *Emergent Strategy* within the next two weeks. Within the next six weeks I will read it and journal about how to bring the principles into my parenting."

"My SMART goal is to find more books that bring in collective liberation concepts. Within the next two weeks I will visit a locally owned bookstore to see what the latest books on the shelves are. I will also talk with the librarian at my kids' school to see if she has any ideas."

Healing justice practice

In *Radical Dharma: Talking Race, Love, and Liberation*, by Reverend angel Kyodo williams, Lama Rod Owens, and Jasmine Syedullah, PhD, Reverend angel shares the Warrior-Spirit Prayer of Awakening,[1] which she developed after the tragedies of 9/11/2001. It is an affirmative response to how she is showing up with regard to the challenges of the world. It keeps me centered and connected and envisioning a just future.

Warrior-Spirit Prayer of Awakening

May all beings be granted with the strength, determination, and wisdom to extinguish anger and to reject violence as a way.

May all suffering cease, and may I seek, find, and fully realize the love and compassion that already lives within me and allow them to inspire and permeate my every action.

May I exercise the precious gift of choice and the power to change that which makes me uniquely human and is the only true path to liberation.

May I swiftly reach complete, effortless freedom so that my fearless, unhindered action be of benefit to all.

May I lead the life of a warrior.

---

1 Rev. angel Kyodo williams, Lama Rod Owens, Jasmine Syedullah, PhD, *Radical Dharma* (Berkeley, CA: North Atlantic Books, 2016), pg. 93–94.

Community of practice questions

1. What have been your successes in talking/reading/taking action with your kids?
2. What have been your struggles?
3. What have been your somatic/body sensations and responses throughout this chapter?
4. Share your SMART goals. How can the group support you in achieving your goals?
5. What else do you want to learn?

Chapter 8

LOOKING BACK AND LOOKING FORWARD

BY ANGELA BERKFIELD

*When I was young I was taught to fear big forces of nature—tornadoes,
thunderstorms, snowstorms, hurricanes. Taught they cause destruction and
devastation. Taught to hide under desks, in basements, stay close to home. For me,
somatic work has been about relearning and reconnecting to the wisdom and life in
natural forces. That what is most alive leads to opening, creating, change. That in
the destruction of something lies a whole new world of possibility—a place where
patterns can finally become unhinged and there's space for something new to take its
place. Not that this doesn't come with loss, grief, devastation, it does. But to see that
there's also resilience, the beauty of survival, the move to create and thrive despite
what surrounds us. To me that's the essence of our fights for liberation.*

—SPENTA KANDAWALLA[1]

*It is our duty to fight for our freedom.
It is our duty to win.
We must love each other and support each other.
We have nothing to lose but our chains.*

—ASSATA SHAKUR, from *Assata: An Autobiography*[2]

Goals

❋ Review all we have covered in this book and recognize our growth and our
growing edges

❋ Set new goals, because this ending is only another beginning

❋ Offer appreciations to ourselves, to each other, and to the collective body of
people who are doing this work

---

1 adrienne maree brown, *Emergent Strategy: Shaping Change*, Changing Worlds (CA: AK Press, 2017),
125–6.
2 Assata Shakur, *Assata: An Autobiography*.

Taking time to reflect

We started this book with a question: As a parent who cares about people and the planet, how do I raise my children to be conscious, connected, and equipped to make change? Throughout the book we've worked together to answer this question. We've taken time to envision a just world, and we all set goals for learning and action that we will do as a family. Let's take a moment to look back at those goals and visions and reflect on our learning.

First, gather any notes you took as you read earlier chapters, journaled about reflection questions, set SMART goals, and so on. Then, set yourself up with a pen and paper, laptop, audio recorder, sketch pad, or whatever tools help you to record your thoughts and reflections.

Using the following questions, you'll reflect on your learning, the goals you set, and the actions you took. It may seem redundant, like reflecting on our reflections, but I've found it a useful way to observe my own growth and notice places where I can take my learning and action to the next level. Taking time to look back on our goals is an important accountability practice. Have we done what we said we would do? If not, what needs to happen for us to follow through? What other support do we need?

1. **What did you learn?** As you worked on the goals through reading this book, what did you learn that was important for your life, your future, your parenting, and your choices in the world? What did you learn about your children? What challenges came up?

2. **Why does this matter?** Why does your parenting matter to you and to the world?

3. **How are you and your children integrating this learning into your lives?** What are you or your family members doing differently as a natural result of the learning from following through with your goals? How has your vision for justice shifted as you've continued learning?

Here's an example of how I've used these questions to reflect on my goals for social justice parenting:

Goal: In the next week I will talk with my white fourth grader about police officers killing Black folks at a rate much higher than white folks. I want him to understand why we are going to the racial justice rally next weekend.

Action: Before the rally, I talked with my son about police and the statistics of police killing Black folks. Together we looked up infographics and more statistics. He had a lot of questions about safety, about fairness, about his Black friends, and about how we could make sure his friends are safe. It was a rare moment of connecting with my son on a deeper level. I learned that he had been paying more attention than I had thought. The following weekend, we went to the rally with signs that said "Black Lives Matter" and marched and chanted with the gathered crowd. Afterwards, we had another conversation to reflect and consider next steps. We came up with a list of questions we wanted to know the answers to. We decided to talk with my son's Black friends and their parents to see what they are doing and how we can support them and work together for justice. We already have a trusting relationship with them, but haven't had this specific conversation yet. We planned to go to the racial justice organizing meetings in our area.

Reflection

What did I learn? Through my goal and my action I learned that when I set a goal I am much more likely to follow through. I learned that setting the goal held me accountable to actually making the rally a much better learning experience for my son, instead of just taking him with me, which is what I've mostly done in the past. I also learned that the conversation beforehand made my son much more likely to go willingly with me to the rally. I learned that my son is paying more attention to national events than I had realized. I learned how to collaborate on researching topics together so that we both can learn about historical and current events as well as current advocacy campaigns. I learned that having hard conversations can strengthen our relationship. The most challenging part of this goal was just getting the conversation started.

Why does this matter? My son and I connected through talking about a hard topic that I had been scared to bring up with him for a long time. I supported him emotionally, and we both gained motivation and courage to take action. This matters for the world because white kids need to know the truth about the disparities in the criminal justice system so they can participate in bringing about social justice.

How am I and my children integrating this learning into our lives? Because of the conversations we had and the actions we took, I have seen my son deepen his relationships with his Black friends. This is supporting him in moving from separation to connection. These relationships are having more impact on him than I can ever know. And it is encouraging me to be braver and go further in my conversations with my kids, and also with friends, family, and coworkers.

Your turn:

Look back at your learning goals for the book and your action goals throughout the course. Choose at least three of the goals you set and record your thoughts on the three prompts. So:

What did I learn?

Why does this matter?

How are my children and I integrating this learning into our lives?

Now that you've reflected on some of the goals you set, take a look at some of the tools and frameworks from Chapter 2 and determine how you've already taken action and how you could continue to do so.

1. Review the Parenting the Whole Child diagram on page 52. Where are these social justice questions showing up in your parenting?

2. Review the anti-bias framework goals and objectives you starred (*see Appendix D: https://www.parenting4socialjustice.com/*).

   a. Star the goals and objectives you have made progress on throughout this book.

   b. Where have you been putting the most time and attention in your parenting?

   c. What can you do to make sure you are active, in your parenting, in all four areas (identity, diversity, justice, and action)?

3. Review the Spheres of Influence worksheet *(see Appendix E: https://www. parenting4socialjustice.com/)* you filled out. What might you add, change, or clarify based on what you've learned since you first did the worksheet?

Overall Reflections:

1. In what ways are you more conscious about parenting 4 social justice than when you started? How about your kids?

Parents at a P4SJ workshop co-facilitated by Shela Linton and Angela Berkfield, 2019, Western Massachusetts.

2. In what ways are you more connected than when you started? How about your kids?

3. In what ways are you more equipped to contribute to social justice change? How about your kids?

4. Set at least one new SMART goal to continue your learning and continue the conversation and action with your kids.

You've got this. and we've got each other!

Oppression is a lot to take in. It is complicated, and we have lots of feelings about it. When we work together, with tools for healing and hard conversations and community practice, we can make things a little better, and a little better means a lot.

Social justice means treating all people with respect, *and* it requires taking organized action for collective liberation. As parents this means teaching our kids to be proud of who they are and to love themselves and respect others, and at the same time providing them with the knowledge and skills necessary to take action for social justice.

Learning about social justice is a lifelong process. We will each continue to expand our learning and incorporate new knowledge as we have new experiences, which will lead us to expanded visions for justice and to new action. We are all going to mess up along the way. We will be held accountable (because

Author Angela Berkfield at a state capital protest in Montpelier, Vermont.

we've set up ways to be held accountable, right?) so that we can grow from those challenging moments. Our kids, however young, are on the journey too.

I am grateful to be on this journey with you and your kids. Our collective commitment to parenting for social justice will have an impact on many future generations. Let's continue widening the circle and inviting more parents and caregivers to join us in our community of practice.

Community of practice questions

1. What have been your greatest learnings throughout this book?

2. What feelings do you have about finishing this book?

3. What have been your somatic/body sensations and responses throughout this chapter?

4. Share your SMART goals. How can the group support you in achieving them?

5. How else would you feel supported in continuing this practice of parenting for social justice?

Healing justice practice

For our last healing justice practice of the book we will offer appreciations. You can do this in writing, or aloud. You can light a candle and make it a ceremony, or do it on the go while chasing your two-year-old around. However you choose to practice appreciations, know that they are powerful.

Let's start by offering appreciations to ourselves. Write or say to yourself, "I appreciate myself . . . "

> For being honest
> For continuing to show up
> For my commitment to doing this work
> For . . .

What else do you appreciate yourself for?

Offering appreciations to our family and the kids in our care (this can be said *to* them if it feels appropriate) . . .

> For being our greatest teachers
> For showing us what it means to love unconditionally
> For being the future generation
> For . . .

Offering appreciations to all the people in the social justice community, including people you know and are organizing with, people you don't know, and those who have come before us in this work . . .

> For being beautiful, wise, resilient, creative, committed
> For never giving up
> For holding a vision for a just world
> For . . .

Now we offer appreciations to Mother Earth and Spirit (however you call Spirit). . .

> For taking care of us, providing what we need
> For being a source of healing
> For inspiring us to action
> For . . .

I appreciate you, dear ones.

Appendix A

SOCIAL JUSTICE FRAMEWORKS

BY ANGELA BERKFIELD

This book comes out of a vast body of thought and teaching based on both research and lived experience. The concept of parenting for social justice is inspired by both pedagogical frameworks (systems of understanding how teaching and learning work) and theoretical frameworks (explanations that help us make sense of the world and that have been repeatedly tested and found consistent over time).

Theoretical and Conceptual Frameworks

Some of the theoretical frameworks important to parenting for social justice thought and action are power analysis, critical consciousness, critical race theory, and social constructionism. We also draw on the concepts of trauma, somatics, and Just Transition to help us make sense of the world and our experiences in it. Some additional theories and concepts that aren't covered in this appendix but appear with explanation within particular chapters are healing justice (Introduction), privilege and oppression (Chapter 1), pracial identity development (Chapter 3), meritocracy (Chapter 4), social model of disability (Chapter 5), intersectionality (Chapter 7), emergent strategy (Chapter 7), and collective liberation (Chapter 7).

Power Analysis

Having a power analysis means recognizing that power exists in nearly every situation and is used in a variety of ways; some for social good, some for personal benefit, and some to control and even harm others. (See Appendix B, p.315, for a definition of power.) When we have a power analysis, we begin to recognize how power is functioning in any given situation. It leads us to ask, "Who is benefitting from this (policy, practice, system, program)? Who is being harmed? Whose interests does this serve?" A power analysis isn't just recognizing that a situation is unfair, or even recognizing who has privilege in any given situation. It is recognizing and naming which group is able to make and implement decisions that benefit them, and which groups are excluded from decision-making and suffer harm from the decisions of others.

For example, an all-white school board with a middle-class culture decides that the after-school program needs to be dropped because of funding. This decision negatively impacts poor and working-class families, who are predominantly families of color. This is not necessarily a malicious decision; even well-intentioned people with power may make harmful decisions because they don't have the lived experience to know how their decisions will impact others. Another way that situation could go is that those who are most impacted by the decision are involved in the decision-making either by having seats on the school board, or by a very intentional process of gathering feedback from families who will be most impacted by the decision. It is likely the outcome will be different, and if it isn't, then it will still be true that the people most impacted had power in making the decision.

There are helpful tools for naming how power is operating in any given situation and for shifting the power dynamics from power-over to power sharing. "To Equalize Power Among Us"[1] is one such tool that can be used to develop a power analysis and shift towards shared power on a personal and a group level.

Just Transition

A tool that is helpful for developing a power analysis and bringing about a power shift at a systems level is the zine developed by Movement Generation, *From Banks and Tanks to Cooperation and Caring: A Strategic Framework for a Just Transition.*[2] This framework was developed over time with a multi-racial collective of folks involved in organizing for economic and environmental justice. The zine describes the current system, which is extractive, encloses wealth for a few, and is based on military power and exploitation of labor. The zine also describes a regenerative system we can all work towards; one that is regenerative, cares for all beings and the earth, values all kinds of work, and honors the sacred, and where decisions are made through deep democracy. It outlines the power shift that is needed to get there, drawing down wealth and decision-making from the top to the local level. Movement Generation is involved in actions to bring about the power shift for a just transition. Many other social justice organizing groups, such as 350.org and workers' centers and Climate Justice Alliance, have also adopted the Just Transition framework to guide their movement work and bring about a power shift.

Critical Consciousness

Critical Consciousness is a framework that was developed in the 1960s by Brazilian educator Paulo Freire to support poor and working-class Brazilians in understanding their reality and fighting for their rights. It has been widely applied in social movements around the world, most often through popular education (see below). "Critical Consciousness refers to the process by which individuals apply critical thinking skills to examine their current situations, develop a deeper understanding about their concrete reality, and devise, implement, and evaluate solutions to their problems."[3] The explicit purpose of this theory is to understand how people can challenge and change oppressive systems and structures, which have resulted in internalized inferiority. Throughout this book we use critical consciousness theory to examine our own

---

1 Margo Adair, Sharon Howell, "To Equalize Power Among Us," Tools for Change, accessed September 20, 2019, https://www.racialequitytools.org/resourcefiles/adair.pdf.

2 Movement Generation, *From Banks and Tanks to Cooperation and Caring: A Strategic Framework for a Just Transition*, accessed September 20, 2019, https://movementgeneration.org/justtransition.

3 Newark Community Collaborative Board, accessed July 2019, https://newarkccb.org/framework/critical-consciousness-theory.

experiences, to name how we and our families have been impacted by social injustice, to recognize the larger systems that are impacting our personal and collective experiences, to reflect on the ways we have contributed to injustice, and to make plans for working personally and collectively for justice. This process supports us in regaining our own sense of personal dignity, as well as our collective ability to make change.

Critical Race Theory

"Critical Race Theory (CRT) asks us to consider how we can transform the relationship between race, racism, and power, and work towards the liberation of People of Color."[4] The five main tenets of CRT[5] are: 1) the centrality and intersectionality of racism, 2) the challenge to dominant ideology, 3) the commitment to social justice, 4) the importance of experiential knowledge, and 5) the use of an interdisciplinary perspective. CRT was developed in the 1970s and 80s by a group of scholars who recognized the limitations of existing frameworks in challenging racism in the legal arena. CRT has continued to develop since then, building and expanding on the foundational work and understanding through critical scholarship.

Our approach in this book has been particularly influenced by the second tenet, challenging dominant ideology. CRT analyzes and challenges mainstream or dominant narratives, which have largely been developed by white men with wealth.[6] CRT tells a counter story that causes us to question the legitimacy of those mainstream stories. An example of the dominant narrative is the story of Christopher Columbus. Many of us were taught that Christopher Columbus "discovered" America, with no mention that many millions of people were already living on this continent and had for millenia. This narrative has been challenged or countered for centuries by those on the margins, the Native people who experienced extreme loss as a result of colonization by Europeans. In more recent years people have succeeded in interrupting the "discovery" narrative of my children's school; the kids are learning about Columbus in a more objective way, and certainly learning about the harm he caused. In some places, Columbus Day has even been replaced by Indigenous Peoples' Day. However, the majority of schools in the U.S. children are still learning that Columbus "discovered" America.

A recent example of dominant and counter narrative is the story of Colin Kaepernick, the first athlete to take a knee during the national anthem at the beginning of a football game. Kaepernick was protesting to draw attention to police brutality against African Americans, providing a counter to the dominant narrative that is silent about this crisis in the U.S.. Some mainstream media outlets vilified him and said that he was "unpatriotic," which became the dominant story about his protest. They did not tell the story of the many athletes, coaches, and fans that support him taking a knee. They did not tell the story of many other athletes before him who have challenged oppression. The consequences of challenging the dominant narrative are usually more violence or marginalization. In this case Kaepernick was quickly silenced and was not signed on to any football team for the next season.

We must question the mainstream narratives, always. Even the mainstream narratives that seem like they are on the side of the people are often backed by big-money interests and so the media can't tell the whole story. They can't talk about who is making profit in any situation,

---

4 Desiree Adaway, blog post, Feb. 2018, https://desireeadaway.com/critical-race-theory.
5 ibid
6 Maurianne Adams, Lee Anne Bell, Diane J. Goodman, Khyati Y. Joshi, Eds., *Teaching for Diversity and Social Justice, Third Edition* (New York: Routledge, 2016). Chapter 1, Lee Anne Bell, pg 17.

they can't tell the story of how much the executive is making in comparison to the others in the company, for to talk about that would counter the dominant narrative. The stories we are told by any mainstream media outlet are not questioning the way that power functions—who labors and who owns, who is harmed and who benefits.

Lee Ann Bell says, "We must look for the counter-narratives that unearth suppressed and hidden stories of marginalized groups, including stories of their resistance to the status quo, and provide evidence as well as hope that oppressive circumstances can change through the efforts of human actors."[7]

You can read more about critical race theory at www.racialequitytools.org.[8]

Social Constructionism

Social constructionist theory says that our understanding of the world is created by and with the people around us and the context we live in; it is not a natural or perfect representation of how things are. And since human understanding and actions have a major impact on how things are, even how things are is not a natural or inevitable truth. If you do an internet search for social constructionism you will find many different explanations and helpful videos for better understanding. Most sociology textbooks include this framework.

Race, gender, ability, and class are examples of socially constructed concepts. They are not innate characteristics of people or natural to the world, but ideas that have been made real by human understanding and actions. They are not essentially true, but because they are widely believed and supported by the current power structures, their impacts on society and on humans are real.

To be able to challenge current constructions, we must recognize that humans have not always thought of these concepts in this way and that we can change the concepts. For example, take the statement "wage pay is a socially constructed concept." Maybe you've been thinking about wage labor as a given. But recognizing wage labor as a social construct makes it possible to think outside the box to imagine what we actually want work to look like and feel like.

Once we recognize that we're treating a social construct as a truth, we can begin to think outside that box. Our vision for change can become huge and radical. Do we just want a higher minimum wage? Or do we want to ensure that all people have what they need to live dignified lives? If it's the latter, then what are the alternatives to wage labor? There are many ideas. Humans are so creative! Check out the Next System Project[9] or Beautiful Solutions[10] to learn about all kinds of outside-the-box thinking, or read *The Fifth Sacred Thing: City of Refuge* by Starhawk.

Trauma

Although everyone has feelings in response to injustice, some of our feelings are much more intense and become embedded in our psyche so that they affect us long after the event that caused the feeling is over. This is called trauma. Experiences that cause trauma can be individual (such as being raped) or collective (such as the rape culture in which one in six women

---

7 Lee Anne Bell, *Storytelling for Social Justice: Connecting narrative and the arts in anti-racist teaching.* (New York: Routledge, 2010).
8 Racial Equity Tools, www.racialequitytools.org.
9 Next Systems Project, www.thenextsystem.org.
10 Beautiful Solutions (www.solutions.thischangeseverything.org) for values, theories, stories, and solutions.

has survived an attempted or completed rape); they can be single-event (the Holocaust, an era of specific state violence against Jews that had an ending point) or ongoing (antisemitism, the oppression of Jews over centuries). Trauma can happen as a result of one event a person experiences, multiple events in a person's experience, or a series of harmful events that harm a whole group of people and are passed from generation to generation through epigenetics and social learning. Trauma has adverse impacts on our mental, physical, emotional, and spiritual well-being. And trauma can be healed.

For the purposes of this book, we want to draw your attention to how oppression of social groups causes trauma. This means that when we are working on healing individual trauma, we need to make the connection to social group oppression. And when we are working on addressing oppression we need to make the connection to collective trauma. Healing individual and collective trauma is a critical piece of ending oppression.

As you engage in this work of thinking about oppression and privilege, your own personal trauma can be reactivated. You might have memories resurface for you that are traumatic and/ or your body might have a trauma reaction (such as pain, intense emotion, or panic) to what you are learning. If this is the case for you, hopefully the healing justice practices throughout the book can help you work through your feelings and reactions. You can also seek support for working through any resurfaced memories from friends, a therapist, a spiritual practitioner, or through other practices that have helped you in the past. Engaging in this curical trauma healing work will help you to support your kids in navigating life situations that can lead to trauma.

To learn more about racial trauma, as well as examples of healing practices you can try for healing racialized trauma, check out *My Grandmother's Hands: Racialized Trauma and the Pathway to Mending Our Hearts and Bodies*, by Resmaa Menakem.[11]

Somatics

Somatics is a system of understanding of how the body, mind, and spirit are all interconnected. Somatics practitioners hold that we need to practice holistic healing to achieve our vision for a just world. So often, we leave the body behind in this work. Somatics draws on ancient knowledge and practices that have more recently become popularized and important in social justice work. The *Healing Justice* podcast[12] has played a large part in this popularization within social justice communities, offering healing practices related to somatics.

Generative Somatics, a national organization dedicated to social justice transformation through somatics work, explains[13]:

> A somatic theory of change helps us understand how personal, collective, and societal systems perpetuate themselves, can be opened and leveraged to transform, and can purposefully be moved toward radically new ways of being, new practices and structures. Somatics purposely elicits resilience and pragmatically builds a "new shape" through body centered transformation. It shows us how to navigate the particularly tricky terrain of "deconstruction" and opening that is a natural part of transformation. Somatic theory and practice helps us embody emotional competency, be generative in conflict, build lasting trust and design practice that is aligned with our commitments and visions for change.

---

11 Resmaa Menakem, *My Grandmother's Hands: Racialized Trauma and the Pathway to Mending Our Hearts and Bodies* (Central Recovery Press, Las Vegas, NV, 2017). If you have a chance to go to hear Resmaa speak or attend a healing retreat, it will be well worth your time.
12 Irresistible podcast.
13 https://generativesomatics.org/our-strategy/.

Many somatic exercises are in the "healing justice practice" section at the end of each chapter, so that we can gain awareness of not only our thoughts and our feelings but also our bodies as places for transformation. Please try these exercises, or do other somatic practices that work for you.

Pedagogical Frameworks

A pedagogy is a philosophy for how to teach in a way that students can best learn and put into practice what they learn. Anti-bias education, popular education, and experiential learning are all pedagogical frameworks that have inspired my workshop facilitation as well as my parenting for social justice. The pedagogy I use also draws on the wisdom of teachers and colleagues whose pedagogies may not have official names.

Anti-bias education (see Chapter 2) is "a pedagogical model for early learning that helps young children recognize, confront, and resist bias and biased attitudes."[14] It has been popularized through the work of Louise Derman-Sparks and Julie Olsen Edwards. On the Teaching for Change website they write:

> Anti-bias curriculum is an approach to early childhood education that sets forth values-based principles and methodology in support of respecting and embracing differences and acting against bias and unfairness. Anti-bias teaching requires critical thinking and problem solving by both children and adults. The overarching goal is creating a climate of positive self and group identity development, through which every child will achieve her or his fullest potential.[15]

While I believe we must go further than anti-bias work, this framework is especially helpful in providing young children with concrete skills that are the basis of acting for social justice.

Popular education, developed by Brazilian educator Paulo Freire in the mid-20th century, comes out of oppressed communities taking action for social change. At the heart of this framework is a belief that we all have something to teach and we all have something to learn. We each bring our own experiences and understanding into a learning experience. And when we commit to unlearning and relearning together, that collective knowledge often leads to critical consciousness and then collective action for justice. This unlearning and relearning for social justice is a collective process. This is why we highly recommend finding or creating a community of practice to expand and deepen your learning. To learn more about popular education, check out *Pedagogy of the Oppressed.*[16]

The Learning Pyramid, which was developed by the National Training Laboratory in the 1960s, demonstrates that learners retain around 90% of what they learn when they teach what they've learned, 75% of what they learn when they practice what they've learned, 50% of what they learn when engaged in a group discussion, 30% of what they learn when they

---

14 Louise Derman-Sparks and Julie Olsen Edwards, *Anti-Bias Education for Young Children and Ourselves* (National Association for the Education of Young Children, 2010).

15 *Anti-bias Education*, Teaching for Change website, retrieved March 8, 2019, www.teachingforchange.org/anti-bias-education.

16 Freire, P. (1972). *Pedagogy of the Oppressed.* New York: Herder and Herder.

see a demonstration, 20% of what they learn from audio-visual, 10% of what they learn from reading, and 5% of what the learn from lecture.[17]

We use the experiential learning cycle[18] throughout this book and suggest following the same cycle as you parent for social justice. It provides a model for putting what you learn into practice, so that you and your kids retain what you learn. Learning is connected to experience, and effective learning includes all four of these components (not necessarily in order): do something, reflect, generalize, plan the next thing to do. No one stage is effective on its own.

1. **First, do something.** Read a book with social justice themes, have a hard conversation, serve food at a soup kitchen, write a letter to a prisoner, talk with a community member, watch your low-income neighbor's kids while the parents work, show up for a racial justice rally, or take any action toward social justice that feels within your reach right now.

2. **Then, reflect.** Reflect on what happened and what you learned. You might use journaling, artwork, video making, and/or music to process and reflect.

3. **Next, generalize.** What does this learning mean in general? How does what I/we saw or heard connect to other learning we've been doing? How does it connect to current events or to history?

4. **Finally, plan.** How will what you've learned influence further action? Make a plan for your next action that includes what you just learned.

5. **Take your next action!**

For more on the experiential learning cycle and how you can use it in your parenting, see Chapter 2. If you want to learn more about experiential learning, a good resource to check out is *Workshops: Designing and Facilitating Experiential Learning* by J.E. Rooks-Harris and S.R. Stock-Ward.[19]

For more on pedagogical and theoretical frameworks, see *Teaching for Diversity and Social Justice* (2016),[20] *Reading for Diversity and Social Justice* (2000),[21] and *Critical Pedagogy, Notes from the Real World*.[22]

---

17 Sean D'Souza, *How to Retain 90% of Everything You Learn,* retrieved July 2019 from https://www.psychotactics.com/art-retain-learning, and The Learning Pyramid, Education Corner, retrieved July 2019 from https://www.educationcorner.com/the-learning-pyramid.html.
18 David A. Kolb, *Experiential learning: Experience as the source of learning and development* (Vol. 1) (Englewood Cliffs, NJ: Prentice-Hall, 1984).
19 Jeff E. Brooks-Harris, & Susan R. Stock-Ward (1999). *Workshops: Designing and facilitating experiential learning*. Thousand Oaks, Calif: Sage Publications.
20 Maurianne Adams, Lee Anne Bell, Diane J. Goodman, Khyati Y. Joshi, Eds. *Teaching for Diversity and Social Justice, third edition*, Routledge, New York, 2016.
21 Maurianne Adams, Warren J. Blumenfeld, D. Chase J. Catalano, Keri "Safire" DeJong, Heather W. Hackman, Larissa Hopkins, Barbara J. Love, Davey Shlasko, Madeline L. Peters, Ximena Zúñiga, Eds. *Readings for Diversity and Social Justice: An Anthology on Racism, Anti Semitism, Sexism, Heterosexism, Ableism, and Classism, 4th Edition,* Rutledge, New York, 2018.
22 Joan Wink, *Critical Pedagogy, Notes from the Real World, Fourth Edition*, Pearson, 2010.

Appendix B

DEFINITIONS

The following concepts, arranged alphabetically, are important for understanding social justice. There are many ways to define these concepts, and how we define them as a society shifts over time. Language is always changing and it is important to be willing to change with it, as well as be changed by it. Still, it is helpful to have a common reference point when talking about concepts; this list of definitions is that common reference point for this book. When we look at this list in five years, we may have a good chuckle because so many definitions are outdated—but you never know, some may have sticking power and even 50 years from now hold true.

We have gotten the below definitions from a variety of sources we trust and have added to them to further explain and contextualize. Sometimes we have personalized the definitions with examples. Our comments are in italics. There are many other words used to talk about social justice that we don't define here. If there are words and concepts that you would like defined, we recommend looking on www.racialequitytools.org,[1] www.genderspectrum.org,[2] or www.coloursofresistance.org/definitions-for-the-revolution.[3]

Ableism is "the normalization of able-bodied persons resulting in the privilege of perceived "normal ability" and the oppression and exclusion of people with disabilities at many levels in society. Normalized bodies are those that are considered in the planning and designing of society under capitalism, because those bodies are deemed profitable to those who rule capitalist society. Ableist thought leads to the planning and designing of communities in ways that deny access to people with disabilities."[4] (Colours of Resistance)

Accountability is a core organizing principle for when people with privilege (race, class, gender, sexuality, ability, citizenship) are working alongside or in solidarity with oppressed peoples. Being accountable to oppressed communities means respecting the leadership of those whose vision and work the activist is trying to support, and having a means of sharing and receiving feedback and constructive criticism. It is a commitment to support and respect others by following through on work, showing up, and generally doing what you say you are

---

1 Racial Equity Tools, www.racialequitytools.org.
2 Gender Spectrum, www.genderspectrum.org.
3 Colours of Resistance, www.coloursofresistance.org/definitions-for-the-revolution.
4 Ibid

going to do. It is a dynamic process that means having a mechanism to make sure that the work the activist does is in line with the broader goals of movement building, self-determination for the community, fighting oppression and white supremacy, and working towards collective liberation."[5] (adapted from the Catalyst Project)

An *ally* is "someone who makes the commitment and effort to recognize their privilege (based on gender, class, race, sexual identity, ability, etc.) and works in solidarity with oppressed groups in the struggle for justice. An ally understands that it is in their own interest to end all forms of oppression, even those from which they may benefit in concrete ways. An ally commits to reducing their own complicity or collusion in oppression of those groups and invests in strengthening their own knowledge and awareness of oppression."[6] (Racial Equity Tools) *This is a definition that continues to shift over time. Many groups are now using the term "accomplice"[7] instead, coined by Mia McKenzie from Black Girl Dangerous,[8] which places the focus on working together to challenge systemic oppression. Whether using "ally" or "accomplice," the point for people with privilege is to support folks who are struggling for resources, decision-making roles, and dignity. Sometimes this support means getting out of the way and sometimes it means speaking out to amplify the voices/actions of those most impacted by harmful systems. And if it doesn't feel like it's hard, then it's probably not enough. Whatever the action, it is important to follow the leadership of the people most impacted by oppression. It also means learning about the ways we are connected to a given issue, the ways we are harmed by it, and why we have a vested interest in working to end the oppression.*

Allyship is "informed, accountable action that helps others survive and thrive in a context of systemic oppression. Often across differences of power/privilege/identity, but sometimes also within groups."[9] (Think Again Training)

Bias is "an attitude, belief, or feeling that results in and helps to justify unfair treatment of a person because of his or her [or their] identity."[10] (Derman-Sparks and Edwards) *We need to recognize and interrupt biases in ourselves, AND we need to change the systems that create and further those biases.*

Biological sex "refers to one's body, the physiological and anatomical characteristics of maleness and femaleness with which a person is born or that develop with physical maturity. Biological sex markers include internal and external reproductive organs, chromosomes, hormone levels, and secondary sex characteristics such as facial hair and breasts. See also *Sex assigned at birth*."[11] (Think Again Training)

BIPOC stands for Black, Indigenous, people of color. The acronym is used for all people of color but specifically highlights Black and Indigenous because of "the unique relationship to whiteness that Indigenous and Black (African American) people have, which shapes the

5 Catalyst Project, Anti-Racism for Collective Liberation, from handout at workshop, October 2008.
6 Racial Equity Tools, retrieved July 2019, https://www.racialequitytools.org/glossary#ally.
7 Indigenous Action, "Accomplices Not Allies: Abolishing the Ally Industrial Complex", May 4, 2014, http://www.indigenousaction.org/accomplices-not-allies-abolishing-the-ally-industrial-complex.
8 Mia McKenzie, "No More Allies", Black Girl Dangerous, September 30, 2013, https://www.bgdblog.org/2013/09/no-more-allies/#.UknTXcPIDVU.facebook.
9 Davey Shlasko, *Trans Allyship Workbook: Building Skills to Support Trans People in Our Lives* (Think Again Training, 2017).
10 Ibid.
11 Ibid.

experiences of and relationship to white supremacy for all people of color within a U.S. context . . . It is used to intentionally undo Native invisibility and anti-Blackness, dismantle white supremacy and advance racial justice." (https://www.thebipocproject.org)

Capitalism is "a system of domination based on class in which the ruling class owns and controls the resources of the society. Capitalism creates the wealth and power for the ruling class through the exploitation of land, waged and unwaged labor, and the oppression of non-ruling class people."[12] *This definition is important because it names power dynamics in capitalism, unlike the Merriam-Webster definition, which defines capitalism as "an economic system characterized by private or corporate ownership of capital goods, by investments that are determined by private decision, and by prices, production, and the distribution of goods that are determined mainly by competition in a free market.[13]" Together, the two definitions describe the features that make capitalism different from other economic systems and also who benefits from that system and who is harmed by it.*

Charity is giving to people in need. It may relieve the momentary effects of oppression, but it does nothing to change the power relations that cause the oppression. It does not return power to the oppressed to liberate themselves from their oppression. Examples of charity are donating food or used clothes to a food pantry, cooking a meal at a soup kitchen, or giving money to the local elder center. These actions are not wrong, but when they are done out of pity, or instead of standing up for justice, they can contribute to the continuation of systems of oppression.

Cisgender is a term for someone who identifies as the gender that's usually associated with their sex assigned at birth. The term cisgender is not indicative of gender expression, sexual orientation, hormonal makeup, physical anatomy, or how one is perceived in daily life. In discussions regarding trans issues, one would differentiate between women who are trans and women who aren't by saying trans women and cis women.[14] (adapted from Trans Student Educational Resources)

Cissexism is "a system of oppression that privileges cisgender people while marginalizing trans people. Also sometimes called cisgenderism or transgender oppression."[15] (Think Again Training)

Class is . . .

- ❀ relative social hierarchical ranking in terms of income, wealth, status, and power.
- ❀ a group of people who share similar roles in the economic system as particular kinds of workers, owners, and/or buyers/sellers/traders/consumers. *Think about the hierarchy of power in those roles: Who labors? Who benefits from the labor of others?*
- ❀ the culture, knowledge, skills, and networks that come along with being part of a particular class group. *Think about the hierarchical ranking of culture, knowledge, skills,*

---

12 Challenging White Supremacy workshop, Glossary of Terms, September 30, 2019. www.cwsworkshop. org/about/6Glossary_of_Terms.PDF. pg. 5.
13 Merriam-Webster, www.merriam-webster.com/dictionary/capitalism.
14 Trans Student Educational Resources, retrieved July 2019, http://www.transstudent.org/definitions.
15 Davey Shlasko, Trans Allyship Workbook: Building Skills to Support Trans People in Our Lives (Think Again Training, 2017).

and networks: What kinds of culture, knowledge, skills, and networks are privileged and awarded? Which kinds are oppressed?

❀ is inextricably connected with gender and race, as well as disability.[16] (adapted from Think Again Training)

Classism "is the policies, attitudes, behaviors, and beliefs that discriminate against and are used to disempower working class and poor people. Classism is one way within a capitalist system that the concentration of power and wealth is maintained. It perpetuates the belief that people are poor because they are lazy and stupid, rather than exposing the nature of the capitalist system that relies upon exploitable classes to thrive."[17] (Catalyst Project)

Collective liberation is "a recognition that each person's liberation is tied up in the liberation of all people, and that racism and white supremacy, along with all other forms of oppression, dehumanize both those they oppress and those who (at least in the short term) profit or are privileged by them."[18] (Catalyst Project) *This concept came out of an Aboriginal activist group in Queensland, Australia, in the 1970s: "If you have come to help me you are wasting your time. But if you have come because your liberation is bound up with mine, then let us work together."*[19]

Colorblind racism is "purporting to not notice race in an effort to not appear to be racist. It asserts that ending discrimination merely requires treating individuals as equally as possible, without regard to race, culture, or ethnicity. Color-blindness actually reinforces and sustains an unequal status quo. By leaving structural inequalities in place, color-blindness has become the 'new racism.'"[20] (Teaching for Diversity and Social Justice)

Colorism "refers to 'within-group and between-group prejudice in favor of lighter skin color.' Emerging throughout European colonial and imperial history, colorism is prevalent in countries as distant as Brazil and India. Its legacy is evident in forums as public as the television and movie industries, which prefer to cast light-skinned people of color, and as private as the internalized thoughts of some Latino, South-Asian or black parents who hope their babies grow up light-skinned so their lives will be 'just a little bit easier.'"[21] (David Knight)

Consent is an agreement between two parties that can be given verbally or nonverbally. Respecting consent means demonstrating care for the needs, boundaries, and autonomy of others. (Leila Raven, see Chapter 6.)

Culture is a shared set of norms, values, and ways of life developed over centuries and millennia to help us make sense of the world around us and survive in it, and/or to take and maintain power. Culture includes language, food, religious beliefs, artistic expression, beliefs about what happens after death, assumptions about the economic system, relationships to nationhood and patriotism, norms about gender and family roles, relationships to work,

---

16 Davey Shlasko & Toby Kramer. 2011. "Class Culture and Classism in Campus and Community Organizing." Paper presented at Presentation at Pedagogies of Privilege Conference, University of Denver. Think Again Training and Consulting: www.thinkagaintraining.com.

17 Catalyst Project, Anti-Racism for Collective Liberation, from handout at workshop, October 2008.

18 Ibid

19 Lilla Watson, as part of Aboriginal activist group, Queensland, Australia, 1970s, https://lillanetwork.wordpress.com/about.

20 Edited by Maurianne Adams, Lee Anne Bell, Diane J. Goodman, Khyati Y. Joshi, Eds. *Teaching for Diversity and Social Justice*, third edition, Routledge, New York, 2016.), pg. 138.

21 David Knight, "What's Colorism? How would your students answer this question?" *Teaching Tolerance*, fall 2015, https://www.tolerance.org/magazine/fall-2015/whats-colorism.

child-raising practices, and so much more. Some parts of a culture are very obvious, like what holidays we celebrate, and others are very deep and hard for us to even notice or articulate when asked, like our beliefs and assumptions about the economic system. A culture is shared within a community, whether large (like an ethnic culture) or small (like a city's unique local culture). Certain aspects of a culture may be very consistent within the community (like using silverware, hands, or chopsticks to eat food) and others can vary widely (like opinions about the best way to raise children). Culture is complex and we have to be careful not to make assumptions about someone's cultural beliefs or practices just because we know one thing about them, like where they live or what language they speak. (for more, see pages 41-43)

Cultural appropriation "is theft of cultural elements for one's own use, commodification, or profit, including symbols, art, language, customs, etc., often without understanding, acknowledgement, or respect for its value in the original culture. Results from the assumption of a dominant (i.e., white) culture's right to take other cultural elements."[22] (Colours of Resistance)

Cultural competency or cultural responsiveness is being aware of one's own cultural identities and views about diversity and justice, and continually interacting with and learning about cultures other than our own in a way that is respectful and responsive and aware of power imbalances. Awareness, attitude, knowledge, and skills are important in the ongoing process of cultural competency. People working for social justice must work on their cultural responsiveness so they don't perpetuate interpersonal oppression. However, the concept of cultural competency is not a stand in for social justice because it does not address the necessity of changing oppressive systems.[23] (ACT for Social Justice)

Decolonization: If colonization is the act of appropriating or forcibly overtaking a place and exerting control over it, then decolonization is recognizing the thinking and beliefs that have justified and resulted from colonization, healing the wounds caused by colonization and embracing cultural traditions, not from the colonizer, but from the original culture. Decolonization means rethinking our connection to each other, to our spirituality, to the land around us, to our language, to our food, to our rituals and ceremonies, to how we manage the distribution of resources and labor, otherwise known as the economy, and all of the institutions within the economy. (adapted from Sherri Mitchell)[24]

Discrimination (behavior) is the differential allocation of goods, resources, and services, and the limitation of access to full participation in society based on individual membership in a particular social group; the unequal and differential treatment of others based on prejudiced thoughts or attitudes, usually resulting in negative or hostile actions towards minority groups in areas of education, employment, accommodation, health care, and access to goods and services.[25] (adapted from Teaching for Diversity and Social Justice)

Diversity is a concept that encompasses acceptance and respect for the uniqueness of each individual. Each person is impacted by many things in life, including the social group they

22 *Colours of Resistance,* Definitions, retrieved July 2019, http://www.coloursofresistance.org/definitions/cultural-appropriation.

23 Angela Berkfield, ACT for Social Justice, retrieved July 2019, http://www.act4socialjustice.com/social-justice-definitions.

24 Sherri Mitchell, *Sacred Instructions: Indigenous Wisdom for Living Spirit-Based Change* (Berkeley, North Atlantic Books, 2018).

25 Edited by Maurianne Adams, Lee Anne Bell, Diane J. Goodman, Khyati Y. Joshi, Eds. *Teaching for Diversity and Social Justice*, third edition, Routledge, New York, 2016, pg. 138.

are born into or in some cases have chosen, race, ethnicity, gender, sexual orientation, socio-economic status, age, physical abilities, religious beliefs, political beliefs, and other ideologies. Diversity practice is the process of understanding each other and moving beyond simple tolerance to embracing and celebrating the rich dimensions of diversity contained within each individual. Diversity is not to be confused with social justice. A respect for diversity is fundamental to our willingness to join the struggle for social justice. However, a respect for diversity does not inherently mean that you recognize the importance of social justice and are fighting for it. (Act for Social Justice, see pages 41-43)

Economic justice is when the economy is organized in such a way that all people and the earth are treated fairly, equitably, and with dignity and respect; they are not exploited or oppressed; and they have what they need to survive and thrive. Making reparations for past harms is a critical component of achieving economic justice, as is political and economically democratic decision-making. This is certainly not possible under the current version of capitalism and arguably not possible under any version of capitalism.[26] (ACT for Social Justice)

Equity is the principle of people putting in what they can and getting back what they need. It goes beyond equality, which implies identical treatment despite differing needs. This principle advocates for policies that account for the impact of systemic oppression.[27] (adapted from ACT for Social Justice) *For example, equity in health care would mean that all people get the health care they need and pay what they are able. One person might need a lot of care but is only able to pay a small amount. One person might only need the basic services, but they can afford to pay a lot. Universal health care is based on the concept of equity. Universal preschool, universal basic income, universal school meals—these are all programs based on the concept of equity.*

Ethnic group refers to a sizable group of humans whose members identify with one another through a common heritage derived from where their ancestors lived (e.g., Puerto Rico, Ireland, India). (Act for Social Justice, see pages 41-43)

Ethnicity refers to the identification of group members based on such shared heritage and distinctiveness that make the group into a "people."[28] (Anti-Bias Education)

Gender can be defined in many ways. "Some people say that gender is something we learn. Some people say that gender is something we are born with. Wherever it comes from, and whatever it is, gender is something that people feel on the inside and something we can show on the outside in the way we dress, the way we act, the things we do, and who we like to be friends with. Gender is also something other people will attribute to us, even if we don't agree with it, because of what they think about how we dress, look, and act. There are lots of different words people use to describe their gender, including words like man, woman, boy, girl, queer, trans, and androgynous. Some Indigenous peoples of North America use the term two-spirit, which is an English word for a very, very old idea that some of us are more than just one thing when it comes to gender."[29]

---

26 Angela Berkfield, ACT for Social Justice, retrieved July 2019, http://www.act4socialjustice.com/social-justice-definitions.
27 Ibid.
28 Louise Derman-Sparks and Julie Olsen Edwards, *Anti-Bias Education for Young Children and Ourselves* (National Association for the Education of Young Children, 2010).
29 Cory Silverberg and Fiona Smyth. *Sex Is a Funny Word: A Book About Bodies, Feelings, and YOU*. New York: Seven Stories Press, 2015.

Gender binary system is the system of beliefs, structures, policies, and practices that assume and assert that there are exactly two genders (male/female), where gender and sex are assumed to be interchangeable. It is a system of exploitation that informs our understanding of our bodies and our assigned and acceptable "roles," and is policed and upheld by heterosexism and patriarchy and closely linked to white supremacy and capitalism.[30] (adapted from Think Again Training) *One way to shift out of the gender binary system is to think of gender as a continuum—there are many different ways to experience gender. You may in time even be able to move past the continuum concept towards infinity! A great quote here is "gender is a playground." This can be so helpful for parents of kids who have all different kinds of expressions—there is no need to assign those expressions to any gender category; kids are just being who they are.*

Gender expression "is our 'public' gender. How we present our gender in the world and how society, culture, community, and family perceive, interact with, and try to shape our gender. Gender expression is also related to gender roles and how society uses those roles to try to enforce conformity to current gender norms."[30] (Gender Spectrum)

Gender fluid people "have a gender or genders that change. Gender fluid people move between genders, experiencing their gender as something dynamic and changing, rather than static."[31] (Gender Spectrum)

Gender identity is "our deeply held, internal sense of self as masculine, feminine, a blend of both, neither, or something else. Identity also includes the name we use to convey our gender. Gender identity can correspond to or differ from the sex we are assigned at birth. The language a person uses to communicate their gender identity can evolve and shift over time, especially as someone gains access to a broader gender vocabulary."[32] (Gender Spectrum)

Gender norms are social expectations about how to dress, what kinds of activities to participate in, and how to act that are imposed on us based on our real or perceived gender. (Leila Raven, see Chapter 6)

Genderqueer is "an identity commonly used by people who do not identify within the gender binary. Those who identify as genderqueer may identify as neither male nor female, may see themselves as outside of or in between the binary gender boxes, or may simply feel restricted by gender labels."[33] (Outright Vermont)

Healing justice "as a movement and a term was created by queer and trans people of colour and in particular Black and brown femmes, centering working-class, poor, disabled and Southern/rural healers. Before 'healing justice' was a phrase, healers had been healing folks at kitchen tables and community clinics for a long time—from the acupuncture clinics run by Black Panthers like Mutulu Shakur in North America in the 1960s and 1970s, to our bone-deep Black, Indigenous, people of colour and pre-Christian European traditions of healing with herbs, acupuncture, touch, prayer, and surgery."[34] (Leah Lakshmi Piepzna-Samarasinha)

---

30 "The Language of Gender," *Gender Spectrum*, retrieved September 20, 2019, https://www.genderspectrum.org/the-language-of-gender.
31 Ibid.
32 Ibid.
33 "Terms and Definitions," *Outright VT*, retrieved September 20, 2019, http://www.outrightvt.org/terms-definitions.
34 Leah Lakshmi Piepzna-Samarasinha, "A Not-So-Brief Personal History of the Healing Justice Movement 2010–16", MICE Magazine, accessed September 20, 2019, http://micemagazine.ca/issue-two/

Heterosexism is "an ideological and social system of compulsory and assumed heterosexuality, based on binary gender, which denies and persecutes any non-heterosexual form of behavior, identity, relationship, or community, and privileges straight people/people who present gender in a normative way. Patriarchy relies on heterosexism to enforce strict gender roles and definitions. Heterosexism upholds 'nuclear' families and punishes other family structures and reproductive choices."[35] (Catalyst Project)

Inclusion is involvement and empowerment, where the inherent worth and dignity of all people are recognized. An inclusive organization promotes and sustains a sense of belonging; it values and practices respect for the talents, beliefs, backgrounds, and ways of living of its members. This term does not account for the fact that most institutions are organized with white, male, middle-class, able-bodied norms, and so people are being included into that context. This is why the concept of recentering is so crucial (see page 313).

Internalized oppression "is the belief in societal negative misinformation about oneself and one's social identity group(s) that leads one to engage in self-restriction, self-limitation, and self-hate."[36] (Anti-Bias Education)

Internalized superiority "is the belief in the entitlement and superiority of oneself and one's social identity group(s), based on societal myths and misinformation. This leads to the justification of mistreatment of groups outside the entitled group."[37] (Anti-Bias Education)

Intersectionality "is the theory that attends to the complexity of identity and experience as constructed by multiple, interlocking systems of power (such as racism, classism, sexism) for the purpose of understanding and shifting those systems of power."[38] (Davey Shlasko)

Intersex "refers to people who are born with any of a range of sex characteristics that may not fit a doctor's notions of binary 'male' or 'female' bodies. Variations may appear in a person's chromosomes, genitals, or internal organs like testes or ovaries. Some intersex traits are identified at birth, while others may not be discovered until puberty or later in life. There are over 30 specific intersex variations and each intersex person is different. People with intersex traits have always existed, but there is more awareness now about the diversity of human bodies. People with intersex bodies, like anyone who may be seen as different, sometimes face discrimination, including in healthcare settings as early as infancy."[39] (InterACT Advocates for Intersex Youth)

Microaggressions are brief and commonplace daily verbal, behavioral, or environmental indignities, whether intentional or unintentional, that communicate hostile, derogatory, or negative slights and insults towards people based on their targeted social group membership within a system of oppression.[40] (Derald Wing Sue, adapted)

---

not-so-brief-personal-history-healing-justice-movement-2010%E2%80%932016.
35 Catalyst Project, Anti-Racism for Collective Liberation, from handout at workshop, October 2008.
36 Louise Derman-Sparks and Julie Olsen Edwards, *Anti-Bias Education for Young Children* and Ourselves (National Association for the Education of Young Children, 2010).
37 Ibid
38 Davey Shlasko (2015), Using the Five Faces of Oppression to Teach About Interlocking Systems of Oppression, Equity & Excellence in Education, 48:3, 349–360, DOI: 10.1080/10665684.2015.1057061.
39 InterACT Advocates for Intersex Youth, https://interactadvocates.org/intersex-definitions.
40 Derald Wing Sue. For more on this see Appendix E.

Neurodivergent "is a term meaning those with mental differences such as autism, depression, ADD, etc. In some contexts the term is used specifically to refer to autistic people, but other groups have adopted it as a catch-all term for having brain function that is different from the 'norm.'" (Rowan Parker, see Chapter 5)

Oppression "is a system that goes far beyond discrimination. It is historically rooted, so it has deep power dynamics. Systems of oppression maintain advantage and disadvantage based on social group memberships, every system of oppression is also a system of privilege. Oppression is always directional, although discrimination can happen in any direction, there is no 'reverse oppression.' Oppression manifests in a variety of ways, including violence, exploitation, marginalization, powerlessness, and cultural imperialism. It operates on internalized, interpersonal, cultural and institutional levels."[41] (Think Again Training)

Organizing builds power to change unjust conditions and power imbalances in society by bringing people together and mobilizing them to create a just change. (ACT for Social Justice)

Patriarchy "is an economic, political, cultural and social system of domination of women, genderqueer, and transgender people that privileges cisgender men. Patriarchy is based on binary definitions of gender (male/female) with strict gender roles. It also relies upon rigidly enforced heterosexuality that places male/straight/non-transgender as superior and women/queer/transgender as inferior. Patriarchy shapes and is shaped by white supremacy, capitalism, and the state. Together, they form interlocking systems of oppression."[42] (Catalyst Project)

People of color: This term refers collectively to the groups that have historically been and currently are targets of racism in the United States—African Americans, Asian-Pacific Americans, Latino Americans, Native Americans, and Arab Americans. Use of the inclusive term "people of color" is not intended to deny the significant differences within this grouping; it is used to challenge white supremacy and to advocate for racial justice for all people who have been oppressed because of false categorizations of race. (ACT for Social Justice)[43]

Poverty is experienced by people who are not able to meet their basic needs of clean water, nutrition, health care, education, clothing, and shelter. Because of discrimination against the poor, poverty of resources often disrupts the basic human need for belonging and connection. Poverty is not natural but rather a consistent feature of the way the economy is structured. In other words, people are not randomly poor; we make policy decisions that create poverty for some groups and benefits for others. Because of the current policies, poverty disproportionately impacts people of color, women and LGBTQIA+ people, and people with disabilities. (ACT for Social Justice)[44] Jaimie Lynn Kessell, the co-author of Chapter 4, defines poverty as a state of being that is caused by a lack of usual or socially acceptable amounts of money (or access to the material possessions that money can buy) and/or an inability to access an appropriate level of resources to sustain one's participation in society. In this state of being the individual or group experiences feelings of guilt, shame, anger, sadness, and inadequacy that affect their quality of life. Generational poverty is simply the continued state of such poverty across the lifespans of multiple generations within a family system.

---

41 For more on this see Chapter 1 and Appendix A.
42 Catalyst Project, Anti-Racism for Collective Liberation, from handout at workshop, October 2008.
43 Angela Berkfield, ACT for Social Justice, retrieved July 2019, http://www.act4socialjustice.com/social-justice-definitions.
44 Ibid.

Power "is a relational term. It can only be understood as a relationship between human beings in a specific historical, economic and social setting. It must be exercised to be visible.

1. Power is control of, or access to, those institutions sanctioned by the state. (Barbara Major, People's Institute for Survival and Beyond, New Orleans)

2. Power is the ability to define reality and to convince other people that it is their definition. (Dr. Wade Nobles)

3. Power is ownership and control of the major resources of a state; and the capacity to make and enforce decisions based on this ownership and control.

4. Power is the capacity of a group of people to decide what they want and to act in an organized way to get it.

5. Power is the capacity to act. (Colours of Resistance)"[45]

(Catalyst Project)

Prejudice is a prejudgment in favor of or against a person, a group, an event, or an idea. A negative prejudgment is often called a stereotype. *Stereotypes* are false, overly simplistic, or unfounded assumptions about a group of people that result in disregard for individual differences among group members—usually, negative preconceptions that characterize each member of that group as being one and the same. (adapted from Think Again Training)[46]

Privilege "is unearned social power accorded by the formal and informal institutions of society to ALL members of a dominant group (e.g., white privilege, male privilege). Privilege is usually invisible to those who have it because they're taught not to see it, but nevertheless it puts them at an advantage over those who do not have it."[47] (Colours of Resistance) *Here's another version . . .* "A privilege is a benefit that some groups of people have access to and other groups do not. Some privileges are benefits that everybody should have and only some people do, while others are benefits that nobody should have and some people do."[48] (Think Again Training) *The second definition can help us determine more concretely what we're talking about when we say "privilege." For example: having clean drinking water is a privilege that everyone should have but only some people do. Having a personal swimming pool is a privilege that nobody should have (because resources are limited and one person having a swimming pool necessarily means others have less water) and only a few people do.*

Queer "is an umbrella term describing a wide range of people who do not conform to heterosexual and/or gender norms; a reclaimed derogatory slur taken as a political term to unite people who are marginalized because of their nonconformance to dominant gender identities and/or heterosexuality; sometimes used as a shortcut for LGBT. Other times it is used to distinguish politically queer people from more mainstream LGBT people. Because of its origin as a derogatory slur, this term should be used thoughtfully. If you're not queer, or for public communications, LGBT is often more appropriate."[49] (Think Again Training)

---

45 Catalyst Project, Anti-Racism for Collective Liberation, from handout at workshop, October 2008.

46 Think Again Training, training handout, May 2018.

47 Colours of Resistance, Definitions, retrieved July 2019, http://www.coloursofresistance.org/definitions/privilege.

48 Think Again Training, training handout, May 2018.

49 Davey Shlasko, Trans Allyship Workbook: Building Skills to Support Trans People in Our Lives (Think Again Training, 2017).

Race is a social and political construction, not a biological fact, yet it has powerful material and psychological consequences in the lives of people from different racialized groups. Race artificially divides people into distinct groups based on characteristics such as physical appearance, ancestral heritage, cultural history, ethnicity, and the social, economic, and political needs of a society at a given time. The idea of race was created centuries ago for the purpose of amassing and maintaining power and wealth for white people, and it has permeated all of the institutions in the U.S. and even around the globe. (ACT for Social Justice)

Racial equity "is the condition that would be achieved if one's racial identity no longer predicted, in a statistical sense, how one fares. When we use the term we are thinking about racial equity as one part of racial justice, thus we also include work to address root causes of inequities, not just their manifestation. This includes elimination of policies, practices, attitudes and cultural messages that reinforce differential outcomes by race or fail to eliminate them."[50] (Racial Equity Tools)

Racial justice "is the systematic and fair treatment of people of all races, resulting in equitable opportunities and outcomes for all. Racial justice, or racial equity, goes beyond "anti-racism." It is not just the absence of discrimination and inequities, but also the presence of deliberate systems and supports to achieve and sustain racial equity through proactive and preventative measures. Racial Justice [is defined] as the proactive reinforcement of policies, practices, attitudes, and actions that produce equitable power, access, opportunities, treatment, impacts and outcomes for all."[51] (Racial Equity Tools)

Racism serves the purpose of maintaining white supremacy and privilege. Racism by white people against people of color is not only those individual acts of hate, but also a system of exclusion, discrimination, and criminalization, which ensures that the elites (while mostly white, the elites are now people of color as well) can maintain their power. Race Prejudice + Power = Racism. (ACT for Social Justice) Or *"A system of advantage based on race."*[52] (see pages 88-91)

Re-centering: "As critical race theorist Kimberle Crenshaw has noted, it is not enough to be sensitive to difference; we must ask what difference the difference makes. Instead of saying, how can we include women of color, women with disabilities, etc., we must ask what our analysis and organizing practice would look like if we centered them in it. By following a politics of re-centering rather than inclusion, we often find that we see the issue differently, not just for the group in question, but everyone."[53] (Andrea Smith)

Redlining "a process in which the Home Owners' Loan Corporation (HOLC), a federal agency, gave neighborhoods ratings to guide investment. This policy is so named for the red or "hazardous" neighborhoods that were deemed riskiest. These neighborhoods were predominantly

---

50 Racial Equity Tools, retrieved July 2019, https://www.racialequitytools.org/glossary#racial-equity.
51 Ibid.
52 Beverly Daniel Tatum, *Why Are All the Black Kids Sitting Together in the Cafeteria?* (New York: Basic Books, 1997, 2017). Pg 87.
53 Andrea Smith, June 1, 2006, http://www.leftturn.org/without-bureaucracy-beyond-inclusion-re-centering-feminism.
55 The Legacy of Redlining: Resources," Urban Displacement Project, retrieved 2020, https://www.urbandisplacement.org/redlining.

home to communities of color, and this is no accident; the "hazardous" rating was in large part based on racial demographics. In other words, redlining was an explicitly discriminatory policy. Redlining made it hard for residents to get loans for homeownership or maintenance, and led to cycles of disinvestment."[55] (Urban Displacement Project)

Reparations: "The harm done through systemic racism has compounded over centuries and is contributing greatly to the racial disparity in outcomes and resources. Not only that, but there has been a massive financial benefit because of this harm done. According to the Movement for Black Lives, reparations consists of five key components: 1) an acknowledgement of harm: apology, public education, memorials; 2) compensation for injury: a good faith attempt to compensate for labor, stolen land, and our lives, and for systemic torture, physical and sexual violence; 3) restitution for harm: restoring rights, property, and citizenship; 4) rehabilitation for past harms: psychological care, childcare, health care, access to quality and free education, acces to quality employement; 5) guarantee that the harms stop: transformation of health care, criminal justice, housing, and all systems."[54] (Movement for Black Lives)

Sex (see *Biological sex* and *Sex assigned at birth*)

Sex assigned at birth: The assignment and classification of people as male, female, intersex, or another sex based on a combination of anatomy, hormones, and chromosomes that is on all ID documents, beginning with a person's birth certificate. It is important we don't simply use "sex" because of the vagueness of the definition of sex and its place in transphobia. (Adapted from Trans Student Educational resources.)

Sexism "is the enforced belief in male dominance and control held in place by systems of power and control that ultimately keep women subordinate to men. These systems of power and control take place at institutional, cultural, and individual levels. Examples of sexism range from denigrating jokes, to objectifying females in the media, to job discrimination, to acts of violence against women."[55] (Reading for Diversity and Social Justice)

Sexual orientation "is an individual's patterns of romantic and/or sexual attraction, in terms of gender. For example, someone may be attracted to people of the same gender as themself, to people of a particular other gender, or to people of all genders. Sexual orientation is not the same as gender expression or gender identity. People of any gender may have any sexual orientation."[56] (Think Again Training)

Social justice: A socially just world meets everyone's basic needs (food, housing, health care, education, job, social security) in a dignified way; guarantees equitable distribution of resources; ensures everyone has a voice in the decisions that affect them; makes sure all people are physically and psychologically safe and secure; treats people from every background with dignity and respect; and supports the development of all people to their full potential. To achieve social justice we must stand in opposition to capitalism, exploitation, white supremacy, and oppression in its many forms. We must engage in a constant practice of creating

---

56 Movement for Black Lives, "What Is Independence Day Without Freedom?" YouTube, July 4, 2019, https://www.youtube.com/watch?v=AsvFV5eDIPg&ab_channel=MovementForBlackLives.
55 Heather W. Hackman, *Readings for Diversity and Social Justice* (NY: Routledge, 2000).
56 Ibid.

and recreating our actions so they are aligned with social justice principles.[57] (ACT for Social Justice, adapted from definitions by Class Action and Janaki Natarajan)

Solidarity is joining people who are struggling for their liberation. It is a commitment to addressing the root causes of injustice and working together for justice, to effectively and resourcefully address the systemic issues that are impacting both people negatively. From a solidarity perspective, when a person with plenty of resources shares resources, it is with deep respect and connection. Sharing happens on the terms of the person whose basic needs have not been met, not the person who has plenty. There is reciprocity, an exchange of skills and resources. There is also accountability for having more resources than is necessary and for shifting those resources towards mutual aid and collective benefit instead of personal benefit. Solidarity shifts unequal power dynamics. Examples of solidarity are leaving a workplace that has discriminated against a black coworker, joining a strike for fair pay, showing up for a rally to demand gender neutral bathrooms.

Somatics is a field of thought recognizing that the body, mind, spirit are all interconnected and we need to practice holistic healing to achieve our vision for a just world. See also *Somatics* Appendix A.

Transgender: "A term for people whose gender identity, expression or behavior is different from those typically associated with their assigned sex at birth. Transgender is a broad term and is good for cis people to use. 'Trans' is shorthand for 'transgender.' (Note: Transgender is correctly used as an adjective, not a noun, thus 'transgender people' is appropriate but 'transgenders' is often viewed as disrespectful.)"[58] (National Center for Transgender Equality)

Transphobia "is irrational fear, discomfort, distrust, or disdain directed towards trans people or trans concepts. This word is used similarly to homophobia, xenophobia, misogyny, etc."[59] (Outright Vermont)

U.S. Imperialism "describes policies aimed at extending the political, economic, and cultural control of the United States over areas beyond its boundaries. It may include military conquest, gunboat diplomacy, unequal treaties, subsidization of preferred factions, economic penetration through private companies followed by intervention when those interests are threatened, or regime change." (Kids Encyclopedia Facts: https://kids.kiddle.co/American_imperialism) *I (AB) find the Beehive Collective out of Maine to be an excellent source for better understanding in a creative and visionary way how U.S. Imperialism works and can be transformed.* (https://beehivedesigncollective.tumblr.com)

Whiteness: "A social construction that has created a racial hierarchy that has shaped all the social, cultural, educational, political, and economic institutions of society. Whiteness is linked to domination and is a form of race privilege invisible to white people who are not conscious of its power. 'Whiteness,' like 'colour' and 'Blackness,' are essentially social constructs

---

57 ACT for Social Justice, 2013. Adapted from a classism definition by Class Action, August 2018, www.classism.org, and from social justice definition from "Social Justice in Intercultural Relations" course syllabus at SIT, taught by Janaki Natarajan, September 2007.

58 National Center for Transgender Equality, retrieved September 2019, https://transequality.org/issues/resources/understanding-transgender-people-the-basics

59 "Terms and Definitions," Outright VT, September 20, 2019, http://www.outrightvt.org/terms-definitions.

applied to human beings rather than veritable truths that have universal validity. The power of Whiteness, however, is manifested by the ways in which racialized Whiteness becomes transformed into social, political, economic, and cultural behaviour. White culture, norms, and values in all these areas become normative natural. They become the standard against which all other cultures, groups, and individuals are measured and usually found to be inferior."* *White includes many different cultures and ethnicities, and even people who don't identify as white, but can pass as white, still benefit from the concept of whiteness. Learning the history of how the concept of whiteness came about in the early days of slavery, for the purpose of maintaining owning class power, is very helpful in realizing that concepts and ideologies change over time. It is time for a change, don't you think?*

White fragility is "discomfort and defensiveness on the part of a white person when confronted by information about racial inequality and injustice. What does it look like? ... the outward display of emotions such as anger, fear, and guilt, and behaviors such as argumentation, silence, and leaving the stress-inducing situation."[60] (Robin DiAngelo)

White privilege "refers to the unquestioned and unearned set of advantages, entitlements, benefits, and choices bestowed on people solely because they are white (or white passing). Generally white people who experience such privilege do so without being conscious of it. A system of white domination that creates and maintains belief systems that make current racial advantages and disadvantages seem normal. The system includes powerful incentives for maintaining white privilege and its consequences, and powerful negative consequences for trying to interrupt white privilege or reduce its consequences in meaningful ways. The system includes internal and external manifestations at the individual, interpersonal, cultural, and institutional levels."[61] *If you are white, then you have privilege, whether you have been aware of it or not. To what degree you have privilege also depends on your other identities—gender, ability, class. To do nothing about it is to collude with the system of oppression.*

White supremacy "is a historically based, institutionally perpetuated system of exploitation and oppression of continents, nations, and peoples of color by white peoples and nations of the European continent, for the purpose of maintaining and defending a system of wealth, power, and privilege."[62] (Challenging White Supremacy workshop) While white supremacy is usually and conveniently associated with the KKK or a "few bad apples," it is actually a system that is built into thinking, action, and systems in the U.S. and around the world, and benefits all people with white skin, but some more than others. It includes everything from indifference ("politics doesn't interest me") to minimization ("we are all one race") to veiled racism (tokenizing POC or Eurocentric curriculum), to racial discrimination (redlining), and acts of violence, which can become as extreme as genocide.

---

*Henry, F., & Tator, C. (2006). *The Colour of Democracy: Racism in Canadian Society*. 3rd Edition Toronto, ON: Nelson. Pg. 46-47, 353.

60 Robin DiAngelo, *White Fragility: Why It's So Hard for White People to Talk About Racism* (Beacon Press, 2018).

61 Racial Equity Tools, retrieved July 2019, https://www.racialequitytools.org/glossary#white-privilege.

62 Glossary of Terms, Challenging White Supremacy Project, retrieved 2016, http://www.cwsworkshop.org/about/6Glossary_of_Terms.PDF.

RESOURCES

There are many great materials out there to support continued learning and action for social justice. This list includes resources mentioned throughout the book, as well as others that have come to our attention since it was written. Of course there are so many more than we have space to share here; our hope is that what follows inspires you to continue on your learning journey. Please see our webiste for a continually updated list.

Curriculum

- *Anti-Bias Education: for Young Children and Ourselves*, by Louise Derman-Sparks and Julie Olsen Edwards, National Association of Education of Young Children, 2010. If you buy one book to help you work with your two- to six-year-old, this should be the one.

- Facing History and Ourselves offers resources that address racism, antisemitism, and prejudice throughout history, helping students connect choices made in the past to those they will confront in their own lives. Some great classroom support here: www.facinghistory.org.

- Rethinking Schools has curriculum resources for all ages, including for early education, about climate change and globalization: www.rethinkingschools.org. We can't recommend it highly enough!

- *Starting Small: Teaching Tolerance in Preschool and the Early Grades*, by Teaching Tolerance of the Southern Poverty Law Center: http://www.tolerance.org/sites/default/files/kits/Teachers_Study_Guide.pdf. This is a free download on the Teaching Tolerance website that features practical activities you can do with your preschoolers and kindergarteners.

- Teaching Tolerance provides many more anti-bias resources for teachers and parents: www.tolerance.org/classroom-resources.

- The Zinn Education Project is chock full of learning materials for classrooms and can be used at home too: https://www.zinnedproject.org.

Books

❀ *Boys Will Be Men: Raising Our Sons for Courage, Caring, and Community*, by Paul Kivel, New Society Publishers, 1999. Although published in the early 90s, this book still provides on-point questions and a solid framework for parenting boys.

❀ *Critical Multicultural Analysis of Children's Literature: Mirrors, Windows, and Doors*, by Maria Jose Botelho and Masha Kabakow Rudman, Routledge Press, 2009. This book offers valuable strategies to help adults guide children in reading dominant narratives of race, class, and gender.

❀ *How to Talk So Kids Will Listen & Listen So Kids Will Talk*, by Adele Faber and Elaine Mazlish, Scribner, 2012. Enthusiastically praised by parents and professionals around the world, the down-to-earth, respectful approach of Faber and Mazlish makes relationships with children of all ages less stressful and more rewarding.

❀ *Privilege, Power, and Difference,* by Allan G. Johnson, McGraw-Hill, 2006. Think of this as a social justice 101 book.

Other Resources

❀ "10 Quick Ways to Analyze Children's Books for Sexism and Racism," by Louise Derman-Sparks and ABC Task Force, from Anti-Bias Curriculum: Tools for Empowering Young Children: www.teachingforchange.org/wp-content/uploads/2012/08/ec_tenquickways_english.pdf.

❀ "How to Talk to Kids About Difficult Subjects," by Caroline Knorr: www.commonsensemedia.org/blog/how-to-talk-to-kids-about-difficult-subjects.

❀ "Let's Talk," by Teaching Tolerance, offers strategies to help adults facilitate difficult conversations with kids about race and racism, as well as gender bias, ableism, and religious and anti-LGBT persecution: www.tolerance.org/sites/default/files/general/TT%20Difficult%20Conversations%20web.pdf.

Media outlets with a social justice lens:

❀ Al Jazeera, www.aljazeera.com.

❀ Democracy Now, www.democracynow.org.

❀ Irresistible, formerly known as the Healing Justice Podcast, has ended, however, you can still find archived episodes with dozens of practices for collective healing and for building a resilient social justice movement. These episodes are well worth a listen. https://irresistible.org

❀ "Unpacking the Knapsack of Privilege," by Peggy McIntosh: deanza.edu/faculty/lewisjulie/WhitePrivilege.pdf.

Parenting for racial justice

Definitions, Tools, Research

- ❋ Background on white, Black, Asian, Latinx, Indigenous, biracial, and multiracial identity development, and much more: https://www.racialequitytools.org/fundamentals/core-concepts/theory.

- ❋ Catholic workers in St. Louis, Missouri, put together an excellent compilation of Racism 101 resources: newsite.karenhousecw.org.

- ❋ Dismantling Racism: 2016 Workbook, by dRworks, offers definitions, historical background, and support for shifting the culture in organizations/workplaces: https://resourcegeneration.org/wp-content/uploads/2018/01/2016-dRworks-workbook.pdf.

- ❋ EmbraceRace hosts frequent webinars on parenting for racial justice: www.embracerace.org.

- ❋ United for a Fair Economy has excellent infographics and reports that illustrate the tangible impact of racism today: faireconomy.org.

Film (clips & features)

- ❋ Brave New Films offers excellent short films that document racism today, such as one on mass incarceration: bravenewfilms.org/racismisreal.

- ❋ "How to Talk About Race" video with Jay Smooth: https://youtu.be/MbdxeFcQtaU.

- ❋ *Kids on Race*, a 2015 video produced by WNYC: https://youtu.be/C6xSyRJqIe8.

- ❋ The feature documentary *I'm Not Racist, Am I?* this documentary follows 12 teenagers from New York City as they talk about race and privilege in a series of workshops and in conversations with friends and family members: http://www.notracistmovie.com.

- ❋ The video "Mighty Times: The Children's March" tells the story of the more than 4,000 Black schoolchildren who deserted classrooms in Birmingham, Alabama, on May 2, 1963, launching a week of powerful mass demonstrations for civil rights: https://youtu.be/5c113fq3vhQ.

- ❋ "The Myth of Race, Debunked" video with Jenee Desmond Harris: https://youtu.be/VnfKgffCZ7U.

- ❋ *Race, the Power of an Illusion* is an outstanding three-part documentary film produced in 2003 by California Newsreel: https://www.racepowerofanillusion.org.

- ❋ *Ruby Bridges* is a 1998 Disney film about the six-year-old who was the first Black child to integrate the all-white schools in New Orleans: https://movies.disney.com/ruby-bridges.

- ❋ In the video "Understanding Race in the 21st Century," PBS correspondent Charlayne Hunter-Gault talks with Rev. David Billings of the People's Institute for Survival and Beyond about the problem of race in America along with possible solutions: https://www.pbs.org/video/understanding-racism-in-the-21st-century-1470184215.

❀ *Unlearning "Indian" Stereotypes* is a DVD produced in 1977 by the Council on Interracial Books for Children and enhanced by Rethinking Schools in 2008: https://www.zinnedproject.org/materials/unlearning-indian-sterotypes.

Books & Articles

❀ "100 Race Conscious Things to Say to Your Child to Advance Racial Justice": http://www.raceconscious.org/2016/06/100-race-conscious-things -to-say-to-your-child-to-advance-racial-justice. *(see Appendix I: https://www.parenting4socialjustice. com/)*

❀ *Between the World and Me*, by Ta-Nehisi Coates, Spiegel & Grau, 2015. Written as a letter to his son in a series of essays, Coates confronts the notion of race in America and how it has shaped American history, often at the cost of Black bodies and lives.

❀ *Brown Girl Dreaming*, by Jacqueline Woodson, Nancy Paulsen Books, 2014. This is a memoir poem about Woodson's childhood, taking places in the South and New York City. While written for youth, it's also an excellent read for adults.

❀ "Characteristics of White Supremacy Culture," by Tema Okun, dRworks: http://www.dismantlingracism.org/uploads/4/3/5/7/43579015/whitesupcul13.pdf. Plus more on white supremacy culture at http://www.dismantlingracism.org/white-supremacy-culture.html. *(see Appendix H: https://www.parenting4socialjustice.com/)*

❀ "Children Are Not Colorblind: How Young Children Learn Race," by Erin Winkler, *PACE*, 2009: https://nmaahc.si.edu/sites/default/files/downloads/resources/children_are_not_colorblind.pdf.

❀ *A Different Mirror: A History of Multicultural America,* by Ronald Takaki, Back Bay Books, 1993. In a lively account filled with the stories and voices of people previously left out of the historical canon, Takaki offers a re-visioning of our nation's past.

❀ *My Grandmother's Hands: Racialized Trauma and the Pathway to Mending Our Hearts and Bodies*, by Resmaa Menakem, Central Recovery Press, 2017. Through the exercises in this book, Menakem helps us recognize where racialized trauma lives in our bodies and take steps toward healing.

❀ *The Guide for White Women Who Teach Black Boys,* by Eddie Moore, Ali Michael, and Marguerite W. Penick-Parks, Corwin, 2018.

❀ "Having the Race Talk with My 4- and 21-Year-Old Sons," by Meilan Carter-Gilkey: https://www.matermea.com/blog/2014/11/16/race-talk-personal-essay.

❀ *How to Be an Antiracist*, by Ibram X. Kendi, OneWorld, 2019. From the basics to the visionary, this book lays out the problem of racism and a roadmap for justice and freedom.

❀ "How to Talk with Kids About the Black Lives Matter Movement," by Laleña Garcia: http://weac.org/wp-content/uploads/2018/02/kid-friendly-language.pdf.

❀ "How Well-Intentioned White Families Can Perpetuate Racism," by Joe Pinsker: https://www.theatlantic.com/family/archive/2018/09/white-kids-race/569185.

❀ *killing rage: Ending Racism*, by bell hooks, Holt Paperbacks, 1996. These 23 essays are written from a Black and feminist perspective, tackling the bitter difficulties of racism by envisioning a world without it.

❀ "Multiracial Bill of Rights," by Maria P.P. Root: www.safehousealliance.org/wp-content/uploads/2012/10/A-Bill-of-Rights-for-Racially-Mixed-People.pdf.

❀ *The New Jim Crow: Mass Incarceration in the Age of Colorblindness*, by Michelle Alexander, The New Press, 2010. This is a must-read book about mass incarceration in the U.S. There's also a companion book for young readers.

❀ "On Mothering White Kids to Know #BlackLivesMatter: Our Silence Is Continued Violence," by Alyssa Dunn: https://www.huffpost.com/entry/on-mothering-white-sons-to-know-blacklivesmatter_b_577e85bce4b03288ddc57d79?te=Atlantic.

❀ *Raising White Kids: Bringing Up Children in a Racially Unjust America*, by Jennifer Harvey, Abingdon Press, 2017. This helpful racism 101 book supports families and educators in raising their children to be active anti-racist allies.

❀ "Talking About Ferguson with Our Little Boys," by Nani Arreaza, an interview with two parents, one Latina and one white: https://parents-together.org/talking-about-ferguson-with-our-little-boys.

❀ Tips for talking to children about race and racism in a 2017 article by Erin Winkler: https://www.buzzfeed.com/erinwinkler/tips-for-talking-to-children-about-race-and-racism.

❀ *Waking Up White: And Finding Myself in the Story of Race,* by Debby Irving, Elephant Room Press, 2014. This nonfiction book shares one woman's honest and unflinching exploration of race in the U.S. and her own white privilege.

❀ *When They Call You A Terrorist: A Black Lives Matter Memoir*, by Patrisse Khan-Cullors and Asha Bandele, Canongate Books, 2018. This powerful book gives insight into how white supremacy has impacted individuals and communities and motivated the authors to respond with love and community.

❀ *White Kids: Growing Up with Privilege in a Racially Divided World*, by Margaret Hagerman, NYU Press, 2018. Hagerman provides a crucial analysis of the "well-meaning" and "colorblind" racism that her subjects perpetuate, stripping down the coded language of suburbia.

❀ *Why Are All the Black Kids Sitting Together in the Cafeteria? And Other Conversations About Race*, by Beverly Daniel-Tatum, Basic Books, 1997, 2017. Written over 20 years ago, this book is still highly relevant, informative, and inspirational.

Support for Organizing for Change

❀ The Black Lives Matter (BLM) website the BLM principles and how we can all support the movement: blacklivesmatter.com.

❀ The Movement for Black Lives consists of over 50 POC-led organizations coming together to organize for change. They have put together a policy platform that is a must-read: https://policy.m4bl.org/platform.

❀ Black Youth Project 100 (BYP100) is a member-based organization of Black youth activists creating justice and freedom for all Black people: byp100.org.

❀ The Gathering for Justice is building a movement to eliminate racial inequities in the criminal justice system: gatheringforjustice.org.

❀ Idle No More, based in Canada, calls on all people to join in a peaceful revolution, to honour Indigenous sovereignty, and to protect the land and water: idlenomore.ca.

❀ Migrant Justice organizes very successfully with undocumented migrant farmworkers in Vermont for basic human rights and dignity, receiving national attention for its work: migrantjustice.net.

❀ #Not1More builds collaboration among individuals, organizations, artists, and allies to expose, confront, and overcome unjust immigration laws: notonemoredeportation.com.

❀ The Root Social Justice Center, based in southern Vermont and working with folks all over the state and region, is building a movement for racial justice by building power for people of color and shifting resources to BIPOC-led organizing: therootsjc.org.

❀ Through community organizing, mobilizing, and education, Showing Up for Racial Justice (SURJ) moves white people to act with passion and accountability as part of a multiracial majority for justice: showingupforracialjustice.org.

❀ Urban Youth Collaborative, led by students, brings together New York City students to fight for real education reform that puts students first, demanding social, economic, and racial justice in our schools and communities: urbanyouthcollaborative.org.

Parenting for economic and class justice

Definitions & Research

❀ Class Action works to end classism and provides helpful tools and training: classism.org.

❀ *Created Equal: A Curriculum for High Schoolers and Middle Schoolers on Class and Classism*, by Phyllis Labanowski and Pamela Freeman: classism.org/programs/created-equal.

❀ The Economic Policy Institute is a think-tank researching issues that impact working Americans: epi.org.

❀ *Economics for the 99%*, a report by the Center for Popular Economics: https://www.populareconomics.org/wp-content/uploads/2012/06/Economics_99_Percent_for_web1.pdf.

- ✤ *From Banks and Tanks to Cooperation and Caring: A Strategic Framework for a Just Transition*: movementgeneration.org/justtransition.
- ✤ *Teaching Economics As If People Mattered*, high school curriculum by Tamara Sober Giecek with United for a Fair Economy: http://www.teachingeconomics.org.
- ✤ United for a Fair Economy offers excellent resources to help us learn about the problem of an unequal economy and solutions for creating a fair economy: faireconomy.org.

Films, Games, Media

- ✤ "A Message from the Future with Alexandria Ocasio Cortez": https://theintercept.com/2019/04/17/green-new-deal-short-film-alexandria-ocasio-cortez.
- ✤ Kids Can Make a Difference offers short film clips about kids learning about and taking action to address root causes of hunger and inequality: www.kidscanmakeadifference.org.
- ✤ The game Spent provides a simulation of the challenging choices (or lack of choices) one has when living in poverty: http://playspent.org.
- ✤ Say the folks behind the Story of Stuff Project, "We have a problem with Stuff: we have too much of it, too much of it is toxic, and we don't share it very well. But that's not the way things have to be." Check out their Story of Solutions: http://storyofstuff.org/movies/the-story-of-solutions.
- ✤ Talk Poverty features a blog, podcast, and more with good info about poverty: https://talkpoverty.org.
- ✤ TESA offers the fun and thought-provoking Co-opoly, "a game of skill and solidarity, where everyone wins—or everyone loses!" https://store.tesacollective.com/co-opoly-the-game-of-co-operatives.
- ✤ Video from Hunger Free Vermont supporting universal school meals: https://youtu.be/kgGyZ41lN18.
- ✤ "Wealth Inequality in America" video by Politizane: https://youtu.be/QPKKQnijnsM.

Books & Articles

- ✤ *Class Matters: Cross-class Alliance Building for Middle-class Activists*, by Betsy Leondar-Wright, New Society Publishers, 2005. A guide to building bridges across class lines and collaborating more effectively in mixed-class social change efforts, this book is full of stories, ideas, tips, and resources.
- ✤ "The Case for Reparations," by Ta-Nehisi Coates: https://www.theatlantic.com/magazine/archive/2014/06/the-case-for-reparations/361631.
- ✤ Essay "Why Is There Poverty?" by Allan G. Johnson: https://www.agjohnson.us/essays/poverty.

⊛ *Hand to Mouth: Living in Bootstrap America*, by Linda Tirado, Putnam, 2014. Tirado articulates what it is to be working poor in America and what poverty is truly like, on all levels.

⊛ Interview with Robert Putnam, "Why You Should Care About Other People's Kids": https://www.pbs.org/newshour/nation/care-peoples-kids.

⊛ *Our Kids: The American Dream in Crisis*, by Robert D. Putnam, Simon & Schuster, 2015. While he doesn't critique the economic system that creates class divisions, Putnam provides an important look at the symptoms and suggests solutions to alleviate the immediacy of the suffering.

⊛ *where we stand: class matters*, by bell hooks, Routledge, 2000. Drawing on her roots in Kentucky and her adventures with Manhattan co-op boards, with this book bell hooks offers personal, straightforward, and rigorously honest reflection on how our dilemmas of class and race are intertwined, and how we can find ways to think beyond them.

⊛ *Without a Net: The Female Experience of Growing Up Working Class*, edited by Michelle Tea, Seal Press, 2004. These fierce, honest, and tender essays cover everything from stealing and selling blood to make ends meet to how feminine identity is shaped by poverty.

Support for Organizing for Change

⊛ Beautiful Solutions is an online platform, book, and training program that elevates strategies for creating the just world we want: https://solutions.thischangeseverything.org.

⊛ The Coalition of Immokalee Workers organizes migrant farmworkers in the U.S. to stand up for their rights: ciw-online.org.

⊛ Community land trusts provide lasting community assets and permanently affordable housing opportunities for families and communities: https://groundedsolutions.org/strengthening-neighborhoods/community-land-trusts.

⊛ Cooperation Jackson is building a solidarity economy in Jackson, Mississippi, anchored by a network of cooperatives and worker-owned and democratically self-managed enterprises: cooperationjackson.org.

⊛ The Democracy Collaborative is a research and development lab for the democratic economy: community-wealth.org/content/worker-cooperatives.

⊛ Economic justice platform of the Movement for Black Lives: https://policy.m4bl.org/economic-justice.

⊛ Equity Solutions hosts cross-class dialogue circles, including virtually, for people of all class backgrounds and experiences to better understand their class stories, build skills for cross-class communication, and gain skills for showing up for economic justice: equitysolutionsvt.com/cross-class-dialogue-circles.

※ Fight for 15 organizes food service workers to push for a $15 minimum wage in the U.S.: fightfor15.org.

※ Grassroots Global Justice Alliance is organizing to build power for poor and working class communities and communities of color in the U.S. and globally: ggjalliance.org.

※ Grassroots International emphasizes human rights to land, water, and food around the world: grassrootsinternational.org.

※ Honor the Earth is protecting Native American lands with the vision of a sustainable future for Native communities: honorearth.org.

※ La Via Campesina organizes millions of peasant farmers and fisher-people around the world: https://viacampesina.org/en.

※ The Landless Workers Movement organizes for land rights in Brazil: http://www.mstbrazil.org/content/what-mst.

※ Movement Generation Justice & Ecology Project is rooted in social movements led by low-income communities and communities of color committed to a "just transition" away from profit and pollution and toward healthy, resilient, and life-affirming local economies: movementgeneration.org.

※ The National Domestic Workers Alliance organizes for economic justice for domestic workers: domesticworkers.org.

※ The New Economy Coalition is a membership-based network that works to accelerate the transition of our economic system from capitalism to a solidarity economy: neweconomy.net.

※ The Next System Project works with researchers, theorists, and activists to create a "next system" that will deliver equitable and just social, economic, and ecological outcomes: thenextsystem.org.

※ Resource Generation organizes young people with wealth and class privilege in the U.S. to become transformative leaders working toward the equitable distribution of land, wealth, and power: resourcegeneration.org.

※ Support for forming (or joining) a timebank, which is when a circle of members agrees to give time and receive credits for services other members provide: timebanks.org/what-is-timebanking.

※ Ujima is a cooperative economic project in Boston: ujimaboston.com.

※ The U.S. Solidarity Economy Network works to connect the elements of the solidarity economy conceptually and practically: ussen.org/solidarity-economy.

※ The Zapatistas have maintained their rights to their ancestral lands in southern Mexico for over two decades: https://www.jacobinmag.com/2016/04/zapatistas-ezln-san-andres-marcos-chiapas.

Parenting for disability justice

Definitions, Tools, Research

❋ Americans with Disabilities Act, under title one of this act employers with 15 or more employees are prohibited from discriminating against people with disabilities: https://www.dol.gov/general/topic/disability/employersresponsibilities.

❋ Autistic Allies, in this Facebook group autistic adults offer information and opinions for parents of autistic children: https://www.facebook.com/autisticallies.

❋ The Helping Hands Foundation provides support for parents of kids with upper limb differences, as well as annual family outings: https://helpinghandsgroup.org.

❋ Helpful guide to recognizing and replacing ableist words you may use in daily conversation: https://www.care2.com/causes/40-alternatives-to-these-ableist-and-oppressive-words.html.

❋ "Ten Principles of Disability Justice," by Patricia Berne, Aurora Levins Morales, and David Langstaff: https://muse.jhu.edu/article/690824.

Film (clips & features)

❋ *The Specials.* This web series documents the lives of several young adults with Down syndrome in their own voices: https://www.the-specials.com.

❋ "What Is Autism?" video with Amythest Schaber: https://www.youtube.com/watch?v=Vju1EbVVgP8.

Books & Articles

❋ "7 Things to Do When Your Kids Point Out Someone's Difference," by Rachel Garlinghouse: themighty.com/2015/04/what-to-do-when-kids-point-at-someone-in-public.

❋ *Care Work: Dreaming Disability Justice*, by Leah Lakshmi Piepzna-Samarasinha, Arsenal Pulp Press, 2018. In this collection of essays, the author explores the politics and realities of disability justice, a movement that centers the lives and leadership of sick and disabled queer, trans, Black, and brown people, with knowledge and gifts for all.

❋ *Count Us In: Growing Up with Down Syndrome*, by Jason Kingsley and Mitchell Levitz, Mariner Books, 2007. At ages 19 and 22, respectively, Jason Kingsley and Mitchell Levitz shared their innermost thoughts, feelings, hopes, and dreams, their lifelong friendship—and their experiences growing up with Down syndrome. Now, 13 years later, the authors discuss their lives since then—milestones and challenges, developments expected and unexpected—in a new afterword.

❋ "De-Stigmatizing Disability: Stereotype-Smashing Kids Books": https://booksforlittles.com/disability-destigmatization.

* "Disability Justice—a working draft," by Patty Berne: http://sinsinvalid.org/blog/disability-justice-a-working-draft-by-patty-berne.

* "Disability Awareness: 10 Things Parents Should Teach Their Kids About Disabilities," by Tiffany Carlingson: huffingtonpost.com/2013/08/02/disability-aware ness-parents-teach-kids_n_3696279.

* "Enterprise Talk: A Handrail to Authenticity," by Tom Drummond: https://tomdrummond.com/leading-and-caring-for-children/enterprise-talk.

* "Interdependency (excerpts from several talks)," by Mia Mingus: https://leavingevidence.wordpress.com/2010/01/22/interdependency-exerpts-from-several-talks .

* "Intelligence Is an Ableist Concept," by Amy Sequenzia: https://ollibean.com/intelligence-is-an-ableist-concept.

* *Nothing About Us Without Us: Disability Oppression and Empowerment*, by James Charlton, California University Press, 2000. This is the first book in the literature on disability to provide a theoretical overview of disability oppression that shows its similarities to, and differences from, racism, sexism, and colonialism.

* "Strive to Be the Person You Want Them to Be," by Tom Hobson: http://teachertomsblog.blogspot.com/2019/02/strive-to-be-person-you-want-them-to-be.html.

* "The Spoon Theory," by Christine Miserandino: https://butyoudontlooksick.com/articles/written-by-christine/the-spoon-theory.

* "Talking to Kids About Disability (and Voldemort)," by Mary Evelyn: whatdoyoudodear.com/talking-kids-disability.

* "Top 10 Inclusive Children's Books," by Sean Stockdale and Alex Strick: https://www.theguardian.com/books/2013/jul/19/alexandra-strick-sean-stockdale-top-10-inclusive-childrens-books.

* "What Disability Justice Has to Offer Social Justice," by Theo Yang Copley: https://www.grassrootsfundraising.org/2011/11/11-3-what-disability-justice-has-to-offer-social-justice-by-theo-yang-copley.

* "What's Disability Justice, Anyway?" by Chelsea Yarborough: http://feministcampus.org/whats-disability-justice-anyway.

Support for Organizing for Change

* Access Is Love provides resources to support a shift to thinking about access as love, instead of as a burden or an afterthought: https://www.disabilityintersectionalitysummit.com/access-is-love.

* The Body Is Not An Apology is an international movement committed to cultivating radical self-love and body empowerment: https://thebodyisnotanapology.com/magazine/this-is-disability-justice.

- The Buddy Walk, sponsored by the National Down Syndrome Society, is a family-friendly annual walk in October in many communities around the U.S.: ndss.org/play/national-buddy-walk-program.
- Disability Visibility Project is amplifying the voices and stories of people with disabilities: https://disabilityvisibilityproject.com.
- Fireweed Collective offers mental health education and mutual aid through a healing justice lens: https://fireweedcollective.org.
- Krip-Hop Nation's mission is to educate the music and media industries and general public about the talents, history, rights, and marketability of hip-hop artists and other musicians with disabilities: kriphopnation.com.
- The National Alliance on Mental Illness is a grassroots organization dedicated to mental health education, family support, and advocacy, hosting walks and conventions, supporting people in advocacy work, and more: www.nami.org.
- Special Olympics is a sports program started in 1968 that gives people with physical and intellectual disabilities a forum for participating in athletics and competition: https://www.specialolympics.org.

Parenting for gender justice

Definitions, Tools, Research

- Gender Spectrum offers resources on gender for all youth, resources for supporting gender expansive children, and more: https://www.genderspectrum.org/audiences/parents-and-family.
- Loveisrespect, a project of the National Domestic Violence Hotline, empowers youth to prevent and end dating abuse: https://www.loveisrespect.org.
- The National Center for Transgender Equality has the latest information about laws and policies affecting transgender people and how we can improve the laws/policies in our area: https://transequality.org/issues.
- Outright Vermont, "working to build a Vermont where all LGBTQ+ youth have hope, equity, and power," offers a helpful list of terms and definitions: http://www.outrightvt.org/terms-definitions.
- Scarleteen is an independent, feminist, grassroots sexuality and relationship education/support organization: https://www.scarleteen.com.
- The youth-led Trans Student Educational Resources created the Gender Unicorn and other great graphics to help kids understand gender: http://transstudent.org/gender.

Film (clips & features)

- "A Call to Men" TED talk with Tony Porter: http://www.ted.com/talks/tony_porter_a_call_to_men.

❀ *The Mask You Live In* is a 2015 documentary on American masculinity: http://therepresentationproject.org/film/the-mask-you-live-in.

❀ *Miss Representation* is a 2011 documentary on how mainstream media and culture contribute to the underrepresentation of women in positions of power and influence in the U.S.: http://therepresentationproject.org/film/miss-representation/about-the-film.

❀ "Rewrite the Story" video by The Representation Project: https://youtu.be/mPAmjWtHHYs.

❀ "Shrinking Women" spoken word by Lily Myers: https://youtu.be/zQucWXWXp3k.

Books & Articles

❀ *American Girls: Social Media and the Secret Lives of Girls*, by Nancy Jo Sales, Vintage, 2017. The dominant force in the lives of girls coming of age in the U.S. today is social media. What is it doing to an entire generation of young women?

❀ "Believe Me the First Time," by Dale Weiss: https://rethinkingschools.org/articles/believe -me-the-first-time.

❀ "Does Your Daughter Know It's OK to Be Angry?" by Soraya Chemaly: http://www.rolereboot.org/culture-and-politics/details/2016-05-daughter-know-ok-angry.

❀ *Dude You're a Fag: Masculinity and Sexuality in High School*, by C.J. Pascoe, University of California Press, 2007. Based on 18 months of fieldwork in a racially diverse working-class high school, this book sheds new light on masculinity both as a field of meaning and as a set of social practices.

❀ *Girls and Sex: Navigating the Complicated New Landscape*, by Peggy Orenstein, Harper, 2016. Orenstein spoke to psychologists, academics, and other experts in the field, as well as 70 young women, to offer an in-depth picture of "girls and sex" today.

❀ *The Macho Paradox*, by Jackson Katz, Sourcebooks, 2006. This book looks at the cultural factors that fuel the tolerance of abuse and violence against women.

❀ "Sex? Sexual Orientation? Gender Identity? Gender Expression?" by Joel Baum and Kim Westheimer: http://www.tolerance.org/magazine/number-50-summer-2015/feature/sex -sexual-orientation-gender-identity-gender-expression.

❀ "The Problem with 'Boys Will Be Boys,'" by Soraya Chemaly: http://www.huffingtonpost.com/soraya-chemaly/the-problem-with-boys-will-be-boys_b_3186555.html.

❀ "When Should Kids Start Learning About Sex and Consent," by Stephanie Auteri: http://www.theatlantic.com/education/archive/2016/04/when-should-kids-start-learning -about-sex-and-consent/480264.

Support for Organizing for Change

❀ The Anti-Defamation League works to stop the defamation of Jewish people and secure justice and fair treatment for all: https://www.adl.org.

- Gender Spectrum offers a number of resources and services to help us create gender-inclusive environments for children and teens: https://www.genderspectrum.org.

- Green Mountain Crossroads, also based in Vermont, connects rural LGBTQ people to build community, knowledge, and power: http://www.greenmountaincrossroads.org.

- Queerly Elementary provides services and resources to help school communities embrace lesbian, gay, bisexual, transgender, and queer diversity: http://queerlyelementary.com.

- The Representation Project inspires individuals and communities to challenge and overcome limiting stereotypes so that everyone, regardless of gender, race, class, age, sexual orientation, or circumstance, can fulfill their human potential: http://therepresentationproject.org.

- The mission of Outright Vermont is to build safe, healthy, and supportive environments for gay, lesbian, bisexual, transgender, queer, and questioning youth ages 13–22: http://www.outrightvt.org.

- The Women's Freedom Center, based in Vermont, is working to end domestic and sexual violence. Its youth educators run workshops and trainings with parents and youth on issues of gender: http://womensfreedomcenter.net.

Parenting for collective liberation

Definitions, Tools, Research

- Extensive background and resources on environmental justice and environmental racism: https://www.ejnet.org/ej/index.html.

- "The History of Environmental Justice in Five Minutes": https://www.nrdc.org/stories/history-environmental-justice-five-minutes.

Film (clips, features) & Audio

- 13th, a documentary about racialized drug policy by Ava DuVernay: https://www.netflix.com/title/80091741.

- Greta Thromberg's speech at the UN Climate Summit in 2018: http://www.youtube.com/watch?v=VFkQSGyeCWg.

- "Me Too Is a Movement Not a Moment," Tamara Burke: https://www.ted.com/talks/tarana_burke_me_too_is_a_movement_not_a_moment.

- "Mending Racialized Trauma: A Body Centered Approach with Resmaa Menakem" episode of Rebecca Wong's Connectfulness Practice podcast: https://connectfulness.com/episode/010-resmaa-menakem-racialized-trauma.

- "A Message from the Future with Alexandria Ocasio-Cortez": https://theintercept.com/2019/04/17/green-new-deal-short-film-alexandria-ocasio-cortez.

* In the documentary *Mossville, When Great Trees Fall*, a centuries-old Black community in Louisiana, contaminated and uprooted by petrochemical plants, comes to terms with the loss of its ancestral home: https://www.pbs.org/video/mossville-when-great-trees-fall-se2q8k.

* The short videos on The Story of Stuff highlight our addiction to stuff and how that addiction is connected to other social and environmental issues. If you apply a collective liberation lens you can connect these videos to many of the issues detailed in *Parenting for Social Justice*: https://storyofstuff.org/movies.

* "The Urgency of Intersectionality" with Kimberle Crenshaw: https://www.ted.com/talks/kimberle_crenshaw_the_urgency_of_intersectionality.

Books & Articles

* "7 Positive Changes That Have Come from the #MeToo Movement," by https://www.vox.com/identities/2019/10/4/20852639/me-too-movement-sexual-harassment-law-2019.

* "19 Youth Climate Activists You Should Be Following on Social Media," by Inma Galvez-Robles: https://www.earthdayorg /2019/06/ 14/15-youth-climate-activists-you-should-be-following-on-social-media.

* *Carbon Pricing: A Critical Perspective for Community Resistance*, by Tamra Gilbertson: https://www.ienearth.org/wp-content/uploads/2017/11/Carbon-Pricing-A-Critical-Perspective-for-Community-Resistance-Online-Version.pdf.

* "Domestic Violence Against American Indian and Alaska Native Women," by the National Coalition Against Domestic Violence: https://www.speakcdn.com/assets/2497/american_indian_and_alaskan_native_women__dv.pdf.

* *Emergent Strategy: Shaping Change, Changing Worlds*, by adrienne maree brown, AK Press, 2017. Inspired by Octavia Butler's explorations of our human relationship to change, *Emergent Strategy* is radical self-help, society-help, and planet-help designed to shape the futures we want to live.

* "#MeToo Brought Down 201 Powerful Men. Nearly Half of Their Replacements Are Women," by Audrey Carlsen, Maya Salam, Claire Cain Miller, Denise Lu, Ash Ngu, Jugal K. Patel, and Zach Wichter: https://www.nytimes.com/interactive/2018/10/23/us/metoo-replacements.html.

* *Pedagogy of the Oppressed*, by Paulo Freire, Herder and Herder, 1972. Freire's work has taken on a special urgency in the United States and Western Europe, where the creation of a permanent underclass in cities is increasingly accepted as the norm.

* *Radical Dharma: Talking Race, Love, and Liberation*, by Rev. angel Kyodo williams, Lama Rod Owens, and Jasmine Syedullah, North Atlantic Books, 2016. This urgent call to action outlines a new dharma that takes into account the ways that racism and privilege prevent our collective awakening.

❀ *Sacred Instructions: Indigenous Wisdom for Living Spirit Based Change*, by Sherri Mitchell, North Atlantic Books, 2018. This book is a powerful weaving of how centuries of violence are impacting our lives and what we can do for healing. (commentary by Angela Berkfield).

❀ *Towards Collective Liberation: Anti-Racist Organizing, Feminist Praxis, and Movement Building Strategy*, by Chris Crass, PM Press, 2013. Organized into four sections, this collection of essays is geared toward activists engaging with the dynamic questions of how to create and support effective movements for visionary systemic change.

❀ "Using the Five Faces of Oppression to Teach About Interlocking Systems of Oppression," by Davey Shlasko: https://www.tandfonline.com/doi/abs/10.1080/1066568 4.2015.1057061.

❀ *Your Silence Will Not Protect You: Essays and Poems*, by Audre Lorde, Silver Press, 2017. Over and over again, in the essays, speeches, and poems collected in this book, Lorde emphasises how important it is to speak up, to give witness.

Support for Organizing for Change

❀ Beautiful Solutions is an online platform, book, and training program that elevates strategies for creating the just world we want: https://solutions.thischangeseverything.org.

❀ Black and Pink is a national prison abolitionist organization dedicated to abolishing the criminal punishment system and liberating LGBTQIA2S+ people and people living with HIV/AIDS who are affected by that system: blackandpink.org.

❀ Catalyst Project is an organization in Oakland, California, that builds multiracial movements for collective liberation: http://collectiveliberation.org.

❀ Climate Justice Alliance was founded in 2013 and is made up of over 70 urban and rural organizations: https://climatejusticealliance.org.

❀ Earth Guardians are taking action for social and climate justice: www.earthguardians.org.

❀ Grassroots Global Justice is an alliance of over 60 U.S.-based grassroots organizing groups comprised of working and poor people and communities of color: https://ggjalliance.org.

❀ The Indigenous Environmental Network is an alliance of Indigenous peoples whose mission is to protect the sacredness of Earth Mother from contamination and exploitation by strengthening, maintaining, and respecting Indigenous teachings and natural laws: http://www.ienearth.org.

❀ The mission of the National Coalition Against Domestic Violence is to lead, mobilize, and raise our voices to demand a change of conditions that lead to domestic violence, such as patriarchy, privilege, racism, sexism, and classism: https://ncadv.org.

❀ The Movement for Black Lives consists of over 50 POC-led organizations coming together to organize for change: https://policy.m4bl.org/platform.

❀ Rising Tide North America supports communities in making a "just transition," in which social and ecological needs are prioritized in the shift to a low-carbon society: https://risingtidenorthamerica.org/features/principles.

❀ Southerners on New Ground builds, sustains, and connects a southern regional base of LBGTQ people to transform the region through strategic projects and campaigns developed in response to current community conditions: www.southernersonnewground.org.

❀ Support the youth who filed a constitutional climate lawsuit, *Juliana v. United States*, against the U.S. government in the U.S. District Court for the District of Oregon in 2015: https://www.youthvgov.org/congress4juliana.

❀ The Sylvia Rivera Law Project is a collective organization founded on the understanding that gender self-determination is inextricably intertwined with racial, social, and economic justice: srlp.org.

❀ The Unist'ot'en Camp is facing a constantly expanding number of companies that have proposed tar sands and fracking gas pipelines through Unist'ot'en territory without consent: https://unistoten.camp/no-pipelines.

❀ United Students Against Sweatshops is the nation's largest youth-led, student labor campaign organization with affiliated locals on over 150 campuses: https://usas.org.

ADDITIONAL RESOURCES

Please visit our website
www.parenting4socialjustice.com
for updated resource lists,
and to view and download Appendices C–L:

Appendix C: Kids at social justice rallies and protests
Appendix D: Teaching for Tolerance: Anti-bias Framework
Appendix E: Spheres of Influence
Appendix F: Microaggressions
Appendix G: White Supremacy Iceberg
Appendix H: Characteristics of White Supremacy Culture
Appendix I: 100 Race Conscious Things to Say to a Child
to Advance Racial Justice
Appendix J: Teaching Tolerance: Teaching Young Children About Race
Appendix K: Just Transition
Appendix L: Childhood Memories Worksheet

Like our Facebook page at
www.facebook.com/parenting4sj

If you would like to engage with other parents around the world
who are practicing parenting for social justice, join our
closed Facebook group Parenting 4 Social Justice:
https://www.facebook.com/groups /2124078564584646.

SOCIAL JUSTICE BOOKS FOR KIDS

Below are kids' books we recommend, organized by chapter topic. Book descriptions are from Goodreads unless otherwise noted. Please see our website (www.parenting4social-justice) for a continually updated book list. Commentary by Goodreads. The commentary by Angela Berkfield is followed by (AB).

Book lists to check out

The Council on Interracial Books for Children offers "10 tips for analyzing books for racism and sexism" to help us think about the books already on our shelves: cmascanada.ca/wp-content/uploads/2011/11/article-10-ways-to-analyze-childrens-books-for-sexism-and-racism.pdf

A Mighty Girl provides book lists, searchable by age, for many different social issues: amighty-girl.com/books

Class Action has a list of books about class for children that is brief and so an accessible place to start: classism.org/resources/resources-for-children

A project of Teaching for Change has a list of environmental justice books for children, young adults, and educators: socialjusticebooks.org/booklists/environment

Lee & Low Books, the largest multicultural children's publishing company, lets you search for books by topic and by age/reading level: leeandlow.com/collections

The San Francisco Public Library lists books by ethnic heritage, specific to Black Lives Matter, and specific to LGBTQ+: sfpl.org/kids#

We Read Too is an app created by Kaya Thomas for finding kids' books by authors of color about people of color: wereadtoo.com

Parenting for racial justice

For Early Readers (preschool and early elementary)
My Grandma/Mi Abuelita, **by Ginger Foglesong Guy, Greenwillow Books, 2007 (pre-K+)**
Follow an imaginative boy and his family as they take a faraway trip above the clouds and across the sea to visit the boy's beloved grandma. Simple words in both English and Spanish provide valuable bilingual vocabulary lessons on every page.

Ten, Nine, Eight, **by Molly Bang, Greenwillow Books, boardbook edition, 1996 (age 1+)**
A counting and going-to-bed book for toddlers that features a Black dad and his daughter at bedtime, dismantling the stereotype that Black fathers are absent and unsupportive.

All the Colors We Are: The Story of How We Get Our Skin Color/Todos los colores de nuestra piel: La historia de por qué tenemos diferentes colores de piel, **by Katie Kissinger, Redleaf Press, 2002 (pre-K+)** This bilingual (English/Spanish) book offers children a simple, scientifically accurate explanation about how our skin color is determined by our ancestors, the sun, and melanin. It is filled with photos that capture the beautiful variety of skin tones, and it supports freedom from myths and stereotypes associated with skin color, helping children build positive identities as they accept, understand, and value our rich and diverse world.

Shades of People, **by Sheila M. Kelly, Holiday House, 2010 (pre-K+)** People come in lots of shades, even within the same family. This exploration of one of our most noticeable physical traits uses vibrant photos of children and words to inspire young people to both take notice and to look beyond the obvious.

Hip Hop Speaks to Children: A Celebration of Poetry with a Beat, **edited by Nikki Giovanni, Sourcebooks, 2008 (pre-K+)** Poetry can have both a rhyme and a rhythm. Sometimes it's obvious; sometimes it's hidden. But either way, make no mistake: poetry is as vibrant and exciting as it gets. Readers will HEAR poetry's rhymes and rhythms in this collection of more than 50 poems and songs, from Queen Latifah to Gwendolyn Brooks, Langston Hughes to A Tribe Called Quest!

Love, **by Matt De La Pena, G.P. Putnam's Sons, 2018 (pre-K+)** This is one of those kids' books that brings on the tears—it is so wonderful. Love is the foundation for all social justice, and this book puts the elusive concept of love into words. One page includes: "And it's love in the made-up stories your uncles tell in the backyard between wild horseshoe throws." The illustrations show all kinds of folks and all kinds of situations. It is amazing. (AB)

Feast for 10, **by Cathryn Falwell, HMH Books for Young Readers, 2003 (age 1+)** A counting book that features an African American family shopping for food, preparing dinner, and sitting down to eat, this is a lively read-aloud text paired with bright collage illustrations.

We March, **by Shane W. Evans, Roaring Book Press, 2012 (pre-K+)** On August 28, 1963, more than 250,000 people gathered in our nation's capital to participate in the March on Washington for Jobs and Freedom, which included Martin Luther King Jr.'s historic "I Have a Dream" speech. Through simple yet compelling illustrations, this book conveys the thrill of the day, brought to life for even the youngest readers.

I'm Your Peanut Butter Big Brother, **by Serena Alko, Alfred A. Knopf, 2009 (pre-K+)** Alko's lyrical and jazz-like text and vibrant illustrations capture the excitement of a new baby for an older sibling, while celebrating the genuine love of family. *Baby brother or sister, will you look like me? I blend from semisweet dark / Daddy chocolate bar and strawberry cream Mama's milk. / My hair is soft crunchy billows of cotton candy. / I'm your peanut butter big-brother-to-be.*

My People, **by Langston Hughes, Atheneum Books, 2009 (age 1+)** Langston Hughes's spare yet eloquent tribute to his people has been cherished for generations. Now, acclaimed photographer Charles R. Smith Jr. interprets this beloved poem in vivid sepia photographs that capture the glory, the beauty, and the soul of being a Black American today.

Giving Thanks: A Native American Good Morning Message, **by Chief Jake Swamp, Lee & Low Books, 1997 (age 1+)** This book offers a special children's version of the Thanksgiving Address, a message of gratitude that originated with the Native people of upstate New York and Canada and that is still spoken at ceremonial gatherings held by the Iroquois, or Six Nations.

Cassie's Word Quilt, **by Faith Ringgold, Alfred A. Knopf, 2002 (pre-K+)** Cassie takes us on a tour of her home, neighborhood, and school, introducing dozens of words along the way. Young readers will love the simple storyline and beautifully designed spreads, each with its own quilt motif.

The Skin I'm In: A First Look at Racism, **by Pat Thomas, B.E.S., 2003 (pre-K+)** This book encourages kids to accept and be comfortable with differences in skin color and other racial characteristics among their friends and in themselves.

Chocolate Me! **by Taye Diggs, Square Fish, 2015 (K–3)** The boy in this book is teased for looking different from the other kids—his skin is darker, his hair curlier. He tells his mother he wishes he could be more like everyone else, and she helps him see how beautiful he truly is.

A is for Activist, **by Innosanta Nagara, Kupu Kupu Press, 2012 (pre-K+)** This is an ABC board book for families that want their kids to grow up in a space where activism in all of its various forms is embraced.

Bein' with You This Way, **by W. Nikola-Lisa, Turtleback Books, 1997 (pre-K+)** An African American girl visits the park and rounds up a group of her friends for an afternoon of fun and playground games. The children discover that despite their physical differences, they are all really the same.

The Other Side, **by Jacqueline Woodson, G.P. Putnam's Sons Books for Young Readers, 2001 (pre-K+)** Clover's mom says it isn't safe to cross the fence that segregates their African American side of town from the white side where Anna lives. But Clover and Anna strike up a friendship and get around the grownups' rules by sitting on top of the fence together. From

Angela Berkfield: I love this book because it illustrates how simple it can be to bridge the divide—and how good kids are at doing it.

***The Chicken Chasing Queen of Lamar County*, by Janice N. Harrington, Farrar, Straus and Giroux, 2007 (pre-K+)** Meet one smart chicken chaser: she can catch any chicken on her grandmother's farm except one—the elusive Miss Hen. From Angela Berkfield: This book is fun to read with my kids, because we used to live on a farm and they spent a lot of time chasing chickens and figuring out ways to catch them. Finding commonality is fun and important.

***Not My Idea: A Book About Whiteness*, by Anastasia Higginbotham, Dottir Press, 2018 (pre-K+)** This book was motivated by an interview with Toni Morrison in which she said, "White people have a very, very serious problem, and they should start thinking about what they can do about it." Also: "Take me out of it." Are we talking with young white children about racism, white supremacy, and white privilege? This book is a helpful way to get the conversation started. (AB)

***Let's Talk About Race*, by Julius Lester, HarperCollins, 2008 (K–3)** Julius Lester says, "I write because our lives are stories. If enough of those stories are told, then perhaps we will begin to see that our lives are the same story. The differences are merely in the details." Now Mr. Lester shares his own story as he explores what makes each of us special.

***Last Stop on Market Street*, by Matt de la Pena, G.P. Putnam's Sons Books for Young Readers, 2015 (pre-K+)** Every Sunday after church, CJ and his grandma ride the bus across town. But one day, CJ wonders why they don't own a car like his friend Colby. Why doesn't he have an iPod like the boys on the bus? How come they always have to get off in the dirty part of town? Each question is met with an encouraging answer from grandma, who helps him see the beauty—and fun—in their routine and the world around them.

For Middle Readers (elementary)
***Rosa*, by Nikki Giovanni, Square Fish, 2007 (pre-K–3)** Excerpt: *She had not sought this moment but she was ready for it. When the policeman bent down to ask "Auntie, are you going to move?" all the strength of all the people through all those many years joined in her. She said, "No."* This is an excellent picture-book account of Rosa Parks' historic choice.

***Fiona's Lace*, by Patricia Polacco, Simon & Schuster/Paula Wiseman Books, 2014 (pre-K–3)** This is an Irish story about poverty, labor, migration, tragedy, perseverance, and resilience. I read it with my kids, then we looked at our family tree and saw that their great-great-great-grandparents came from Ireland. Knowing our history is crucial for understanding the way forward. Our brains and bodies have been colonized, and it takes a lot to look at the painful history of the USA—land theft, genocide, and slavery. It also takes a lot of work to keep our family's stories alive; they can so easily become assimilated into the "white" story. (AB)

***The Great Migration: An American Story*, by Jacob Lawrence, HarperCollins, 1993 (grade 1+)** This is a simple and powerful book that can help illustrate connections between race and class and causes of migration. (AB)

Rad American Women A to Z, **by Kate Schatz, City Lights Publishers, 2015 (grade 2+)** American history was made by countless rad—and often radical—women. Twenty-six diverse individuals are profiled in this book, including artists and abolitionists, scientists and suffragettes, rockstars and rabble-rousers, and agents of change of all kinds. Young readers will be captured by the bright visuals and easily modified texts, while the subject matter will stimulate and inspire high-schoolers and beyond.

Show Way, **by Jacqueline Woodson, G.P. Putnam's Sons Books for Young Readers, 2005 (pre-K–3)** In this story, which spans generations, Soonie's great-grandma was just seven years old when she was sold to a big plantation without her ma and pa, and with only some fabric and needles to call her own. She pieced together bright patches with names like North Star and Crossroads, patches with secret meanings made into quilts called Show Ways—maps for slaves to follow to freedom.

Moses: When Harriet Tubman Led Her People to Freedom, **by Carole Boston Weatherford, (grade 1+)** This book tells the story of Harriet Tubman's courage and faith that freed many souls from the bondage of slavery. While telling of Harriet's courageous acts, the book focuses more on her faith in God and internal battle with trusting His timing.

Sky Sisters, **by Jan Bourdeau Waboose, Kids Can Press, 2000 (pre-K+)** This book covers themes of sisterhood, connection with nature, and Ojibway culture and language, and can spark some great conversation with kids. Also, you get to "see" the northern lights!

Crown: An Ode to the Fresh Cut, **by Derrick Barnes, Bolden, 2017 (K+)** This book is so much fun! I love it! The author says it "focuses on the humanity, the beautiful, raw, smart, perceptive, assured humanity of black boys/sons/brothers/nephews/grandsons, and how they see themselves when they highly approve of their reflections in the mirror." (AB)

Sitting Bull: Lakota Warrior and Defender of His People, **by S.D. Nelson, Abrams, 2015 (grade 2+)** This book is an accessible history of the very difficult story of white expansion into native territory in the dakotas. It has beautiful illustrations and is told mostly in Sitting Bull's words. Powerful and important. (commentary by Angela Berkfield)

The World Is Not a Rectangle: A Portrait of Architect Zaha Hadid, **by Jeanette Winter, Beach Lane Books, 2017 (pre-K+)** I have to admit I did not know who Zaha Hadid was, and it was so fun to learn about this incredible Iranian woman through a children's book. This is a good example of a way to do some research with your kids. (commentary by Angela Berkfield)

The Word Collector, **by Peter H. Reynolds, Orchard Books. 2018 (pre-K+)** We need diverse books, and this is a particularly good one. A young Black boy is collecting words. He does such an amazing job of it that it makes me want to collect words too! (AB)

I am Harriet Tubman, **by Brad Meltzer, Dial Books, 2018 (K+)** Yes! Harriet Tubman was amazing and this book is so super cool and inspiring and just—wow! This book shows the strength, brilliance, and generosity of the spirit, and how awful slavery was, but mostly the resilience in the face of it. It shows white people in solidarity with black folks, too, which is important for our kids to see, and for me to see too! (AB)

Malcolm X: A Fire Burning Brightly, **by Walter Dean Myers, Amistad, 2003 (grades 2–5)**
This is a compelling account of the life of one of the most controversial and misunderstood men of the 20th century. From the troubled childhood of Malcolm Little to the assassination of Malcolm X, Myers shows the influences on and the personal strengths of this fiery leader.

Parenting for economic justice

For Early Readers (preschool and early elementary)
A House Is Not a Home, **by Anne Liersch, North-South Books, 1999 (pre-K+)** Winter is coming and the animals are busy building a house to keep themselves warm and cozy. The hares gather stones from the field, Hedgehog helps Wild Boar get wood from the forest, Deer lays the stone wall, and Fox mixes the concrete in this book that shows how cooperation and compromise are important tools when it comes to building friendships.

Love As Strong As Ginger, **by Lenore Look, Atheneum Books for Young Readers, 1999 (pre-K+)** Katie loves to show her grandma how to dress a Barbie, and GninGnin loves to show Katie how to make rice dumplings. More than anything, Katie longs to go with GninGnin to work, to crack a mountain of crabs alongside her at the crab cannery. One day Katie gets her wish, but nothing is the way she'd imagined—and she develops an understanding of the sacrifices her grandma has made to give her granddaughter a brighter future.

Two White Rabbits, **by Jairo Buitrago, Groundwood Books, 2015 (pre-K+)** In this moving story, a young child describes her and her father's travel north toward the U.S. border. They travel mostly on the roof of a train known as The Beast, but the little girl doesn't know where they're going. As many thousands of people, especially children, in Mexico and Central America continue to make the arduous journey to the U.S. border in search of a better life, this is an important book.

The Streets Are Free, **by Kurusa, Annick Press, 1981, fifth printing 2014 (pre-K+)** Based on a true story about the barrios on the outskirts of Caracas, Venezuela, this is such a powerful story of kids taking things into their own hands and getting what they need. (commentary by Angela Berkfield)

Brave Girl: Clara and the Shirtwaist Factory Maker's Strike of 1909, **by Michelle Markel, Balzer + Bray, 2013 (K+)** This picture book is about Ukrainian immigrant Clara Lemlich and the plight of immigrants in America in the early 1900s. It tackles topics of activism and the U.S. garment industry and the timeless fight for equality and justice.

Muskrat Will Be Swimming, **by Cheryl Savageau, Tilbury House, 1996 (pre-K+)** This is a gorgeous book with themes of poverty, Native American worldviews, respecting the natural world, bullying, and finding our own power. It is such a good book. (AB)

Spuds, **by Karen Hesse, Scholastic Press, 2008 (pre-K+)** This is a heartwarming story set in the backwoods of Maine that glows with integrity, love, and true family values. Ma's been working so hard, she doesn't have much left over. So her three kids decide to do some work on their own: in the dark of night, they steal into their rich neighbor's potato fields in hopes of collecting the strays that have been left to rot.

Town Is by the Sea, **by Joanne Schwartz and Sydney Smith, Groundwood Books, 2017 (pre-K+)** This book tells the story of a young boy who is the son of generations of coal miners and will likely be a coal miner himself when he grows up. It holds hardness and beauty simultaneously. (AB)

Those Shoes, **by Maribeth Boelts, Candlewick, 2009 (pre-K+)** *But all the kids are wearing them!* Any child who has ever craved something out of reach will relate to this warm, refreshingly realistic story. All Jeremy wants is a pair of "those shoes," the ones everyone at school seems to be wearing. But Jeremy's grandma tells him they don't have room for "want," just "need," and what Jeremy needs are new boots for winter. Jeremy eventually realizes that the things he has—warm boots, a loving grandma, the chance to help a friend—are worth more.

The Teddy Bear, **by David McPhail, Square Fish, 2005 (pre-K–K)** A young boy loses a beloved teddy bear, which is then found by a homeless man. As time passes, the boy forgets about his bear, and the bear is as treasured by the man as he was by the boy. Circumstances bring them together and the little boy is able to react with compassion.

Yertle The Turtle, **by Dr. Seuss, Random House Books for Young Readers, 1958 (pre-K+)** Dr. Seuss provides this amazing social commentary in the form of rhyming turtles. My kids love this one. In real life it takes more than a sneeze to topple tyrants and tyrannical systems, nevertheless this story provides an illustration of the climb to the top and what it's like to be on the bottom of the pile. (AB)

The Dumpster Diver, **by Janet S. Wong, Candlewick, 2007 (pre-K+)** Anyone can dive for treasure in the ocean, but Steve dives for it in his neighborhood dumpster! As he delves into the trash each weekend, he encourages his young neighbors (a.k.a. the Diving Team) to see the potential in what others throw away. With a bit of imagination, trash can be transformed into treasure—and as the Diving Team soon discovers, it might even help a friend in need.

Night Job, **by Karen Hesse, Candlewick, 2018 (pre-K–3)** When the sun sets, Dad's job as a school custodian is just beginning. What is it like to work on a Friday night while the rest of the city is asleep? Newbery Medalist Karen Hesse's quietly powerful story of a boy and his father is tenderly brought to life by G. Brian Karas in this luminous tribute to an enduring, everyday sort of love.

For Middle Readers (elementary)
Harvesting Hope: The Story of Cesar Chavez, **by Kathleen Krull, HMH Books for Young Readers, 2003 (grade 1+)** When Cesar Chavez led a 340-mile peaceful protest march through California, he ignited a cause and improved the lives of thousands of migrant farmworkers.

But Cesar wasn't always a leader; as a boy, he was shy and teased at school. His family slaved in the fields for barely enough money to survive. Cesar knew things had to change, and he thought maybe he could help change them.

La Frontera: El Viaje con Papa/My Journey with Papa, **by Deborah Mills, Alfredo Alva, and Claudia Navarro, Barefoot Books, 2018 (K+)** This is a true story told in English and Spanish of when Alfredo and his father immigrated from Mexico to the U.S. (AB)

Brick by Brick, **by Charles R. Smith Jr., Amistad, 2013 (grade 1+)** Did you know that the original White House, to be the home of George Washington, was built with slave labor? This book tells the story in verse. It makes the connection between slave labor and profit very clear (most kids books don't do that). It provides a clear example of the intersection between race and class in a way young kids can easily understand. (AB)

Each Kindness, **by Jacqueline Woodson, Nancy Paulsen Books, 2012 (grade 1+)** Chloe and her friends won't play with the new girl, Maya, who wears hand-me-downs and plays with old-fashioned toys. Every time Maya tries to join Chloe and her gang, they reject her. Eventually, Maya stops coming to school altogether. When Chloe's teacher talks about how even small acts of kindness can change the world, Chloe is stung by the lost opportunity for friendship and thinks how much better it could have been if she'd shown Maya a little kindness.

¡Sí, Se Puede!/Yes, We Can!: Janitor Strike in L.A., **by Diana Cohn, Cinco Puntos Press, 2005 (grade 2+)** This bilingual story is set against the backdrop of the successful janitors' strike in Los Angeles in 2000. Every night, Carlitos sleeps while his mother cleans as a janitor in one of the skyscrapers in downtown LA. Eventually his mother explains that she can't make enough money to support him and his abuelita the way they need and so she and the other janitors have decided to go on strike. Carlitos and the kids in his class join the marchers with a special sign!

The Hundred Dresses, **by Eleanor Estes, HMH Books for Young Readers, 2004 (grade 4+)** At the heart of this story is Wanda Petronski, a Polish girl who is ridiculed by her classmates for wearing the same faded blue dress every day. Wanda claims she has 100 dresses at home, but everyone knows she doesn't and bullies her mercilessly. The class feels terrible when Wanda is pulled out of the school, but by that time it's too late for apologies. Maddie, one of Wanda's classmates, decides she is "never going to stand by and say nothing again."

Crenshaw, **by Katherine Applegate, Feiwel & Friends, 2015 (grade 4+)** Jackson's family has fallen on hard times. There's no more money for rent, and not much for food either. His parents, his little sister, and their dog may have to live in their minivan. Again. Author Applegate shows in unexpected ways that friends matter, whether real or imaginary.

I Can Hear the Sun, **by Patricia Polacco, Puffin Books, 1999 (grade 1+)** A boy visits a park every day, where he helps the park's caretaker look after the geese. He is from a home for homeless children, and when he finds out that he is to be moved to a permanent placement, away from the geese he loves, he taps into some incredible magic and flies away with the geese. A tear-jerking combination of magic and realism. I have a hard time reading any of Patricia Polacco's books without crying, and this one is no different. (AB)

Just Juice, **by Karen Hesse, Scholastic Paperbacks, 1999 (grade 2+)** Letters and numbers still don't make sense to Juice Faulstich. She'd rather skip school and spend the day at home in the North Carolina hills. But when the bank threatens to repossess her family's home, Juice faces her first life-sized problem.

YA
Note: Mature 9- and 10-year-olds could read these books or adults could read aloud with them.

The Benefits of Being An Octopus, **by Ann Braden, Skypony, 2018 (grades 3–7)** Written by a friend of mine, this book is being held up nationally as one of the best books for having complex conversations with middle-schoolers about rural poverty, gun violence, domestic violence, and the opiate crisis. It is also being used by fourth- and fifth-grade teachers because these are issues that students are dealing with. It is a book about finding voice and power and allies. It is a book about being an ally. It is worth reading as an adult too! (AB)

The Mighty Miss Malone, **by Christopher Paul Curtis, Yearling, 2013 (grade 6+)** "We are a family on a journey to a place called Wonderful" is the motto of Deza's family. Deza is the smartest girl in her class in Gary, Indiana, singled out by teachers for a special path in life. But the Great Depression hit Gary hard, and there are no jobs for Black men. When Deza's beloved father leaves to find work, the family goes in search of him and ends up in a Hooverville outside Flint, Michigan. The twists and turns of their story reveal the devastation of the Depression.

The Whispering Road, **by Livi Michael, Putnam Juvenile, 2005 (grade 6+)** It's hard to find books that approach poverty from a resiliency and systems perspective (rather than deficit or blame), and this book does an excellent job. While Michael is writing about the realities of poverty in the mid-19th century, it is not hard to draw comparisons to today. Joe and the wonderful friends he meets along the way do an excellent job of telling the story of poverty as something that presses upon the poor instead of initiating with the poor. It was hard to put the book down. (AB)

Song of the Trees, **by Mildred Taylor, Puffin Books, 2003 (grade 4+)** With the depression bearing down on her family and food in short supply, Cassie Logan isn't sure where her next meal will come from. But there's one thing she knows will always be there—the whispering trees outside her window, a steady source of comfort to her. When Mr. Andersen tries to force Big Ma to sell their valuable trees, Cassie can't sit by and let it happen. She knows her family needs the money, but something tells her that they need the trees just as much.

Parenting for disability justice

For Early Readers (preschool and early elementary)

My Friend Isabelle, **by Eliza Woloson, Woodbine House, 2003 (pre-K+)** This is a heart-warming story of two friends, Charlie and Isabelle. Charlie tells about the things they like to do together and also how he and Isabelle, who has Down syndrome, are different. The book encourages readers to think about what makes friendships special and how our differences can make the world more interesting.

Hands and Hearts, **by Donna Jo Napoli, Harry N. Abrams, 2014 (pre-K–2)** A mother and daughter spend a sunny day at the beach together, where they swim, dance, build sandcastles, and, most importantly, communicate. But their communication is not spoken; rather, it is created by loving hands that use American Sign Language. Readers will learn how to sign 15 words using American Sign Language with the help of sidebars that are both instructive and playful.

I Can, Can You? **by Marjorie W. Pitzer, Woodbine House, 2004 (age 1+)** This is a delightful board book full of babies and toddlers with Down syndrome going about the business of their lives. Presented in crisp, uncluttered full-colour photographs, these children swim, take a bottle, share, eat spaghetti, laugh, play in the park, and more . . . looking adorable all the while!

The Animal Boogie, **by Debbie Harper, Barefoot Books, 2000 (ages 0–5)** This book features children from many cultures and differently abled children. The rhymes and music encourage children to experiment with movement. Everyone will want to get up and dance to this toe-tapping favourite!

Susan Laughs, **by Jeanne Willis, Henry Holt & Co, 2000 (pre-K+)** Told in rhyme, this story follows Susan through a series of familiar activities. She swims with her father, works hard in school, plays with her friends… It's a portrait of a busy, happy little girl, and it's not until the end of the story that we learn Susan uses a wheelchair. Told with insight, and without sentimentality, here is an inspiring look at a spunky girl whose physical disability is never seen as a handicap.

Max the Champion, **by Sean Stockdale and Alex Strick, Frances Lincoln, 2013 (pre-K+)** Max loves sports. As he gets up, eats breakfast, and heads off to school, he dreams of competing in world-class sporting events. This is an inclusive picture book that shows disabled children and children without disabilities mixing and enjoying different sports in a natural way.

My Silent World, **by Nette Hilton, Hachette Australia, 2009 (pre-K+)** This is a lyrical description of how a deaf child treasures her silent world and how it's changed by a cochlear implant, which she sees at first as an intruder.

Zoom! **by Robert Munsch, Cartwheel, 2004 (pre-K+)** Young daredevil Lauretta puts her brand new wheelchair to the ultimate test—and saves her brother!

Cinderella's Magical Wheelchair: An Empowering Fairy Tale (Growing with Love), **by Jewel Kats, Loving Healing Press, 2011 (pre-K+)** In a kingdom far, far away lives Cinderella. As expected, she works endlessly for her cranky sisters and stepmother. She would love to attend the royal costume ball and meet the prince, but her family is dead set against it. In fact, they've gone so far as to trash her wheelchair! But an unexpected magical endowment to her wheelchair launches an enchanted evening and a dance with the prince. This fairytale shows that people with disabilities can overcome abuse.

For Middle Readers (elementary)

King for a Day, **by Rukhsana Khan, Lee & Low Books, 2014 (K+)** In two fierce battles, Malik takes down the kites flown by the bully next door. Then Malik moves on, guiding Falcon into leaps, swirls, and dives, slashing strings and plucking kites from the sky. By the end of the day, Malik has a big pile of captured kites—but then the bully reappears, trying to take a kite from a nearby girl. With a sudden act of generosity, Malik finds the perfect way to help the girl.

Not So Different: What You Really Want to Ask About Having a Disability, **by Shane Burcaw, Roaring Brook Press, 2017 (grades 1–4)** Shane Burcaw was born with a rare disease called spinal muscular atrophy, which hinders the growth of his muscles. This hasn't stopped him from doing the things he enjoys (like eating pizza and playing sports and video games) with the people he loves, but it does mean that he routinely relies on his friends and family for help.

Joey Pigza Swallowed the Key, **by Jack Gantos. Harper Trophy, 2001 (grades 5–6)** The first in a five-book series about a boy with ADHD and his family, this book finds Joey dealing with some challenging family dynamics, such as alcoholism and separated parents.

Rules, **by Cynthia Lord, Scholastic Press, 2006 (grades 4–7)** Twelve-year-old Catherine just wants a normal life, which is near impossible when you have a brother with autism and a family that revolves around his disability. But the summer Catherine meets Jason, a paraplegic boy, and Kristi, the next-door friend she's always wished for, it's her own shocking behavior that turns everything upside down and forces her to ask *what is normal?*

Alchemy and Meggy Swann, **by Karen Cushman, Clarion Books, 2010 (grades 3–7)** Meggy Swann has just come to London with her only friend, a goose named Louise. Meggy's mother was glad to be rid of her, and her father, who sent for her, doesn't want her after all. Meggy is appalled by London—dirty and noisy, full of rogues and thieves, and difficult to get around in (not that getting around is ever easy for someone who walks with the help of two sticks).

Wonder, **by RJ Palacio, Alfred A. Knopf, 2012 (grades 3–7)** August Pullman was born with a facial difference that up until now has prevented him from going to a mainstream school. Starting fifth grade at Beecher Prep, he wants nothing more than to be treated as an ordinary kid. The story begins from Auggie's point of view but soon switches to include the POVs of his classmates, his sister and her boyfriend, and others. These perspectives converge in a portrait of one community's struggle with empathy, compassion, and acceptance. (There is extensive critique of this book by disability communities, which is crucial to look up and reflect on while reading. AB)

Al Capone Does My Shirts, Al Capone Shines My Shoes, **and** *Al Capone Does My Homework,* **by Gennifer Choldenko, Puffin Books, 2006 (grades 5–6)** This is a series of books focused on Moose's family in the 1930s, who lives on Alcatraz where Moose's father works as a guard. Little sister Natalie is autistic. The books do a great job of portraying full characters with lots of depth.

Paperboy, **by Vince Vawter, Delacorte Press, 2013 (grades 5–6)** This story takes place in Memphis in 1959. "Little Man" Victor, an 11-year-old boy who stutters, takes over his best friend Rat's paper route while Rat is visiting his grandparents. Little Man has various encounters with Rat's customers, with the paper route posing challenges and introducing Little Man to life's daily obstacles.

El Deafo, **by CeCe Bell, Harry N. Abrams, 2014 (grades 3–7)** Starting at a new school is scary, even more so with a giant hearing aid strapped to your chest! At Cece's old school, everyone in her class was deaf. Here she is different. This funny and perceptive graphic-novel memoir about growing up hearing-impaired is also an unforgettable book about growing up, and all the super and super-embarrassing moments along the way.

Insignificant Events in the Life of a Cactus, **by Dusti Bowling, Sterling Children's Books, 2017 (grades 3–7)** Aven Green loves to tell people she lost her arms in an alligator-wrestling match or a wildfire in Tanzania, but the truth is she was born without them. And when she moves with her parents across the country, she knows she'll have to answer questions about her body over and over again. Her new life takes an unexpected turn when she bonds with Connor, a classmate who also feels isolated because of his own disability.

The Autism Acceptance Book: Being a Friend to Someone with Autism, **by Ellen Sabin, Watering Can Press, 2006 (grades 1–4)** This is an activity book, a conversation starter, and an educational tool that helps kids learn to embrace people's differences and treat others with respect, compassion, and kindness. It teaches children about autism, helps them imagine how things might feel for those with autism, and encourages them to think about how they can show understanding and acceptance of people with autism.

Parenting for gender justice

The following book descriptions are from www.genderspectrum.org unless otherwise noted.
For Early Readers (preschool and early elementary)

All of Me! A Book of Thanks, **by Molly Bang, The Blue Sky Press, 2009 (age 1+)** In colors as bright as sunshine, Caldecott Honor Illustrator Molly Bang presents a young child who is thankful for the world around them.

Neither, **by Airlie Anderson, Little, Brown Books for Young Readers, 2018 (pre-K–3)** In this colorful and touching story that celebrates what makes each of us unique, a little creature that's not quite a bird and not quite a bunny—it's "neither"—searches for a place to fit in.

C is for Consent, **by Eleanor Morrison, Phonics by Finn, 2018 (age 1+)** Finn's parents encourage him to make his own choices about receiving and offering physical affection. This book teaches babies, toddlers, parents, and grandparents that it is okay for kids to say no to hugs and kisses and that what happens to a person's body is up to them—helping children grow up confident in their bodies, comfortable with expressing physical boundaries, and respectful of the boundaries of others.

How Mamas Love Their Babies, **by Juniper Fitzgerald, The Feminist Press at CUNY, 2018 (pre-K–3)** Illustrating different ways that mothers provide for their children—including by dancing at a strip club—this children's book is the first to depict a sex-worker parent. By introducing and normalizing the idea of bodily labor, it provides an expanded notion of working mothers overall and challenges the idea that only some types of work result in good or appropriate parenting.

My Body! What I Say Goes! **by Jayneen Sanders, Educate to Empower Publishing, 2016 (pre-K–4)** The crucial skills taught in this book will help children protect their bodies from inappropriate touch, empowering them to say in a strong and clear voice, "This is my body! What I say goes!" In-depth discussion questions will further enhance learning and help initiate important family conversations about body autonomy.

Families, Families, Families! **by Susanne Lang and Max Lang, Random House, 2015 (age 2+)** A host of animals portray all kinds of families: "If you love each other, then you are a family."

Truly Willa, **by Willa Naylor, Createspace, 2016 (pre-K+)** This book, written by eight-year-old Willa, who's a transgender girl, tells Willa's story of growing up transgender and how she becomes an advocate for other transgender children.

All I Want to Be Is Me, **by Phyliss Rothblatt, CreateSpace Independent Publishing, 2011 (pre-K+)** This book shows the diverse ways young children experience and express their gender, giving voice to those who don't fit into narrow gender stereotypes and just want to be free to be themselves. It offers a wonderful way for children to learn about gender diversity, embracing different ways of being, and being a true friend.

A Fire Engine for Ruthie, **by Lesléa Newman, Clarion Books, 2004 (pre-K+)** Nana has dolls and dress-up clothes for Ruthie to play with, but Ruthie would rather have a fire engine.

Goblinheart, **by Brett Axel, East Waterfront Press, 2012 (pre-K+)** Using "fairy" and "goblin" in lieu of female and male, this is a timely allegorical fairytale. A youngster named Julep, who lives in a forest tribe, insists on growing up to be a goblin rather than a fairy. The tribe learns to accept that Julep is a goblin at heart, eventually coming around to support the physical transition that must be made for Julep to live as a goblin.

I am Jazz, **by Jessica Herthel, Dial, 2014 (pre-K+)** This is the story of a transgender child based on the real-life experience of Jazz Jennings, who has become a spokesperson for transgender kids everywhere.

Look Like a Girl, **by Sheila Hamanaka, Harper Collins, 1999 (pre-K+)** In this book, exuberant girls seem to burst both the limits of the page and the confines of traditional expectations. Each child, while engaging in typical childhood activities, is imagining a life as free and wild as that of a tiger, dolphin, mustang, condor, or wolf.

Roland Humphrey Is Wearing a WHAT? **by Eileen Kiernan-Johnson, Huntley Rahara Press, 2012 (pre-K+)** This is the story of a little boy's quest to be his authentic self, dressed in pink and festooned with sparkles, in a world that frowns upon boys who like "girly" things. Written in verse, it playfully raises important questions about gender norms, acceptance, and friendship.

Tutus Aren't My Style, **by Skeers, Linda. Dial. 2010 (pre-K+)** Emma loves lizards and pirates and cowboy boots, so when a package arrives from Uncle Leo, she doesn't know what to do with the ballerina costume inside. "I don't know how to be a ballerina," she says. But when she decides to make her own rules about how to be a ballerina, Emma's style prevails in her triumphant dance debut.

Virgie Goes to School with Us Boys, **by Elizabeth Fitzgerald Howard, Aladdin, 2005 (pre-K+)** The youngest and the only girl in a family of five boys, Virgie works hard to convince everyone she is old enough, strong enough, and smart enough to attend the school set up by the Quakers for recently freed blacks in Jonesborough, Tennessee. She eventually convinces her family that she can make the seven-mile walk to board at school each week and handle the job of "learning to be free."

When Kayla Was Kyle, **by Amy Frabikant, Avid Readers Publishing, 2013 (pre-K+)** Kyle doesn't understand why the other kids at school call him names. He looks like other boys but doesn't feel like them. Can Kyle find the words to share his feelings about his gender—and can his parents help him to transition into the girl he was born to be?

Are You a Boy or Are You a Girl? **by Sarah Savage, Jessica Kingsley Publishers, 2017 (grades 1–2)** This book leaves it up to the reader to decide the gender of the main character. It includes all forms of gender expression, and it allows parents and children to begin to break down the barriers of gender and to talk about what different stereotypes and roles mean to them.

Sparkle Boy, **by Leslea Newman, Lee & Low Books, 2017 (K–3)** When older boys at the library tease Casey for wearing "girl things," Jessie realizes that Casey has the right to be himself and wear whatever he wants. Why can't both she and Casey love all things shimmery, glittery, and sparkly? Here is a sweet, heartwarming story about acceptance, respect, and the freedom to be yourself in a world where any gender expression should be celebrated.

The Paper Bag Princess, **by Robert Munsch, Annick Press, 1980 (pre-K–2)** The Princess Elizabeth is slated to marry Prince Ronald when a dragon attacks the castle and kidnaps Ronald. In resourceful and humorous fashion, Elizabeth finds the dragon, outsmarts him, and rescues Ronald—who is less than pleased at her un-princess-like appearance.

***What Makes a Baby*, by Cory Silverberg, Triangle Square, 2013 (K–3)** This book teaches kids about conception, gestation, and birth in a way that works regardless of whether or not the kid in question was adopted, conceived using reproductive technologies at home or in a clinic, through surrogacy, or any of the other wondrous ways we make babies these days. It doesn't gender people or body parts.

***When Aidan Became a Brother*, by Kyle Lukoff, Lee & Low Books, 2019 (pre-K–3)** After he realized he was a trans boy, Aidan and his parents fixed the parts of life that didn't fit anymore, and he settled happily into his new life. Then Mom and Dad announce they're going to have another baby, and Aidan wants to do everything he can to make things right for his new sibling from the beginning—from choosing the perfect name to creating a beautiful room to picking out the cutest onesie. But what does "making things right" actually mean?

For Middle Readers (elementary)
***A Quick Guide to Queer and Trans Identities*, by J.R. Zuckerberg and Mady G, Limerence Press, 2019** Covering the essential topics of sexuality, gender identity, coming out, and navigating relationships, this guide explains the spectrum of human experience through informative comics, interviews, worksheets, and imaginative examples. It's a great starting point for anyone curious about queer and trans life, and helpful for those already on their own journeys!

***Sex Is a Funny Word: A Book about Bodies, Feelings, and YOU*, by Cory Silverberg and Fiona Smyth, Triangle Square, 2015 (grades 2–5)** A comic book for kids that includes children and families of all makeups, orientations, and gender identies, *Sex Is a Funny Word* is an essential resource about bodies, gender, and sexuality that is much more than the "facts of life" or "birds and the bees."

***The Gender Wheel*, by Maya Christina Gonzales, Reflection Press, 2018 (grades 2–5)** This body-positive book depicts a wide range of bodies and goes into the origins of the current binary gender system. It addresses how we can learn from nature to see the truth that has always existed and envision a new story that includes room for all bodies and genders.

***The Misfits* (series), by James Howe, Atheneum Books for Young Readers, 2003 (grades 5–7)** "Kids who get called the worst names oftentimes find each other. That's how it was with us. Skeezie Tookis and Addie Carle and Joe Bunch and me. We call ourselves the Gang of Five, but there are only four of us. We do it to keep people on their toes. Make 'em wonder. Or maybe we do it because we figure that there's one more kid out there who's going to need a gang to be a part of. A misfit, like us."

***Rickshaw Girl*, by Mitali Perkins, Charlesbridge Publishing, 2008 (grades 2–5)** Ten-year-old Naima longs to earn money to help her poor Bangladeshi family, but her talent in painting traditional patterns, or alpanas, is of no use. Disguised as a boy to drive her father's rickshaw, she wrecks the vehicle, threatening the family's sole livelihood. Her solution is to steal away, disguised as a boy, to a repair shop and offer her services painting decorations on the rickshaws. She's surprised to find the owner is a woman.

Wandering Son, Volumes 1–6, **by Shimura Takako, Fantagraphics, 2011–13** Fifth grade: threshold to puberty. Shuichi Nitori and his new friend Yoshino Takatsuki have happy homes and loving families and are well liked by their classmates. But they share a secret that complicates a time in life that is awkward for anyone: Shuichi is a boy who wants to be a girl, and Yoshino is a girl who wants to be a boy. Takako portrays Shuishi and Yoshino's private journey with affection, sensitivity, gentle humor, and grace.

Parenting for collective liberation

Many books don't fit into just one category—and some books, though they may address a single issue, are excellent for use in talking about how other issues are connected.

Most books by Patricia Polacco (pre-K+) Polacco finds ways to describe human connection and resilience that inspire me (and hopefully my kids) to be the kind of human who is creating the fabric of social justice by how I am with other people. She seamlessly weaves in class, race, gender, sexuality, ability, ageism, religion, language, immigration, and more in the most inspiring stories. These are just some of her many wonderful books I started reading to my kids when they were three or four years old: *Mrs. Katz and Tush, The Blessing Cup, Chicken Sunday, Thank you Mr. Faulkner, Thunder Cake, Pink and Say, Mr. Lincoln's Way, Mrs. Mack, In Our Mothers' House.* (commentary by Angela Berkfield)

For Early Readers (preschool and early elementary)
My Friends, Mis Amigos, **by Taro Gomi, Chronicle Books, 2006 (age 1+)** Here's a book about the value of making friends with everyone!

Counting on Community, **Innosanto Nagara, Triangle Square, 2015 (age 1+)** Counting up from one stuffed piñata to ten hefty hens—and always counting on each other—in this book children are encouraged to recognize the value of their community, the joys inherent in healthy and eco-friendly activities, and the agency they possess to make change.

Feminist Baby, **by Loryn Brantz, Disney-Hyperion, 2017 (age 1+)** Feminist Baby likes pink and blue; sometimes she'll throw up on you! Feminist Baby chooses what to wear, and if you don't like it she doesn't care! Here's a refreshing, clever board book about a girl who's not afraid to do her own thing and wants to make as much noise as possible along the way!

Baby Feminists, **by Libby Babbott-Klein, Viking Books, 2018 (age 1+)** Before Ruth Bader Ginsburg, Mae Jemison, Frida Kahlo, and others were change-making feminists, they were... babies! In this board book that's perfect for budding feminists, lift the flaps to discover what these iconic figures might have looked like as adorable babies and toddlers. It's an inspiring message that any baby can grow up to make the world a better place for all genders.

Dreamers, **by Yuyi Morales, Neal Porter Books, 2018 (pre-K+)** In 1994 Yuyi Morales left her home in Xalapa, Mexico, and came to the U.S. with her infant son. She left behind nearly everything she owned, but she didn't come empty-handed. She brought her strength, her work, her passion, her hopes and dreams...and her stories.

Malala Yousafzai: Warrior with Words, **by Karen Leggett Abouraya, StarWalk Kids Media, 2014 (K+)** There are many good books about Malala; her story is an important one to tell. She is a school-aged girl in Pakistan who has been a global advocate for girls' access to education. This book doesn't teach collective liberation, but it provides a great opportunity to talk about global issues and how education for girls in Pakistan is connected to education in the U.S. and people here who don't have access to education. This kind of critical thinking is what is needed for collective liberation. (AB)

Young Water Protectors: A Story About Standing Rock, **by Aslan Tudor and Kelly Tudor, self-published, 2018 (K+)** At age eight, Aslan Tudor arrived in North Dakota to help stop a pipeline. A few months later he returned—and saw the whole world watching. Read about his inspiring experiences in the Oceti Sakowin Camp at Standing Rock—what happened there and why.

For Middle Readers (elementary)

A River Ran Wild, **by Lynne Cherry, Harcourt Books, 1992 (pre-K–4)** Cherry traces the ecological evolution of New England's Nashua River: how it was respected by generations of Native Americans, polluted and ultimately deadened in the wake of the industrial revolution, and restored in recent years through the efforts of concerned citizens.

Sila and the Land, **by Shelby Angalik, Ariana Roundpoint, and Lindsay DuPré, Ed-Ucation Publishing, 2017 (grades 1–6)** This book doesn't claim to represent any specific cultures or teachings, but instead encourages children and youth to seek out knowledge from the territories they are living on. It also aims to inspire other young Indigenous writers and illustrators to believe in their gifts and the power of their stories, and it provides recommendations for readers to learn more and take action.

RAD Women Worldwide, **by Kate Schatz, Ten Speed Press, 2016 (K+)** Featuring an array of figures, from Hatshepsut (the great female king who ruled Egypt peacefully for two decades) and Malala Yousafzi (the youngest person to win the Nobel Peace Prize) to Poly Styrene (legendary teenage punk and lead singer of X-Ray Spex) and Liv Arnesen and Ann Bancroft (polar explorers and the first women to cross Antarctica), this is a progressive and visually arresting book.

The Birchbark House **(series), by Louise Erdrich, Hyperion Books, 2002 (grade 1+)** Nineteenth-century American pioneer life was introduced to thousands of young readers through Laura Ingalls Wilder's Little House books. With The Birchbark House, this same period is seen through the eyes of the spirited, seven-year-old Ojibwa girl Omakayas. The sole survivor of a smallpox epidemic on Spirit Island, Omakayas, then a baby, was rescued by a fearless woman named Tallow and welcomed into an Ojibwa family on Lake Superior's Madeline Island, the Island of the Golden-Breasted Woodpecker.

A Young People's History of the United States, **by Howard Zinn, Triangle Square, 2009 (grade 4+)** The viewpoints of workers, slaves, immigrants, women, Native Americans, and others are rarely included in books for young people. Beginning with a look at Christopher Columbus through the eyes of the Arawak Indians and ending with the current protests against continued American imperialism, Zinn presents a radical new way of understanding America's history. In so doing, he reminds readers that America's true greatness is shaped by our dissident voices, not our military generals.

A Different Mirror for Young People: A History of Multicultural America, **by Ronald Takaki, Seven Stories Press, 2012 (grade 4+)** A longtime professor of ethnic studies at the University of California at Berkeley, Ronald Takaki was recognized as one of the foremost scholars of American ethnic history and diversity. Rebecca Stefoff, who adapted Howard Zinn's best-selling *A People's History of the United States* for younger readers, turned the updated 2008 edition of Takaki's multicultural masterwork into *A Different Mirror for Young People.*

ACKNOWLEDGEMENTS

To my kids, Birch and River, this book is for you, and because of you.

My deepest gratitude to these dear people in my life:

My mom and dad—you gave me the building blocks that made this possible. You are amazing!

My husband and best friend, Richard, who provides endless support.

My grandpa, an Iowan, corn farmer, Baptist pastor, and Republican, who told me, "MLK Jr. was a man ahead of his time. I had a lot of respect for him."

My aunt Jane Ann, who taught me how to swear in French and think critically about the world around me.

To my teachers and mentors: Janaki Natarajan, the teacher who broke it all apart and put it all together again, and Dottie Morris, a constant source of inspiration, wisdom, and compassion.

Those people who I don't know, but whose way of seeing the world has profoundly influenced me: bell hooks, Beverly Daniel Tatum, Alice Walker, Toni Morrison, Rev. angel Kyodo williams, Sherri Mitchell, adrienne maree brown, Assata Shakur, Rigoberta Menchú, and many more truth seekers and wisdom sharers.

All of the people along the Thai-Burma border who taught me about true action for justice.

The Bad-Ass Babes: Hun Taing, Ei Ei Samai, Kya Kowalczyk, Farah Council, Shiri Barr, Layli Samimi-Moore, Theresa Anderson, and Umra Omar. Keep on rockin' it around the globe!

My co-conspirators: Mikaela Simms, who has spent many hours talking things through with me, and who still hasn't given up on me; Shela Linton, a constant source of inspiration to show up for racial justice with the utmost integrity; Deb Witkus, for modeling play and embodying social justice; Davey Shlasko, editor of this book and co-conspirator extraordinaire; and Kendra Colburn, for being honest with me and so so patient.

The Root Social Justice Center Collective members throughout the past eight years, who have truly shown me what it means to work collectively for justice: Shela Linton, Alex Fischer, Mel Motel, Shea Witzo, Ezlerh Oreste, and Vanessa Santana.

To that boyfriend who taught me to ask critical questions of the Bible and Christianity, which then propelled me to ask deeper questions about everything.

All of the parents I've talked with over the past decade about all of the challenges and joys of parenting, and particularly the members of the "Boob Club," who have been there through it all—Enza, Marcella, Dana, Sara, and Abi.

All of the parents who have participated in the P4SJ chats, for taking action in your families and for encouraging the continuation of the work that resulted in this book.

All of the parents who contributed their experiences and wisdom to this effort.

To Dede Cummings and Green Writers Press, for believing in this project when it was still quite messy. And for seeing us across the finish-line, with a stellar layout design!

And a special thanks to Kristen Elde who saw this book through to completion during my intense journey with breast cancer in 2020/21.

Each person who has touched my life has changed me. While there is no way I can thank each person by name, you are present in this book and I offer you deep gratitude.

And to spirit for guidance, wisdom, and opening.

Author Angela's kids on a camping trip in 2015.

AUTHOR BIOS AND FAMILY PHOTOS

ABIGAIL HEALEY

Abigail Healey is white, cisgendered, and middle-class raised. She is the mother of two children, one of whom is limb-different and Hard of Hearing, and both of whom are creative, wild and kind. She currently works with elders, providing activities and gardening at a residential care facility. She is constantly seeking ways to engage her children in critical thinking, big questions, justice, and change-making. She started her social justice work decades ago with cardboard puppet theater and loves the way that bringing creativity into activism makes it feel like a new world is possible. She lives with her family in southern Vermont.

Angela Berkfield

Angela Berkfield, a social justice educator and activist, is a parent of two young boys who are advantaged because of race, class, gender, and ability. In her words, "I have a tall task in raising kids who have privilege to move through the world honoring principles of equity and justice. I've aimed to center social justice in my parenting from day one. The more caregivers I can partner with on this journey, the better!" Angela has taught in a variety of settings over the past two decades and is a co-founder of the

Root Social Justice Center, ACT for Social Justice, and

Equity Solutions. She has an MA in social justice from the School for International Training. She believes that a world where everyone can thrive is possible, and coming.

Brittney Washington

Brittney Nicole Washington is a Southern Queer Black Artist + Mama + Art Therapist + Doula + Strategist + Troublemaker. Brittney's multidisciplinary approach to her craft applies an understanding that 1) our most important responsibility is dismantling the power arrangements that maintain structural oppression and

poverty; 2) everyone has different points of entry into politicization and social justice movements;

and 3) art is a portal toward healing, imagination, and movement for that purpose.

As an artist, Brittney uses painting, illustration, and filmmaking to uplift BIPOC experiences and perspectives in media. Her work decolonizes ideas of normality and invites radical empathy across difference. As a racial justice strategist and cultural organizer, Brittney facilitates nationwide to illuminate the historical events that shape our current experiences of racialized poverty, trauma, and disconnection. She curates arts-based spaces where folks can be brave, vulnerable, and imaginative about how to bend our world toward justice together. She also serves as a visual arts producer for various movement groups in the DC-area..

Chrissy Colón Bradt

Chrissy Colón Bradt is an educator and mom to two children under the age of 6. As an Afro-Latina in an interracial marriage, Chrissy is keenly aware of her family's intersecting identities and privilege. She strives to support her children in developing a positive racial and ethnic identity, and in taking joy in this one precious life. Chrissy serves as an educator and director of equity and inclusion at

an independent school and is on the board of The Courage of Care Coalition and The Root Social Justice Center. She holds a BA in comparative ethnic studies from Barnard College and an M.Ed. in special education from Hunter College.

Jaimie Lynn Kessell

Jaimie has spent her entire life dealing with the consequences of being born into generational poverty—hunger, prejudices, and a lack of access to connections and capital that would facilitate an upwards movement of social class. One of Jaimie's life goals is to raise her four children—ages 16, 13, 6, and 7 months—with the

knowledge necessary not only to propel themselves out of poverty but to help create a world in which all people have access to what they need, not just to survive, but to thrive.

Leila Raven

Leila Raven is an Afro-Caribbean descended, mixed-race queer mama parenting using a consent-based, non-hierarchical approach. From 2015 to 2018, she was the director of DC-based grassroots organization Collective Action for Safe Spaces (CASS), where she worked to create community-based strategies to interrupt patriarchal violence and state violence in public spaces.

Leila sees the family as an important site of resistance against oppression and seeks to uplift alternatives to the nuclear family structure to promote collective responsibility for the safety and well-being of whole communities.

Rowan Parker

Rowan Parker has worked in early childhood education and early childhood development for over a decade. He is white and transgender; he is neurodivergent and has a chronic pain condition. Rowan currently works in Early Intervention as a Developmental Specialist, assessing young children for thera-

peutic needs, but his favorite part of the job is helping parents learn to understand and work with their children. He continues his work with children as a foster parent with his partner. Rowan has a Master's in Education from Western Governors University.

PARENTING FOR SOCIAL JUSTICE

RAISING A NEW GENERATION OF CHANGE MAKERS